Advances in Regional Demography

ADVANCES IN REGIONAL DEMOGRAPHY: INFORMATION, FORECASTS, MODELS

Edited by
P. Congdon and P. Batey

*Published in
association with the
Regional Science Association
(British Section)*

Belhaven Press
A division of Pinter Publishers
London and New York

© The Editors and contributors, 1989

First published in Great Britain in 1989 by
Belhaven Press (a division of Pinter Publishers).
25 Floral Street, London WC2E 9DS

British Library Cataloguing in Publication Data
A CIP catalogue record for this book is available from the
British Library

ISBN 1 85293 046 2

Library of Congress—Cataloging-in-Publication Data
Advances in regional demography: information, forecasts, models /
    edited by P. Congdon and P. Batey.
       p. cm.
    "Published in association with the Regional Science Association
    (British Section)."
    Includes index.
    ISBN 1-85293-046-2
    1. Population geography. 2. Population forecasting.
    3. Migration, Internal – Mathematical models. 4. Regional planning.
    I. Congdon, P. II. Batey, Peter W. J. III. Regional Science
    Association. British Section. IV. Title: Regional demography.
    HB 1951.A34   1989
    304.6—dc19   89-197 CIP

Printed and bound in Great Britain by SRP Ltd, Exeter

CONTENTS

PART III Models for Settlement and Redistribution

PART IV Models for Migration in the Labour Market

LIST OF FIGURES

LIST OF TABLES

LIST OF CONTRIBUTORS

Peter Batey, Department of Civic Design, University of Liverpool, Liverpool L69 3BX, UK

Peter Boden, Department of Geography, University of Leeds, Leeds LS2 9JT, UK

Tony Champion, Department of Geography, University of Newcastle, Newcastle, NE1 7RU, UK

Peter Congdon, Population and Statistics, London Research Centre, 81 Black Prince Road, London SE1, UK

Ian Corner, Building Research Establishment, Garston, Watford, Hertford-shire WD2 7JR, UK

Gerard Evers, Department of Personnel Management Sciences, Faculty of Sociology, University of Tilburg, PO Box 90153, NL–5000 LE Tilburg, The Netherlands

Tony Fielding, School of Social Sciences, University of Sussex, Brighton BN1 9QN, UK

Robin Flowerdew, Department of Geography, University of Lancaster, Lancaster LA1 4YB, UK

Jean Forbes, Glasgow Centre for Planning, Livingstone Tower (Floor 10), University of Strathclyde, Glasgow G1 1XH, UK

Andrew Lovett, Department of Geography, University of Lancaster, Lancaster LA1 4YB, UK

Robert McNown, Department of Economics, University of Colorado, Boulder, Colorado 80309–0484, USA

Shane Nugent, National Capital Development Commission, PO Box 373, Canberra 2601, Australia

Peter Phibbs, Department of Town and Country Planning, University of Sydney, NSW 2006, Australia

David Plane, Department of Geography and Regional Development, University of Arizona, Tucson, Arizona 85721, USA

Helen Rampa, Department of Immigration, Local Government and Ethnic Affairs, PO Box 879, Canberra 2616, Australia

Philip Rees, Department of Geography, University of Leeds, Leeds LS2 9JT, UK

John Rhodes, PA Cambridge Economic Consultants, 1 Gresham Road, Cambridge

Andrei Rogers, Population Program, University of Colorado, Boulder, Colorado 80309–0484, USA

Peter Rogerson, Department of Geography, State University of New York, Buffalo, New York 14260, USA

Terry Sincich, Department of Information Systems and Decision Sciences, College of Business Administration, University of South Florida, Tampa, Florida 33620, USA

Stanley Smith, College of Business Administration, University of Florida, Gainesville, Florida 32611, USA

John Stillwell, Department of Geography, University of Leeds, Leeds LS2 9JT, UK

Peter Tyler, Department of Land Economy, University of Cambridge, 19 Silver Street, Cambridge, UK

Les Worrall, Policy Unit, Wrekin Council, PO Box 213, Malinslee House, Telford, Shropshire TF3 4LD, UK

Chapter 1

EDITORIAL INTRODUCTION

Peter Congden and Peter Batey

THE FRAMEWORK OF REGIONAL DEMOGRAPHY

Regional demography is concerned with describing the structure and evolution of human populations not only within the age-time framework of single-region demography, but in terms of space (Rogers, 1975). In addition to the analysis of stocks of human population subject to vital events, regional demography is concerned with interdependence between regions as reflected in directional migration flows between them. It thus goes beyond closed and open single-region models by allowing for gross migration flows both internal to the system and externally (through foreign emigration and immigration), and by including their contribution to the past evolution and future projections of the growth of regional populations (Rees and Wilson, 1977). Multi-regional demographic models thus enhance the significance of regional economic differentials which underlie the often considerable variation in regional components of demographic change, particularly migration. They recognise the household and economic processes that underlie regional differences in population growth, and in so doing expand the frame of reference events (transitions, exits, entries) and statuses (employment, marital, regions) in the life cycle of the individual or household. In this way, multi-regional demography can be embedded within the ambit of multi-state demography, which recognises the possibility of recurrent transitions between states as well as the vital events of the classical cohort-component model (Ledent, 1980).

The present book intends to investigate recent issues in spatial demography and to explore potential new directions for research. The earliest developments in this field stressed extension of formal demographic analysis to the multi-regional situation, such as the development of a multi-regional projection matrix (Isserman, 1985). The aims here are wider. One object is to set regional demography in the broader explanatory context of regional science, for example, by exploring economic-demographic interactions and by assessing their implications for spatial population redistribution and for the parameters describing such redistribution (Plane, 1988). Another and related intention is to assess the contribution of demographic research and information to the formation of spatial policy, an interplay which should ideally be symbiotic (Ter Heide, 1984). The impetus to analytic research is frequently provided by problems of policy with regard to the spatial distribution of population, housing and employment; examples include the research contribution to the development of policies to reverse population and employment loss in particular regions or in inner metropolitan areas, and attempts to match local and regional housing supply with anticipated household formation.

Single-region or -nation demography has been primarily concerned with the evolution and projection of fertility and mortality patterns, with perhaps an allowance for net migration. Thus different 'demographic regimes' defined on the basis of birth and death rates are used to assess position in terms of the demographic transition (Woods, 1986), while in the projection context, a population closed to migration is exposed to a fixed schedule of fertility and mortality (Rogers, 1975; Keyfitz, 1968). However, the recognition of demographic interactions between regions and of the processes underlying them has implications for describing the evolution of populations, for analysing population structures and for demographic projection.

Migration between regions is the main force underlying the population redistributions which accompany urban transition: that is, centralisation as societies develop and industrialise, with a later phase of decentralisation from mature urban centres. The most recent analysis points towards interregional population deconcentration as a further stage in spatial urban transition (Korcelli, 1986). Migratory shifts are often linked to significant stages in the career development of individuals and in the formation and dissolution of households, so expanding on the 'vital events' framework of single-region demography. For example, decentralisation has been depicted in terms of mobility caused by shifts in housing demand associated with life-cycle transitions (such as family formation and marriage). Again, the major phase in the counterurbanisation in the 1970s has been attributed both to the surge of household formation associated with the coming of age of the large post-war birth cohorts (Greenwood, 1985), and to the growth and increased migratory potential of the retirement age cohorts.

Analysis of spatial population structure and the mechanisms of redistribution takes account both of the wider frame of events or stages in household and career development at micro level, and of macro-level differences between and within regions in the availability and structure of employment and housing. Thus the evaluation of human capital models of migration depends both on individual life-cycle characteristics which affect lifetime returns to migration, and on regional economic differentials (Isserman, 1985; Sjaastad, 1962). Again, the development of migration schedules for inflow to and outflow from urban centres illustrated the role of an expanded set of lifetime events: such schedules may exhibit labour dominance (reflecting migration on entry to the labour market or at early career stages), child dependence (reflecting family migrations at mid-career), and retirement migration peaks (Rogers and Castro, 1986).

In the projection context, a multi-regional life table incorporating regional survivorship and outmigration probabilities has been developed as one basis for a multi-regional population-projection matrix (Rogers, 1975), though spatial accounting of population change has also been proposed (Rees and Wilson, 1977). The multi-regional approach focuses on the interdependent populations of different regions, and associates gross flows between these populations with the appropriate populations at risk (Rogers, 1986b). The multi-regional projection process involves multiplication of the multi-regional population by a growth matrix which allows for increments through both births and immigration, and for decrements through deaths and emigration. Recent work on such projections has modified the underlying assumptions of the multi-regional matrix approach. This may involve relaxing the basic Markovian assumptions: for example, to reflect non-stationarity in the interregional migration transitions (see Chapter 15, by Plane and Rogerson). Or it may involve a redefinition of the 'state space': for example, by treating the household rather than the individual as the decision-making unit (Harsman and Snickars, 1983), or by incorporating economic-demographic interactions (Madden and Batey, 1986).

METHODS AND ISSUES

The methods of regional demography include simple classification, ecological correlation and regression, and formal modelling of the components of past and future regional population paths. An example of classification is provided by the delineation of phases of urban transition, with the balance between centralisation and counterurbanisation reflected in the correlation between net migration and settlement size (Fielding, 1982).

The ecological analysis of cross-sectional or temporal analyses of regional demographic indices is illustrated by studies of local mortality differences in terms of socio-economic and enviromental factors; by analysis of fertility differentials over time and space in terms of regional economic fluctuations, and social and household characteristics (Isserman, 1985; Coward, 1986); and by simultaneous equation models which relate migration differentials between areas to spatio-temporal differentials in growth in unemployment, earnings and so on (Greenwood, 1975).

Evolution and projection of regional populations

More formal models for the evolution, distribution and projection of regional populations involve a consideration of the effects of all components of change in difference equations with subscripted indices (for age, time, region, etc.) with a generalisation to matrix equivalents. In practice such models are usually estimated and applied for discrete age groups and time intervals, though there is an analogous representation in continuous age and time (see, for example, Rogers, 1975, Chapter 5.5). A distinction may be made between methods based on demographic accounts and those centred on the multi-regional life table (Rees and Wilson, 1977; Ledent, 1980). The former employ the concept of transitions, the latter that of moves. Thus survivorship rates based on transition and movement data are calculated differently and may have different interpretations in terms of probabilities (Rees, 1986).

Currently much discussion is focused on the extent to which parameterised rather than observed rates can be used to represent the extensive sets of rates involved in multi-regional models, so that the full model is replaced by sub-models expressed in a relatively few parameters. One approach is to relate observed values in basic parameters to a standard schedule for mortality or marital fertility (Coale and Demeny, 1966; Brass, 1980). However, a functional approach is more flexible in the multi-regional situation. Searches for a mathematical law for fertility and mortality have been long-standing, while there has more recently been investigation of regularities in age-specific migration schedules. The utility of parameterised schedules in multi-regional projections has also been studied (Rogers, 1986a; Bates and Bracken, 1982). Much work remains to be done in the area of extrapolation of parameterised model schedules in the projection context.

Households and population

A further issue, of particular importance in the policy context of planning housing development, is the link between regional population and household modelling and projection. In the former, the focus is on the individual, with age and sex as the main dimensions. In the latter, the focus in on the household head and household composition, with additional categories such as marital status, of importance. It has been argued that household formation has been neglected in regional analysis, and that many micro-decisions treated as occurring at the individual level are in fact taken in household units (Harsman and Snickars, 1983). This is important in several contexts, such as housing-demand forecast, residential relocation and fertility. The pressures on housing in urban areas and growth regions implied by household projections are often the area of greatest public discussion: a current example is the pressure for housing development in South-East England following recent upward revisions in the projected number of households by central government.

Demo-economic models

Regional population and household growth takes place within and is constrained or stimulated by economic conditions. Conversely, demographic change has an impact on economic conditions, both on labour supply and the demand for goods and services, and so may act to enhance or reduce regional economic imbalances. Thus economically active migrants are attracted to regions with growing employment opportunities, though the extent to which migration is equilibrating in the labour market depends on whether it is generally a movement between growth regions or from decline to growth regions (see Chapter 11). Again, the impacts of selective migration (for example, retirement migration or gentrification) on demand in the receiving area can be considerable. The endogeneity between economic and demographic change is particularly important in explaining and forecasting recent trends in the spatial distribution of population. Examples are net migration to non-metropolitan areas (which peaked in the 1970s) and some tendency to 're-urbanisation' in the 1980s, primarily through migration shifts. At the national level there is generally a reasonable probability of forecasts being accurate without the need for an exact specification of the linkages between demographic and economic sub-systems. However, the same cannot be said about the regional level. Here factors such as migration, unemployment and differential labour-force participation rates are of greater importance in relation to the sizes of the population and economy concerned. Within regions an additional element, the supply and consumption of housing, must be taken into account because of its effect on migration and headship rates.

SECTIONS AND THEMES

The chapters of this book are intended to pursue the above issues and their methodological representation in greater detail. Most attempt to explore and explain demographic–geographic interrelationships through empirical analysis as well as discussing issues of measurement and definition. The intention may be broadly described as to provide an overview of regional demography in both method and practice, but with particular attention to potential future development.

The arrangement of sections is intended to represent a conceptual progression from regional demographic information systems, which set the basic parameters for demographic analysis and policy formulation; through sub-national forecasts and projections, which while recognising regional interdependencies, are of necessity goal-orientated and require standardised methods for several regions or localities; to a consideration of a range of models of trends and structure, that provide a broader consideration of underlying processes and assumptions, and thereby provide guidance as to the validity of data or forecast-orientated methods.

DEMOGRAPHIC INFORMATION FOR SPATIAL PLANNING

The development of demographic information systems for local planning (Part I) is closely bound up with other developments in the methodology of regional demography discussed above. For example, information systems have been developed based on demographic accounting principles, with an explicit recognition of spatio-temporal dimensions, and a double-bookkeeping approach to ensure consistency between periods and regions (Scheurwater, 1984). Information systems are intended for use in continuous updating of inputs for policy planning, and for the evaluation of existing plans and projections.

Changes in population levels and structure, in household size and composition and in the spatial distribution of social groups all have direct implications for the provision of public services and facilities. It follows, therefore, that effective stategic planning by public bodies will require the support of an up-to-date, accurate and locally-specific information base. In Chapter 2, Worrall comments on the inadequacies of nationally available local-area statistical series for urban planning and research. The ten-year gap between population censuses presents particular problems in the analysis of urban change to inform urban policy development. Worrall focuses on an alternative source of local-population data available from enhanced electoral registration counts. A limited number of local authorities have been carrying out annual surveys of this kind for some time. The chapter reports on analyses of these registration-based surveys for Telford New Town, and demonstrates the very substantial changes in household structure and employment status that have occurred since the early 1980s, when the last national population census was undertaken.

The theme of population information systems is continued by Forbes in Chapter 3, which looks specifically at the problem of measuring and annual monitoring of migration. Forbes argues convincingly that the most appropriate way of observing migration patterns is by means of a population register or monitor which records the precise origin and destination of a move at the time it takes place. Storing information at the level of the individual gives the maximum degree of flexibility in aggregation which should suit all spatial levels and zone types. A population monitor is likely to prove useful in strategic planning as a practical tool for managing service delivery. It should also help considerably in academic research concerned with the process of migration. Forbes goes on to discuss the feasibility of implementing the population monitor, indicating the particular benefits of data sources in Scotland. Detailed records of tenancy changes and privately owned property transactions are kept as a matter of routine.

The relationship between the provision of facilities and the changing age structure of city neighbourhoods is the subject of Chapter 4, by Nugent and Rampa. This examines small-area population change in Canberra, a planned city which has experienced rapid growth since the early 1960s. Even in a new town, planners are unable to regulate the distribution of demographic characteristics between neighbourhoods. Much more important are the effects of market forces and the processes of demographic change. In Canberra it is the ageing of the initial population, rather than the impact of population turnover, which is the major determinant of demographic characteristics at small-area level. Suburbs are observed to progress through the family life cycle in a similar manner to and at the same pace as individual families. Nugent and Rampa look at the implications this has for the planning of school provision and review the options that are available for policy-makers in managing the supply of school places and in influencing the age structure of particular neighbourhoods through the price, type and market sector of housing.

DEMOGRAPHIC FORECASTS AND PROJECTIONS AT SUB-NATIONAL LEVEL

Part II considers recent developments in population and household projections, particularly those of importance at sub-national level. Methods to extrapolate future populations generally involve an algorithm incorporating rates or parameters and assumptions about the future path of such rates or parameters.The designation of this set of methods as 'projection' or 'forecast' is problematic. In theory, a distinction can be drawn between, on the one hand, forecasts, which involve a judgement as to the most likely future, and, on the other, projections, which are merely the numerical consequences of conditional statements about the future ('what if' or 'if . . . then' statements) (Isserman, 1984). In practice, planners may treat projections as if they were forecasts, tending to blur the distinction. In any case, the demographer's choice of assumptions and techniques may be seen as a judgement, implicit or explicit, of the most likely future (Pittenger, 1978).

Forecast accuracy

Given the uncertainty involved in choice of technique and assumptions about future rates and parameters, potential users of projections may be interested not only in the central projection but in the bounds of accuracy of this central figure. Discrepancies between projected results and reality may be categorised into chance or random deviations and systematic deviations (such as those associated with a new disease, medical breakthroughs, or unseen economic events) (Hoem, 1973). In principle, random deviations are amenable to statistical methodology, leading to the interpretation of projections as central measures in a probability distribution, with 'confidence intervals' attached around such measures, though with the caveat that intervals based on past trends cannot in theory be applied to the future.

Various methods have been proposed for population projection as a stochastic process with an error structure providing information on the degree of accuracy. Sykes (1969) proposes, for example, that the elements of the Leslie population transition matrix be treated as random variables, while time-series models for population parameters have as one of their motivations the development of a range of confidence around the parameter — for example, the work of Lee (1974) on forecasts of the total fertility rate. The chapter by Smith and Sincich may be regarded as an empirical investigation of the nature and determinants of the distribution of forecast errors in sub-national projections, and of the stability of this distribution over time. One motivation for this and related work is to develop confidence intervals for current projections on the basis of the accuracy of projections made in the past (Willekens, 1984).

Thus the evidence of this chapter by Smith and Sincich, at US state level, and of earlier work by Smith (1987), at US county level, is that forecast accuracy is lower the longer the projection horizon, the higher the growth rate of the area, and the smaller the size of the area. While there is no overall evidence of forecast bias, in the sense of a systematic difference between forecast and actual central forecasts, there may be biases for certain types of area (for example, high-growth states) and evidence that certain types of technique are more likely to lead to such biases (see also Isserman, 1977). The construction of empirical confidence intervals is supported by evidence of stability in absolute errors.

Household projection

An evaluation of forecast accuracy is one feature of Chapter 6, by Corner, on the headship-rate method of household projection. This chapter is also concerned with possible alternative methods of household projection based on the dynamics of individual households. Forecast accuracy is assessed by a comparison of actual households in 1981 with a projection based on extrapolation of headship rates in 1971. Accuracy is shown to be high except in the South-East region of Britain, where the large fall in households which occurred in London during the 1970s was underpredicted (though see Chapter 11, by Congdon and Champion, on signs of a reversal in London's population and households in the 1980s as deconcentration has waned).

Differential trends between regions in the number of households are shown by Corner primarily to reflect changes in regional population rather than differential trends in the overall headship rate, which increased uniformly in all regions. However, for policy purposes the balance between different types of household (household composition by size, age and marital status of household head, and child dependency) is fundamental. Regional differences in the evolution of household composition are (unlike the number of households) primarily linked to differences in the patterns of household headship between regions and in the evolution of such differentials.

As the chapter by Smith and Sincich shows, forecast accuracy may be related to choice of technique. One question is whether the accuracy of household projections would be enhanced by the adoption of alternative methods of household projection which more explicitly recognise economic–demographic interactions. These include econometric models for headship rates, and structural models which reflect the dynamic nature of household formation and dissolution. Thus household transition matrices for moves between states defined by household/demographic categories can be used in household projections in the same way as the multi-regional Leslie matrix is used in regional population projections (Harsman and Snickars, 1983). Household transition behaviour differs between regions just as headship rates do. Akkerman (1985) has developed a household-composition matrix approach to the multi-regional projection of population and households simultaneously. One rationale for such methodological developments is that individuals migrate as part of households rather than independently of each other, as is implicit in the multi-regional and population-transition matrix (see also Chapter 14, by Flowerdew and Lovett).

Corner discusses the application of a 'life-cycle' headship rate, derived from large-sample data but retaining some of the advantages of dynamic structural models based on the behaviour of individual households. This approach attempts to account for the behaviour of the headship rate of particular birth cohorts as they pass through time (see also Corner, 1987). Two possible approaches to implementation are discussed: an accounting method for the elements of the numerator and denominator of the headship rate; and the expression of the life-cycle headship rate as a parameterised function of age and year of birth.

Parameterized model schedules

The development of such parameterized schedules for demographic events or transitions has several motivations: an assessment of forecast accuracy; an insight into demographic processes through substantive interpretation of parameter values; and the potential for simplification, particularly in the projection context . There has been a long tradition of use of mortality and fertility functions in demographic projections. The development of multi-regional projections has also stimulated parameterisation of migration schedules (Bates and Bracken, 1982). Rogers (1986a) argues for population projection based on parameterised model selection for all the demographic components in a multi-regional/multi-state context. He presents there a method for regressing model schedule parameters on gross transition rates (overall levels of fertility, migration and marriage) which is used to project model schedules.

An alternative approach, outlined by McNown and Rogers in Chapter 7, is to use time-series forecasts of all model schedule parameters rather than simply extrapolate the gross transition rate (cf. Lee, 1974). A model mortality schedule is used to describe patterns of mortality during the middle of the century (up to 1970), and then time-series equations are derived for each parameter and used to forecast future parameter values and thereby future mortality schedules. The Heligman–Pollard model for mortality by age has eight parameters with ready interpretations and forms the basis for mortality forecasts (Rogers, 1986a, p. 50).

While changes in mortality are generally more gradual than those in fertility and migration (so, incidentally, providing a justification of time-series methods), there are important trends both in the overall mortality level (the crude death rate) and more particularly in mortality by age (for example, a recent increase in young adult mortality). Forecast schedules based on time-series forecasts of mortality parameters are shown to give a better fit to observed mortality shifts in mid-century than the traditional fixed rates assumption. This type of parameter forecast has obvious extensions in regional projections in view both of different mortality patterns between regions, and the multi-regional implications for the distribution of life expectancy by region (Rogers, 1975).

Integrated demographic-economic forecasts

For some time now, there has been recognition among analysts of the need to produce regional forecasts of population, employment, housing demand and other key activities that relate to a common set of assumptions and are informed by the knowledge of the relationship between these various activities. In fact, almost 30 years ago, Isard (1960) drew attention to the importance of drawing together the separate activities of population, employment and transport in a multi-region system. This classic work devotes an entire chapter, 'Channels of Synthesis', to an exploration of the concepts involved in integrated regional modelling. More recently, Wegener (1986) has taken this conceptual scheme a stage further, identifying the variables and linkages that would need to be included in an idealised, comprehensive regional forecasting model. Ledent (1986) has provided an excellent discussion of the problems of achieving statistical consistency and identifiability in designing and constructing integrated models of employment, population, the labour force and unemployment. Work by Bracken (1982) has addressed the question of how integrated modelling frameworks can be modified to take account of the uncertainties associated with particular forecasts.

Planning practitioners have also come to accept the importance of integrated demographic-economic forecasting, although progress has varied considerably between local authorities. Breheny and Roberts (1981) carried out a survey of the forecasting methodology adopted by structure planning authorities in Britain during the 1970s and found little evidence of consistent, integrated forecasts. They drew attention to some of the dubious forecasts that had been made and to the serious consequences this had for long-term strategic land-use planning. Nevertheless, it is also possible to quote examples of good practice. The Munich integrated forecasting system has supported decision-making in that city since the early 1970s (Schussman, 1984), while in Britain, three local authories—Gloucestershire (Breheny and Roberts, 1978); the Grampian Region (Cockhead and Masters, 1984); and Greater Manchester (Dewhurst, 1984)—have developed systems which have proved their worth among practitioners over many years.

Such systems embody a variety of different modelling approaches. These range from simple accounting schemes, as in the case of the Gloucestershire framework, to extremely elaborate econometric modelling schemes. Ledent (1982) has shown how demographic and economic models can be combined to give a 'minimal demoeconomic model' suitable for long-range population forecasting. A sophisticated attempt to model demo-economic linkages using econometric techniques is the ECESIS model, and inter-regional model designed to forecast population for the 50 states of the USA (Beaumont *et al.*, 1985).

The Cambridge Regional Model for integrated forecasting described by Tyler and Rhodes in Chapter 8 places emphasis on the growth of labour demand at the regional and sub-regional levels, and the effect this has on labour supply as a result of its influence on migration, commuting and labour-force participation rates. Meeting the criticisms of Breheny and Roberts (1981) and others, the model incorporates explicit linkages between labour supply and demand. The basic approach is demonstrated in conceptual terms by reference to a set of labour-market balance sheets which encapsulate the changes in the levels of key activities between census dates. Tyler and Rhodes illustrate the application of the Cambridge model by describing a forecasting exercise in South-East England where the aim was to produce sub-regional forecasts of population and employment. These forecasts were then extended to provide estimates of household formation and of the demand for dwellings.

Integrated modelling has also proved useful in impact assessment where the aim is to establish the effects of policies and proposals upon certain key variables in an urban and regional system. Micro-simulation techniques have proved particularly valuable for this purpose and have the benefit of enabling demo-economic linkages to be specified at a high degree of detail (Orcutt *et al.*, 1976; Clarke *et al.*, 1981). Input–output analysis, too, has provided a fruitful approach to demo-economic impact assessment. Traditionally, regional input–output tables have been designed to permit only the most rudimentary form of demo-economic analysis, because the main function of the table has been to record the transactions between industrial sectors. Usually just one row and one column are devoted to household income and expenditure.

Recent research has demonstrated several ways in which the input–output model can be extended to include a disaggregated household sector embodying detailed demographic and labour-market characteristics. The work of Van Dijk and Oosterhaven (1986) represents the most sophisticated attempt so far to incorporate demographic characteristics, as part of a socio-economic assessment of the impact of migration in the northern Netherlands. Batey (1985) has provided a systematic comparison of the various forms of demographic-economic extended input–output models, while Batey and Weeks (1989) present an empirical evaluation of the effects of household disaggregation in such models. Finally, Madden and Batey (1986) show that it is possible to embed extended input–output models within a wider integrated forecasting system, suitable for producing short- to medium-term regional forecasts of population, employment and unemployment.

Phibbs offers in Chapter 9 a critique of conventional economic impact analyses based on regional input–output models. He points to the need for closer attention to the relationship between population change and the demand for services. His preferred model structure, an extended input–output framework, includes a modified inter-industry model in which the population-services linkage in removed so that it can be handled more sensitively in a separate sub-model. The context for the application of Phibbs's model is quite different from that of the Cambridge Model. His examples are drawn from non-metropolitan regions in which small settlements are experiencing large proportional changes in employment. The magnitude of these changes is such that special attention must be paid to the effects on the local housing construction industry of influxes of population, moving into the locality to take up new job opportunities. Phibbs's model is also notable for the care that is taken in matching new jobs to the available local labour force, so that precise estimates can be made of the economic activity composition of in-migrants.

MODELS FOR SETTLEMENT AND REDISTRIBUTION

The importance of migration in population change when the spatial dimension is recognised, and the role of economic–demographic interactions, are apparent in theories for spatial population shifts between and within regions, particularly in developed societies. In single-nation demography, the focus is on demographic transition in terms of fertility and mortality regimes, or on the replacement of secular fertility decline by fertility fluctuation around replacement level. Analogous issues arise in regional demography: for example, that of convergence or divergence in regional fertility (O'Connell, 1981). However, the distinct feature of sub-national population analysis is the paramountcy of net migration as the source of differences in regional population growth, and of age-selective migration as well as past waves of births as a major source of differences in age structure (Fielding, 1982; Robert and Randolph, 1983, p. 92).

Of particular concern in recent spatial demography have been shifts in the balance of growth between metropolitan and non-metropolitan regions. There are certain definitional problems here: for example, urban growth beyond outdated boundaries may be represented as rural growth (Gordon, 1979; Congdon and Shepherd, 1986), while reclassification of non-metropolitan areas as metropolitan may also have a distorting effect (Fuguitt *et al.*, 1988). Despite such questions of definition, the main consensus is that during the 1950–80 period both Western Europe and North America experienced major shifts in favour of non-metropolitan growth. This has been represented in a number of ways: as an urban–rural shift, as a shift from urbanisation to counterurbanisation (Fielding, 1982), and as a shift from decentralisation to extended deconcentration, from either metropolitan or non-metropolitan cores (Robert and Randolph, 1983; Lichter and Fuguitt, 1982).

In support of the idea of a shift from urbanisation to counterurbanisation is the finding that in several countries a positive relationship in the 1950s between net migration (or overall population growth) and settlement size or density, had by the 1960s and 1970s changed to a negative relationship. It may be argued that this shift primarily reflects changes in the pattern of interregional migration in favour of less densely populated, less urbanised regions. In the more confined migration fields of some countries a more appropriate framework might be seen as a shift from decentralisation from large urban cores, while remaining within their commuting shed or daily urban system, towards deconcentration beyond the economic influence of the large centre. This has been seen as a clean break with previous metropolitan development (Vining and Strauss, 1977).

Superimposed on these shifts are redistributions between regions (to some degree independent of the rural–urban differential) such as the North–South shifts apparent in both Britain and the United States—see Chapter 15, by Plane and Rogerson. Also apparent are changes in the nature of metropolitan decentralisation itself, as the metropolitan system becomes more fragmented (see Gordon *et al.*, 1986; and Chapter 11).

There is recent evidence from a number of countries that the main phase of counterurbanisation has now passed and that there may even be instances of 'reurbanisation'. Thus during 1980–5, 36 per cent of non-metropolitan counties in the US lost population as against 20 per cent in 1970–80 (Engels, 1986). Of those non-metropolitan counties still gaining population, those with the highest commuting rates to metropolitan centres had higher growth. In other countries this reversal may not be so pronounced in that the metropolitan growth rate has not yet overtaken the non-metropolitan rate as it has in the US. However, the differential has been sharply reduced, suggesting an end to the clear-cut counterurbanisation of the 1970s (Courgeau, 1986).

Explaining counter- and reurbanisation

There have been various explanations for the counterurbanisation phenomenon and for its waning in the 1980s. Chapter 10, by Fielding, discusses possible sources of counterurbanisation advanced by other studies: changes in individual aspirations and residential preferences; deconcentration of employment opportunities; and policy changes. There is evidence from a number of studies that residential preferences of certain footloose groups (such as retirement migrants) or certain highly skilled workers may play a leading role in counterurbanisation (Bourne, 1980); that employment growth in non-metropolitan areas may have led population growth to some degree (Briggs and Rees, 1982); and, at least in some countries, that policy favoured the growth of small urban areas (Congdon and Shepherd, 1986). While not denying the importance of such factors in certain contexts, Fielding proposes that the primary underlying influence is the emergence of a new spatial division of labour. In particular, spatial fragmentation of different parts of the production process—with, for example, corporate control in large metropolitan centres, and routine production in peripheral or rural areas—is seen as determining recent population redistribution.

Such changes in the spatial division of labour can also be proposed as a source of metropolitan employment revival or even growth in the 1980s (often in marked contrast to earlier trends). These changes include the concentration of corporate control and growth producer services in metropolitan areas, and the waning of the main phase of manufacturing deconcentration—with some tendency to high-technology growth in certain metropolitan regions. They may in turn be seen as one source of metropolitan population revival, though other explanations—such as the impact of the recession of the early 1980s, and the role of new housing—are examined in Chapter 11, by Congdon and Champion, in the context of London's 'turnround'. Plane and

Rogerson pursue a related theme, tracing the slowdown in net migration to the energy-rich sunbelt of the south-west central US to the energy crisis of the early 1980s and its impact on job-linked migration. It is notable, however, that signs of metropolitan revival in capital cities (London, Paris) or high-tech centres (Boston) do not usually imply a return to urbanisation in the sense of a positive relationship of growth to size.

Selective migration and counterurbanisation

A major component in non-metropolitan growth in the 1960s and 1970s were shifts in selective migration patterns: for example, a cessation of net out-migration of young economically active migrants from non-metropolitan areas, and a move to net in-migration of both the economically active age groups (particularly among high-incomes more skilled categories) and of retirement age groups (again among the higher-income groups). It has been suggested that elderly migration was most important in the earliest phase of counterurbanisation (Briggs and Rees, 1982). The retirement migration component has been more important in some types of non-metropolitan region than others, with well-recognised retirement regions being apparent—for example, the South West of Britain.

Chapter 12, by Rees, Stillwell and Boden, assesses the contribution of elderly migration to population redistribution in Britain, and measures changes in non-metropolitan preferences of the elderly over time. The authors use a multi-regional components framework, adapted from shift-share techniques (comparing regional components of change with those expected on the basis of national rates). A components framework for evaluating the relative importance of *in-situ* ageing as against elderly migration is applied by Rees and his co-authors to projected changes in the elderly over the next 50 years. Their results on the components of change in elderly age structures in non-metropolitan migration may be compared with those of Clifford *et al.* (1983), while some studies have used locational characteristics to specifically explain elderly counterurbanisation (Heaton *et al.*, 1981).

MODELS FOR MIGRATION IN THE LABOUR MARKET

The feature distinguishing multi-regional from single-region demography is the explicit recognition of migration flows between regions and between localities within regions. There is evidence that migration is the most important influence on local population change, and accordingly a high correlation between regional net migration rates and rates of overall population growth. There has been extensive work, primarily by economists and economic geographers, using economic differentials (for example, in wages and unemployment) to explain regional and local migration structures, with little attention to projection. By contrast, within the demographic tradition the focus had been on extrapolation of constant origin-specific migration transition rates, without reference to causal processes. The contribution of regional science would be towards an integration of the behavioural perspective into the modelling and projection of interregional migration and thereby of regional population change.

The migration decision takes place at the level of the individual person or household and theories of micro-economic decision-making form the basis for behavioural migration modelling at both micro an macro levels, though there are caveats to complete parallelism (van der Veen and Evers, 1983). The neo-classical approach to individual migration choices was in terms of regional wage differentials, with high wages in areas of excess labour demand serving to attract immigrants. The human-capital perspective of Sjaastad (1962) provided a more complete view in terms of the expected lifetime returns to the individual or household of moving to different destination areas or staying in the current area of residence. This model accounts for empirical regularities such as the decline in migration rates with age (as the time horizon for returns to migration shortens). The use of the random utility model (Domenich and McFadden, 1975) provided a further step towards realism in that while systematic influences on the expected utility of migration are represented (and imply conventional utility maximisation), so also are random differential preferences representing individual heterogeneity. Assuming a particular form for the distribution of such errors leads to a multinomial logit specification adapted to choice between discrete alternatives (see   Chapter 13, by Evers).

Decomposition of the migration decision

The tractability and realism of models for individual migration behaviour may often be increased by the decomposition of the migration decision into a series of stages. The most common characterisation is in terms of a decision to move from a particular origin, followed by a choice of destination conditional on the decision to move and on the origin. This sequence underlies the use (for example, in demographic projections) of the traditional Markov model of stationary transition probabilities for destination choice. More complex search theories of migration behaviour may pose a sequence such as (a) the probability of being in search, (b) the probability, conditional on search, of receiving an opportunity in a particular area, and (c) the probability, conditional on receiving an offer, of accepting it (Molho, 1986). This type of nesting of migration decisions in turn implies a particular methodology, such as the nested logit for the choice of whether to move, of a particular neighbourhood and of a particular dwelling type and unit, as in the work of Onaka and Clark (1983).

In practice, the choice to migrate may coincide with (or precede or follow) decisions to relocate workplaces, or enter or leave the labour market, and may involve choices in both labour and housing markets. The choices involved may be treated as either simultaneous (in the statistical sense) or sequential. For example, joint (simultaneous) probability models of migration and job change have been proposed by Congdon (1988) and Krumm (1983). Evers presents a sequential-choice approach to the modelling and estimation (at micro level) of substitution and complementarity relationships between migration and commuting decisions. These choices, handled within a multinomial logit framework, involve four kinds of decision: (a) whether it is useful to supply one's labour outside the present region of residence; (b) if so, whether it is then useful to make a partial or total displacement (a partial displacement involving the retention of either existing workplace or residence); (c) in the case of partial displacement, whether one commutes and/or migrates; and (d) choice of destination.

Gravity migration models

A micro-based analysis such as this is essential to the evaluation of the relative impact of personal (life-cycle) as against area factors on migration. However, there are computational problems in modelling directly at an individual level, and a frequent lack of suitable data (namely, retrospective migration histories). Analysis and forecasts of migration, particularly those incorporating interactions with aggregate employment and housing markets, are usually undertaken at macro level. Spatial interaction or gravity models of migration are a frequently used framework for analysis at aggregate level, and reflect (as do discrete-choice micro models) the set of competing destination regions facing migrants from different origins. They posit that flows between localities or regions are a function of the population or employment 'mass' as the origin and destination, and of the relative economic attractiveness of origin and destination (for example, relative employment growth or new housing), combined with a distance-deterrence function which expresses the greater cost of longer moves.

Gravity models may be used to test a wide variety of economic hypotheses about migration. For example, they were used by Lowry (1966) to explain interregional migration in terms of 'mass' labour-force sizes, and wage and unemployment differences, while Gordon and Vickerman (1982) propose a multi-stream decomposition of the gravity model to reflect different search fields associated with local, regional and national migration streams. Gravity models may be singly or doubly constrained to reproduce observed migration totals and so reflect the competing destinations nature of migration. They may be estimated by maximum entropy (Wilson, 1971), or by the principles of general linear models (Flowerdew and Aitken, 1982; Liaw and Ledent, 1987; Congdon, 1989).

Chapter 14, by Flowerdew and Lovett, is concerned with a particular aspect of the gravity modelling of migration flows, namely migration variability in excess of that expected under the Poisson assumption of independence between individual migrants. They argue that migration by individual persons is generally undertaken as part of a household unit, so that extra-variation in individual person migration behaviour will be reduced if the household size distribution of movers is explicitly recognised. A generalised linear modelling approach is used, with the independent variables as in the baseline gravity model (distances and population masses) but with the Poisson model compounded with the distribution of household size. In broad terms the general linear model, whether applied to individual demographic event histories or to aggregate count data, may be seen as a potential approach to the problem of population heterogeneity in demographic parameters, and thereby to the endogenising of parameter change in projections (Willekens, 1984).

Migration simultaneity

The gravity model of migration interactions is not generally used, however, in the reciprocal modelling of demoeconomic relationships. Gravity models are demand-orientated in the sense that migration is a response to employment or housing differentials, whereas a mixed demand–supply orientation is the distinguishing criterion of models of migration endogeneity in labour and/or housing markets (Ledent, 1986). Early simultaneous equation models corrected for simultaneity bias in demand-orientated models by recognising the reciprocal relations between employment and migration in the regional context (Greenwood, 1975) or between employment, housing and migration in the local context (Greenwood, 1980). However, there is now recognition of the endogeneity between migration and other forms of labour-supply adjustment, such as changes in commuting or indigenous participation (van der Veen and Evers, 1983; Congdon, 1983; Chalmers and Greenwood, 1985). Such endogeneity is likely to be most important in the overlapping labour markets of heavily urbanised regions. It may not be fully incorporated in the demometric approach (Ledent, 1978). The chapters by Congdon and Champion and Evers both discuss the simultaneous character of different types of labour supply mobility.

Migration forecasts

For the purpose of migration forecasting, simultaneous eco-demographic relationships may be included in large-scale econometric models or in input–output models. However, these do not usually take account of the full information available on the structure and evolution of place-to-place flows. The traditional Markov assumption often used in migration projections is of stationarity in transition probabilities, these probabilities being derived from an origin perspective. The Markov procedure separates the migration decision into a decision or propensity to migrate and a subsequent choice of destination. These stages may be modelled as a generation and distribution component, respectively, and the stationarity assumption modified in a projection context (Ament and van der Knaap, 1985; Willekens and Baydar, 1986). The contrasting gravity model incorporates both origin and destination variables within a behavioural context, but has limited usefulness for forecasting. Plane (1982) and Plane and Rogerson (1985) have proposed destination-weighted modifications of the Markov model to reflect the shifting attractiveness over time of potential destinations: such weighting may be in terms simply of population or of a measure of labour-market opportunity.

Chapter 15, by Plane and Rogerson, considers two methods which may be used in the analysis and projection of changing interregional migration structures, while retaining the origin-destination perspective, and applies them to an analysis of recent shifts in migration to and from the South-West Central area of the US. The constant causative matrix technique (Rogerson and Plane, 1984) may be used to forecast the transition matrix at time $t + 1$ given information on observed transition matrices for $1, 2, \ldots, t$; this technique provides for a relaxation of the stationarity assumption of the Markov model while retaining interregional dependencies. The adaptation of shift-share techniques to the decomposition of interregional migration may be used to assess change in relative attractiveness of a region as a migration destination, or relative retentiveness as an origin. Such changes in competitive position may be distinguished from proportional shift: the extent to which past patterns of migration 'specialisation' are favourable to accelerating growth through migration in the current period.

FUTURE DEVELOPMENTS

The advance of regional demography lies in methods of sub-national demographic monitoring and projection which are regio-scientifically valid and of utility in policy-making. The analysis of the above chapters suggests that this will involve an extension of regional demographic models more closely to represent both the underlying processes and the structure of the data. For example, investigation of decision-making processes points towards a household- as well as an individually based demography (Chapter 6). Improved techniques for representing demographic data are also becoming available, for example, general linear models (Chapter 14) or time-series extrapolation of graduated parameters (Chapter 7). However, multi-regional demography will also require an integration of monitoring, forecasting and planning systems (Willekens, 1984); for example, by incorporating simulation in a forecasting framework (via sensitivity analysis or impact assessment), or by using monitoring systems to update forecasts (Chapter 3). Again, the need to integrate forecasts and planning implies, for one thing, projections at small-area level (Platek *et al.*, 1987), which can then be aggregated both to functional and planning units.

Such considerations imply that the future of multi-regional demography lies in the integration of the demography of households or members of the labour force with the multi-state demography of individuals. Explanation in terms of underlying processes as opposed to analysis of data structures will thus play an increased role. However, the practical application of methodological improvements, for example, in regional and local demographic projections by government agencies, will continue to be constrained by the requirements of strategic planning and by the adequacy of available demographic information in relation to model requirements.

REFERENCES

Ahlburg, D. (1986) 'Forecasting regional births: an economic-demographic approach' in A. Isserman, (ed.), *Population Change and the Economy*. Boston: Kluwer Nijhoff.

Akkerman, A. (1985) 'The household composition matrix as a notion in multiregional forecasting of population and households'. *Environment and Planning*, vol. 17A, pp. 355–71.

Ament, D. and van der Knapp, A. (1985) 'A two state model for the analysis of intraurban mobility processes', *Environment and Planning*, vol. 17A, pp. 1201–16.

Bates, J. and Bracken, I. (1982) 'Estimation of migration profiles in England and Wales', *Environment and Planning*, vol. 14A, pp. 889–900.

Batey, P. (1985) 'Input–output models for regional demographic-economic analysis: some structural comparisons', *Environment and Planning*, vol. 17A, pp. 73–99.

Batey, P. and Weeks, M. (1989) 'The effects of household disaggregation in extended input–output models', in R. Miller, K. Polenske and A. Rose (eds), *Frontiers of Input–Output Analysis: Commemorative Papers*. New York: Oxford University Press.

Beaumont, P., Isserman, A., Macmillen, D., Plane, D. and Rogerson, P. (1985) 'The ECESIS economic-demographic inter-regional model of the United States', in A. Isserman (ed.), *Population and the Economy: Theory and Models*. Boston: Kluwer Nijhoff.

Bourne, L. (1980) 'Alternative perspectives on urban decline and population deconcentration', *Urban Geography*, vol. 1, pp. 39–52.

Bracken, I. (1982) 'New directions in key activity forecasting'. *Town Planning Review*, vol. 53, pp. 51–64.

Brass, W. (1980) 'The Relational Gompertz Model of Fertility by Age of Woman' in *Regional Workshop on Techniques of Analysis of World Fertility Survey Data*. Occasional Papers 22. London: WFS.

Breheny, M. and Roberts, A. (1978) 'An integrated forecasting system for structure planning', *Town Planning Review*, vol. 49, pp. 306–18.

Breheny, M. and Roberts, A. (1981) 'The forecasts in structure plans', *The Planner*, vol. 67, pp. 102–4.

Briggs, R. and Rees, J. (1982) 'Control factors in the economic development of nonmetropolitan America', *Environment and Planning*, vol. 14A, pp. 1645–66.

Chalmers, J. and Greenwood, M. (1985) 'The regional labour market adjustment process: determinants of changes in the rate of labour force participation, unemployment and migration', *Annals of Regional Science*, vol. 19, pp. 1–17.

Clarke, M., Keys, P. and Williams, H. (1981) 'Microsimulation in socio-economic and public policy analysis' in H. Voogd (ed.), *Strategic Planning in a Dynamic Society*. Delft: Delftsche Uitgevers Maatschappij.

Clifford, W., Heaton, T. and Lichter, D. (1983) 'Components of change in the age composition of non-metropolitan America', *Rural Sociology*, vol. 48, pp. 458–70.

Coale, A. and Demeny, P. (1966) *Regional Model Life Tables and Stable Populations*. Princeton, NJ: Princeton University Press.

Cockhead, P. and Masters, R. (1984) 'Forecasting in Grampian: three dimensions of integration', *Town Planning Review*, vol. 55, pp. 473–88.

Congdon, P. (1983) 'A model for the interaction of migration and commuting', *Urban Studies*, vol. 20, no. 2, pp. 185–96.

Congdon, P. (1988) 'The interdependence of geographic migration with job and housing mobility in London', *Regional Studies*, vol. 22, no. 2, pp. 81–93.

Congdon, P. (1989) 'Modelling migration flows between areas: an example for London using the Census and OPCS Longitudinal Study', *Regional Studies*, vol. 23, no. 2.

Congdon, P. and Shepherd, J. (1986) 'Modelling population changes in small English urban areas', *Environmen and Planning*, vol. 18A, pp. 1297–1322.

Corner, I. (1987) 'Household projection methods', *Journal of Forecasting*, 6, pp. 271–284.

Courgeau, D. (1986) 'Vers un ralentissement de la 'déconcentration urbaine' en France?', *Population et Société*, vol 41, pp. 1–4.

Coward, J. (1986) 'The analysis of regional fertility patterns' in R. Woods and P. Rees (eds), *Population Structures and Models*. London: Allen & Unwin.

Dewhurst, R. (1984) 'Forecasting in Greater Manchester: a multi-regional approach', *Town Planning Review*, vol. 55, pp. 453–72.

Domenich, T. and McFadden, D. (1975) *Urban Travel Demand: A Behavioral Analysis*. Amsterdam: North Holland.

Engels, R. (1986) 'The metropolitan/nonmetropolitan population at mid-decade'. Paper presented to Population Association of America, Annual Meeting, California.

Evers, G and van der Veen, A. (1985) 'A simultaneous non-linear model of labour migration and commuting', *Regional Studies*, vol. 19, pp. 217–29.

Fielding, A. (1982) 'Counter urbanisation in Europe', *Progress in Planning*, vol.17, pp. 1–54.

Flowerdew, R. and Aitkin, M. (1982) 'A method of fitting the gravity model based on the Poisson distribution', *Journal of Regional Science*, vol. 22, pp. 191–202.

Fuguitt, G., Heaton, T. and Lichter, D. (1988) 'Monitoring the metropolitanization process', *Demography*, vol. 25, pp. 115–28.

Gordijn, H., Heida, H. and Ter Heide, H. (1984) 'Monitoring migration and population redistribution' in H. Ter Heide and F. Willekens (eds), *Demographic Research and Spatial Policy*. London: Academic Press.

Gordon, I. and Vickerman, R. (1982) 'Opportunity, preference and constraint: an approach to the analysis of metropolitan migration', *Urban Studies*, vol. 19, pp. 247–61.

Gordon, P. (1979) 'Deconcentration without a "clean break" ', *Environment and Planning*, vol. 11A, pp. 281–290.

Gordon, P., Richardson, H. and Wong, H. (1986) 'The distribution of population and employment in a polycentric city: the case of Los Angeles' *Environment and Planning*, A18, pp. 161–173.

Greenwood, M. (1975) 'A simultaneous equations model of urban growth and migration', *Journal of the American Statistical Association*, vol. 70, pp. 797–810.

Greenwood, M. (1980) 'Metropolitan growth and the intrametropolitan location of employment, housing and labour force', *Review of Economics and Statistics*, vol. 62, pp. 491–501.

Greenwood, M. (1985) 'Human migration: theory, models and empirical studies', *Journal of Regional Science*, vol. 25, pp. 521–42.

Hårsman, B. and Snickars, F. (1983) 'A method for disaggregate household forecasts', *Tijdschrift voor Economische en Sociale Geografie*, vol. 74, pp. 282–90.

Heaton, T., Clifford, W. and Fuguitt, G. (1981) 'Temporal shifts in the determinants of young and elderly migration in nonmetropolitan areas', *Social Forces*, vol. 60, pp. 41–60.

Hoem, J. (1973) 'Levels of error in population forecasts'. *Artikler fra Statistisk Sentralbyrå*, no. 61. Oslo: Central Bureau of Statistics.

Isard, W. (1960) *Methods of Regional Analysis*. Cambridge, MA: MIT Press.

Isserman, A. (1977) 'The accuracy of population projections for subcounty areas', *Journal of American Institute of Planners*, vol. 43, no. 3, pp. 247–59.

Isserman, A. (1984) 'Projection, forecast and plan', *Journal of American Institute of Planners*, vol. 50, pp. 209–21.

Isserman, A. (1985) 'Economic-demographic modelling with endogenously determined birth and migration rates: theory and prospects', *Environment and Planning*, vol. 17A, pp. 25–45.

Keyfitz, N. (1968) *Introduction to the Mathematics of Population*. Addison Wesley: Reading, MA.

Korcelli, P. (1986) 'Migration and urban change' in A.Rogers and F. Willekens (eds), *Migration and Settlement: a Multiregional Comparative Study*. Dordrecht: D. Reidel, pp. 323–52.

Krumm, R. (1983) 'Regional labour markets and the household migration decision', *Journal of Regional Science*, vol. 23, pp. 361–76.

Ledent, J. (1978) 'Regional multiplier analysis: a demometric approach', *Environment and Planning*, vol. 10A, pp. 537–60.

Ledent, J. (1980) 'Multistate life tables: movement versus transition perspectives', *Environment and Planning*, vol. 12A, pp. 533–62.

Ledent, J. (1982) 'Long-range regional population forecasting: specification of a minimal demoeconomic model with a test for Tucson, Arizona', *Papers of the Regional Science Association*, vol. 49, pp. 37–67.

Ledent, J. (1986) 'Consistent modelling of employment, population, labour force and unemployment in the statistical analysis of regional growth' in P. Batey and M. Madden (eds), *The Integrated Analysis of Regional Systems*. London Papers in Regional Science 15. London: Pion.

Lee, R. (1974) 'Forecasting births in post-transition populations', *Journal of the American Statistical Association*, vol. 69, pp. 607–17.

Liaw, K. and Ledent, J. (1987) 'Nested logit model and maximum quasi-likelihood method', *Regional Science and Urban Economics*, vol. 17, pp. 67–88.

Lichter, D. and Fuguitt, G. (1982) 'The transition to nonmetropolitan deconcentration', *Demography*, vol. 19, pp. 211–21.

Lowry, I. (1966) *Migration and metropolitan growth*. San Francisco: Chandler.

Madden, M. and Batey, P. (1986) 'A demographic-economic model of a metropolis' in R. Woods and P. Rees (eds), *Population Structures and Models*. London: Allen & Unwin.

Molho, I. (1986) 'Theories of migration: a review', *Scottish Journal of Political Economy*, Vol. 33, pp. 396–419.

O'Connell, M. (1981) 'Regional fertility patterns in the United States: convergence or divergence?', *International Regional Science Review*, vol. 6, pp. 1–14.

Onaka, J. and Clarke, W. (1983) 'A disaggregate model of residential mobility and housing choice', *Geographical Analysis*, vol. 15, pp. 287–304.

Orcutt, G., Caldwell, S. and Wertheimer, R. (1986) *Policy Exploration through Microsimulation*. Washington, DC: The Urban Institute.

Pittenger, D. (1978) 'The role of judgment, assumptions, techniques and confidence limits in forecasting population', *Socio-economic Planning Sciences*, vol. 12, pp. 271–6.

Plane, D. (1982) 'An information theoretic approach to the estimation of migration flows', *Journal of Regional Science*, vol. 22, pp. 441–56.

Plane, D. (1987) 'The geographic components of change in a migration system', *Geographical Analysis*, vol. 19, pp. 283–99.

Plane, D. (1988) Review of R. Woods and P. Rees (eds), *Population Structures and Models*, Allen & Unwin, 1986, *Annals of Regional Science*, vol 22, no. 1, pp. 109–12.

Plane, D. and Rogerson, P. (1985) 'Economic-demographic models for forecasting interregional migration', *Environment and Planning*, vol. 17A, pp. 185–98.

Platek, R., Rao, J., Sarndal, C. and Singh, M. (eds) (1987) *Small Area Statistics: an International Symposium*. Wiley: Chichester.

Rees, P. (1986) 'Developments in the modelling of spatial populations' in R. Woods and P. Rees (eds), *Population Structures and Models*. London: Allen & Unwin.

Rees, P. and Wilson, A. (1977) *Spatial Population Analysis*. London: Edward Arnold.

Robert, S. and Randolph, W. (1983) 'Beyond decentralization: the evolution of population distribution in England and Wales, 1961–1981', *Geoforum*, vol. 14, pp. 75–102.

Rogers, A. (1975) *Introduction to Multiregional Mathematical Demography*. New York: Wiley.

Rogers, A. (1986a) 'Parameterized multistate population dynamics and projections', *Journal of the American Statistical Association*, vol. 81, pp. 48–61.

Rogers, A. (1986b) 'Population projections', in A. Rogers and F. Willekens (eds), *Migration and Settlement: A Multiregional Comparative Study*. Dordrecht: D. Reidel, pp. 211–63.

Rogers, A. and Castro, L. (1986) 'Migration', in A. Rogers and F. Willekens (eds), *Mirgration and Settlement: A Multiregional Comparative Study*. Dordrecht: D. Reidel, pp. 157–208.

Rogerson, P. and Plane, D. (1984) 'Modelling temporal changes in flow matrices', *Papers of the Regional Science Association*, vol. 54, pp. 147–64.

Scheurwater, J. (1984) 'Towards a spatial demographic information system' in H. Ter Heide and F. Willekens (eds), *Demographic Research and Spatial Policy*. London: Academic Press.

Schussman, K. (1984) 'Forecasting methods and the Munich infrastructure planning system', *Town Planning Review*, vol. 55, 435–52.

Sjaastad, L. (1962) 'The costs and returns of human migration', *Journal of Political Economy*, vol. 70, pp. 80–93.

Smith, S. (1987) 'Tests of forecast accuracy and bias for county population projections', *Journal of the American Statistical Association*, vol. 82, pp. 991–1003.

Sykes, Z. (1969) 'Some stochastic versions of the matrix model for population dynamics', *Journal of the American Statistical Association*, vol. 64, pp. 111–30.

Ter Heide, H. (1984) 'Demographic research questions arising from spatial policy in the Netherlands' in H. Ter Heide and F. Willekens (eds), *Demographic Research and Spatial Policy*. London: Academic Press.

Van der Veen, A. and Evers, G. (1983) 'A simultaneous model for regional labor supply, incorporating labor force participation, commuting and migration', *Socioeconomic Planning Sciences*, vol. 17, pp. 239–50.

Van Dijk, J. and Oosterhaven, J. (1986) 'Regional impacts of migrants' expenditure: an input-output vacancy chain approach' in P. Batey and M. Madden (eds), *Analysis of Regional Systems*. London Papers in Regional Science, 15. London: Pion.

Vining, D. and Strauss, A. (1977) 'A demonstration that the current deconcentration of population in the U.S. is a clean break with the past', *Environment and Planning*, vol. 9A, pp. 751–8.

Wegener, M. (1986) 'Integrated forecasting models of urban and regional systems' in P. Batey and M. Madden (eds), *Integrated Analysis of Regional Systems*. London Papers in Regional Science 15. London: Pion.

Willekens, F. (1984) 'Spatial policy and demographic research opportunities' in H. Ter Heide and F. Willekens (eds), *Demographic Research and Spatial Policy*. London: Academic Press.

Willekens, F. and Baydar, N. (1986) 'Forecasting place-to-place migration with generalized linear models' in R. Woods and P. Rees (eds), *Population Structures and Models*. London: Allen & Unwin.

Wilson, A. (1971) 'A family of spatial interaction models, and associated developments', *Environment and Planning*, vol. 3A, pp. 1–32.

Woods, R. (1986) 'Spatial and temporal patterns' in R. Woods and P. Rees (eds), *Population Structures and Models*. London: Allen & Unwin.

PART 1

DEMOGRAPHIC INFORMATION FOR SPATIAL PLANNING

Chapter 2

URBAN DEMOGRAPHIC INFORMATION SYSTEMS*

L. Worrall

INTRODUCTION

The last decade has witnessed considerable change in urban population structures, in the size, composition and economic status of households and in the
spatial distribution of social groups within and between urban areas and their
hinterlands. A knowledge of the nature of these changes, of their interrelationships and of the socio-economic context in which these changes are taking
place both nationally and sub-nationally is of fundamental importance to
those organisations which are concerned with the management of urban
change, with the provision of services and with the development of responsive
and effective social policy. Within local government, accurate and regular
information on demographic, social and economic change and the implications of these changes on urban socio-spatial form, is an essential input to
strategic planning (Black, 1984; 1985).

It is within the context of growing information needs that the cancellation
of both the 1976 and 1986 Censuses and the inadequacy of nationally available
statistical series for urban planning and research must be seen. A ten-year gap
in the collection of information is clearly inadequate, given the rapidity and
selectivity of the process of urban change (Redfern, 1988). Nationally available information sources do not permit an analysis of urban change at a level of
detail sufficient to inform urban policy development.

The pressure of demand for more information, and in some cases a concern
about the accuracy of central government's estimates of the population of
local authority areas, has caused those local authorities which are more active
in social policy to develop alternative sources of social and demographic information. The primary purpose of this chapter is to describe how, in Telford,
policy-relevant information on urban social and demographic change has
been collected, organised and analysed.

The chapter comprises four main sections: first, a review several urban
and regional population information systems; second, a description of the
Telford population information system; third, a discussion of how the Telford
system has been used to provide the spine for an integrated urban information

*I acknowledge the (former) Central Research Unit at Telford Development Corpor-
ation (now Prism Research) and the Planning Department at Shropshire County
Council who are jointly involved with the Policy Unit at Wrekin Council in the collection of data. I also acknowledge the many local authorities who sent me information
on their attempts to implement EERPS.

system; and finally, a discussion of how the integrated system has been used to explore aspects of urban change and their interrelationships at both the whole-town and the small-area levels.

LOCAL POPULATION INFORMATION SYSTEMS IN THE UK

The stimulus for the development of local systems

The cancellation of the 1976 and 1986 mid-term Censuses created major gaps in the UK information base for urban planning and research. In 1976 the perceived need for current, small-area socio-demographic information prompted several local authorities to develop alternative information sources. Two media for information collection emerged: household-based sample surveys to replicate the format, scale and design of the aborted 1976 Census and a more innovative solution which comprised a comprehensive population survey carried out in conjunction with the annual electoral registration process.

In 1976 several local authorities developed what have become known as 'Enhanced Electoral Registration Population Surveys' (EERPS). Since then a minority of local authorities have incorporated what was originally a Census replacement device into the information-collection regimes they use to support their policy planning processes: Strathclyde Regional Council and Wrekin Council are two examples of this (Black 1984; Worrall 1986, 1988).

The EERPS approach: an outline

The Electoral Register is compiled in October each year using a standard form which is sent to each dwelling unit. The EERPS methodology exploits an existing administrative process by incorporating within it an ancilliary but separate data-collection exercise. There are two variants of the basic approach: the first uses a self-completion questionnaire (as in Telford) and the second uses face-to-face interviews (as in Strathclyde and Tameside). In both these cases, the EERPS methodology aims at 100 per cent coverage of occupied dwellings. Usually the complexity and scope of the questionnaire are kept to a minimum in order to maximise response. While there is a legal obligation to complete the electoral registration form, the completion of the questionnaire is voluntary. The EERPS method provides an estimate of population normally resident in households. To estimate the total population of an area, a parallel survey of the institutional population must be undertaken.

The desire to enumerate all people in all households is an optimistic objective given the voluntary nature of the survey and so it is essential to produce an estimate of the total number of occupied dwellings in order to assess the achievable response, to develop confidence intervals for the derived population estimates and to weight the raw data to account for non-response. While it is possible to produce a reliable estimate of the response rate for households, it is impossible, without using call-back quality-control checks, to be certain that households have responded correctly. The process may be susceptible to selective non-response which can blur accuracy of the results by producing an inaccurate estimate of total population and its age and sex profile and also by producing an inaccurate image of household composition.

At the household level the propensity to respond has been found to vary with a range of respondent attributes. Hardie (1985) found that households with young families were less likely to respond and in a survey conducted in Oldham in 1986 response was lowest in the inner-urban core which had a high concentration of ethnic minorities. It is usually those social groups and areas which are in greatest need in terms of the provision of services that have the lowest response rates. In addition, faulty questionnaire design may further bias the representativeness of what is, in effect, a self-selecting sample. EERPS need to achieve both a high global response and a spatially uniform response if the potential for error is to be minimised.

A review of EERPS in practice

Since the mid-1970s many local authorities have either undertaken EERPS or evaluated the technique. EERPS have been conducted in a wide range of urban and regional environments. It must be conceded that EERPS have not been successful in all cases: in Nottingham a calibration of the 1981 survey results against the 1981 Census revealed major discrepancies. There is a strong relationship between the type of electoral canvass and the probability of success: Vincent (1981) attributed the success of the Tameside exercise to 'linking the survey to an efficient electoral registration procedure which does not rely on householders for the completion or return of the forms'.

The Strathclyde Voluntary Population Survey is a variant of the EERPS approach and it is the largest regularly undertaken voluntary population survey in the UK, with 2.4 million people having been enumerated in the 1983 survey. It is conducted mainly by face-to-face interview with a postal approach only being used in the more remote areas. This accounts for the high and spatially uniform pattern of response. In common with the Nottingham survey, Black (1985) identified a problem with the enumeration of households with young children, and in particular he found that 0-year-old children were undercounted. Because of the computerised ageing routine used to generate the age profiles for subsequent years, a cumulative undercount of children will have occurred. OPCS VS1 tabulations can be used to produce a more reliable estimate of the total number of 0-year-olds.

Enhanced Electoral Register Population Surveys achieved widespread use in the 1970s but their use has not generally persisted into the 1980s. There have been problems with the accuracy of the approach and is some cases this has led to the discontinuation of EERPS. Telford, Strathclyde, Tameside, Portsmouth, Shropshire and Hampshire are examples of where the approach has been most successful. A common feature of these successful cases is that the surveys are implemented regularly: in Telford and Strathclyde the surveys are annual, and in Shropshire, Tameside, Portsmouth and Hampshire they are biennial.

Summary

The main advantage of the EERPS approach is that it is a cost-effective method of data collection (England *et al.*, 1985). Given a robust data-collection technique, EERPS produce accurate, small-area population estimates and a continuous flow of socio-demographic information for the monitoring of urban and regional change. The main limitation of EERPS is that they have, on occasion, produced unreliable population estimates: this has been caused both by residents' unwillingness to respond at all and by selective non-response. There have been problems with the enumeration of young children and with response rates in inner-city areas with large ethnic minority populations. The success of the approach is highly dependent on the type of electoral registration process used: postal methods are least effective and the best results are produced by door-to-door collections or interviews.

A method developed originally for the whole of Shropshire in 1976 has been made considerably more eleborate in the Telford area because of the desire to take an integrated approach to the monitoring of the demographic, social and economic development of Telford New Town. Developments have taken place in questionnaire design and implementation, in the range and sophisticaton of the output produced and in the linkages to other local information systems and secondary source material. It is this more elaborate system which is described in the next section.

THE TELFORD POPULATION INFORMATION SYSTEM

In conjunction with the annual electoral canvass, a questionnaire is delivered to and collected from each household in Telford. The detailed data-collection and analysis process in shown in Figure 2.1. While the questionnaire is implemented at the household level, it is structured on a person-by-person basis. A household is defined as the occupants of a single housing unit: the 'common housekeeping' criterion used to define households in the Census cannot be applied (OPCS, 1983). Three data items are collected on each person: age (single year), sex and work status. The work status variable identifies whether a person is employed or not, with employed being defined as having worked for eight or more hours in the previous week.

A count of occupied (and vacant) dwellings is also undertaken within the survey process to generate zonal weights to apply to the raw data to account for non-response. The Population Survey provides a count of those normally resident in households (the 'domestic' population). In order to produce an estimate of total population, an annual Institutional Survey is also undertaken. (In 1987 the domestic population of Telford was 111,473, and the institutional population was 878.)

Each form is geographically referenced using a hierarchical coding system which is used to assign responding households to one of 100 'survey zones'. In 1987, the average survey zone had a population of 1,100 people and contained 410 households. Survey zones can be aggregated into electoral wards and to approximate other types of spatial unit relevant to urban planning (such as school catchment areas and postcode sectors).

The accuracy of the results depends on the representativeness of the sample

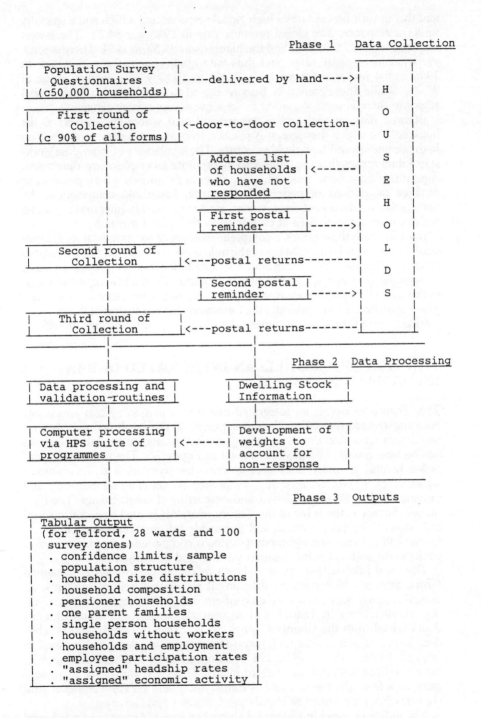

Figure 2.1 The Telford population survey: methodology

and this in turn necessitates a high global response and a high and a spatially uniform response. The global response rate in 1986 was 94.7%. The lowest response was 88.5% in 1978 and the highest was 95.5% in 1984. There is some variation in response rates (and thus data quality) across survey zones. In 1986, zonal response ranged from 78.8% to 100% with a median value of 96.0%. While the Population Survey has always achieved a high global response there is some variation in response across survey zones.

Because data on each individual are collected within the context of the household in which they live, it is possible to construct a variety of tables on both population and household structure. The availability of individual work-status data means that the tables also incorporate an employment dimension. Algorithms have been designed, using Census definitions where possible, to produce tabulations of population structure, household composition, the household distribution of employment, assigned headship rates and economic activity rates for each area at each level in the spatial hierarchy.

In addition to these tables, a comprehensive set of social indicators is produced for zones and wards. Many of the indicators are based on those available from the Census. Most important, the Population Survey provides a base, disaggregated by age, sex and employment status, for the production of social indicators when the survey is used in conjunction with other data sources. The Population Survey provides the foundation for an integrated urban information system for the measurement of socio-demographic change in Telford.

THE TELFORD MODEL: AN INTEGRATED URBAN INFORMATION SYSTEM

The 'Telford model' is an integrated urban information system which has been constructed to monitor the development of Telford. It contains data on population structure, on social issues, on vital events, on the labour market and on households. The model is shown as Figure 2.2. The framework comprises several spatially orientated information systems and data sources which support research, provide a comprehensive set of social indicators and provide the data for the modelling and forecasting of urban change. The Population Survey is the spine of the Telford model: it is used to produce social indicators, to support research and to provide information and assumptions for modelling in its own right, but its value is compounded when it is used in conjunction with other information systems and data sources.

The local information systems shown in Figure 2.2 comprise an annual Crime Survey which contains data on all prosecuted Telford residents, an annual Employment Survey which contains data on all employment-generating establishments in Telford, and an operational database which contains data derived from the County Council Social Services Department on children at risk of non-accidental injury. (The systems are described in detail in Worrall, 1986a; 1986b: 1987a; 1987b) Two nationally available data sources have also been built into the Telford model. These are ward-level unemployment data from the Department of Employment and OPCS ward-level vital statistics from the Office of Population Censuses and Surveys.

The indicator panel in Figure 2.2 shows the range of zone- and ward-level indicators which are available from the Telford model. They are used to

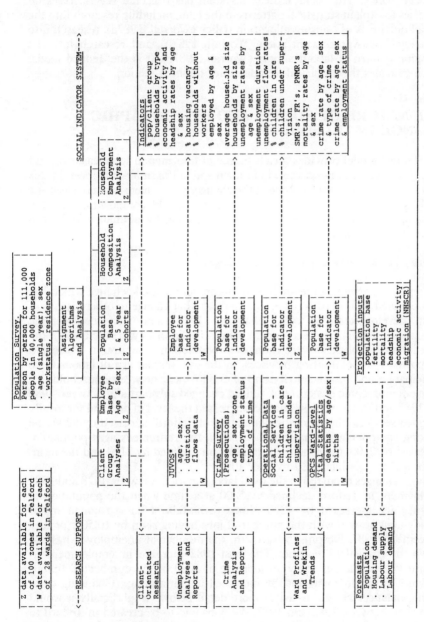

Figure 2.2 An integrated urban information system: the Telford model

* The nationally available JUVOS system superceded a local Unemployment Survey in October 1982.

measure the pace, scale and selectivity of urban change, to analyse the impact of policy, to identify emerging issues and to identify the common pathological characteristics of social groups and neighbourhoods as an input to the design of social policy. The social indicator system has triggered several research exercises to explain statistical patterns in the data, including research into the spatial outcomes of housing allocation policy (Worrall, 1987a), research into changing employer concentration (Worrall, 1987b), and research into the changing pattern of labour supply (Worrall, 1987c). It is the Telford model which provides the empirical foundation of the next section.

THE NATURE OF SOCIAL AND DEMOGRAPHIC CHANGE IN TELFORD

The Telford model provides a rich source of information for measuring and analysing urban change at the whole-town and at the small-area level. In this section, I propose to review some of the changes which have taken place at the whole-town level (in particular changing household composition and the changing labour-market position) before examining social change in Telford at the small-area level.

An overview of change at the whole-town level

An important aspect in the analysis of urban demographic change which has been pursued in Telford is the ability to relate that change to other aspects of urban development. Between 1980 and 1987 there were considerable demographic, social and economic changes in Telford (Worrall, 1987c): the most important of these were changes in population structure, in household composition, in commuting balances, in the age–sex pattern of labour-force participation and in the distribution of employment between households.

The demographic structure of Telford changed substantially between 1980 and 1987 and many of these changes increased the level of demand for locally provided services: the domestic population of Telford increased by 8200, the working-age population increased by 7100, the retirement ages population increased by 2200, the school-age population declined by 2100 and the number of under-fives increased by over 1000.

Major changes occurred in the local labour market: between 1978 and 1982 employment in Telford declined by 5800 at a time when the population of working age increased by 4200. Since then Telford has sustained major employment growth with the number of jobs having risen by 10,500 (or 25.7 per cent) to 1987. Despite this growth, the number of unemployed has not shown an equivalent decline. The post-1982 increase in employment in Telford was accompanied by an increase of 5000 in the number of Telford residents in employment and by increased in-commuting. (Changing commuting balances are discussed in more detail below.) Superficially it would seem that, between 1982 and 1987, two jobs had to be created in Telford to get one Telford resident into employment. In January 1988, male unemployment was 16.9 per cent and Telford had the second highest unemployment rate of the travel-to-work areas in the West Midlands Region.

This brief summary of recent socio-demographic change in Telford in the period from 1980 to 1987 shows that the scale of change has been substantial and these these changes have had major implications for the design of effective and responsive social policy and for the planning of services. In order to explore the impact of change further, I propose to examine recent change in household composition and in the Telford labour market more fully.

Changing household composition in Telford, 1980–7

Elsewhere (Worrall, 1987c), I used the concept of the *minimal household unit* (MHU) as a medium for exploring changes in household composition in Telford between 1980 and 1986. In the present work, the objective is again to examine changing household composition using the MHU as a medium for analysis but to explore in some detail the situational characteristics of certain household types.

An examination of Table 2.1 reveals that there have been significant changes in household composition in Telford since 1980: the number of one parent families increased by over 76% and the number of lone non-pensioner households increased by over 60%. The percentage of households which comprised a person living alone increased from 17.5% in 1980 to 21.8% in 1987. One of the major implications of changing household structures is its effect on the demand for housing in general and certain types of dwelling unit in particular. Even in a New Town context the increasing demand for housing for the elderly has been considerable. The number of pensioner-only households increased by over 1000 between 1980 and 1987, but what is more important is that certain more vulnerable pensioner household types came to account for a greater share of pensioner households: for example, the number of over-75s living alone increased from 1650 in 1980 to 2150 in 1987.

In 1980, 5.9% of children aged under 16 lived in one-parent families; by 1987 this had increased to 11.1%. Given the need to develop policies for this client group it is important to be able to identify the situational characteristics of this type of household. In 1987 one-parent families were predominantly (92%) female headed with 78% of these heads not being in employment. One-parent families were found to be spatially concentrated. In 1987, 11% of Telford's one parent families resided in one ward (the ward accounted for 5.5% of households in Telford).

This brief analysis of recent household change in Telford has illustrated the type of social and demographic analysis which can be conducted within the Telford model and the use of the concept of the MHU as a medium for analysis. In the next subsection I describe some of the recent changes which have taken place in the Telford labour market again to illustrate the analysis which has been carried out using locally collected data.

The changing local labour market, 1980–7

The conventional wisdom in economic planning is that employment creation is the panacea for both economic and social problems. If this is so then the failure of Telford's unemployment rate to respond to employment growth and the failure of various social indicators to respond to the upswing in Telford's

Table 2.1 The Changing Household Composition of Telford, 1980–7

Household type	1980	1981	1982	1983	1984	1985	1986	1987
One-parent family	975	1 074	1 177	1 265	1 387	1 517	1 655	1 717
Lone adult non-pensioner	2 604	2 857	3 154	3 465	3 685	3 799	4 082	4 184
Lone adult pensioner	3 727	3 926	4 143	4 272	4 468	4 586	4 693	4 885
Couple, no children	6 519	6 475	6 389	6 470	6 547	6 708	6 949	7 225
Pensioner couple	4 486	4 588	4 774	4 807	4 902	4 945	5 013	5 122
Couple with dependent children	10 598	10 523	10 382	10 348	10 279	10 145	9 944	9 762
Total simple households	28 909	29 443	30 019	30 627	31 268	31 700	32 336	32 895
3+ adults with dependent children	3 115	2 928	3 208	3 159	3 141	3 182	3 066	3 062
3+ adults, no dependent children	3 694	3 948	4 007	4 241	4 401	4 615	4 854	5 145
OTHER	497	501	516	491	501	525	519	499
Total complex households	7 306	7 377	7 731	7 891	8 043	8 322	8 439	8 706
Total households	36 215	36 820	37 750	38 518	39 311	40 022	40 775	41 601
Average household size	2.851	2.830	2.797	2.764	2.740	2.725	2.700	2.680

economic health are paradoxes which require some explanation. What is important is not to focus upon the volume of employment created but to examine the distributional issue of who is getting the jobs. In this subsection, I argue that the employment created in Telford has not benefited *all* Telford's residents and that many of the benefits of job creation in Telford have leaked into Telford's hinterland.

An explanation of the failure of unemployment to sustain a decline equivalent to the volume of jobs created can be sought, first, in an analysis of the changing distribution of employment between households; second, in the changing pattern of labour-force participation; and third, in changing commuting balance between Telford and its hinterland.

A fundamental change has taken place in the way that employment is distributed between households. Between 1980 and 1986 households became increasingly polarised into zero- and multi-worker household (see Table 2.2): in 1980, zero-worker households accounted for 18.34% of non-pensioner households, multi-worker households accounted for 38.65%, with the one-worker household being dominant (43.01% of non-pensioner households). By 1986, zero-, one- and multi-worker households accounted for 30.61%, 33.93% and 35.46%, respectively: the multi-worker household had become dominant despite the fact that male unemployment had increased from 8% in 1979 to 25% in 1985.

Between 1986 and 1987, the number of multi-worker households continued its upward trend to account for 37.62% of non-pensioner households: for the first time since 1980 the number of zero worker households broke its upward trend to decline by about 400 (to 28.91% of non-pensioner households). Between 1980 and 1987, the two main trends in the household distribution of employment were that employed became increasingly concentrated in multi-worker households and that unemployment became increasingly concentrated in zero-worker households.

Just as there was a change in the distribution of employment among households, there were also changes in the age–sex pattern of labour supply. For males, the all-age participation rate (16–64) declined from 76.8% in 1980 to 68.1% in 1987, reaching a low of 63.9% in 1984. The female all-age (16–59) participation rate increased from 41.6% in 1983 to 47.2% in 1987. A large proportion of the increase in female participation was accounted for by increases in participation rates for 20–44-year-olds. This phenomenon can be related to the simultaneous increase in the number of zero- and multi-worker households between 1980 to 1986 by means of the 'discouraged worker hypothesis' (Worrall, 1987c). This implies that the spouses of employed males are more likely to enter employment than the spouses of unemployed males.

The third means of explaining the failure of the number of employed residents to respond to employment growth is to examine Telford's changing commuting balance. From the Population Survey the total number of residents in employment can be identified and this can be used in conjunction with information from the Employment Survey on the total number of jobs in Telford and the volume of in-commuting into Telford to measure change in the commuting balance.

The pattern of commuting flows across Telford's boundaries changed after 1982. In 1982, there were 10 900 cross-boundary flows comprising 7400 out-flows and 3500 in-flows. By 1987 the volume of cross boundary flows had

Table 2.2 The Changing Distribution of Employment between Non-pensioner Households in Telford 1980-7

Household type	1980	1981	1982	1983	1984	1985	1986	1987
Zero-worker households	5 430	6 448	8 113	9 048	9 556	10 014	10 065	9 665
One-worker households	12 735	12 232	11 665	11 465	11 310	11 083	11 154	11 191
Multi-worker households	11 442	10 854	10 422	10 326	10 547	11 193	11 659	12 577
Non-pensioner households	29 607	29 534	30 200	30 839	31 413	32 290	32 878	33 433

increased to 16 700. Out-flows increased marginally to 3800 but in-commuting increased to 12 900. In 1982, 18.9% of jobs in Telford were taken by in-commuters but by 1987 this had increased to 26.3%. The number of Telford residents employed in Telford also increased (by 4850 from 31 500 in 1982 to 36 350 in 1987). By 1987 both Telford residents and the residents of Telford's hinterland had become increasingly dependent on the New Town as a workplace: the *proportion* of Telford residents in employment who worked outside Telford had declined from 10.1% in 1982 to 9.5% in 1987.

The disparity between employment growth in Telford and the growth in the number of employed residents raises questions about the relative employability of Telford residents compared to the residents of its hinterland and about the potential mismatch between the skill requirements of the jobs being created and the skill and educational endowments of the local labour force. The coexistence of large numbers of zero- and multi-worker households also raises distributional issues about the concentration of employment in some households and the concentration of unemployment in others.

The social, economic and demographic trends identified in Telford from 1980 are fundamentally relevant to the development of urban policy. The trends raise questions about the relative employability of Telford residents, about the leakage of the direct *and* indirect effects of employment creation from Telford, about the social consequences of the changing distribution of employment between households and about meeting the housing and other welfare needs of different population groups and household types.

The analysis of urban change at the small-area level

Having identified the direction and scale of social economic and demographic change at the whole-town level it remains to examine the impact of some of these changes at the small-area level and to examine what effects these changes have had on individual neighbourhoods. It is important to be able to monitor intra-urban variations in welfare in order to develop responsive urban policy, to identify emerging social problems and to ensure that resources are being targeted on those social groups and neighbourhoods with the greatest need.

In order to monitor small-area social change, four social indicators for each of 98 survey zones were selected: they, together with a range of basic statistics to describe the changing distributions of the indicators between 1980 and 1987, are shown in Table 2.3. The analysis gives some indication of the extent and nature of social change within Telford over that period.

From Table 2.3 it can be seen that there are wide intra-urban differences in social conditions within Telford: in 1987, male unemployment ranged between 16.71% and 60.07% and the one-parent family indicator ranged between 0% and 23.89%. Over the whole period, and particularly from 1980 to 1986, evidence of substantial intra-urban social change can be found on all indicators: the mean, the range and the standard deviation of the one-parent families indicator increased continuously though it retained roughly the same degree of positive skewness; the mean and the standard deviation of the crime indicator increased continuously and it became more positively skewed; the range of the male unemployment indicator widened from 28% in 1980 to 47% in 1986 and became more positively skewed.

Table 2.3 Some basic statistics of socio-spatial change

Indicator*	Min	Max	Mean	SD	Skewness
OPF__80	0.000	18.634	5.769	3.634	0.805
OPF__82	0.000	20.091	6.815	4.103	0.692
OPF__83	0.000	22.421	7.789	4.487	0.696
OPF__84	1.176	23.684	8.756	4.907	0.653
OPF__85	1.501	27.053	9.409	5.323	0.838
OPF__86	1.948	28.087	10.266	5.608	0.792
OPF__87	0.000	23.890	10.420	5.942	0.426
CRM__80	n/a	n/a	n/a	n/a	n/a
CRM__82	0.000	15.201	4.710	3.421	0.827
CRM__83	0.000	18.781	5.413	4.267	1.188
CRM__84	0.000	24.891	5.968	4.994	1.456
CRM__85	0.000	22.861	6.298	5.110	1.309
CRM__86	0.301	25.398	6.460	5.193	1.466
CRM__87	0.000	19.385	6.290	4.898	0.862
ZWH__80	4.918	34.017	18.545	6.498	0.129
ZWH__82	7.331	48.746	27.441	10.454	0.235
ZWH__83	7.664	55.513	29.909	11.620	0.319
ZWH__84	8.158	61.317	31.053	12.577	0.259
ZWH__85	8.479	61.181	31.805	12.024	0.302
ZWH__86	9.873	62.305	31.492	12.311	0.438
ZWH__87	8.312	56.747	30.112	11.418	0.376
MUN__80	10.165	38.197	23.363	5.718	0.081
MUN__82	16.058	59.058	33.809	9.014	0.284
MUN__83	19.378	60.396	36.487	10.182	0.220
MUN__84	16.637	61.638	36.887	11.034	0.176
MUN__85	18.108	62.722	36.634	11.228	0.304
MUN__86	14.914	61.905	35.547	10.986	0.379
MUN__87	16.710	60.070	33.470	10.010	0.393

*The small-area indicators used have the following definitions:
OPF__*yy* 0–15s in one parent families (%)
MUN__*yy* males aged 16–64 *not* in employment (%)
CRM__*yy* prosecution rate for males aged 16–64 (%)
ZWH__*yy* non-pensioner households with no workers (%)

Between 1986 and 1987 there were the signs of a break in the trend: the range of all indicators narrowed; the degree of intra-urban variation in crime rates, male unemployment and the precentage of zero-worker households (as shown by the standard deviation) declined and, in addition, the OPF, CRM and ZWH measures became less positively skewed.

The basic statistics show that significant change occurred in the socio-spatial form of Telford between 1980 and 1987. Until 1986, there was a general trend towards increasing ranges, increasing means and increasing standard deviations: all these factors point to a divergence in the social conditions within Telford between 1980 and 1986 with the begining of a reversal of this trend in 1987.

CONCLUSIONS

The main purpose of this chapter was to show that the ability to acquire knowledge about the many dimensions of urban change depends primarily upon the existence of well-designed and well-managed information systems to provide decision-makers and urban analysts with the data they need. Within the UK the cancellation of the last two mid-term Censuses and the generally poor quality of nationally available information sources on small-area demographic, social and economic issues mean that much of the information needed to support the development of effective and responsive urban policy does not exist. This lack of systematically organised and regularly available information has prompted some urban and regional planning authorities to develop their own sources of information to measure social, demographic and economic change.

From the review of EERPS applications it was found that the approach had not been successful everywhere. In those areas where the approach had been regularly applied it was found that it had generated accurate and usable information. In the Telford case, data generated using an EERPS has been used as a spine for an integrated urban information system in which locally collected data and secondary source material are used in conjunction with each other.

The Telford model was shown to provide a rich source of information for the analysis of change at both the whole-town and the small-area levels. The material presented was included primarily to illustrate the analytical potential of the Telford model but it did reveal a number of issues which are fundamentally relevant to the development of urban policy. At the whole-town level the analysis showed that the demands on local government have increased considerably in the 1980s and in particular from a rising number of elderly people and an increasing number of people in vulnerable groups such as children in one-parent families and households lacking economic support.

The analysis raised issues about the functioning of the local labour market: particularly concern about the labour-market processes which appear to be concentrating employment in some households and unemployment in others and also a concern about the relative employability of Telford's residents given the disparity between local employment growth and the growth in the number of employed residents. At the small-area level, it was shown that wide disparities exist in the levels of several social indicators within Telford and that social conditions had tended to diverge between 1980 and 1986 with those areas which were already deprived deteriorating relative to the Telford-wide norm.

Given that most contemporary social problems tend to be manifest within urban areas, it is disappointing that the Telford model should be the exception rather than the rule, in that it is unique within the UK. The complexity of urban problems, together with the considerable economic and social costs of making wrong decisions, necessitate the development of information systems to support public policy-making. Within the UK this challenge has been largely unmet.

BIBLIOGRAPHY

Black R. (1984) *Instead of the 1986 Census: The Information Needs of Local Authority Policy Making. Local Authorities Research and Intelligence Association: Papers delivered to the 1984 Conference.* Birmingham: INLOGOV.

Black R. (1985) 'Instead of the 1986 Census: the potential contribution of enhanced electoral registers', *Journal of the Royal Statistical Society*, vol. 148, no. 4, pp. 287–316.

England J., Hudson K., Masters R., Powell K and Shortridge J. (1985) *Information Systems for Policy Planning in Local Government.* London: Longman.

Hardie P. (1985) 'Using Operational Data to Supplement the Census', *BURISA*, no. 68, pp. 4–5.

OPCS (1983) *The Family*. Occasional Paper 31. London: OPCS.

Redfern P. (1988) *A Study of the Future of the Census of Population: Alternative Approaches.* Luxembourg: The Statistical Office of the European Communities.

Vincent R. (1981) 'ERE Population Surveys—What makes them worthwhile', *BURISA*, no.51, pp. 13–15.

Worrall L. (1985) 'Social and economic research in an English New Town: local information systems', *Environment and Planning*, vol. 12B, pp. 277–86.

Worrall L. (1986a) 'Information Systems for Policy Planning in a Shire District', *BURISA*, no. 72, pp. 8–10.

Worrall L. (1986b) 'The analysis and management of urban change: the role of local information systems', *Journal of Economic and Social Measurement.* 14(4), 257–270.

Worrall L. (1987a) 'Information systems development and the analysis of urban change'. Unpublished PhD thesis, Department of Civic Design, University of Liverpool.

Worrall L. (1987b) 'Information systems for urban labour market planning and analysis', in I. Gordon (ed.), *Unemployment, the Regions and Labour Markets: Reactions to Recession.* London Papers in Regional Science, no. 17. London: Pion.

Worrall L. (1987c) 'Population information systems and the analysis of urban change', *Town Planning Review.* 58(4), 411–425.

Worrall L. (1988) *Information System Development and the Management of Urban Change.* LARIA Occasional Paper, no.2.

Chapter 3

MIGRATION MONITORING AND STRATEGIC PLANNING

Jean Forbes

MIGRATION, POLICY AND THE NEED FOR MONITORING

Migration is the outcome of a process of decision-making by individuals acting alone or as a household unit. A move from an origin to a destination traces an observable path in the visible world. The distance and direction of the path reflects the migrant's response, in his decision-making, to the social, economic and environmental forces which together surround and shape his perception of the need to move, his capacity to choose among preferred destinations and his ability to realise his intentions. The same forces also define and determine the range of opportunities open to potential movers, and are interwoven with both the 'structuring context' and the 'behavioural response' (Woods, 1983).

Political forces structure the whole of society and, through strategic planning, modify the configuration of the environment. Both context and behavioural response are thus embedded within policy and politics. Lewis (1982) has reviewed academic research into migration. Migration is observed at various spatial scales: intra-national (between regions of the nation); intra-regional (between localities within regions); and intra-locality. (This may arbitrarily select particular ages and stages of migrants since an individual may move at different scale levels at different stages in one lifetime.) In most cases, the observations relate to moves between spatially aggregated territorial units, counted at one particular time, for example, at Census year. The study of migration is thus imprisoned in a data environment which is of restricted value for the task in hand. First there is the unsolved cartographic problem which arises when data are aggregated into spatial units for mapping. The problem is evident enough when one is mapping static data such as presence or absence of an item within an area, but becomes very difficult when mapping *movement* between areal units, as Figure 3.1 demonstrates. The maps shown were all made from the same basic data using different areal meshes (Forbes, 1984). The resulting portrayals of both volume and direction of move are so different from each other that one wonders which (if any) represents reality.

In temporal terms, Kosinski (1975) notes that there is a fundamental difference between a continuous record (a kind of movie film) of a dynamic process like migration, and a 'snapshot' which, at one time, asks for details of previous

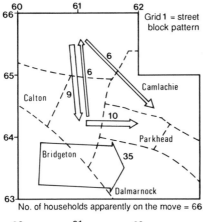

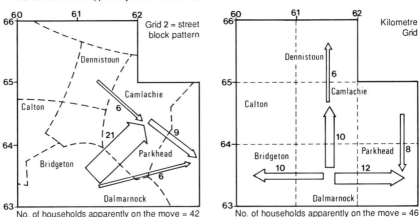

Figure 3.1 Demonstration of the effect of the size and shape of areal unit mesh on the apparent volume and direction of migration flows. All three maps use the same base data (adapted from Forbes 1984).

residence within a specified previous period such as one year. The observation of migration in a pre-set time block of some particular scale, conditions the sensitivity of the record in exactly the same way as does the shape, and scale of aggregation, of spatial recording unit mesh. 'The longer the time interval, the less accurate becomes the migration measure as an indicator of mobility level' (Rogers and Castro, 1986, p. 158).

The ideal way of observing the patterns of migration would be by way of a population register which would record the precise origin and destination of a move at the time it takes place. Since this basic recording would be at the level of the individual, all spatial levels of study could be serviced through simple aggregation. Equally, longitudinal studies could be packaged into desired aggregations of time blocks. If, as in Sweden, each person had an identity in the record it would be possible to follow individual 'life paths' in these longitudinal studies (Hägerstrand, 1972).

The difference between the register (or monitor) type of approach and the snapshot (or census) approach affects the kinds of study which can be based upon the data. Snapshot data of pre-set time blocks, aggregated into pre-set territories, leave research wholly dependent on those data as they stand and on the apparent patterns they portray in space and time. The research task has to be developed within the constraints of the data, and contributions to theory are circumscribed by this. By contrast, with unaggregated data it would be possible to construct hypotheses for testing and to extract the data in any spatial and/or temporal aggregation which fitted the task.

Penetration of the hidden processes of migration requires studies based on interviews at the level of the decision-making household. The pattern of moves observed and mapped by whatever method constitutes the sampling frame within which process studies can be grounded. If the frame is inadequate in its spatial precision and/or temporal up-to-dateness, the essential task of finding the movers to interview is difficult and the sample studies cannot be clearly related to their regional context.

Flexible, precise and up-to-date data, such as would be available from a migration monitor, would serve two important client groups. First, it would serve academic research into process. This research, with its ability to deliver clearer and more timely understanding of this process, would itself have two uses. One would be to serve theory-building and the other would be to contribute directly to the work of strategic planners of societal and environmental change. In addition to a research-derived understanding of process, this latter group requires a basis of data for diagnosing routine managerial problems and assessing the impact of policy. These data must follow events closely in the time dimension.

'Strategic planning' is a term usually applied at regional level. It connotes the task of designing the spatial patterns of housing accommodation, services, employment and transportation, for the population, together with the programming of these developments. The strategic planning task requires co-ordination of the policies for social and economic and physical development and the making of a design for their combined location in regional space such that the overall living environment is made as good as possible for all the citizens. It is thus a process of fitting environments to people, and of managing this 'fit' so that it serves peoples' needs, area by area, and within reasonable spans of time. Its whole rationale rests upon knowing where the population is at any one time, what its structure is, predicting changes by small area, and identifying areas or groups in difficulty.

The task of the strategic planner is to develop policy for overall improvement and to manage the day-to-day implementation of existing policies. This needs data which precisely track spatial movements about the region, on an up-to-date basis to enable routine administration to be efficient and quick to respond to crises; to permit study of the efficacy or otherwise of existing service delivery routines and housing-development activity; and to provide a basis for comprehensive evaluation of policy impacts and for related policy adjustments or review.

The product of academic research into the process of migration would, if delivered quickly, shed light on the relationships between households, services and environment. This would enable the components of policy to be better fine-tuned to locality or group needs.

A working model of the process of migration is necessary to clarify the design principles of a monitor, to aid the interpretation of any monitored record and to guide the use of the monitor as a sampling frame. The whole study of process must weigh factors of society and factors of place, since both together comprise the 'living environment' in which people tread their life paths.

Since there is a reasonable case for monitoring migration, it is worth examining further the design implications.

POSSIBLE STRUCTURE FOR A REGIONAL MONITORING SYSTEM

Design items

The ideal monitor should permit spatially precise and temporally continuous tracking of household moves. In the absence of a national-level system of population registration in the UK, it is evident that any monitoring will have to be confined to the regional or even sub-regional level, be set up and run by such interested parties as can join together for the purpose and will thus be available to feed into research and management only at this local level. However, this enforced localising of effort need not, indeed should not, be of merely parochial significance. The basic principles of structure and function in the design of a monitor will be similar in their logic whatever the scale of territory within which the monitor will operate. Its output data, being precise and continuously recorded, would open the way to research findings and management procedures which should have more than local applicability.

The design elements which need to be considered are:
(a) the potential input data, its nature and availability;
(b) the system of spatial and temporal referencing;
(c) the management of regular data reporting to the central monitoring unit;
(d) the tasks of the monitoring unit;
(e) the procedures for using the output from the record

Potential input data

Records of moves through the housing stock make up the most accessible data dealing with individual household moves. The degree of accessibility varies between public and private sectors throughout the UK. In the public sector the District Councils, being the housing authorities, routinely record the old and new address of a tenant (and thus a household) who transfers from one house to another within their stock. New tenants entering the stock are similarly recorded. This is effectively migration data, although data are collected for other administrative reasons.

In the private sector, Scotland has the unique advantage of the historic Register of Sasines. This is a public record which documents every property transaction. Although not existing to record migration, the Register of Sasines does do this since the documentation of each transaction includes the old and the new address of any house buyer. The record has some snags requiring careful interpretation, for example, the fact that the buyer is not always moving (McCleery, 1980). These are far outweighed by the geographic totality and temporal continuity of the coverage.

Such a public record is absent in England. Some records of moves do exist, most notably the family practitioner records of changes of address of doctors' patients. These records are held by the local health authorities but are subject to strict confidentiality constraints which require them to be preaggregated before release to researchers. This diminishes the value of the record for fine-grained monitoring. Records of changes of address also exist within the electricity authorities' systems for purposes of collection of payments, but not in an easily collatable form.

In England tracking of private-sector moves will have to be a complicated orchestration of such varied local sources of information as can be found, including data from estate agents as well as public bodies. The very variety of these sources may preclude early development of a true monitoring system at household level.

In the private rented sector the difficulties of tracking household movement are uniformly great throughout the UK. Short of finding and entering into a regular reporting agreement with every private landlord, of whom there is a multitude, there seems to be no secure way of tracing the moves through this stock. The degree of difficulty this poses is in proportion to the quantity of total stock affected. Scotland gains here, for historical reasons. In Glasgow, for example, only 10% of the stock is in 'the private rental sector', a proportion low enough that its absence from a monitoring system would not invalidate the general usefulness of that system.

With the Scottish data it is possible to test monitoring ideas at the scale of a conurbation. This chapter draws on preliminary studies for a proposed experimental migration monitor for the Greater Glasgow area, covering a population of about 1.5 million. In summary, in the public sector the Glasgow data can give origin address, destination address, and the number of rooms at each; in the private sector it can give origin address, destination address (though with no data on size of house)[1], and the price paid for the house.

The system of spatial and temporal referencing

The Glasgow data are recorded in their source records, by ordinary postal address and by date of transaction. For purposes of monitoring, a single spatial and a single temporal referencing system must be agreed and all data conformed to it at the point of input to the monitor. This is symbolised in Figure 3.2 as the 'coding screen'.

The most elegant and stable system of locational referencing available to us is the National Grid system. The virtues of the system are:

(a) it can provide a 'point' level of locational referencing which uniquely identifies a building;
(b) it provides systems of spatial aggregation which are either higher orders of the grid itself, or customer-specified through point-in-polygon procedures whereby a chosen spatial area is defined by a string of point references defining its shape on the map;
(c) it lends itself to computer manipulations and graphic output, since it simultaneously defines positions in mathematical space as well as geographic space;
(d) it never changes, thus commending itself for any kinds of study which require longitudinal comparisons over a spread of years.

The Chorley Report (1987) commended the use of the geocoding system of the National Grid when practicable because of its flexibility and capability of linking various data sets (recommendations 37–40). Practicability is conditioned by two interacting factors: the availability of a gazetteer which lists the point reference of each conventional address; and the size of the data set expected to be involved in any single monitor. Without a gazetteer, every origin and every destination would need to be individually digitised or (worse) determined by eye from large-scale maps at the time of input. This cumbersome procedure would only be worth undertaking with a small study area and would even then be tiresome and costly to sustain over time. The most effective remedy in these circumstances is to make a local gazetteer.

A gazetteer exists for the administrative city of Glasgow, but not yet for any suburbs beyond the boundary. From the gazetteer tape, the point reference (or geocode) could be added automatically as the origin and destination addresses were being typed routinely for input as part of existing office procedures. A program is available to do this. This automated procedure is usable only where the record-keeping has been computerised. In non-computerised authorities, a gazetteer in hard copy form would greatly assist the task of geocoding manually since it can be used at input like a telephone book.

The cost–benefit calculations about geocoding for migration study need to be reckoned in association with the overarching calculations about the value of geocoding a local authority's whole information system.

The ideal circumstance for the migration monitor would be the existence of comprehensive computerised gazetteer coverage, *and* computerised routine record-keeping. In the Greater Glasgow area these circumstances are approached. The data from the Register of Sasines are collated and computer-stored regularly for the Strathclyde region area by the Department of Land Economics at Paisley College of Technology. Hence for monitoring purposes this record at Paisley is similar in form to the city's and the surrounding districts' record of moves through public sector houses. The only missing piece in the jigsaw is a gazetteer for areas outside the city.

Temporal referencing, by contrast with spatial referencing, is a simple issue. We all use the same calendar and clock. What remains to be decided is the most useful temporal frequency with which to enter data in the monitoring unit archive. Since the contributory data are recorded at the level of the day date, it would be easy to standardise into totals per calendar month.

The management of data

Since both the potential data suppliers and the potential users of the monitor are likely to be varied, two central elements in the system must be: first, a steering group representing the local authorities and research agencies to form policy guidance and to exercise collective 'weight' with the official bodies and institutions in which they work as individuals and which are potentially data contributors and/or users; and second, a technical monitoring unit located on organisationally 'neutral ground', like in a university or college, where it can stand slightly outside any inter-agency tensions and be more clearly visible and accessible to a wider public.

The steering group would advise on the appropriate procedure for gather-

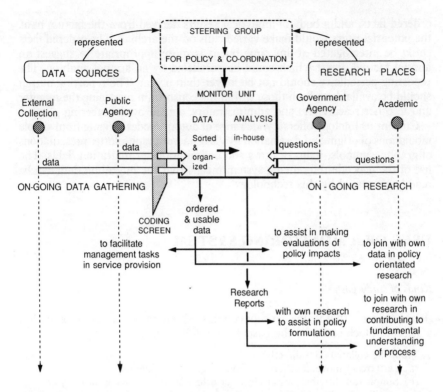

Figure 3.2 Outline structure for the migration monitor, showing data sources and potential output paths

ing the data in the central archive on a regular basis whether from computerised or non-computerised sources. Such data would then need to be entered into the computer archive as a recurring input operation at the unit. As shown in Figure 3.2, it is suggested that there would be two kinds of work to be done by this unit: one, the routine archive work, which would involve the receiving, collating and inputting of data to the computer, and the outputting to prospective users of some ordered expressions of quantity and pattern of movement; the second kind of work would be some basic routine analysis of the factual record, for example, numbers moving particular distances or numbers moving across tenure-type boundaries, and the outputting of this to users.

Whether as archive or source of analysis, the monitoring unit's essential reason for existence would be to provide a *service*, to all *bona fide* users, in public authorities or universities.

Procedures for using the record

The monitoring unit's work would need to be arranged to permit responses to be made to the potential clients, indicated on the right hand side of Figure 3.2. Given that there would be two streams of output, a body of sorted and ordered facts, and a body of analytical results derived from the factual base, the potential users would make varied calls on the archive. The ordered facts could be interrogated at any time but it is more appropriate to suggest an annual factual digest which could be paralleled by an annual analysis. The reporting periodicity should not be longer than a year. The reporting output should be available to both those within the consortium managing the monitor and to other researchers and administrators, agreed by the steering group.

Current technology offers a wide range of output modes ranging from simple tabulations of origin and destination to VDU and/or graph-plotter presentations of graphs, symbols, maps of flows and delimitations of migration fields. The use of the geocode referencing system means that the migration data can be readily processed by this technology.

USES OF A MONITORING SYSTEM

Kinds of study possible

At any one time (that is, in snapshot conditions) portrayals of migration within a selected block could be the basis for the following:

1. From the collated data directly:
   (a) Patterns of movement (arrows from origin to destination).
   (b) Simple dot distributions of places or origin of those moving into any area specified by the point-in-polygon procedure.
   (c) Superimposition of such distributions on maps of location of aspects of the 'environment':
      (i) service points;
      (ii) age and tenure of housing stock;
      (iii) patterns of accessibility to transport networks.

2. From partially analysed data:
   (a) Graphical analysis of distance versus number of moves.
   (b) Migration fields (measures of diminishing intensity of moves with increasing distance from importing area).
   (c) Distribution of turnover (relationship between net change per enumeration unit and the number of inhabited houses) (see Robertson, 1982).
   (d) Migration (or vacancy) chains (see Clark, 1984).

All such portrayals of pattern could be as wide as the monitor area, but, by virtue of the precision of the spatial referencing, it would be possible to 'zoom' in on particular sub-areas and enlarge the pattern to reveal the fine texture of local movements.

Patterns portrayed over time (the 'movie-film' conditions) would allow all the above studies to be replicated over a succession of observation times:

1. Studies in time dimension: a particular type of moving group may be sampled and studied at sample times (for instance, cross-tenure movers) wherever they are found within the study area.
2. Studies in space and time: particular localities may be selected and studied by way

of replications of sample interviews to lend depth to the spatial patterns of change within them and/or between them and the rest of the study area.

As data accumulate in the record the possibilities offered by the data as a spatial or temporal *sampling frame* increase. Sample studies of process require interview-based work at the level of the decision-making unit (that is, the household). The proposed spatial precision would permit accurate targeting of the interview visits. Sampling could be related to broad groups (such as those moving to new built areas, or from public to private housing) or to particular locales (such as suburbs or central area rehabilitated houses). The up-to-dateness of the monitor would allow movers to be found reasonably soon after the move, while the decision-making would still be in mind and could be discussed.

Knowledge applied to tasks

Figure 3.3 suggests the range of tasks to which monitored data could be linked. There would be two major kinds of people involved, as indicated at the bottom of the figure: those in government (central or local); and those in academic research institutions. These cover three types of task between them (the central one being overlapped by both): implementation of service policy and routine management thereafter; discernment of problems and consequent policy formulation; and contribution to overall theoretical understanding of the processes in society.

The kinds of data use noted above are given again in the column headings of Figure 3.3. Reading vertically under each heading, the information is shown progressing through the kinds of study already described, *en route* to its destination in servicing the range of managerial, policy and theoretical research tasks. These lines of developing knowledge may travel directly to the tasks, or may be supplemented as they proceed, by being linked to '*Other data sets*' and '*Other studies*'. These other sources of knowledge are listed in the second row of the diagram matrix.

The most significant kind of 'other data' would be base population data which may be available routinely from the electoral registration process and its associated 'enhancements'. The social work and education departments of a local authority, and local health authorities, have large bodies of socially significant data linked to house addresses which may bear upon or may be influenced by the migrations within the region. If geocoding was used by several departments of a local authority each could analyse its own record for its own purposes within its confidentiality boundaries, while still being able to cross-link to the data sets of others at an agreed level of aggregation to conceal individual cases. Institutional data on the distribution and state of the housing stock and local and structure plan commitments relative to new development would both influence and help to explain migration patterns.

'Other studies' by other agencies, if related to the studies coming from partial analysis of the migration data, could create considerable new knowledge of population and socio-environmental relationships within the overall process of urban change. This in turn could feed into both policy-making and theoretical research.

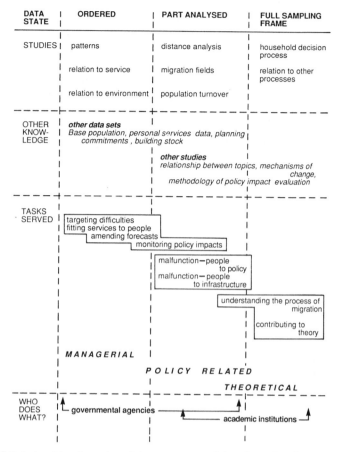

Figure 3.3 Relationship of monitored data to managerial, policy-related and theoretical study tasks

MIGRATION DATA AND LOCAL GOVERNMENTAL TASKS

The tasks which could be serviced by monitored migration data are shown slanting diagonally across the centre of Figure 3.3, symbolising the overlapping progression from managerial tasks through to theoretical developments. These tasks which fall within the ambit of local governmental agencies are as follows.

1. Managerial tasks:
   (a) Perception of areas of difficulty; indicated by excessive out-movement or rapid turnover.
   (b) Fine-tuning service provision to population by area with minimum time-lag, thus effecting technical economy and consumer satisfaction.
   (c) (Linked to the above) refining small-area population forecasts as well as authority-wide forecasts (linked to strategic service planning).
   (d) Acting as a component in overall housing need projections.

2. Policy-forming tasks:
   (a) Definition of population-related problems for the whole territory of the authority, for example, major inter-locality shifts or inter-tenure shifts.
   (b) Applying understanding of process of migration (derived from links to research studies) to development of policies for new development or rehabilitation and to the general improvement of areas perceived to be in need.
   (c) Assessment of infrastructure planning implications in terms of needed quantity and desired location.
3. Policy impact measuring:
   (a) Acting as part of an overall system of monitoring social, economic and environmental policy impacts. Routine recording of volume and destination of migration into newly-built housing would reveal the extent of the effects of a development strategy, such as that in Strathclyde region which seeks to contain new development on brownfield sites within the existing settlement outline (Cowan, 1986).
   (b) Contributing to overall periodic evaluation of the effectiveness of current policy, for example a declared policy such as that in the Glasgow Eastern Area Renewal (GEAR) project to attract young people into an area to improve the age structure.

In relation to the monitoring and evaluation of local authority policy, the periodic reporting from the migration monitor should be timed to coincide with critical points in the administrative and political cycles of local government. Annual monitoring reports could be connected directly to the beginning of the annual budget deliberations of the authority each autumn. Every fourth migration report could be linked to the four-year electoral cycle, and contain records of the preceding four years' analysis of both pattern and process.

Sample studies of the migration process, reinforced by studies of other processes, would create a better understanding of the mechanisms of local social change, and of the interweaving roles of social, economic and physical planning factors. This work would have practical benefit to strategic planners concerned with the steering of regional change, as well as providing an important underpinning for the development of theory.

THE MIGRATION MONITOR AND RESEARCH TASKS

While the monitor would provide a uniquely valuable sampling frame it will be necessary to have some outline theory or model in mind to enable the research *foci* to be selected so as to maximise the use of the frame. The following paragraphs and Figure 3.4 sketch the outlines of a possible model.

The context within which migrants form their decisions is a complex amalgam of macro- and micro-factors. Macro-factors are social, economic and physical, and structure the potential choice of the household and are beyond its power to control. Micro-scale factors relate to the household itself. Some of them are 'given', like age, personality, health, and some are profoundly influenced by the macro-structures, for example, education (and aspiration) level and income. The amalgam produces the household's perceptions of its present conditions, shapes its capability to 'respond' through its decision to move, and frames its choice of alternative home and its actual moving. Holm and Öberg (1984, p. 70) express these as 'an exposure phase, a search phase, a decision phase and a realized phase'.

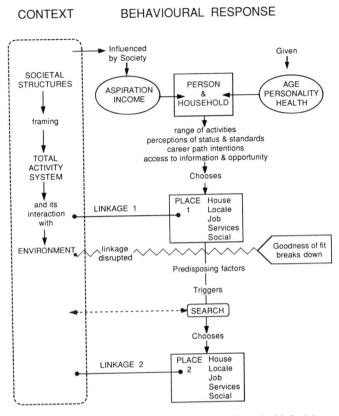

CONTEXT   BEHAVIOURAL RESPONSE

Figure 3.4 Outline model of elements and stages in a household decision to move

Figure 3.4 distinguishes between the given factors and those influenced by society. It lists some of the resulting characteristics which shape the propensity to move (such as perception of status).

The model indicates that each person in society is an actor requiring space for the accommodation of his activities. Activities take place in the physical environment and the aggregate of all citizens' activities demands, and obtains, a constantly changing modification of the visible world for activity location. Each person has a characteristic range of his own activities determined by age, aspiration and income. He is thus involved, in however small a way, in the constant dialogue between activity space demand and environmental supply. The relationship between activity system and environment is symbolised on the left of Figure 3.4.

Through the structured world of the aggregate activities–environment relationship each individual moves between home and activity places or (more rarely) from one home to another in pursuit of a 'best fit' between his lifestyle and the world around him. The individual (or in a more complicated way, the household) 'plugs in' to all the sites in the city at which his (its) activities can be pursued within the finite span of time given in the waking day (Carlstein, 1978; Lenntorp, 1976) and within reasonable reach of home. Strategic planning policy's task is to identify localities or groups suffering 'bad fit' at the present time and to act to change some aspect of the organisation or spatial or temporal structure of the activities involved, to improve the 'fit' in the future.

Planning policy, like all aspects of macro decision-making, inevitably alters the social-economic-environmental context within which the next round of individual decisions will be made. At the same time, official perception of today's discontents becomes an input to tomorrow's planning policy formulation.

In such a complex landscape of interrelated factors it is essential to be able to follow the actual moves of households in space *and* through time, if one is to win understanding of the process of migration. The time dimension is especially significant. People respond differently to external factors according to particular conjunctions of their career paths and their life-cycle stage. That personal progression through stages is itself borne on the back of the larger progression of societal change through calendar time which alters the mix of context factors. The visible environmental context, changing slowly in time, may vary markedly between localities in a single region. Only with a migration monitor can one hope to obtain a research sampling frame which is not itself the product of one time or one small locality.

The behavioural response to context

Figure 3.4 condenses the decision to move into a choice between Place 1 and Place 2. Each place has characteristics of: house (its size and quality); locale (its 'amenity'); job (its accessibility); service pattern (its range and accessibility); and social associations (character and variety). Cullen and Phelps (1978) indicate that the transition out of Place 1 to any other place is a two stage process. First the move is decided upon and made when the place utility at Place 1 breaks down, or, in our terms here, when the 'fit' between the household's activity pattern and the surroundings ceases to be a good 'fit'. Following a move, the household adapts to its new place and 'plugs in' to the new social and physical environment. It will only be disposed to move again when the household's own character changes and/or the context changes and 'good fit' breaks down again. (Note Petersen's, 1970, observation that some people move to improve their circumstances and others move to maintain their existing level of well-being).

Table 3.1 suggests the range of factors which could lead to a move, noting those which 'predispose' to a feeling of discontent and those more sudden events which 'trigger' action. This simplistic model conceals within it the effects of countervailing factors, such as lack of an alternative place at the right time or lack of sufficient finance, which can both delay action indefinitely.

The whole elaborate process of looking for Place 2 demonstrates the interplay between spatial and aspatial scanning. The spatial search is for the right place at which the household's activities can continue to be pursued with the minimum of disruption, (intra-regional migration involves many short distance moves; in Glasgow in 1974 over 50 per cent of all moves involved distances of less than 2 km—see Forbes *et al.*, 1977, p. 12). The aspatial search seeks the right house at the right price. Both kinds of search will be profoundly influenced by the characteristics of the searcher and especially by his

Table 3.1 Predisposing and trigger factors

	Predisposing factors which lead to discontent if changed away from the 'good fit' condition	Trigger factors (examples)
Personal and household	• Age/structure • Health • Aspiration • Income • Perceived status	• Child leaves home for job. • Sudden illness; death or birth in family. • Aspiration outruns present conditions. • Loss of job. • New housing opportunity occurs.
Social connections	• Proximity to relatives • Proximity to friends • Links to local social groups • Good neighbours	• Relatives leave. • Friends leave. • Social groups close down. • Quarrel with neighbours.
Environmental attachments	• School of choice nearby • Shops of choice nearby • Several family links to various services • Family long established in city sector	• Service closes. • Family links to locality disconnected.

access to information. (Studies reviewed by Clark (1982)). Migration is thus a highly constrained process in which the factors balance out differently for every potential moving household. Sample studies of the decision to move will require to pursue the factors. Responses will inevitably be filtered through differentially reliable memories and variable value systems and decisions made with partial knowledge.

The presence of a migration monitor would allow sample studies to be located in various localities at one time and/or replicated in selected areas over a span of time. Table 3.2 gives examples of kinds of study.

Since both the local authority work on policy-related analysis and research work on process can be bound together via the common data framework, migration-research findings could be speedily incorporated into the policy-making process. Strategic planning for improving services and environment will be able more securely to identify the levers of change which will have the best effect in meeting the citizen's perceived needs.

Table 3.2 Potential areas for research within the process of migration

	(i) Characteristics of movers		
Context structuring the	(ii) Social and economic	influences on	the movers the socio-economic environment and its opportunities
	(iii) Strategic planning policy	influences on	movers physical environment and opportunities
	(iv) The background environment: services and amenities and the role of planning policy in influencing		
Behavioural response	(v) Decision elements		predisposing trigger
	(vi) Searching and choosing		role of information role of place connectedness

CONCLUSION

A range of possible uses of monitored data has been described, demonstrating that there are important tasks for it in local authority management of strategic services and land-use planning; in problem perception, policy-making and policy-impact evaluation; and in fundamental research into the dynamics of regional change as exemplified in movements of the population. The method of monitoring proposed here is necessarily rather roundabout since it depends on data collected for a housing purpose. A national system of registration of population would allow migration to be tracked routinely and would obviate the necessity to compile local monitors in what can only be a rather labour-intensive manner.

If a migration monitor will be laborious to set up, is it worth doing? The answer will vary from interest group to interest group and region to region. There are, surprisingly, arguments of cost effectiveness which can be made in its favour. These stem from the pre-monitor step of persuading various data collectors of the value of using point geocode referencing. Once accepted, this would allow several data sets thus referenced to be cross-related accurately *and* flexibly by chosen area. This would serve as the stable background against which intra-urban migration could be plotted and its causes and effects studied rigorously.

The short-term costs of setting up a geocoded system would be mostly 'once-for-all' capital costs and must be viewed in the context of the lower maintenance costs thereafter, relative to those incurred in running the existing unco-ordinated systems. In addition, enormous savings of costly staff time may be expected to accrue to both local government and research work. The factual underpinning for both would be capable of being provided quickly by the automated system, freeing analysts from time-consuming data collection.

In the population field, for example, officers in some local authorities have been involved in recent years in time-consuming wrangles with central government on the contentious topic of calculating housing needs and land requirements. The argument has turned on statistical forecasts of population related to area—calculations which can never reach a state of being securely 'right' or 'wrong' since they are based on coarsely aggregated data with little time dimension and with little means of modifying for small-area migration. Maclennan (1987) has trenchantly criticised current methods of calculation of housing need and has entered a strong plea for improvement in the data base and in particular for a clearer temporal logic in the data collection, in the interests of more effective strategic plan making for housing provision. Given a migration monitor in being, population research projects, whether policy-related or theoretical, could start into their analyses from the beginning of their allotted time. Delayed starts are common at present, because so much time is taken up wrestling data into usable form. In any weighing of 'cost effectiveness' this is wasteful on a vast and continuing scale. It is these costs which must be set against the short-term costs of constructing a new system of migration monitoring. The long-term gains for both policy and research have been outlined in this chapter. The technology is already to hand. It is time to exploit it.

NOTE

1. This information exists for valuation purposes but has been deemed highly confidential and is not released by the Assessor even to other departments of the same regional council. This is a serious omission. Change of house size is known in the public sector (where data can be obtained) to be associated with a majority of household moves. In 1974, 70% of all public sector moves in Glasgow involved a change of house size (Forbes *et al.*, 1979, p. 8). House size is therefore an important element in any ideal monitoring of migration-related data.

BIBLIOGRAPHY

Carlstein, Tommy (1978), 'Innovation, time allocation and time-space packing' in T. Carlstein, D. Parkes and N. Thrift (eds), *Human Activity and Time Geography*. London: Edward Arnold.

Chorley, Lord (chairman) (1987), *Report of Committee on the Handling of Geographic Information*. London: HMSO.

Clark, Eric (1984), 'Vacancy chains and life cycle theory' in *Scandinavian Population Studies*, 6:1, Studies in Migration. Stockholm: The Scandinavian Demographic Society, pp. 85–92.

Clark, W. (1982) Recent research on migration and mobility: a review and interpretation. *Progress in Planning* vol 18 no. 1.

Cowan, Max (1986), 'Development of owner-occupied housing in Strathclyde region 1975–85', *Scottish Planning Law and Practice*, no. 17, February, p. 56.

Cullen, Ian and Phelps, Elizabeth (1978), 'Patterns of behaviour and responses to the urban environment' in William Michelson (ed.), *Public Policy in Temporal Perspective*. The Hague: Mouton, pp. 165–82.

Forbes, Jean (1984), 'Problems of cartographic representation of population change', *Cartographic Journal*, vol. 22, December, pp. 93–102.

Forbes, Jean, Lamont, Douglas and Robertson, Isobel M. L. (1979), *Intra-urban Migration in Greater Glasgow*. Glasgow: Scottish Development Department, Central Research Unit.

Hägerstrand, Torston (1972), 'On the definition of migration', *Yearbook of Population Research in Finland*, XI, pp. 63–72.

Holm, Einar and Öberg, Sture (1984), 'Migration in Micro and Macro Perspectives', *Scandinavian Population Studies*, 6:1, Studies in Migration. Stockholm: The Scandinavian Demographic Society, pp. 61–84.

Koskinski, L. A. (1975), 'Data and measures in migration search' in L. A. Kosinski and R. M. Prothero, *People on the move*. London: Methuen, pp. 107–19.

Lenntorp, Bo (1976), 'Paths in space-time environments', *Lund Studies in Geography*, Series B, 44.

Lewis, G. J. (1982), *Human Migration: A Geographical Perspective*. London: Croom Helm.

McCleery, Alison (1980) The Register of Sasines as a source of migration data. *BURISA Newsletter*, no. 46, pp. 16–17.

Maclennan, Duncan (1987), *Demand for Housing: Economic Perspectives and Planning Practices*. Edinburgh: Scottish Office.

Petersen, W., (1970), 'A general typology of migration' in Clifford J. Jansen (ed.), *Readings in the Sociology of Migration*. Oxford: Pergamon, pp. 49–68.

Robertson, Isobel M. L. (1982), 'Population turnover in Glasgow: an approach by co-ordinate references', *Town Planning Review*, vol. 53, no. 1, pp. 79–89.

Rogers, A. and Castro, L. J. (1986), 'Migration data, rates and schedules' in A. Rogers and F. J. Willekens (eds), *Migration and Settlement: A Multiregional Comparative Study*. Dordrecht: D. Reidel.

Woods, Robert (1983) Towards a general theory of migration, in White, P. and van der Knapp, B. (eds), *Contemporary Studies of Migration*. Norwich: Geobooks.

Chapter 4

DEMOGRAPHIC CHANGE AT THE SMALL-AREA LEVEL: IMPLICATIONS FOR THE PLANNING OF CANBERRA*

Shane Nugent

Helen Rampa

INTRODUCTION

In general, demographic change within urban areas is very poorly understood. . . . Understanding changes that have occurred in the past is needed before the future can be projected with any confidence. Land use planners need to understand processes of change, not simply be provided with projections of the results (Neutze, 1984, p. 98).

While history does not provide a certain guide to the future, an assessment of past demographic changes can provide valuable insights in planning for the future. This is particularly so in planning for small areas, where demographic change is likely to be most dramatic and where planning decisions have the greatest impact on the everyday lives of residents. This chapter explores the processes of small-area demographic change in Australia's capital city, Canberra, and discusses the implications of these processes for the planning of Canberra.

BACKGROUND

Development of Canberra as one of the world's few wholly planned cities commenced in 1913 as a compromise between the claims of Sydney and Melbourne to be the seat of government of the newly federated Commonwealth of Australia. Progress was slow, and by the late 1950s Canberra had a

This chapter has benefited from the comments and suggestions of many people at the NCDC, in particular John Giles, Colin Adrian and Ian Woolcock, and draws on Malcolm Beer's research into ageing of suburbs during his time with the NCDC.

* The views expressed in it are those of the authors and do not necessarily represent the views or policies of the NCDC or of the Department of Immigration, Local Government and Ethnic Affairs. It was originally prepared when Ms Rampa was employed with the NCDC.

population of only about 40 000, with many government functions still located in either Sydney or Melbourne.

The National Capital Development Commission (NCDC) was established in 1958 to accelerate Canberra's development, and was given the responsibility to plan, develop and construct the infrastructure necessary to serve a growing population. This integration of the planning and development functions enables the NCDC to determine the location and timing of new land development. The NCDC is responsible for the construction of government schools and other community facilities in conjunction with client authorities and is thus directly involved in the planning of these facilities.

With a few exceptions, the basic building block of planning in Canberra is the neighbourhood or suburb of about 1000 to 1200 dwellings. Each suburb is focused on a local shopping centre and primary school. Clusters of about 20 suburbs comprise a district centred on a major shopping centre, government offices and other facilities.

Population forecasting and demographic analysis play an important part in the NCDC planning and development process. Forecasts of Canberra's total population growth for the forthcoming ten years are reviewed annually. These forecasts are used to prepare a land-development programme to accommodate forecast housing requirements, which in turn is used to forecast future population levels in each suburb. The forecast rate of population growth in new suburbs forms the basis for assessing future needs for schools, shops and other community facilities.

RECENT DEMOGRAPHIC TRENDS IN CANBERRA

The demographic structure of the total Canberra population provides the context for the analysis of changes occurring at the small-area level. Since the establishment of the NCDC in 1958, Canberra's population has grown from just over 41 000 to an estimated 258 900 as at June 1986. Annual growth has fluctuated markedly in line with changing economic conditions. Population growth in Canberra over the past 20 years has gone through three distinct phases. The decade from 1966 to 1976 was a boom period with average annual growth of 10 800 persons (7.8 per cent). This was followed by a period of reduced growth up to 1983 when the average annual increase was around 4800 persons (2.2 per cent). More recently, higher growth rates have returned, with an estimated increase between 1983 and 1986 of 9300 persons per annum (3.8 per cent).

The sequence and scale of residential land development in Canberra reflects the fluctuations in metropolitan population growth over time. As shown in Figure 4.1, a large part of Canberra was settled during the period of high population growth from 1966 to 1976. This includes the districts of Woden and Weston Creek (to the south), Belconnen (to the north-west) and parts of Tuggeranong (far south). Less rapid growth, particularly from 1976 to 1983, is reflected in a reduction in new suburban development since 1976.

These phases of population growth in Canberra have been largely due to changes in levels of net migration. As almost 60 per cent of Canberra's employment is in the public sector, these fluctuations have been largely attributable to the impact of changes in federal government expenditure and

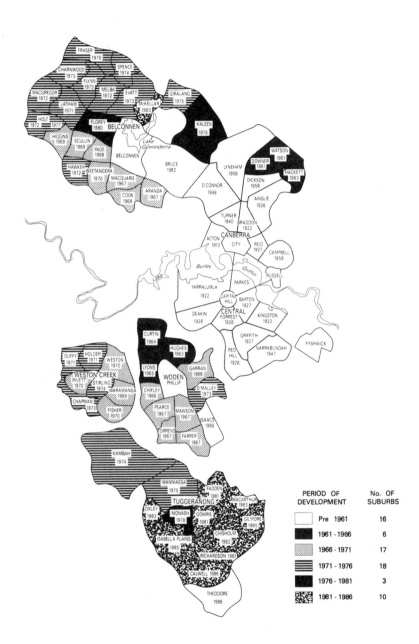

Figure 4.1 Development of Canberra suburbs

employment policies. While the levels of net migrant flow have varied, the age profiles of migrants have remained relatively constant, with concentrations in the young adult groups, though an increase in the number of older persons moving to Canberra has been evident in recent years.

Natural increase has remained relatively stable over recent years. While the number of females in the reproductive ages (15–44 years) has increased, particularly during the period of high migration in the late 1960s and early 1970s, the declining fertility rates during the 1970s have resulted in a relatively constant number of annual births. Mortality has remained at a low level.

These processes have resulted in a relatively young age profile, as shown in Figure 4.2. However, the narrowing of the age pyramid base reflects a declining proportion of the population at pre-school and school age.

SPATIAL VARIATION AND PROCESSES OF DEMOGRAPHIC CHANGE

At the broad metropolitan level, land-use planning can do little more than respond to the demands created by population growth. However,

while planning can do little to influence the total volume of growth it can do something about where within the region it occurs. The stronger land use planning is, relative to the land market, in determining the direction and timing of urban development, the more it will be able to determine intra-urban population trends (Neutze, 1984, p. 93).

Canberra has a strong and integrated planning and development system. The NCDC is responsible for most land development and thus has a high degree of influence over the location of new land release, residential development and therefore population growth. This planning system combines with metropolitan demographic trends to produce distinctive patterns of demographic change and of spatial variation in demographic characteristics.

Canberra's integrated planning and development system allows for the release of developed residential land, and so new population settlement, to be concentrated in only a few small areas at any one time. The population of these areas as a consequence builds up extremely rapidly. This is illustrated by the development of the district of Tuggeranong, which grew from commencement in 1974 to an estimated population of 52 500 at June 1986, and is expected to increase to a population of almost 90 000 by 1996. The build-up of population at small-area or suburban level is even more dramatic. It is usual for a suburb to grow from first settlement to up to 5000 people over a period of about three years. This rapid build-up of population results in economies in land development and facilitates the early provision of services such as schools, shops and a wide range of other community facilities.

While knowledge and control of the total population of suburbs is vital to planners, the demographic characteristics of that population are of equal importance, particularly for the planning of facilities to serve specific age groups. Even in a planned city such as Canberra, planners are unable directly to control the distribution of these characteristics. Rather, the distribution of demographic characteristics is a product of market forces and the processes of demographic change. There are two major influences on the process of small-

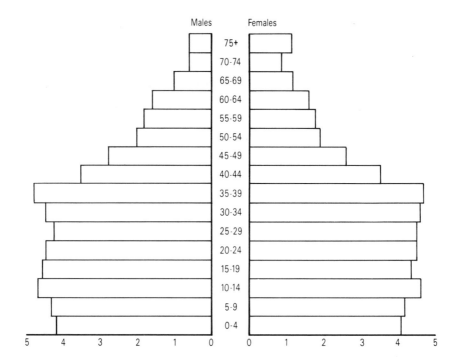

Figure 4.2 Canberra age distribution, 1986

area demographic change: ageing of the initial population; and population turnover through migration.

New suburbs on Canberra's fringe are settled predominantly, but not exclusively, by young couples with young children or who are about to commence having children. Due to the rapid occupation of new suburbs, these areas tend to have a generally homogeneous population in the young family age groups. This means that populations of new areas are typified by large proportions of the population in the 0–4 and 25–29 years age groups, and a high percentage of couples and head, spouse and dependant(s) families. This pattern has been repeated in newly developed suburbs over the past 30 years. It is the ageing of this initial population which remains the major determinant of demographic characteristics at small-area level. Canberra suburbs therefore tend to progress through the family life cycle in the same way as and at a similar rate to individual families. The stages involved are:

1. A family formation stage typified by high birth rates and thus increasing population, and by a high proportion of pre-school-aged children.
2. A stable family stage as families are completed, with declining birth rates and large numbers of school-aged children.
3. A maturing stage during which children leave school and begin to leave home. Substantial population decline would be anticipated during this stage. Historically the populations of Canberra suburbs have started to decline after about seven to ten years, after reaching a peak average household size of about 3.6 persons per household.

4. An aged population stage typified by few children and large numbers of ageing couples and single-person households.

While this ageing pattern is dominant, intra-urban migration has the effect of adding some diversity to the demographic character of a suburb. Major migration trends in Canberra appear to parallel those in other cities, including:

- Movement of young couples (perhaps with young children) from rented accommodation to owner-occupied dwellings, often in new suburbs.
- Movement of families, often with teenage children, to larger and higher standard housing.
- Young adults leaving the family home either to form new families (generally in new suburbs) or to live in single or rented group accommodation (often in inner areas).

In addition, in Canberra the development of medium-density housing five to ten years after initial settlement tends to attract young singles, couples, groups and the like, to the suburb. The development of such housing, however, is not evenly spread over all suburbs and is mostly concentrated around the major employment centres.

The overall impact of this migration is to increase heterogeneity and thus reduce the size of peaks in age and family-structure distributions as the initial populations of suburbs age. Migration can also serve to hasten the onset of population decline as completed families are replaced by a more diverse population.

The current spatial distribution of demographic characteristics in Canberra is the product of this complex series of processes. This distribution may be summarised as follows:

- The inner suburbs developed prior to 1960 are characterised by a relatively stable mature population with few children. Young adults without children also form a significant part of the population in these areas. The population of the inner suburbs has declined by over 20 per cent in the past 15 years.
- Suburbs settled during the 1960s and 1970s in Woden, Weston Creek and Belconnen have low birth rates, low and declining numbers of young children, and high proportions of teenagers.
- Newer suburbs, mostly in the southern district of Tuggeranong, have the typical new suburb profile of young families.

This concentric pattern of demographic profiles is common to other cities. However in Canberra the rapidity of initial settlement is reflected in the speed of consequent demographic change. This may be illustrated by examining the history of demographic change in a selection of suburbs at different stages of development. The suburbs chosen as examples of the processes of small-area demographic change are Ainslie, Pearce, Fisher and Giralang, the locations of which are shown in Figure 4.1.

Ainslie is one of Canberra's oldest suburbs, having been first settled in 1926 (though parts were developed as late as the 1950s), and provides an example of a mature suburb. Pearce was first settled in 1967 and Fisher in 1970—these provide examples of suburbs currently passing through the maturing stage of demographic change. Giralang was established in 1975 and thus, at the 1976 and 1981 Censuses, demonstrates the early stages of the demographic change process. Figures 4.3–4.5 show changes in a number of demographic indicators in these suburbs over the period 1966-81.

Of particular significance is the rapid decline in the population aged 0–4

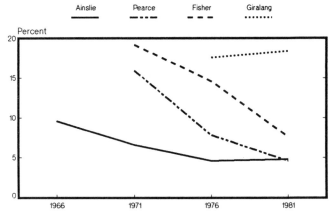

Figure 4.3 Trends in the proportion aged 0–14, selected Canberra suburbs
Source: Censuses 1966–81

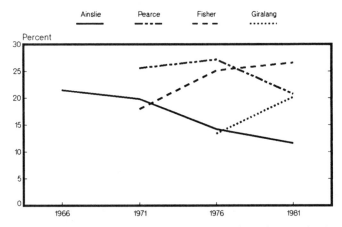

Figure 4.4 Trends in the proportion aged 5–14, selected Canberra suburbs
Source: Censuses 1966–81

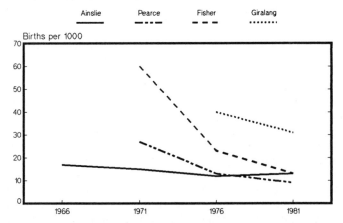

Figure 4.5 Trends in crude birth rates, selected Canberra suburbs
Source: Birth Registrations

and in the crude birth rate in Pearce and Fisher, from high levels typical of newly settled areas to levels similar to those in the mature suburb of Ainslie over a ten-year period. This would be expected to be the forerunner of declines in the 5–14 years age group—indeed this is already evident in Pearce. These suburbs were among those developed in the rapid-growth period of the late 1960s and early 1970s and are representative of a large number of areas in Woden, Weston Creek and southern Belconnen undergoing similar demographic change.

This rapid ageing, whereby populations may change from very young to mature within a single generation, provides a challenge to Canberra's planners to accommodate the impacts of demographic change.

THE IMPLICATIONS FOR PLANNING—AN EXAMPLE OF PLANNING FOR THE PROVISION OF SCHOOLS

Demographic change at the surburban level has wide-ranging implications for the planning of age-specific facilities and services. A useful method of illustrating this point is by employing examples of areas undergoing demographic change and examining the effect on a specific aspect of planning, in this case schools planning.

The planning of school provision is chosen as an example for the following reasons:

- Since schools serve specific small age groups (5–12 years for primary schools), their enrolments are extremely responsive to changes in the demographic profile of their catchment area.
- Catchments for primary schools generally comprise single suburbs. At this level the population is most homogeneous and hence the impacts of demographic change most pronounced.
- Very good data are available on school enrolments in Canberra. The Australian Capital Territory Schools Authority (ACTSA) conducts annual school censuses which, since 1981, have provided information on the number of children attending a particular school and living in a particular suburb. This allows detailed analysis of enrolments by suburb and by school.

Schools planning is, for these reasons, considered ideal in exemplifying the implications of demographic change at a small-area level.

Data on government primary schools provide a good indication of the current school enrolment situation in Canberra. Table 4.1 shows the recent trends in enrolments by district of residence of the students. Given that there has been no substantial change in the proportion of students attending non-government primary schools, the decline in enrolments in Canberra as a whole reflects the ageing of the population. High primary school enrolments in the early 1980s were a result of high fertility and migration levels through the 1960s and early 1970s. These large cohorts have since passed through primary school. Tuggeranong is the only district to have experienced any substantial increase in enrolment numbers in the first half of the 1980s, while enrolments in Woden Valley have almost halved. The total district trends, however, hide the suburban fluctuations, as even in the older areas of Canberra Central there are a variety of trend curves. For example the number of government primary school students resident in the inner Canberra

Table 4.1 Trends in government primary school enrolments, Canberra, 1981–86

DISTRICT	1981	1986	Change (%)
North Canberra Central	2 119	1 788	−15.6
South Canberra Central	1 283	1 281	−0.2
Woden Valley	3 050	1 866	−38.8
Weston Creek	3 717	2 370	−36.2
North Belconnen	4 858	4 907	+1.0
South Belconnen	5 244	3 753	−28.4
Tuggeranong	3 784	5 566	+47.1
TOTAL	24 055	21 531	−10.5

suburb of Ainslie has increased slightly from 288 in 1981 to 304 in 1986, while the number living in the nearby suburb of Watson suffered a decline from 307 to 164 over the same period. It is at this small area level where changes are the most dramatic and where planning for these changes is most vital.

An analysis of pupil generation rates, the number of school students per dwelling in an area, clearly shows the changes in demand for a school in an area as the population of that area moves through the traditional family life cycle. The basic pattern is as follows:

- Primary school demand peaks 10–15 years after first settlement and is followed by a rapid decline in numbers of school students.
- A plateau is reached after about 20 years when school enrolments are stabilised by population turnover.
- The pattern of changes in the pupil generation rate has remained fairly constant over recent years, although a lowering of the peak has been experienced.

The changes in the number of school students in a suburb are of course directly linked to the overall demographic changes occurring in the suburb. The four suburbs cited previously—Ainslie, Pearce, Fisher and Giralang— illustrate the effects of demographic change on school enrolments by providing a snapshot of suburbs at different stages of the demographic change process, and highlight the problems of planning for the peak enrolment period as well as the decline which will inevitably follow. Figure 4.6 shows the trends in the number of government primary school students resident in these suburbs.

As can be seen, the estimated number of primary school students resident in Ainslie declined rapidly from 1970 to 1980 in line with a falling crude birth rate in the suburb and the declining size of the 5–14 years age group. The stable number of school students between 1981 and 1986 reflect the small increase in the crude birth rate in Ainslie.

School enrolments in Pearce have undergone a steady decline over the 16-year period from 1970 to 1986, a result of the fall in the crude birth rate in the suburb and the out-migration of young families over the inter-censal period 1976 to 1981. Since 1976 the number of government primary school students resident in Pearce has declined by over 60 per cent.

The number of primary school students living in Fisher is estimated to have peaked around 1976 and has shown a rapid decline of over 50 per cent over the five years from 1981 to 1986. The quick succession from initial settle-

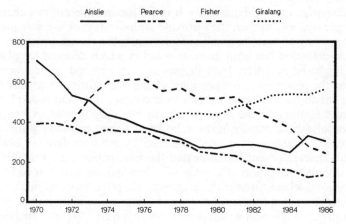

Figure 4.6 Trends in government primary school enrolments, selected Canberra suburbs. Source: Schools censuses

ment to peak enrolments and rapid decline, occurring over only a ten-year period, is due to the dramatic change in the crude birth rate in Fisher.

Being a more recently settled suburb, Giralang is still experiencing increasing numbers of school students, though was probably near its peak in 1986 as crude birth rates declined between 1976 and 1981.

It is only in recent years that the phenomenon of rapidly declining school enrolments, as illustrated by the cases of Pearce and Fisher, has been seen as a problem in Canberra. This is due to two major factors. First, until recent years substantial enrolment declines had been restricted to a few older suburbs of Canberra. However the processes of demographic change mean that a large number of suburbs settled during the boom period of the late 1960s and early 1970s (such as Pearce and Fisher) have recently experienced sizeable school enrolment declines. This has increased the magnitude of the problem and made it more obvious. Second, resource constraints over recent years have meant that more attention has been paid to the economic and educational viability of small schools.

The problem can be addressed from either a supply or demand viewpoint. The supply of schools is mainly the responsibility of the education planners, such as the ACTSA, while the demand for schools is more the product of land-use planning and therefore can be modified by planning bodies, such as the NCDC.

As a response to declining enrolments, education planners have paid considerable attention to options to modify the supply of schools to maintain larger, more viable, schools. In existing areas this means the closure of schools, an option which inevitably creates great dissent within the community.

In planning for the education facilities in new areas in Canberra, various options to modify the supply of schools to accommodate the impacts of demographic change are being considered. These options may be grouped into two major categories: those which include schools being planned from the start to be closed or converted to other uses after a set period; and those which involve planning larger schools, either serving larger neighbourhoods or a combination of neighbourhoods. It is not the intention of this chapter to assess these options. Rather, they provide an indication of the way planners are now starting to react to small-area demographic change processes.

Far less attention has been given to ways in which demand for places in schools might be modified, both in existing suburbs and in new areas, by modifying the processes of demographic change. In existing areas this means adopting urban consolidation policies to encourage infill and redevelopment and attract families to the area. Canberra has only limited experience of urban consolidation, mainly in the suburbs of Kingston and Griffith, where large areas of housing have been replaced by medium-density dwellings. While this redevelopment has increased the total population of the area and led to increased utilisation of a range of urban infrastructure, it has had no impact on local school enrolments. In general, the price, type and market sector of dwellings provided as a consequence of urban consolidation policies seem likely to attract single people and second-home buyers—groups which seldom have school-aged children.

In planning new areas for the future, the obvious solution to peaks in demand for schools would be to prolong the demographic change process by substantially increasing the period during which each new suburb is settled. This could be achieved by spreading new land development across a large number of development fronts at any one time. Such an initiative would involve a fundamental change to the NCDC's current planning and development policies. The current system has many advantages, notably in facilitating the early provision of schools and other services. These advantages need to be weighed against the long-term costs as demand for these services declines as a result of the processes of demographic change.

CONCLUSION

Schools are but one of many facilities for which planning is affected by small-area demographic change. Others include child health centres, sporting entertainment and recreation facilities, and, at the other end of the life cycle, senior citizens' clubs and other facilities for the aged. Indeed, demographic change is an important consideration in planning for the provision of any facilities which predominantly serve particular age groups.

A particular feature of demographic change processes in Canberra is the rapidity of change. This results in equally rapid change in requirements for facilities such as schools, leading to underutilisation of comparatively new facilities. This problem is likely to become more severe over the next few years as the bulk of Canberra suburbs settled in the period 1966–76 progress through the demographic ageing process.

The speed of demographic change in Canberra is a direct consequence of the planning and development system, whereby whole suburbs are established within a few years. While recognising the considerable advantages of this system, planners should also be aware of its consequences. The planning system creates a need to plan suburbs and their facilities not only for the initial population, but for a population whose characteristics will change rapidly.

Further investigation is needed into the advantages and disadvantages of various options for the utilisation of community facilities over time.

While the rapidity of small-area demographic change in Canberra is a unique consequence of Canberra's planning system, the lessons to be learned are applicable to planning throughout Australia and elsewhere. The main lesson is that the analysis of demographic change is an essential input to planning and that demographers have an important role in the development of planning policy.

POSTSCRIPT

Since this chapter was prepared the Australian government has announced that future land development in Canberra is to be undertaken by the private sector. Mechanisms for achieving this while maintaining the NCDC's control over the location of new population settlement are currently being developed.

Also since preparation of this chapter, the ACTSA have released for public discussion proposals to close or amalgamate a number of government schools in Canberra. Pearce and Fisher primary schools, discussed in this chapter, are among those proposed for closure. The proposed school closures have been widely opposed within the community. The ACTSA is currently assessing the public response to its proposals.

BIBLIOGRAPHY

Adrian, C. (1983) *Canberra. A Social Atlas. Atlas of Population and Housing, 1981 Census, vol. 1*. Canberra: Division of National Mapping and the Australian Bureau of Statistics in association with the Institute of Australian Geographers.

Adrian, C. (1985) *Canberra: A Demographic and Socio-economic Profile*. Canberra: Australian Institute of Urban Studies.

Australian Bureau of Statistics (1981) *Census of Population and Housing*, Canberra: ABS (various published and unpublished data)

Australian Bureau of Statistics (1986) *Australian Demographic Statistics, March and June quarters 1986*. Catalogue no. 3101.0, Canberra: ABS.

Committee to Review Primary Education in ACT Government Schools (1981) *Primary Children in the ACT*, Canberra: Canberra Publishing and Printing Co.

Encel, S. and Lepani, B. (1971) *Education and Planning in a New City: An Opportunity for Campbelltown*. Sydney: Urban Systems Corporation Pty. Ltd.

Foskett, R. A. (1977), *Canberra—The Last of the Great Growth Centres—Implications for Education Planning*, Address to the Institute of Educational Administration, Canberra.

National Capital Development Commission (1977), *Canberra: Demographic and Social Background*, Technical Paper 7, March 1975 revised May 1977, NCDC, Canberra.

National Capital Development Commission (1982), *ACT School Situation*, Urban Economics Branch, Canberra.

National Capital Development Commission (1985), *28th Annual Report*, NCDC, Canberra.

Neutze, M. (1984), 'Population issues and physical planning'. *Journal of the Australian Population Association*. Vol. 1 pp. 89-98.

O'Neill, C. J. and Ramsay, P.D.K. (1979), 'Educational Futures: The implications of demographic change for educational policy.' *New Zealand Journal of Educational Studies*, Vol. 14 pp. 107-123.

Rowland, D. T. (1980) 'Demographic changes in the Australian Capital Territory:

Recent developments affecting primary school enrolments', in *Report to the Australian Capital Territory Schools Authority, Review of Primary Education in ACT Government Schools*.

Rowland, D. T. (1983) *Population and Educational Planning. The Demographic Context of Changing School Enrolments in Australian Cities*, ERCD Report no. 36. Canberra: Australian Government Printing Service.

Young, C. (1985) *Exploring the Demography of the ACT*. Canberra: Australian Government Publishing Service.

PART II

DEMOGRAPHIC FORECASTS AND PROJECTIONS AT SUB-NATIONAL LEVEL

Chapter 5

STABILITY OVER TIME IN THE DISTRIBUTION OF POPULATION FORECAST ERRORS*

Stanley K. Smith
Terry Sincich

INTRODUCTION

A number of studies in recent years has investigated empirical approaches to the production and use of confidence intervals for population projections. Some have used time-series models in which historical population data were fitted to autoregressive or moving average processes, and future values were made to depend on a weighted average of past values and a random error term (see, for example, Lee, 1974; Saboia, 1974; Voss *et al.*, 1981). Others have focused directly on the errors of projections made in the past (for example, Keyfitz, 1981; Smith, 1987; Stoto, 1983). Under either of these approaches, the critical assumption underlying the construction and use of confidence intervals for population projections is that the distribution of forecast errors remains stable over time.

Is that a reasonable assumption? To date, very little research has been directed toward answering this question. In the present study we analyse the distribution of population forecast errors for US states for a number of different time periods during the twentieth century. Our objectives are twofold: to determine the extent to which these distributions have remained stable over time and to evaluate the validity of using data on the distribution of past forecast errors to predict the distribution of future forecast errors. First, we describe the data and techniques used to make the population projections analysed in this study. Next, we discuss the characteristics of forecast errors and the stability of those errors over time. Then we use data on the distribution of past forecast errors to construct empirical confidence limits and test their performance in predicting the range of future forecast errors. Finally, we draw several conclusions regarding stability in the distribution of forecast errors over time and the potential usefulness of developing empirical confidence limits for population projections.

Demographers often draw a distinction between the terms 'projection' and 'forecast'. A projection is typically defined as the numerical outcome of a specific set of assumptions regarding future trends, whereas a forecast indicates the specific projection that the author believes is most likely to provide

*Permission to reproduce this article from *Demography* 25 (3) 1988, is gratefully acknowledged.

an accurate prediction of future population (see Irwin, 1977; Isserman and Fisher, 1984; Keyfitz, 1972). In this chapter 'projection' refers to the future population implied by a particular technique and data set, and 'forecast accuracy' refers to the percentage difference between a projection and the Census-enumerated population for the same year. In other words, projections are treated as if they were indeed forecasts of future population.

DATA AND PROJECTION TECHNIQUES

The data used in this study were the final population counts from each decennial Census from 1900 to 1980, for each of the 50 states in the USA (United States Bureau of the Census 1983). These data refer to total population only; no analysis was performed on the age, sex or race distribution of the population. The following terminology, based in part on Cohen (1986), is used to describe population projections:

Base year: the year of the earliest observed population size used to make a projection.

Launch year: the year of the latest observed population size used to make a projection.

Target year: the year for which population size is projected

Base period: the interval between the base year and the launch year

Projection horizon: the interval between the launch year and the target year.

For example, if data from 1900 and 1910 were used to project population size in 1920, then 1900 would be the base year; 1910, the launch year; 1920, the target year; 1900–10 the base period; and 1910–1920 the projection horizon.

Four primary projection techniques were used. The first was linear extrapolation (LINE), which assumes that a population will increase (decrease) by the same number of persons in each future year as the average annual increase (decrease) during the base period:

$$P_t = P_1 + x/y \ (P_1 - P_b) \tag{5.1}$$

where P_t is the state population projection for the target year; P_1 is the state population in the launch year; P_b is the state population in the base year; x is the duration in years of the projection horizon; and y is the duration in years of the base period.

The second technique was exponential extrapolation (EXPO), which assumes that a population will grow (decline) at the same annual rate in each future year as during the base period:

$$P_t = P_1 \exp \ (rx) \tag{5.2}$$

where r is the average annual growth rate during the base period.

In the third and fourth techniques, state population data were expressed as shares of national population data. Under the shift-share technique (SHIFT), state shares of national population were calculated for the base year and launch year and were extrapolated into the future by assuming that the average annual absolute change in each state's share of national population observed during the base period would continue throughout the projection horizon. The extrapolated state shares were then applied to an independent projection of national population to provide state population projections:

$$P_t = P_{jt} \left[\frac{P_1}{P_{jl}} + x/y \left(\frac{P_1}{P_{jl}} - \frac{P_b}{P_{jb}} \right) \right]$$

(5.3)

where P_{jt} is the national population projection for the target year; P_{jl} is the national population in the launch year; and P_{jb} is the national population in the base year.

Under the share-of-growth technique (SHARE), state shares of national population growth during the base period were calculated. Projections were made by assuming that these shares would be the same throughout the projection horizon as they were during the base period:

$$P_t = P_1 + \left(\frac{P_1 - P_b}{P_{jl} - P_{jb}} \right) \left(P_{jt} - P_{jl} \right)$$

(5.4)

The SHIFT and SHARE techniques each require an independent projection of national population. Since no widely accepted set of national projections was produced in the early part of this century, a new set had to be constructed. This was done by applying the LINE and EXPO techniques to the US population and using an average of the results as a national projection.

It should be noted that the SHIFT and SHARE techniques have two sources of error: one caused by errors in projecting state shares of national population and the other caused by errors in the national projections themselves. The latter source of error is minor. An alternate set of projections from SHIFT and SHARE was made using Census enumerations of the national population for the target years instead of projections. The results from this alternate set of state projections differed only slightly from those reported in this chapter. National projections rather than Census data were used in the present analysis because when the SHIFT and SHARE techniques are used for population projections, they must utilize projections rather than Census counts of the larger-area population.

A fifth technique was evaluated as well. Projections from this technique (AVE) were simply the averages of the projections produced by the four primary techniques.

Simple projection techniques have a long history, having been used by such notable persons as Benjamin Franklin, Thomas Jefferson and Abraham Lincoln (Dorn, 1950, p. 315). They are still frequently used for local population projections (Federal-State Cooperative Program, 1984) but are no longer commonly used for projections of state or national populations, having been replaced by more sophisticated cohort-component and economic-demographic techniques. These more sophisticated techniques, however, have been developed and used for state-level projections only within the last several decades (see, for example, US Bureau of the Census, 1957; US Bureau of Economic Analysis, 1974). Projections from these techniques are therefore not available for most decades of this century. Creating such projections specifically for this study would have been prohibitively expensive or even impossible, given the lack of relevant data. Consequently it was necessary to base the present analysis on the simple projection techniques described above.

The simplicity of these techniques does not negate their usefulness, however. A number of studies have concluded that simple extrapolation techniques produce short- to medium-term forecasts of total population that are at least as accurate as those produced by more sophisticated techniques (see Ascher, 1978; Greenberg, 1972; Kale *et al.*, 1981; Murdock *et al.*, 1984; Siegel, 1953; 1972; Smith, 1984; White, 1954). Furthermore, the more sophisticated techniques themselves are typically based on extrapolations of one type or another (such as migration rates, birth rates and survival rates for cohort-component projections; employment trends for economic-based projections). The functional forms of these extrapolations are often similar to those of the simple extrapolation techniques. If applied to the same base periods, then, the projections from the more sophisticated techniques would most likely be similar to those analysed in this study (Smith, 1987).

The advantages of using simple projection techniques for the present analysis are that they require very little base data, they can be applied at low cost, and they can be applied retrospectively to produce a large number of consistent projections that are comparable over time. We believe these simple techniques provide a useful vehicle for testing stability in the distribution of population forecast errors over time.

ANALYSIS OF ERRORS

Projections for each of the 50 states were made for ten- and 20-year horizons, using ten-year base periods and the five techniques described above. Projections were made from every base period since 1900, yielding seven sets of ten-year projections and six sets of 20-year projections. These projections were then compared with decennial Census counts for each target year. The resulting differences are called forecast errors, although they might have been caused partly by errors in census enumeration as well as by errors in the forecasts themselves. Throughout this chapter the term 'error' refers to percentage error rather than to absolute numerical error.

General characteristics

Two measures were used to provide a general description of forecast error characteristics. Mean absolute percentage error (MAPE) is the average percentage error when the direction of error is ignored. This provides a measure of forecast accuracy. Mean algebraic percentage error (MALPE) is the average percentage error when the direction of error is accounted for. This provides a measure of bias: a positive error indicates a tendency for projections to be too high and a negative error indicates a tendency for projections to be too low.

To provide an overall picture of forecast error characteristics, errors were aggregated from all seven sets of ten-year projections and all six sets of 20-year projections. This provided a pooled sample of errors from 350 ten-year projections and 300 20-year projections. Tables 5.1 and 5.2 summarize these errors for each technique, with states divided according to population size in the launch year (Table 5.1) and rate of population growth during the base period (Table 5.2).

A number of consistent patterns can be seen in these tables. Forecast accuracy declined as the projection horizon increased; forecast accuracy increased as the size of the base population increased; and forecast accuracy declined as

Table 5.1 MAPE and MALPE by technique, population size and length of projection horizon

Technique	Population size*	MAPE Projection horizon 10 Years	20 Years	MALPE Projection horizon 10 Years	20 Years
LINE	<1 million	9.5	17.3	−1.2	−3.3
	1–3 million	6.0	11.9	−1.4	−2.3
	>3 million	5.5	9.1	−0.2	−1.4
	Total	7.0	13.0	−1.0	−2.4
EXPO	<1 million	11.6	26.8	3.7	12.2
	1–3 million	7.4	16.3	1.2	5.9
	>3 million	6.6	13.5	2.3	6.3
	Total	8.5	19.1	2.3	8.1
SHIFT	<1 million	9.9	18.3	−0.2	−0.5
	1–3 million	6.2	12.3	−0.7	−0.1
	>3 million	5.8	9.8	0.7	1.2
	Total	7.3	13.7	−0.1	0.1
SHARE	<1 million	10.6	21.6	0.0	0.1
	1–3 million	7.0	14.3	−1.3	−2.0
	>3 million	6.0	11.1	0.7	1.1
	Total	7.9	15.9	−0.2	−0.4
AVE	<1 million	10.3	20.3	0.6	2.1
	1–3 million	6.6	13.4	−0.6	0.4
	>3 million	5.9	10.5	0.9	1.8
	Total	7.6	15.0	0.2	1.4

*Population size in launch year

the rate of population growth during the base period increased. These patterns were found for all five techniques and for both ten- and 20-year projections. Similar patterns have been found in many other studies (see, for example, Irwin, 1977; Isserman, 1977; Schmitt and Crosetti, 1951; 1953; Smith, 1987; Stoto, 1983; White, 1954).

There was no evidence of any overall bias in these projections. The total sample MALPE was slightly negative for LINE, slightly positive for EXPO and virtually zero for SHIFT and SHARE. In no instances were total sample MALPEs significantly different from zero. There was no evidence of a consistent relationship between population size and bias (Table 5.1), but there was strong evidence of a consistent relationship between growth rates and bias (Table 5.2). For every technique in both the ten- and 20-year projections, MALPEs increased as the rate of growth during the base period increased. Differences in MALPEs by rate of growth were frequently very large. A positive relationship between bias and population growth during the base period has been noted previously for projections of counties in the US (Smith, 1987). 1987).

Table 5.2 MAPE and MALPE by technique, rate of growth and length of projection horizon

Technique	Rate of Growth* (%)	MAPE Projection Horizon 10 Years	MAPE Projection Horizon 20 Years	MALPE Projection Horizon 10 Years	MALPE Projection Horizon 20 Years
LINE	<10	5.7	10.8	−3.0	−6.2
	10–20	5.6	10.4	−0.5	−2.2
	>20	10.9	19.2	1.3	2.6
	Total	7.0	13.0	−1.0	−2.4
EXPO	<10	5.6	10.6	−2.7	−5.2
	10–20	5.9	11.4	1.1	2.4
	>20	16.4	41.1	11.5	34.5
	Total	8.5	19.1	2.3	8.1
SHIFT	<10	5.7	10.9	−2.8	−5.4
	10–20	5.8	10.9	0.3	0.3
	>20	11.7	21.2	3.2	7.7
	Total	7.3	13.7	−0.1	0.1
SHARE	<10	6.5	14.2	−4.7	−11.2
	10–20	5.6	10.6	0.1	−0.7
	>20	13.0	25.2	5.9	15.1
	Total	7.9	15.9	−0.2	−0.4
AVE	<10	5.8	11.4	−3.3	−7.0
	10–20	5.7	10.8	−0.2	−0.1
	>20	12.8	25.5	5.5	15.0
	Total	7.6	15.0	0.2	1.4

*Rate of growth during base period

A number of studies have concluded that the choice of projection technique generally has little impact on the overall forecast accuracy of short- to medium-term population projections, once the base period and projection horizon have been fixed (see Ascher, 1978; Kale *et al.*, 1981; Smith, 1984; White, 1954). The present study supports that conclusion. Differences in forecast accuracy among alternate techniques were found to be quite small in most instances. The overall MAPEs for the ten-year projections were between 7.0% and 8.5% for all five techniques, while the 20-year projections displayed a somewhat wider range of 13.0% to 19.1%. EXPO was the technique with the largest errors, particularly for the 20-year projections and for states with populations of less than 1 million or growth rates of greater than 20%. Other than these results for EXPO, however, the errors for the different techniques were quite similar. Furthermore, the patterns relating forecast errors to size of place, rate of growth and length of projection horizon were much the same for all five techniques.

Stability over time

The pooled sample data summarized in Tables 5.1 and 5.2 provide an overall picture of the error characteristics for state population projections during the twentieth century. The results regarding accuracy, bias and the effects of population size, growth rate and length of projection horizon are consistent with the findings of many other studies. However, these results tell us nothing about trends in forecast accuracy and bias over time. What patterns can be seen when each set of projections is viewed individually?

Table 5.3 shows MAPEs and MALPEs for ten-year projections, for each technique and each target year from 1920 to 1980. Several conclusions can be drawn from this table. First, the largest MAPEs were for the first set of projections (1920). This was true for all five techniques, most notably for EXPO. Second, there were no persistent biases in these projections. For each technique MALPEs were positive for about half the target years and negative for about half. Third, for target years after 1920 there were no apparent trends in accuracy or bias. MAPEs and MALPEs did not become systematically larger or smaller over time, but rather fluctuated up and down. Finally, after 1920 MAPEs and MALPEs did not differ dramatically by target year or by technique. On the contrary, they typically fell within a fairly narrow range. Similar results regarding MAPEs and MALPEs were found in an analysis of 20-year projections for target years 1930–80 (not shown here).

A constant mean is a necessary but not a sufficient condition to establish the stability of a distribution over time. Measures of the dispersion of errors around the mean must also be considered. Table 5.4 shows the standard deviations for absolute and algebraic forecast errors for each of the seven sets of ten-year projections. For all five techniques (especially EXPO), standard deviations were quite large for 1920 but considerably smaller thereafter. There were no major differences among techniques regarding the size of standard deviations, nor was there any apparent trend over time. In all instances, standard deviations were larger for algebraic than absolute errors because algebraic errors account for both size and direction of error.

We are not primarily concerned in this study with differences in errors among alternative projection techniques. Consequently, the analysis throughout the remainder of this chapter will focus on projections coming solely from the AVE technique. Narrowing the focus to a single technique eliminates duplication and simplifies exposition, permitting a more detailed discussion of the empirical results than would be possible if all five projection techniques were considered individually. An analysis of errors from the other four techniques was also performed (not shown here), and the results were quite similar to those reported here for AVE.

Stem-and-leaf plots (Tukey, 1977) in Figure 5.1 show the distributions of algebraic forecast errors for the seven sets of ten-year projections for the AVE technique. For each target year, the distribution is mound-shaped and symmetric, except for occasional outliers (for example, errors of 76 per cent in 1920 and 40 per cent in 1930). All seven distributions appear to be roughly normal. In fact, formal tests of normality (Shapiro and Wilk, 1965) reveal that the null hypothesis of a normal distribution cannot be rejected at a 5% level of significance for any target years except the two earliest, 1920 and 1930.

Stem-and-leaf plots for absolute forecast errors were also generated. Not

Table 5.3 MAPE and MALPE for ten-year projections, by technique and target year

Target Year	LINE	EXPO	SHIFT	SHARE	AVE
MAPE					
1920	8.4	15.6	9.5	11.0	10.9
1930	6.6	7.3	6.7	7.4	7.0
1940	6.5	8.6	7.1	7.8	7.5
1950	7.9	7.3	7.8	7.8	7.7
1960	6.9	5.6	6.6	6.7	6.4
1970	4.4	7.3	5.0	6.0	5.6
1980	8.4	7.9	8.3	8.5	8.2
MALPE					
1920	5.2	14.1	7.1	7.9	8.6
1930	−1.4	1.2	−0.6	−0.8	−0.4
1940	3.5	5.9	4.4	3.8	4.4
1950	−6.8	−5.9	−6.6	−6.6	−6.5
1960	−5.2	−2.6	−4.5	−4.7	−4.2
1970	1.3	5.4	2.4	2.0	2.8
1980	−3.7	−1.7	−3.1	−3.3	−2.9

surprisingly, they revealed skewed (non-normal) distributions, truncated at zero. The interested reader can use the data shown in Figure 5.1 to construct plots for absolute forecast errors by disregarding the signs of the errors and starting the scale at zero.

To evaluate the stability of error distributions over time, we must focus on both means and variances. With θ representing the parameter of interest (mean or variance), we test three alternate hypotheses regarding stability:

1) H_1: $\theta_{1920} = \theta_{1930} = \ldots = \theta_{1980}$

2) H_2: $\theta_t = \theta_a$

3) H_3: $\theta_t = \theta_{t-10}$ (5.5)

where $t = 1920, 1930, \ldots, 1980$; and a is all target years between 1920 and 1980 (except t) combined.

H_1 tests the hypothesis that means (variances) of forecast errors are identical for all seven target years (1920–80). This hypothesis is the most stringent of the three considered. H_2 tests the hypothesis that the mean (variance) of forecast errors for target year t is identical to the mean (variance) for the distribution of errors from all six other target years combined. For H_2, then, seven different tests were conducted, one for each target year. H_3 tests the hypothesis that the mean (variance) of forecast errors for target year t is identical to the mean (variance) for the previous target year $(t-10)$. For H_3 six different tests were conducted, one for each pair of consecutive target years.

Due to the non-normal distributions of algebraic errors for 1920 and 1930 and of absolute errors for all target years, tests of means were conducted using

Table 5.4 Standard deviations for ten-year projections, by technique and target year

Target Year	LINE	EXPO	SHIFT	SHARE	AVE
Standard Deviations for Absolute Percentage Errors					
1920	10.7	23.4	11.9	14.8	15.1
1930	7.0	8.7	7.2	8.0	7.6
1940	5.0	7.5	5.3	5.9	5.8
1950	7.0	6.5	6.9	6.8	6.8
1960	6.3	5.0	6.0	5.5	5.5
1970	4.1	7.9	4.4	5.5	5.0
1980	5.5	5.8	5.5	5.8	5.5
Standard Deviations for Algebraic Percentage Errors					
1920	12.6	24.4	13.5	16.7	16.6
1930	9.5	11.3	9.9	10.9	10.3
1940	7.5	9.8	7.8	9.1	8.5
1950	8.2	7.8	8.1	8.0	8.0
1960	7.8	7.1	7.7	7.2	7.3
1970	5.9	9.3	6.3	7.9	7.0
1980	9.4	9.7	9.5	9.9	9.5

well-known non-parametric alternatives to the traditional analysis-of-variance F-test. The Kruskal–Wallis H-test was used to test equality of means for H_1 and the two-sample Wilcoxon rank sum test was used for H_2 and H_3. For testing the equality of variances, Conover *et al.* (1981) have shown that a variation of Levene's (1960) approximate F-test is one of the most powerful and robust procedures. We chose this modified Levene test (where the modification involved replacing the sample mean with the sample median) to test for the equality of variances.

The results of these tests are summarized in Table 5.5, which shows the p-values associated with each of the three hypotheses. p-values greater than or equal to 0.05 indicate that the hypothesis of equal means (or variances) cannot be rejected at the 5% level of significance. Looking first at absolute forecast errors, the top panel of Table 5.5 shows that we cannot reject the hypothesis (H_1) that the mean errors for all seven sets of projections were identical, but we must reject the hypothesis that all seven variances were identical. On this most stringent test, then, the hypothesis regarding stability of absolute forecast errors must be rejected for one of the two parameters under consideration.

For the second and third hypotheses, the results are more favourable for the notion of stability over time in the distribution of absolute forecast errors. The hypothesis (H_2) that the mean (variance) for target year t is identical to the mean (variance) for all other years combined must be rejected for only one out of seven sets of projections (1980 for the mean and 1920 for the variance). Even greater stability is found when testing the third hypothesis (H_3), that the mean (variance) for one target year is identical to the mean (variance)

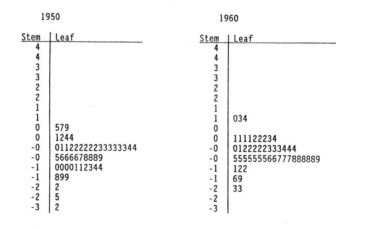

```
        1920                          1930                              1940
Stem | Leaf                   Stem | Leaf                      Stem | Leaf
  4  | 9    (High=76)           4  |                             4  |
  4  | 11                       4  | 0                           4  |
  3  | 7                        3  |                             3  |
  3  |                          3  |                             3  |
  2  | 677                      2  |                             2  |
  2  |                          2  | 4                           2  | 013
  1  | 558                      1  |                             1  | 788
  1  | 1                        1  | 003                         1  | 01111123
  0  | 55555688999              0  | 55566667                    0  | 566778899
  0  | 111222223444             0  | 22223334                    0  | 001223334444
 -0  | 0011222233              -0  | 000112233333444            -0  | 0111223
 -0  | 6889                    -0  | 55557777                   -0  | 566778
 -1  | 2                       -1  | 02                         -1  |
 -1  |                         -1  | 78                         -1  | 34
 -2  |                         -2  | 24                         -2  |
 -2  |                         -2  |                            -2  |
 -3  |                         -3  |                            -3  |
```

```
                1950                                  1960
        Stem | Leaf                          Stem | Leaf
          4  |                                 4  |
          4  |                                 4  |
          3  |                                 3  |
          3  |                                 3  |
          2  |                                 2  |
          2  |                                 2  |
          1  |                                 1  |
          1  |                                 1  | 034
          0  | 579                             0  |
          0  | 1244                            0  | 111122234
         -0  | 01122222233333344             -0  | 0122222333444
         -0  | 5666678889                    -0  | 555555566777888889
         -1  | 0000112344                    -1  | 122
         -1  | 899                           -1  | 69
         -2  | 2                             -2  | 33
         -2  | 5                             -2  |
         -3  | 2                             -3  |
```

Figure 5.1 Stem and leaf plots for algebraic percentage errors (AVE) for ten-year projections, by target year

1970

Stem	Leaf
4	
4	
3	
3	
2	5
2	
1	7
1	00234
0	556667899
0	0111122222333333444
-0	011223344
-0	679
-1	0
-1	5
-2	
-2	
-3	

1980

Stem	Leaf
4	
4	
3	
3	
2	
2	
1	55
1	0124
0	57889
0	133344
-0	1122334444
-0	566777777899
-1	00001
-1	5577
-2	0
-2	9
-3	

Note: The numbers for the stem indicate the first digit for each forecast error and the numbers for the leaf indicate the second digit (e.g., an error of 10 percent is indicated by stem = 1 and leaf = 0). Each plot shows 50 errors, one for each state.

Figure 5.1 *cont'd*

for the previous target year. This hypothesis must be rejected for only one out of six target years for means (1980) and cannot be rejected for any target years for variances.

With respect to algebraic forecast errors, the evidence regarding stability is much weaker. For H_1, we must reject the hypotheses that both the means and variances from all seven sets of projections were identical. For H_2, the hypothesis of equality of means must be rejected for six of the seven comparisons and the hypothesis of equality of variances must be rejected for three of the seven comparisons. For H_3, the hypothesis of equality of variances must be rejected for only one of the six target years (1980), but the hypothesis of equality of means must be rejected for five of the six target years (all except 1960).

We replicated these tests for states divided into size categories ($<$ 1 million, $\geqslant$ 1 million) and growth-rate categories ($<$ 20%, $\geqslant$ 20%).[1] The results were much the same as those reported above. Although means and variances were considerably different for small states than large states, and for rapidly-growing states than slowly-growing states, within each size or growth-rate category the hypothesis of equality of means and variances for absolute errors could not be rejected in most instances, whereas the algebraic errors the hypothesis of equality of variances had to be rejected in a number of instances and the hypothesis of equality of means had to be rejected in almost all instances.

We also replicated the tests for 20-year projections with a 20-year base period. (For projections with a 20-year horizon, a 20-year base period provided somewhat greater accuracy and stability than a ten-year base period.) Although the means and standard deviations for twenty-year projections were approximately twice as large as for ten-year projections, the results regarding

Table 5.5 π-values for tests of stability of means and variances over time for ten-year AVE projections

Hypothesis*	Absolute Percentage Error Means	Variances	Algebraic Percentage Error Means	Variances
H₁	0.13	<0.01	<0.01	0.02
H₂				
1920	0.92	<0.01	<0.01	0.01
1930	0.42	0.56	0.81	0.55
1940	0.46	0.66	<0.01	0.51
1950	0.63	0.95	<0.01	0.20
1960	0.42	0.21	<0.01	0.03
1970	0.05	0.12	<0.01	0.03
1980	0.02	0.33	0.02	0.93
H₃				
1930	0.63	0.05	<0.01	0.16
1940	0.29	0.89	<0.01	0.83
1950	0.90	0.71	<0.01	0.53
1960	0.35	0.25	0.25	0.41
1970	0.41	0.71	<0.01	0.94
1980	<0.01	0.55	<0.01	0.03

*Hypothesis H_1: means (variances) are identical for all seven target years.
Hypothesis H_2: mean (variance) for target year t is identical to mean (variance) from distribution for all other target years combined.
Hypothesis H_3: mean (variance) for target year t is identical to mean (variance) for target year $t-10$.
p-values greater than 0.05 indicate that the hypothesis cannot be rejected at the 5% level of significance.

stability over time for absolute and algebraic errors were virtually the same as those reported in Table 5.5.

We conclude from these results that there was a high degree of stability over time for both the means and variances of absolute forecast errors for state projections during the twentieth century. There was somewhat less stability for the variances of algebraic forecast errors, and no stability at all for mean algebraic forecast errors. Since the MALPE is a measure of bias, this tells us that the study of past forecast errors cannot help us predict the overall tendency for a current set of projections to be too high or too low.[2] A number of other studies have drawn similar conclusions (among them Kale *et al.*, 1981; Smith, 1984; Stoto, 1983). The stability for both the means and variances of absolute forecast errors, however, provides evidence that the study of past forecast errors may help us predict the level of accuracy of current population projections, even if we cannot predict their bias.

EMPIRICAL CONFIDENCE LIMITS

The second objective of this study is to evaluate the validity of using data on the distribution of past forecast errors to create confidence intervals for population projections. The results presented in the previous section suggest that the critical assumption underlying the construction and use of empirical confidence intervals—that the distribution of errors remains stable over time—is reasonably well satisfied in this sample for absolute forecast errors. How can these results be used to construct and test confidence intervals?

Williams and Goodman (1971) have suggested a method for constructing 'empirical confidence limits' based on the distribution of past forecast errors. We have modified and adopted this technique because it can accommodate any error distribution, including the asymmetric and truncated distributions of absolute forecast errors found in this sample. The Williams and Goodman approach also permits an assessment of the confidence limits; that is, we can compare the actual number of errors falling inside the limits with the expected number.

For each of the seven sets of ten-year projections, absolute forecast errors were ranked and the 90th percentile error (the asbolute percentage error that was larger than exactly 90% of all absolute percentage errors) was determined. The 90th percentile errors for each target year are shown in the second column of Table 5.6. We followed three different approaches in using these errors to construct 90% confidence limits:

1. The 90th percentile error from target year $t-10$ was used as a forecast of the 90th percentile error in target year t.
2. The 90th percentile error from the distribution of errors from all other target years was used as a forecast of the 90th percentile error in target year t.
3. The 90th percentile error from the distribution of errors from all other target years (excluding 1920) was used as a forecast of the 90th percentile error in target year t.

The first two approaches were selected to correspond to null hypotheses H_3 and H_2, as described in the previous section. The third approach was selected to eliminate the effects of several unusually large outliers in the error distribution for 1920. If the distribution of absolute forecast errors remains stable over time, 90th percentile errors based on past error distributions (or, in the case of the second and third approaches, error distributions both preceding and following the target year) should provide accurate predictions of the 90th percentile error for the target year. Since we expect 90 per cent of the absolute forecast errors to fall below this value, the predicted 90th percentile error for any target year may be thought of as a one-sided (upper) confidence limit with an associated confidence coefficient of 0.90.

To assess the accuracy of these three approaches to the construction of empirical confidence limits, we compared the predicted with the actual 90th percentile errors for each target year from 1920 to 1980 and computed the proportion of absolute forecast errors that fell within the predicted value. These results are shown in the last six columns of Table 5.6. In general, the results are quite satisfactory, especially in light of the small sample size. In most instances the proportion of errors falling within the predicted confidence limit was quite close to 90 per cent. Using data from all other target years generally provided a more accurate confidence limit than using data solely from

Table 5.6 Actual and predicted 90th percentile errors for AVE technique, by target year

Target Year	Actual 90th Percentile Error	Distribution of Errors from Previous Target Year		Distribution of Errors from all other Target Years		Distribution of Errors from all other Target Years (excl. 1920)	
		Predicted 90th Percentile Error	Actual Errors Less than Predicted Error (%)	Predicted 90th Percentile Error	Actual Errors Less than Predicted Error (%)	Predicted 90th Percentile Error	Actual Errors Less than Predicted Error (%)
1920	36.4	–	–	15.1	82	–	–
1930	17.8	36.4	98	16.6	88	15.0	88
1940	17.6	17.8	92	16.7	90	15.0	88
1950	18.8	17.6	88	16.6	88	15.0	88
1960	14.3	18.8	94	17.4	94	15.3	92
1970	13.2	14.3	92	17.7	98	16.6	96
1980	15.1	13.2	82	17.4	94	15.2	92

the previous target year, and excluding the first set of projections (target year 1920) further improved accuracy. For this third approach, between 88% and 92% of errors fell within the predicted 90% value for all target years except 1970, when 96% were within the predicted value.[3]

These empirical confidence limits appear to be neither too wide nor too narrow. For some target years more than 90% of the errors fell within the predicted value, while for other years fewer than 90% fell within the predicted value. The target years with too many errors within the predicted values essentially offset the years with too few. Summing over all target years, 91.0% of actual errors fell within the predicted value using the first approach to confidence limits; 90.6% using the second approach; and 90.7% using the third approach.

The same three approaches to empirical confidence limits were applied to 20-year projections with a 20-year base period (not shown here). Although the 90th percentile errors were larger than for the ten-year projections, the relationships between actual and predicted errors were quite similar to those shown in Table 5.6.

We also constructed empirical confidence limits for states grouped by population size ($<$ 1 million, $\geqslant$ 1 million) and growth rate ($<$ 20%, $\geqslant$ 20%). The results for large states ($\geqslant$ 1 million) and slowly-growing states ($<$ 20%) were very similar to the results shown in Table 5.6: actual 90th percentile errors corresponded very closely to predicted 90th percentile errors. For small states ($<$ 1 million) and rapidly growing states ($\geqslant$ 20%), however, predicted 90th percentile errors differed considerably from actual 90th percentile errors. These less satisfactory results can be attributed to the more volatile nature of population growth in small and rapidly-growing states and—perhaps more important—to the very small sample sizes for these categories (between five and 19 states per decade).

CONCLUSIONS

Can confidence intervals really be made for population projections? Under the formal definition of confidence intervals, the answer is 'no': confidence intervals cannot be constructed because the probability distribution of future forecast errors is unknown (and unknowable) at the present time. It is possible, however, to look at forecasts made in the past to see how accurate they were in predicting population change. If current projection techniques are similar to those used in the past, and if the degree of uncertainty is about the same in the future as it was in the past, we can assume that future forecast errors will be drawn from the same distribution as past errors (Keyfitz, 1981, p. 587). Data on the distribution of past forecast errors can therefore be used to construct empirical confidence limits for population projections.

The critical assumption underlying the construction and use of empirical confidence limits is that the distribution of forecast errors remains stable over time. The present study has shown that the distribution of absolute forecast errors for states remained quite stable over the decades of the twentieth century (especially since 1920). This finding is quite powerful, given the tremendous fluctuations in population growth caused by world wars, depressions, baby booms and countless other events that occurred during this century. It gives us reason to believe that just as data on past population trends can frequently provide reasonably reliable short- to medium-term population forecasts, so might data on past forecast errors be able to provide useful predictions of the distribution of future forecast errors. Indeed, the empirical confidence limits tested in this study were quite successful in predicting the range of future errors.

This study has also shown that the distribution of algebraic forecast errors was not at all stable over the course of the twentieth century. Although standard deviations remained moderately stable over time, mean algebraic errors varied dramatically and unpredictably from one decade to the next. In this sample, then, data on the bias of past projections did not provide a reliable basis for predicting the bias of current projections. The approach taken in this study is not likely to be useful for predicting the overall tendency for a particular set of population projections to be too high or too low.

There are many different ways to produce confidence intervals for population projections (see Cohen, 1986; Land, 1986). Each approach has its own unique characteristics. Within each approach, different projection techniques imply different confidence intervals as well. Future research must therefore evaluate various approaches to constructing confidence intervals, focusing on the effects of using different projection techniques, base periods, projection horizons, and so forth. The results of the present study imply that such research will be very useful. While we may never be able to forecast future *populations* with a high degree of accuracy, we may be able to develop relatively accurate forecasts of the *distribution of errors* surrounding our point forecasts. Indicating the potential range of errors surrounding population forecasts may be the most useful service the producers of population projections can provide to their users.

NOTES

1. It would also be interesting to replicate these tests for states divided by size of place and rate of growth simultaneously. Smith (1987) reported some important interactions between these two variables. Unfortunately, the sample size used in this study is too small to permit such an analysis.
2. This refers to bias for an entire set of projections. There is evidence that extrapolative projection techniques have predictable biases for places with extreme growth rates during the base period (Smith, 1987).
3. We also looked at 50th, 75th and 95th percentile errors. For 95th percentile errors, the results were very similar to those reported in Table 5.6. For 50th and 75th percentile errors, however, there were larger differences between the actual and predicted number of errors falling below the predicted value than is shown in Table 5.6. We believe the reason for this is that errors are more tightly bunched around the 50th and 75th percentile errors than around the 90th and 95th percentile errors. Therefore relatively small differences between the actual and predicted values of percentile errors can cause relatively large differences in the number of errors falling below the predicted value.

REFERENCES

Ascher, William (1978) *Forecasting: An Appraisal for Policy-makers and Planners.* Baltimore, MD: Johns Jopkins University Press.

Cohen, Joel (1986) 'Population forecasts and confidence intervals for Sweden: a comparison of model-based and empirical approaches', *Demography*, vol. 23, no. 1, pp. 105–26.

Conover, W. J., Johnson, M. E. and Johnson, M. M. (1981) 'A comparative study of tests for homogeneity of variances, with applications to the Outer Continental Shelf bidding data', *Technometrics*, vol. 23, no. 4, pp. 351–61.

Dorn, Harold F. (1950) 'Pitfalls in population forecasts and projections', *Journal of the American Statistical Association*, vol. 45, no. 251, pp. 311–34.

Federal-State Cooperative Program for Population Projections (1984) *State Survey on Population Projections.* Sacramento: California Department of Finance, Population Research Unit.

Greenberg, Michael (1972) 'A test of combination of models for projecting the population of minor civil divisions', *Economic Geography*, vol. 48, no. 2, pp. 179–88.

Irwin, Richard (1977) *Guide for Local Area Population Projections.* Technical Paper, no. 39. Washington, DC: US Bureau of the Census.

Isserman, Andrew (1977) 'The accuracy of population projections for subcounty areas', *Journal of the American Institute of Planners*, vol. 43, no. 3, pp. 247–59.

Isserman, Andrew and Fisher, Peter (1984) 'Population forecasting and local economic planning: the limits on community control over uncertainty'. *Population Research and Policy Review*, vol. 3, no. 4, pp. 27–50.

Kale, Balkrishna, Voss, Paul, Palit, Charles and Krebs, Henry (1981) 'On the Question of Errors in Population Projections'. Paper presented at the annual meeting of the Population Association of America, Washington, DC.

Keyfitz, Nathan (1972) 'On future population', *Journal of the American Statistical Association*, vol. 67, no. 338, pp. 347–63.

Keyfitz, Nathan (1981) 'The limits of population forecasting', *Population and Development Review*, vol. 7, no. 4, pp. 579–93.

Land, Kenneth C. (1986) 'Methods for national population forecasts: a review', *Journal of the American Statistical Association*, vol. 81, no. 396, pp. 888–901.

Lee, Ronald D. (1974) 'Forecasting births in post-transition populations: stochastic renewal with serially correlated fertility', *Journal of the American Statistical Association*, vol. 69, pp. 607–17.

Levene, H. (1960) 'Robust tests for equality of variances' in I. Olkin (ed.), *Contributions to Probability and Statistics*. Palo Alto, CA: Stanford University Press, pp. 278–92.

Murdock, Steve H., Leistritz, F. Larry, Hamm, Rita R., Hwang, Sean-Shong and Parpia, Banoo (1984) 'An assessment of the accuracy of a regional economic-demographic projection model', *Demography*, vol. 21, no. 3, pp. 383–404.

Saboia, Joao (1974) 'Modeling and forecasting population by time series: the Swedish case', *Demography*, vol. 11, no. 3, pp. 483–92.

Schmitt, Robert and Crosetti, Albert (1951) 'Accuracy of the ratio method for forecasting city population', *Land Economics*, vol. 27, no. 4, pp. 346–8.

Schmitt, Robert and Crosetti, Albert (1953) 'Short-cut methods of forecasting city population', *Journal of Marketing*, vol. 17, no. 4, pp. 417–24.

Shapiro, S. S. and Wilk, M. B. (1965) 'An analysis of variance test for normality (complete samples)', *Biometrika*, vol. 52, pp. 591–611.

Siegel, Jacob S. (1953) 'Forecasting the population of small areas', *Land Economics*, vol. 29, no. 1, pp. 72–88.

Siegel, Jacob S. (1972) 'Development and Accuracy of Projections of Population and Households in the United States', *Demography*, vol. 9, no. 1, pp. 51–68.

Smith, Stanley K. (1984) *Population Projections: What Do We Really Know?* Monograph

No. 1, Gainesville, FL: Bureau of Economic and Business Research, University of Florida.

Smith, Stanley K. (1987) 'Tests of forecast accuracy and bias for county population projections', *Journal of the American Statistical Association*. 82, pp. 991-1003.

Stoto, Michael (1983) 'The accuracy of population projections', *Journal of the American Association*, vol. 78, no. 381, pp. 13-20.

Tukey, J. W. (1977) *Exploratory Data Analysis*. Reading, MA: Addison-Wesley.

United States Bureau of the Census (1957) 'Illustrative projections of the population, by state, 1960, 1965 and 1970', *Current Population Reports*, Series P-25, no. 160.

United States Bureau of the Census (1983) 'Number of Inhabitants' in *1980 Census of Population*, PC80-1-A1. Washington, DC: US Government Printing Office.

United States Bureau of Economic Analaysis (1974) *Area Economic Projections 1990*. Washington, DC: US Government Printing Office.

Voss, Paul, Palit, Charles, Kale, Balkrishna and Krebs, Henry (1981) *Forecasting State Population Using ARIMA Time Series Techniques*. Madison: Applied Population Laboratory, University of Wisconsin.

White, Helen R. (1954) 'Empirical study of the accuracy of selected methods of projecting state population', *Journal of the American Statistical Association*, vol. 49, no. 267, pp. 480-98.

Williams, W. H. and Goodman, M. L. (1971) 'A simple method for the construction of empirical confidence limits for economic forecasts', *Journal of the American Statistical Association*, vol. 66, no. 336, pp. 752-4.

Chapter 6

DEVELOPING CENTRALISED HOUSE-HOLD PROJECTIONS FOR NATIONAL AND SUB-NATIONAL AREAS

I. E. Corner

INTRODUCTION

For many goods and for services such as health care and education it is natural to measure demand in terms of numbers of individuals. In such cases projections of population, usually disaggregated into particular age and sex groups, are an indispensable input to any forecast of future demand. In other situations, however, the unit of demand is the household rather than the individual, and household, rather than population, projections are required. In the UK household projections are of particular interest in the Department of the Environment (DoE) and local authorities because of their involvement with housing policy. This chapter describes the method used by the DoE to project households in England and Wales and some of the thinking behind it. It also examines how well the method performs and discusses some possibilities for further developments.

HOUSEHOLD TRENDS

It is suitable to start the discussion with a review of some of the current main trends in household formation. Not only are these of interest in their own right but they also illustrate some of the factors which must be taken into account by a household projection model. Throughout the discussion figures given for years up to 1981 are Census-based estimates, whereas those for later years are projections which incorporate population and marital status projections with 1985 as base year.

If the average size of households were to remain constant the total number of households would vary in direct proportion to the population. It follows that population change is an important component in forecasting household numbers. However, Figure 6.1 shows that it is not the only one. Over the period 1971-2001 the number of households increases much more rapidly than the adult household population, particularly after the mid-1980s. It follows, therefore, that average household size is decreasing or, equivalently, that the proportion of adults who head households—the overall adult headship rate—is increasing. In fact, it can be seen from Figure 6.1 that the main growth in the overall adult headship rate lags behind the most rapid

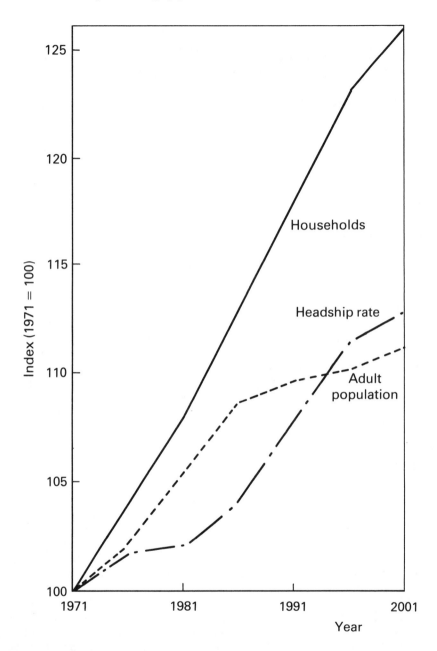

Figure 6.1 Index of household, population and headship rate growth in England and Wales, 1971–2001

period of growth in the adult population by about eight to ten years. This can be attributed to the fact that children born during the baby boom of the late 1950s and the 1960s would reach adulthood during the 1970s and early 1980s—thus causing a rapid increase in the adult population during this period—but would not, in any great numbers, form households of their own until some years later.

A sub-national breakdown of trends in household numbers reveals marked differences between different regions. In Figure 6.2 regions have been combined, for ease of presentation, into four areas: the North (consisting of the North-East, North-West, and Yorkshire and Humberside regions); the East and South (the East Midlands, East Anglia and South-West regions and the South-East outside of Greater London); Greater London; and the West (Wales and the West Midlands region).

Household growth is greatest in the East & South with steady, but smaller increases in the West and the North. In Greater London there is a decline in households during the 1970s but growth from the early 1980s onwards, resulting in a modest overall growth for the 30-year period. Table 6.1 shows that the pattern in Greater London is fairly typical of urban areas in general. Among metropolitan districts and London boroughs, taken as a whole, household growth over the period is only 8%, mostly occurring in the 1980's. By contrast there is steady growth in the rest of the country amounting, overall, to 38% of the 1971 total.

Table 6.1 suggests that, while the magnitude of the growth in household numbers is heavily dependent on both headship rate and population increase, the origin of these regional variations lies in differential rates of population growth rather than of headship rate change. As with households, the growth of the adult population base over the period 1971–2001 is most rapid in the East and South followed by the West, the North and, finally, Greater London. In the case of Greater London there is, over, the 30-year period, a decline in the adult population base, although this is concentrated in the 1970s with comparative stability thereafter. This regional variation in population change contrasts with the growth in overall adult headship rates which is much less variable among the areas considered. Similarly the slower rate of household growth in the more urban areas, represented by the aggregation of metropolitan districts and London boroughs, can be explained by the decline in adult population there, which contrasts with a steady growth in the rest of the country. Overall headship rates increase at roughly the same rate in both urban and rural areas.

If the intention in projecting households is to estimate housing demand it is important to form a picture of the type, as well as the number, of dwellings required. It would, for example, be inappropriate to respond to a rapid growth of retired one-person households by building more three- and four-bedroomed family-style houses. It is therefore of interest to consider trends amongs different types of household. For the purposes of illustration, six types of household, covering a variety of housing requirements, are considered:

MC<30: a married couple, with or without children, with the husband younger than 30.

MC30+: a married couple, with or without children, with the husband aged 30 or over.

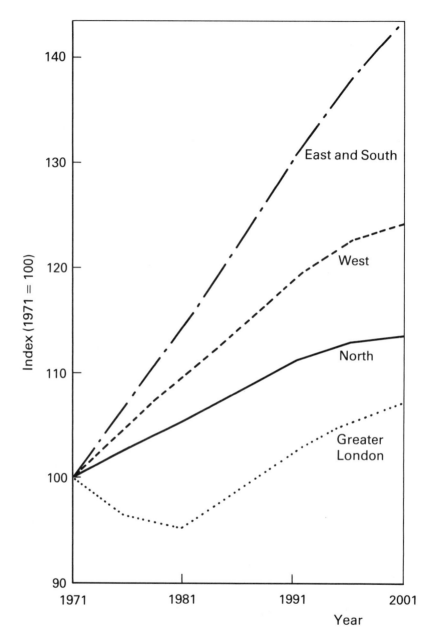

Figure 6.2 Index of sub-national household growth, 1971–2001

1P⟨RET: one person, younger than retirement age, living alone.
1PRET+:   one person, of retirement age, living alone.
LP⟨45:   a lone parent, younger than 45, living with children.
Oth⟨30:   an 'other' type of household whose head is younger than 30.[1]

Table 6.1 Regional variation of population, headship rates and household trends (percentage change, 1971–2001)

Area	Adult population	Headship rate	Households
North	2	11	14
East and South	27	13	44
Greater London	−8	16	7
West	9	14	24
Metropolitan districts and London boroughs	−6	14	8
Rest of England and Wales	22	12	38

Figure 6.3 shows that the national trends for these household types vary widely. The number of young married couples falls dramatically over the period, reflecting the trend towards cohabitation as an alternative or a prelude to marriage and possibly a tendency to marry at a later age than was once the case. On the other hand, the number of older married-couple households remains fairly constant. One-person households increase steadily in both of the age groups considered. The numbers of lone parent and 'other' households grow rapidly until the 1990s, after which time lone-parent households level off and 'others' decrease.

Headship rates specific to each of these household types can be defined as the proportion of the 'at risk' population who are heads of household of the specified type. For example, the headship rate of type MC<30 is the proportion of adults younger than 30 who are heads of married-couple households. Table 6.2 suggests that the differential growth in households of the various types is due mainly to headship, rather than population, effects. Married-couple headship rates fall in both of the age groups considered, but more dramatically among the under-30s where the trend combines with the declining population base to reduce the number of young married-couple households by almost two-thirds over the 30-year period. In the higher age group the decline in the married-couple headship rate is negated by population increase and, as a result, there is little change in the household total. Owing to growing headship rates households of the other types considered are all increasing rapidly in number. These headship-rate trends can be seen as reflections of a variety of social and economic changes including accelerated rates of divorce and cohabitation, greater independence of the elderly and an increased desire—and economic capability—among single people to form independent households.

Table 6.3 shows that there are also considerable regional variations in household-type-specific headship rates. In particular, Greater London stands out in relation to the rest of the country as having lower married-couple rates and a greater concentration of one-person, lone-parent and 'other' households. This situation is reversed in the East and South and in the West. The North has a particularly high rate of retired one-person households and the

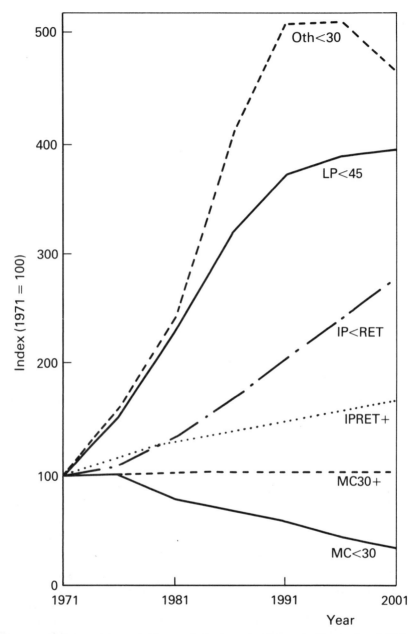

Figure 6.3 Index of household growth by household type in England and Wales, 1971-2001

highest rate for young married couples among the four areas considered, but is close to the national levels for each of the other household types. The headship characteristics of Greater London are reflected, to a lesser extent, in metropolitan areas in general and contrast with the prevailing pattern in the counties.

Table 6.2 Trends in population, headship rates and households of various types (percentage changes, 1971–2001)

Headship group	'At risk' population	Headship rate	Households
MC<30	−9	−62	−65
MC30+	19	−13	4
1P<RET	10	152	177
1PRET+	17	44	69
LP<45	11	254	296
Oth<30	−9	415	368

Table 6.3 Differentials from national headship rates for various regions and household types, 1981

Area	MC<30	MC30+	1P<RET	1PRET+	LP<45	Oth<30
North	0.006	−0.002	−0.002	0.020	0.001	−0.007
East and South	0.005	0.011	−0.006	−0.015	−0.003	−0.001
Greater London	−0.032	−0.034	0.026	0.015	0.008	0.027
West	0.005	0.004	−0.005	−0.010	−0.001	−0.008
Metropolitan districts and London boroughs	−0.011	−0.016	0.010	0.019	0.005	0.007
Rest of England and Wales	0.007	0.009	−0.006	−0.011	−0.003	−0.004

THE DoE HOUSEHOLD PROJECTION METHOD

Where projections are made by some central agency such as the DoE constraints apply which would be irrelevant or of lesser importance were they made locally. First, as manpower and computing resources are limited and a large number of projections is required, methods must be robust, mechanical and computationally efficient. It is not feasible either to check manually that each and every projection behaves 'reasonably' or to intervene in the computer system to deal with odd cases for which the method is not suitable. Any method used must therefore apply to all situations and be as well behaved as the quality of the data warrants. Second, comparable areas should be treated in a comparable way. If, for example, the projections were to be used to allocate limited resources between different regions it would be desirable to apply the same projection method to all areas involved. An important implication is that the data sets used must be available on a similar basis for all comparable projection areas, and the possibility of incorporating locally available data sets, or of taking into account special conditions which prevail in individual local areas, must therefore be discounted. Third, data of adequate quality must be available for all projection areas.

A number of more specific criteria which should be met by any centrally operated household projection model are highlighted by the earlier discussion of household trends: it should take into account both the effects of population growth and of changing patterns of household formation; it should be applicable at national and sub-national levels; and it should produce projections for separate household types.

To satisfy these various criteria the DoE household projection model is based on the headship-rate method. In essence this approach applies a projected headship rate to an exogenous population projection and consequently takes explicit account of the contributions of changes in population and household-formation patterns.

In general a headship rate specific to a particular household type and base population group can be defined as the proportion of members of the population group who head households of the specified type. In the DoE model projections are made of household heads disaggregated by age, sex, marital status and the type of household they head, by applying projected headship rates for each category to corresponding population projections disaggregated by age, sex and marital status. Estimates of numbers of households of each type are made by summing the appropriate household heads and invoking the one-to-one correspondence between household heads and households.

One of the main attractions of the headship-rate method—in the context in which the DoE model is used—is the extensive availability of most of the requisite data sets and exogenous projections, allowing projections to be made for England and Wales at national level and for all regions, counties, metropolitan districts and London boroughs.

Projections of home population, disaggregated into 15 age categories and the two sexes, and covering all projection areas, are prepared every two years. They use the most up-to-date population base available and incorporate assumptions set by the Office of Population Censuses and Surveys (OPCS) on fertility and mortality rates, and sub-national migration assumptions prepared by OPCS and DoE in consultation with local authorities. These are further disaggregated into three marital-status groups by applying factors derived from the Government Actuary's projections of population by marital condition. As these are available only for England and Wales, sub-national estimates of marital status factors assume constant differentials from the national figures, based on the 1981 Census. Projections of population in private households are then made by subtracting estimates of institutional population—assumed constant at the 1981 Census level in each age, sex and marital status category.

Data for projecting headship rates are derived from the Censuses for the years 1961, 1966, 1971 and 1981. For England and Wales these are supplemented by data derived from the annual Labour Force Surveys carried out since the last Census. Ten per cent samples of the Census data are used except in the case of 1966 when the 'Census' was itself a 10% sample survey and the full data set is available. For each of seven headship types in each age, sex and marital status category the time series of headship-rate data is extrapolated by fitting a scaled tanh curve by least squares. As headship rates must necessarily be between 0 and 1 the asymptotes of the projected curve are constrained to lie within this interval. Weighting procedures can be used to perturb the projected curve to achieve continuity with the data values, to allow for sampling error and to apply fixed user-defined weights if required.

The fact that independent projections are made for England and Wales at national level and for all regions, counties, metropolitan districts and London boroughs gives rise to inconsistencies—in the sense that the projected number of households in any given area is not normally equal to the sum of the household projections for its constituent sub-areas. This is the result of the non-linearity of the headship rate extrapolations and, in the case of England and Wales, methodological differences in that data are more finely disaggregated by age and that additional data, from the Labour Force Survey, are incorporated. To counteract this problem a constrained optimisation method is used to modify the projections for the constituent sub-areas of each area to sum to the total for the area, while maintaining the population totals within each age, sex and marital-status category.

This procedure is referred to as 'regional controlling'. In practice it is applied in stages in a top-down manner. Separate projections for England and for Wales are first modified to agree with the projections for England and Wales (projected together). At the next stage the projections for the English regions are calibrated to the controlled projections for England and those for the Welsh counties are altered to sum to the controlled figures for Wales. This procedure is continued down the 'tree' of projection areas—the controlled projections for each area being used to calibrate the projections of its sub-areas.

Revised household projections are published every two years and generally cover 15-20 years. The most recent cover the period up to 2001. They use 1985-based population and marital status projections and data from the Labour Force Surveys of 1983, 1984, 1985 and 1986. The DoE publication of these projections (DoE, 1988) gives full details of the definitions and disaggregation levels used and the mathematical formulations used for regional controlling and in extrapolating headship rates. The basic model has been used to produce the three most recent sets of projections published by the DoE and experience has shown it to be generally robust without requiring excessive resource input.

PERFORMANCE OF THE PROJECTION MODEL

In order to examine the performance of the model a simulated set of projections has been made. Household composition data from the 1961, 1966 and 1971 Censuses were used to project 1981 headship rates. 'Projected' population totals for 1981 were set to the 1981 enumerated private household totals, and the institutional population was assumed to be zero. Marital-status figures for England and Wales in 1981 were likewise set to the values for the private household population enumerated in the 1981 Census. The resulting household 'projections' were then compared with the enumerated figures for 1981. This was effectively a test of the household projection method in all of its aspects apart from the adequacy of the institutional population projections which, by virtue of using private household population totals, were effectively omitted from the test. It did not, however, take account of errors in the exogenous projections of total population and of marital status at the national level.

The error in the projected total number of households in England and Wales was roughly 49,000, or 0.3% of the total number of households in 1981. However, a better measure of performance is achieved by comparing the error with the actual household change between 1971 and 1981. On this basis the percentage error was 4.5%. For sub-national areas a comparable summary indicator of projection error is given by the expression

$$\frac{\Sigma \ (\text{error in 1981 projection/actual 1981 value})^2}{\Sigma \ (\text{actual change 1971–81/actual 1981 value})^2} \times 100\% \qquad (6.1)$$

where the summations are over the areas (regions, counties or metropolitan districts/London boroughs) under consideration. For total household numbers this statistic takes the values 1.5% for regions, 1.2% for non-metropolitan counties and 13.3% for metropolitan districts/London boroughs. Closer examination shows that the method produced very good projections at regional level with one exception—the South-East. This was mainly because of an underestimate of the magnitude of the decrease in households in Greater London (84,000 projected as against 162,000 actual). Projections for non-metropolitan counties are almost uniformly good and, although those for metropolitan districts and London boroughs are more variable, particularly in those areas which experienced a decrease, they are still a good fit to the true situation. The performance of the model in projecting households of more specific types was also considered. In particular the household types MC⟨30, MC30+, 1P⟨RET, 1PRET+, LP⟨45, and Oth⟨30, as defined earlier, were examined. The results, in terms of the error indicator used above, are given in Table 6.4. They are generally good, with values of less than 10% in two-thirds of the tests, and none exceeding 50%. The results are generally poorest for metropolitan districts and London boroughs, which is perhaps to be expected as these include the smallest areas considered and are probably the areas in which household trends are most volatile. Considering results for different household types, the poorest are for 1P⟨RET and Oth⟨30.

FURTHER DEVELOPMENTS

In view of this discussion of the performance of the model it may be asked whether further methodological development is likely to lead to significantly improved projections. If this question is addressed in the narrow sense of working with the same data sets, with the same aim of making absolute predictions at national, regional and local level, then there may not be scope for great improvement. However, it is perhaps time to ask whether models should be developed to address a wider range of questions. The current method extrapolates past trends in household composition. It does not take explicit account of such factors as income and housing supply which are undoubtedly related to household formation, but implicitly assumes that they too will follow future trends which are consistent with past behaviour. Effectively the aim is to project a 'natural' growth of households, one which would be expected in a fairly stable housing market. This is valuable information as

Table 6.4 Projection error indicators for different household types

	Regions	Counties	Metropolitan districts/ London boroughs
MC<30	4.8	9.2	10.6
MC30+	1.4	1.6	5.8
1P<RET	5.0	8.0	49.1
1PRET+	0.9	2.7	6.5
LP<45	2.5	3.2	18.3
Oth<30	31.3	41.2	42.9

it can be used by policy-makers to set targets for housing provision, and the indications are that the model generally carries out the task well. Nevertheless the aim is a limited one. The model cannot, for example, predict the effect on household formation of a rapid change in the employment level and the consequent change in income distribution. There is therefore a need to develop models of household formation which can take account of the effects of specific changes in related social and economic factors.

A direct approach to this task is to build econometric models to explain headship rates—or other indicators of patterns of household formation—in terms of other variables such as household income, the costs of housing services and marriage and divorce rates (see, for example, Smith *et al.*, 1984). A common difficulty encountered with this approach arises from the interdependence of the explanatory variables, complicating the determination of the primary causes of change. In this context Ermisch and Overton (1984) have stressed the importance of constructing an underlying theory of household formation which can then be tested empirically. Their work is in terms of minimal household units (MHUs)—individuals or family units—and seeks to explain the propensity to form separate households in terms of social and economic variables.

An alternative, less direct, approach is 'based upon the idea that *structural* issues in household modelling have to be resolved before any *substantial* relationships can be studied adequately' (Keilman, 1988). The primary aim is an understanding of the dynamics of household formation in terms of processes such as marriage, divorce and leaving the parental home. Subsequent investigation can then concentrate on the links between these processes and social economic conditions. A common approach to modelling of this nature is based on the concept of a transition matrix. Members of a given cohort, at a given time, are partitioned into a number of 'states' defined in terms of their demographic and household membership characteristics. The transition matrix defines the probabilities of an individual moving between any pair of states, or of leaving the system, in a particular time period. If transition matrices and patterns of migration into the cohort can be estimated for all cohorts and for the time period relevant to the projection interval then future numbers of individuals within each state can be estimated. A number of such models have been constructed. That developed by Holmberg,

Hårsman, Snickars and others (Hårsman and Snickars, 1983) defines the states principally in terms of the size of the household to which an individual belongs. Their framework can also be extended to derive a multi-regional model. Heida and Gordijn (1985) use the categories 'child', 'single', 'married (or cohabiting)', 'formerly married (cohabiting)' and 'in an institution', while Murphy (1985) classifies individuals by headship.

Micro-simulation models (Nelissen, 1987) have a similar aim of studying the structural relationships of household formation. In general, a sample of individuals is selected and described by demographic and household variables, and Monte Carlo methods are used to simulate the future development of the sample in terms of these characteristics. Again the emphasis is on the processes of household formation.

In developing a model intended for the centralised projection of households it is essential to bear in mind the criteria which were outlined earlier. A particularly limiting constraint concerns the availability of data, especially for sub-national areas. Most of the econometric models developed require a fairly long time series of data. In the UK the only sources which provide a reasonable number of points for parameter estimation are comparatively small-scale surveys such as the General Household Survey (GHS), which do not permit a detailed level of disaggregation or sub-national investigation. Ermisch and Overton use a micro-analytical framework which uses a dichotomous dependent variable and information relating to individuals. This avoids the need for time-series data but their formulation in terms of MHUs restricts the data sources available to them. The dynamic models of the processes of household formation require data on the transitions of individuals between the states defined in the model. A few such data sets have been constructed by matching records of individuals from two or more Censuses or surveys but this is an expensive procedure compared with the collection of cross-sectional data. The most promising development in the UK, in this respect, is the OPCS Longitudinal Study which matched the 1971 and 1981 Census records of a sample of roughly 1 per cent of the population. This data source was used by Murphy (1985). However because data were available for only one time period he was obliged to model transitions as time-independent for projection purposes. Micro-simulation methods also model transitions in the demographic and household characteristics of individuals and are therefore similarly constrained by the need for sophisticated and extensive data sets.

LIFE-CYCLE HEADSHIP

An alternative method, currently being developed at the Building Research Establishment, seeks to retain the benefits of the current model deriving from its use of large-sample data, while introducing some of the advantages of the dynamic models. It is based on the concept of a life-cycle headship rate. This may be explained with the aid of an example. Consider the cohort of males born in the year b and define a married headship rate for the cohort by

$$h = \frac{\text{married household heads in the cohort}}{\text{total cohort numbers}} = \frac{m}{n}. \qquad (6.2)$$

h, m and n will all vary with the age, a, of the cohort and so

$$h(a) = \frac{m(a)}{n(a)} . \tag{6.3}$$

In the period during which the cohort ages from a to a +1 there will be changes in both the numerator and the denominator of this quotient. Additions to the group of married heads within the cohort are possible by married non-heads becoming heads (H_n), single people marrying and becoming heads of household (H_s), widowers or divorcees remarrying and becoming heads of household (H_w and H_d) and entries as married household heads by in-migration and from the institutional population (H_i). The group can be left by transition to non-head (N_n), widowhood (N_w), divorce (N_d), out-migration or institutionalization (N_i) or death (N_m). Additions to the cohort will be by in-migration or from the institutional population (A_i) and losses will be through out-migration and institutionalisation (P_i) and mortality (P_m). At the cohort age a + 1 the headship rate is therefore

$$h(a +1) = \frac{m(a)+H_s+(H_n-N_n)+(H_w-N_w)+(H_d-N_d)+(H_i-N_i)-N_m}{n(a)+(A_i-P_i)-P_m} \tag{6.4}$$

A qualitative view of the function h can be gained by examining the major terms in this expression. If mortality rates can be assumed not to differ too greatly between married household heads and other cohort members then the terms N_m and P_m can be neglected. Likewise, if the net change brought about by migration and movements to and from institutions is small, the terms H_i, N_i, A_i and P_i will not be of primary importance in a qualitative analysis.

For ages corresponding to young adults, say 16–35, the dominant term in the expression will be H_s, as many cohort members marry and establish their own households. h will therefore tend to increase rapidly. The terms N_n, H_w and N_w will be small enough to neglect. H_n represents the situation where married couples, having lived as part of another household, possibly with parents, set up their own household. This will be a small effect, except possibly at the lower end of the age range, but will reinforce the effect of H_s. H_d and N_d will assume greater importance towards the end of the age range. Of the two, N_d will be dominant and will tend to flatten the curve as a increases.

In the middle years, say 35–60, H_s will be much smaller. The largest term will probably be N_d, although this will be largely balanced by H_d (remarriages), and H_s. Towards the end of this period N_w (widowhood) may begin to acquire some significance. However the overall effect during this period is one of stability, the various processes largely cancelling each other out, and so h will be relatively flat in this range.

Beyond 60 the dominant term will increasingly be N_w and h will begin to fall again. In general h will therefore increase rapidly up to the age of about 35, then level off and, after the age of about 60, start to fall again. For different cohorts the precise curve will alter slightly, as regards its turning points and its maximum value for example, but will retain its overall general shape.

One approach to using life-cycle curves to make household projections would be to estimate the various terms in the above expression for h. How-

ever, this method shares the problem faced by the transition-matrix methods—
the restricted availability of data. Rates would have to be estimated for each
cohort and for each future age of interest. In many cases, very little evidence
is available even regarding past values of these rates, and it seems doubtful
whether such a method would prove very successful.

An alternative approach is to model the headship rates by a mathematical
function, h, of the two variables a (age) and b (year of birth), depending on a
number of parameters $p_1, p_2, \ldots, p_n$:

$$h(a,b) \simeq f(a,b;p_1, p_2, \ldots, p_n)$$

The mathematical form of the approximating function f is chosen to be
appropriate to the shape of the life-cycle curve. Model curves currently being
experimented with are based on polynomials, spline functions or sums of
certain rational functions transformed by a logit operator, T, of the form

$$T(u) = \frac{1}{1 + e^u} . \tag{6.6}$$

Once the form of the life-cycle curve has been fixed the problem reduces to
one of estimating the parameters $p_1, p_2, \ldots p_n$. This can be done by fitting to
data from past Censuses. Estimates of headship rates for any age, a, and time,
t, are then available from the fitted curve as $f(a, t-a)$.

This approach of fitting a two-variable function (that is, a surface) to the
data is analogous to drawing a relief map of a geographical area. The map-
maker will have data (measurements of the height of the land above sea level)
at certain map coordinates. The surface he fits to these data is the land surface which he will represent graphically in terms of contours. In the same way
a 'contour map' of headship rates can be drawn. In this case the map coordinates are represented by the year of birth b and the age a of a particular
cohort. The data values are the Census headship rates which are known for
particular coordinates on this 'map', and the function of the life-cycle model is
essentially to use these data to draw the contours. Life-cycle headship-rate
curves for specific cohorts can be examined by drawing sections taken parallel
to the a-axis of this map. Sections parallel to the b-axis give headship-rate
time series for specific age groups (as are projected by the extrapolation
method currently used). Diagonal sections, with $a + b = t = $ constant, give
headship rate age-profiles at specific points in time.

While this curve-fitting approach tackles the problem of lack of data, it is
likely to obscure the relationship between the life-cycle curves and the household-formation processes. One means of overcoming this may be to frame the
parametric forms in such a way that the parameters have practical meaning in
demographic terms, such as 'the age at which the marriage rate attains its
maximum value', or 'the maximum proportion of married couples who live as
part of another household'. Such an approach has been applied in other contexts such as the modelling of schedules of demographic rates (Rogers, 1986)
and of household-state transition probabilities (Heida and Gordijn, 1985). A
further possibility (Corner, 1987) relies on a three-part strategy in which the
life-cycle method is used in conjunction with a standard transition-matrix
approach. The life-cycle method is first used to form a base set of projections.

Then the household transitions which would have to take place to give this projected pattern of household development are estimated. These form a base set of transitions which define the processes leading to the modelled household life-cycle development. At the third stage, the effects of modifying specific transition rates can be examined using a standard transition-matrix approach with states defined in terms of headship status.

CONCLUSION

The household projection model used by the DoE has been developed with a practical purpose firmly in mind. In particular, it is designed to provide projections disaggregated by household characteristics for a large number of areas ranging, in size, from England and Wales down to individual metropolitan districts and London boroughs. This goal imposes certain constraints, particularly regarding resource inputs and the nature and quality of the data used. The model is a disaggregated version of the headship rate method which allows the use of large-sample cross-sectional data derived from Censuses, and exogenous population projections. Experience has shown that the method is robust and efficient in terms of resources, and tests of its predictive power have been encouraging.

The main shortcoming of the model is its limited capacity to predict the impact on household formation of postulated changes of a social or economic nature. This failing is a result of the way headship rates are projected and the limited understanding of their behaviour in relation to other variables, rather than an inherent weakness of the headship-rate method framework. In order to expand the model's capabilities in this type of analysis within the constraints imposed by its original purpose, a method which projects characteristic life-cycle patterns of headship rates is being developed. The analysis of these life-cycle patterns by econometric methods and in terms of the processes of household formation will lead to a more transparent projection model capable of wider use in a policy-making context.

NOTE

1. This category of household, as used in the DoE household projection system, covers a variety of household types, generally groups of two or more related or unrelated adults who may be sharing or cohabiting.

REFERENCES

Corner, I. E. (1987) 'Household projection methods', *Journal of Forecasting*, vol. 6, no. 4, pp. 271–84.

Department of the Environment (1988) *1985 Based Estimates of Numbers of Households in England, the Regions, Counties, Metropolitan Districts and London Boroughs 1985–2001*. London: DoE.

Ermisch, J. and Overton, E. (1984) *Minimal Household Units*. Research paper 84/1. London: Policy Studies Institute.

Hårsman, B. and Snickars, F. (1983) 'A method for disaggregate household forecasts',

Tijdschrift voor Economische en Sociale Geographie, vol. 74, no. 4, pp. 282–90.

Heida, H. and Gordijn, H. (1985) 'Een prognosemodel voor de huishoudenson-twikkeling in Nederland' (A projection model for household development in the Netherlands), *Planning: Methodiek en Toepassing*, vol. 24, pp. 2–13.

Keilman, N. (1988) 'Dynamic household models', in Keilman, N., Kuijsten, A. and Vossen, A. (eds) *Modelling Household Formation and Dissolution*, pp. 123–138. Oxford: Clarendon Press.

Murphy, M. (1985) *Housing and Demographic Change*. ESRC report (ref. D00250012).

Nelissen, J.H.M. (1987) *Household Formation by Microsimulation: the Dutch Household Structure Generated*. Tilburg University Sociology Department, Working Paper Series, no. 18 (paper presented to the European Population Conference, Jyväskylä, Finland, 11–16 June).

Rogers, A. (1986) 'Parameterized multistate population dynamics and projections', *Journal of the American Statistical Association*, vol. 81, no. 393, pp. 48–61.

Smith, L. B., Rosen, K. T., Markandya, A. and Ullmo, P. (1984) 'The demand for housing, household headship rates, and household formation: an international analysis', *Urban Studies*, vol. 21, pp. 407–14.

Chapter 7

TIME-SERIES ANALYSIS FORECASTS OF A PARAMETERISED MORTALITY SCHEDULE*

Robert McNown
Andrei Rogers

INTRODUCTION

Projections of mortality rates are an essential ingredient of the demographic forecasting exercises that are regularly carried out by institutions such as the United Nations, the World Bank, the US Bureau of the Census, and the US Social Security Administration. Normally, the projected rates are applied to an observed population disaggregated by age, within a cohort-survival framework, to yield a forecast of the total number of deaths and of the surviving population.

The problem addressed in this chapter is the method used to forecast the age-specific mortality rates. Generally, such forecasts are carried out by generating 'scenarios' of the expected future trajectory of mortality rates, often using informed judgement or an extrapolation of past trends. Frequently, individual age-specific rates are extrapolated into the future, despite Keyfitz's (1982, p. 743) warning:

If one were to extrapolate the age-specific death rates, age by age using virtually any formula, one would obtain highly irregular rates within a very few cycles of projection. On a straight-line projection age by age, many ages would soon show negative death rates. One plainly ought to summarize the rates into some minimum parameter set.

In this chapter, we follow Keyfitz's advice and forecast the entire age pattern of mortality. The pattern is described by means of a mathematical representation called a *model mortality schedule*, which is specified with the aid of a relatively small number of parameters. Forecasts of future mortality

*A number of individuals contributed in various ways to the preparation of this chapter. Foremost among them was Kathy Gard who, as research assistant to the project, carried out a prodigious amount of data-processing work with good cheer, for which we are most grateful. Thanks also go to Alice Wade of the Social Security Administration for supplying the data and to Larry Heligman of the United Nations Population Division for providing the software (included in MORTPAK) for the Heligman–Pollard model. The authors also wish to acknowledge with thanks the accurate typing of Carrie Andree. An early version of this chapter was presented at the 27th meeting of the Western Regional Science Association, 24–28 February 1988, in Napa, California, where we benefited from the insightful comments of our discussant, John Long, of the US Bureau of the Census. This research is being supported by the National Science Foundation under Grant no. SES-8705591 to Andrei Rogers, Principal Investigator.

regimes are obtained by projecting the temporal evolution of each of these parameters.

The use of model schedules, expressed in terms of a small number of parameters, to smooth and describe schedules of age-specific rates is a common practice in demography. A large number of such functions have been proposed and fitted to mortality, fertility and migration data, for example, and the results have been widely applied to data-smoothing, interpolation, comparative analysis, data inference, and forecasting. The relevant literature on model schedules is vast and entry into it can be made from such representative publications as Brass (1971); Coale and Trussell (1966); Coale and Demeny (1974); and Rogers and Castro (1981).

The role of model schedules in population analysis is at least twofold. First, model schedules allow one to condense an enormous amount of information about transitions between states of existence or the occurrences of vital events in each year into a few parameters. Second, model schedules provide a manageable number of interpretable descriptive statistics, for each demographic transition or vital event in each year, the time series of which can be the basis for econometric analysis and forecasting.

During the past several years, a number of scholars have experimented with the application of autoregressive integrated moving average (ARIMA) methods to demographic data, especially to fertility series (Carter and Lee, 1986; Land, 1986; Lee, 1974; 1975; McDonald, 1979; 1981; Miller, 1984; Saboia, 1977). And recently, Thompson *et al.* (1987) have modeled the entire curve of age-specific fertility rates by using a model schedule approach and a multivariate time series model for projections. To our knowledge, however, no one has yet adopted such an approach to the modeling of mortality series. We carry out such an exercise in this chapter.

The organisation of our exposition is as follows. First, we review the demographer's well-known life-table framework for analysing survivorship and introduce alternative specifications of model mortality schedules. Next, we examine more fully the characteristics of a particularly effective mathematical representation of such schedules: the Heligman–Pollard model mortality schedule. Then we use this model schedule to describe patterns of mortality for the US during this century. A time-series analysis of these data is then presented and followed by a forecast of future US mortality. Finally, the chapter concludes with an assessment and discussion of future research directions.

MODELING THE SURVIVORSHIP OF A BIRTH COHORT

Let l (0) denote an arbitrary fixed number of babies of the same sex, born at a given moment in time, $t = 0$, say. Imagine that after exactly x years, decrements due to death have reduced the size of the original cohort to l (x) survivors. The number of deaths experienced by the cohort during the age interval $(x, x+h)$ is l $(x) - l$ $(x+h)$, and the exposure in terms of person-years (persons times years) is h l (x). As the age interval is reduced to zero, in the limit the ratio of these two quantities defines the actuarial 'force of mortality' at each exact age x:

$$u(x) = \lim_{h \downarrow 0} \frac{l(x) - l(x+h)}{hl(x)} = -\frac{d}{dx} \ln [l(x)] \tag{7.1}$$

where $\ln [l(x)]$ denotes the natural logarithm of $l(x)$.

Integrating the associated differential equation

$$u(x)dx = -d[\ln l(x)] \tag{7.2}$$

gives the well-known actuarial formula:

$$l(x) = l(0) \exp \left[-\int_0^x u(t)dt \right]. \tag{7.3}$$

Let $_nq_x$ denote the conditional probability of dying during the age interval $(x, x+n]$ given survival until age x. Then

$$_nq_x = \frac{l(x) - l(x+n)}{l(x)} = 1 - {_np_x} \tag{7.4}$$

where $_np_x$ is the corresponding conditional probability of surviving n years, and

$$l(x) = l(0)_np_0{_np_n} \cdots {_np_{x-n}} \tag{7.5}$$

Notice that if $l(0)$ is set equal to unity, $l(x)$ becomes interpretable as the unconditional probability of surviving from birth to exact age x.

Demographers often estimate $_nq_x$ from observed age-specific annual mortality rates m_x, using the classical formula (Keyfitz, 1968).

$$_nq_x = \frac{nm_x}{1 + \dfrac{n}{2} m_x} \tag{7.6}$$

When the mortality data refer to single years of age, the subscript n usually is eliminated, a practice we shall follow in this chapter.

MODEL MORTALITY SCHEDULES

The search for mathematically specified 'laws of mortality' has attracted the attention of actuaries, demographers and others fascinated by the powerful regularity in age profile that is exhibited by schedules of age-specific death rates (or probabilities) in different societies over time. The first attempt was apparently that of DeMoivre around 1725, who suggested that the probability of survival from birth to age x could be expressed as a linear function of age (Keyfitz, 1982):

$$l(x) = 1 - x/w \tag{7.7}$$

where w denotes the highest attainable age. A more realistic representation for the adult ages was offered by Gompertz (1825) who suggested the exponential:

$$u(x) = ac^x = a \exp{(bx)} \tag{7.8}$$

for the curve of age-specific death rates (*intensities*). Not until a half-century later did a realistic expression for mortality *at all ages* appear in the literature. The Danish actuary Thiele (1872) was the first to suggest the decomposition of the U-shaped intensity curve into its three constituent components—early-life mortality, $u_1(x)$, middle-life mortality, $u_2(x)$, and late-life mortality, $u_3(x)$:

$$u(x) = u_1(x) + u_2(x) + u_3(x). \tag{7.9}$$

Thiele chose the Gompertz function in equation (7.8) to represent both childhood and old-age mortality (a negative and a positive exponential, respectively) and selected a scale-modified normal probability density function to model middle-life mortality:

$$
\begin{aligned}
u_1(x) &= a_1\exp{(-b_1 x)} \\
u_2(x) &= a_2\exp{(-\tfrac{1}{2}b_2(x - c)^2)} \\
u_3(x) &= a_3\exp{(b_3 x)}
\end{aligned}
\tag{7.10}
$$

where all seven parameters a_i, b_i, and c are assumed to be positive.

Experimental work carried out at the International Institute for Applied Systems Analysis (Rogers and Planck, 1983) explored the fit of a multiexponential model similar to Thiele's, but with the middle-life mortality component specified by the double exponential distribution of Coale and McNeil (1972):

$$u_2(x) = a_2\exp{\{-\alpha_2 (x-\mu_2) - \exp[-\lambda_2 (x-\mu_2)]\}} \tag{7.11}$$

Mode and Busby (1982) put forward yet another variation of the Thiele decomposition by adopting a parabolic function for the middle-life mortality component:

$$u_2(x) = a_2 - b_2 (x-c)^2 \tag{7.12}$$

and Siler (1983) simplified matters even more by assuming $u_2(x)$ to be constant, a_2, say.

Finally, Heligman and Pollard (1980), although following Thiele's decomposition approach, chose a somewhat different set of component curves and a different (discretised) dependent variable:

$$f_x = A^{(x+B)^C} + D \exp{[-E(\ln x - \ln F)^2]} + GH^x \tag{7.13}$$

where f_x is the ratio of the conditional probability of dying, q_x, to its complement, p_x; the use of this ratio for f_x permits q_x to take on values between zero and one only.

THE HELIGMAN–POLLARD MODEL MORTALITY SCHEDULE

Equation (7.13) is defined for $x > 0$ only; for $x = 0$, Heligman and Pollard apparently set

$$f_0 = \frac{q_0}{p_0} = A^{B^C} + G. \tag{7.14}$$

They interpret the parameters of their model in the following way. The parameter A is a close approximation to q_1, B reflects the difference $q_0 - q_1$, and C is a measure of the rate of mortality decline during childhood (the higher the value of C, the faster is the decline of q with age). Parameter D indicates the level of middle-life mortality (the 'accident hump') and E and F refer to its dispersion and location, respectively. Finally, G denotes the level of late-life mortality at age zero, and H represents the rate of increase of that mortality.

As Heligman and Pollard point out, the parameter B is a measure of age displacement that identifies the location of infant mortality within the range $(q_1, \frac{1}{2})$. When $B = 0$, and if the value of G is small enough to be ignored, $q_0 = \frac{1}{2} = p_0$, irrespective of the values taken on by A and C. When $B > 0$ (its value is normally close to zero) the higher the value of B, for a fixed C, the closer q_0 is to q_1. Finally, the effect of B on the values of model mortality rates other than for age zero is negligible.

The middle-life mortality component is represented by a curve that is similar to the log-normal function; it is hump-shaped and centred with maximum value D, at age $x = F$, declining on either side of this age. Although it is a symmetric function of $\ln x$, it is asymmetric with respect to x, declining more slowly for the ages above $x = F$. Normally, the central value, $x = F$, is located somewhere in the early 20s among males, and anywhere from ages 40 to 60 among females. Typically, the variance around this central value ($\sigma^2 = 1/E$) is much smaller for males than for females.

Finally, the late-life mortality component in equation (7.13) is a simple Gompertz function. But Heligman and Pollard also offer an alternative specification, which we adopt in this chapter. To allow for the normally observed curvature away from the Gompertz curve among mortality rates at the oldest ages, they suggest a modified Gompertz function in which the late-life component GH^x is replaced by

$$u_3 = \frac{GH^x}{1 + GH^x}, \tag{7.15}$$

a quantity that is always less than unity. In this alternative specification they also set $f_x = q_x$. Despite the appeal of using the ratio $f_x = q_x/p_x$, in order to limit the range of q_x between 0 and 1 for all x, we follow Heligman and Pollard's alternative specification in this chapter for three reasons. First, in mortality age profiles that exhibit no 'accident hump' at the middle-life ages, the computer algorithm may fit a hump at much older ages to account for the curvature that may remain in q_x at those ages. Second, the computer software that we use in this study was provided to us by Heligman, courtesy of the

Population Division of the United Nations. That software assumes that $f_x = q_x$. Finally, according to Heligman and Pollard (1980, p. 60), the two alternative specifications produce results that are almost identical.

To estimate the eight parameters in their model schedule, Heligman and Pollard search for estimates that minimise the sum of squares

$$
SS_x = \sum_{x=0}^{w} \left[\frac{\hat{q}_x - q_x}{q_x} \right]^2
$$

where $\hat{q}_x$ is the fitted (model schedule) value at age x, q_x is the observed mortality rate, and w is the last year of age (or the starting age of the last age group). 'The observed rates above 85 were excluded from the calculation because they appeared to be less reliable' (Heligman and Pollard, 1980, p. 51). The same procedure is followed in this chapter.

To demonstrate the use of the formula in equation (7.13) with $f_x = q_x$ and the modification for u_3 set out in equation (7.15), we fitted the model to the Australian data on male mortality presented in the Appendix of the Heligman and Pollard (1980) article. The comparison of the Heligman–Pollard estimates with our own confirms the similarity of the two alternative specifications (McNown and Rogers, 1988, Table 1). Furthermore, aggregated data (at five-year age intervals) seem to yield parameter estimates that in most instances also come close to the corresponding disaggregated estimates (using single-year-of-age data). That is, the loss of information regarding age profile due to aggregation does not appear to introduce a significant bias (with the possible exception of the B and E parameter estimates).

MORTALITY IN THE UNITED STATES, 1900–85

A history of mortality decline

The history of mortality in the USA during this century may be characterised as a sequence of two periods of sharp decline separated by a 14-year period of very modest reductions in mortality levels. The crude death rate (CDR) declined dramatically during the first period, dropping from its 17.2 per thousand level in 1900 to a relative low of 9.2 per thousand in 1954, at which point it leveled off until 1968 and then again resumed its previous decline, dropping to a new low of 8.5 per thousand in 1979 and leveling off once again (Klebba *et al.*, 1973; National Center for Health Statistics, 1986).

This recent stall in the historical pattern of mortality decline is a consequence of the shifting age composition of the US population, which has been growing older. Correcting for this shift by standardisation yields age-adjusted death rates that are more accurate indicators of true mortality levels, because they take into account variations in the age composition of the population. The age-adjusted death rate resumed its historical pattern of decline after 1968, dropping to 5.5 per thousand in 1985, the lowest ever recorded in the US.

Another index of mortality levels that controls for changes in population age composition is the period expectation of life at birth, a measure that standardises the age-specific rates by weighting them with the age composition of the stationary (zero-growth) life-table population. The evolution of this index is inversely related to that of the age-adjusted crude death rate, but it tells the same story in a different way.

The expectation of life at birth in 1900 was 46.60 years for males and 48.95 years for females. By 1985 these two life expectancies had increased to 71.2 and 78.2 years, respectively. The historical pattern of life expectancy also shows a stall in mortality decline during the 1954–68 period, which is largely a feature of male mortality (Faber and Wade, 1983).

According to Crimmins (1981, p. 251), the two periods of rapid US mortality decline (she focuses only on the 1940–77 period) were caused by different factors:

In the 'first' period, much of the decline was due to a reduction of deaths from the diseases that were cured with antibiotics and similar drugs. Much of the recent decline is accounted for by decreases in cardiovascular diseases. This is the first time in history that mortality declines have been dominated by decreases in diseases of old age or degenerative diseases. Because this is so, we may be beginning a new era of mortality decline, which, if it continues, will lead to large increases in life expectancies at older ages.

Thus, the early period of mortality decline was largely due to reduced death rates from infectious and parasitic diseases, and from influenza and pneumonia—diseases of the young. The recent decline on the other hand, is mostly a consequence of reductions in deaths attributable to cardiovascular diseases and deaths from other causes at the older ages. Such shifts are concealed in the temporal patterns of aggregate indicators of mortality levels.

Another significant shift within the broad general pattern of mortality decline is offered by the death rates of those aged 15–44 years during the 1960s. The nearly stable CDRs of this period conceal the different patterns exhibited by this middle-life age group, in contrast to the early- and late-life segments of the population. The latter two age groups exhibited appreciably lower death rates, but these declines were in large part cancelled by the marked increases in the death rates of the middle-life age group. These increases in the mortality levels of teenagers, young adults, and persons entering the middle years of life were due in large part to increases in the death rates of men in those age groups, although substantial increases were also observed in female death rates at ages 15–24 (Klebba *et al.*, 1973).

A parameterised description of the history of mortality decline

The history of mortality decline during the 1900–85 period can be concisely described by the history of the eight parameters defining the Heligman-Pollard model. To fix the character of the description, consider the numerical results for males at two moments in time: 1900 and 1980, say. For ease of comparison, we reproduce in Figure 7.1 the two sets of parameter values and illustrate their associated age patterns of mortality.

Examining the contrasting age profiles in Figure 7.1, one is immediately struck by the sharp decline in infant mortality over the 80-year interval. Correspondingly, all three early-life mortality parameters show marked declines,

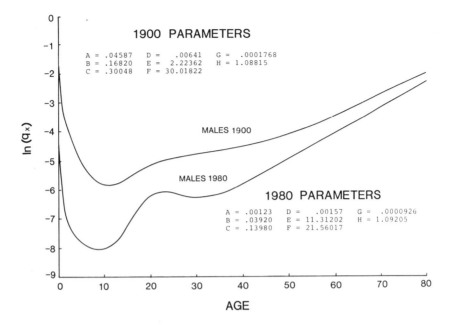

Figure 7.1 Probabilities of dying at each age (q_x): US males: 1900 and 1980

indicating a reduction in level (the dramatic reduction in A), a narrowing of the gap between q_0 and q_1 (the decline in B), and a corresponding reduced rate of decrease from q_0 to q_1 and beyond (the drop in C).

Changes in the age pattern of middle-life mortality are captured by the three parameters D, E and F. They indicate that the height of the hump declines (the drop in D), its maximum shifts to a much younger age (the reduction in F), and the spread, or variance, around this peak value is much narrower (the increase in E).

Finally, late-life mortality, as described by the Gompertz curve, starts at a lower initial value (the decline in G), but it grows at a faster pace (the slight increase in H). Consequently, the combined effect of the two changes is difficult to gauge without a numerical calculation. According to Figure 7.1, however, old-age mortality in 1980 fell moderately below old age mortality 80 years earlier.

Although the above comparison across an 80-year interval shows a decrease in the numerical values of all parameters except E and H, the path of the decline in between 1900 and 1980 is definitely not a straight line. Figures 7.2 and 7.3 reveal that the individual parameter trajectories over the several decades vary considerably. For example, parameters A, B and C decline rapidly from 1900 to the mid-1940s, then level off, with B exhibiting a slight upward slope since 1960. These three patterns define a regime of early-life mortality that has decreased dramatically in level during the first half of this century and has sharply reduced its rate of decline since that time.

Parameters D, E and F show a mixed pattern. Except for two sudden peaks, due to the dramatically increased male mortality during the influenza epidemic of 1918 and the Second World War, D (like A, B and C) declines from 1900 to the early 1940s, levels off, and then shows a modest increase. F follows the same general pattern, but one without the two distinct peaks. E, on the other hand, exhibits a sudden and dramatic increase during the early 1940s, and then begins a gradual decline. This suggests that both the level and the peak age of mid-life mortality have essentially stabilised since the Second World War, following significant declines during the first four decades of this century. But the spread (or dispersion) of mortality probabilities around the peak age decreased dramatically shortly after 1940 and is now gradually increasing.

Finally, G and H exhibit a temporal evolution that also indicates a 'break with the past' around 1940. During the first four decades of this century, G was generally increasing, whereas H was decreasing; during the second four decades, this pattern was reversed. Apparently the initial base *level* of senescent mortality first increased and then decreased, whereas the *rate* of increase with age of senescent mortality first decreased and then increased. Because both parameters determine the rates of late-life mortality, it is difficult to unconfound their individual contributions.

TIME-SERIES MODELS AND FORECASTS OF MODEL SCHEDULE PARAMETERS

Plots of the model schedule parameters for the entire 1900–83 period show a sharp change in pattern for every parameter during the early 1940s (see Figures 7.2 and 7.3). Although this shift raises some interesting questions concerning the behaviour of mortality, it also poses major problems for modelling and forecasting the parameters. We experimented with time-series models of the parameters, both including and excluding the observations before 1941, and discovered that models based on the more complete sample had inferior diagnostic statistics and out-of-sample forecasts. Using only post-1940 data reduces the number of observations below desired limits for time-series modelling because statistics used in model identification and model coefficients tend to be estimated with large standard errors. Despite these problems, we have employed the shorter sample in the modelling and forecasting analysis presented here, allowing forecast performance to override considerations of statistical insignificance in the decision to retain parameters.

Univariate time-series models for each of the parameters were identified and estimated according to the methods of Box and Jenkins (1976), using the 30 observations from 1941 to 1970. The final models are reported in Table 7.1. Of the eight parameters, only C was found to be most appropriately modelled as a random walk without drift, so the forecast for C is that of no change.

All parameters required a logarithmic transformation and a differencing of at least order one to achieve stationarity. The logarithmically transformed

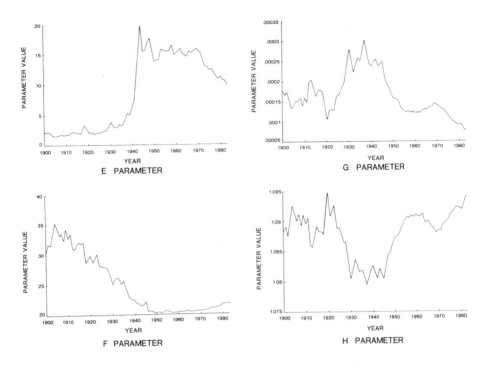

Figure 7.2 Heligman–Pollard parameters A–D: 1900–83, males

series tend to show less heteroscedasticity, and this transformation also sets a lower bound of zero on parameter forecasts.

To the extent that forecast horizons required in demographic forecasting are rather long, proper modelling of trend is a crucial component of time-series analysis. Forecasts from univariate time-series models tend to converge fairly quickly to the long-run trends incorporated in the models, which may be either deterministic and global or stochastic and local. With the exception of C and D, all parameters have been modelled with trend components. First-differenced models with a constant term, such as those used to model G and H necessarily contain a deterministic trend. For G and H the trend is weak and statistically insignificant, but it has been retained because it improves forecasting performance. For these two series the forecasts approach the constant rate of change given by the value of the constant term. In the models of A, B, E, and F stochastic trends have been introduced through use of a second differencing transformation. Forecasts of these parameters converge to a constant value determined by the last several observations in the sample.

All models reported in Table 7.1 show satisfactory diagnostics as summarized by the Q-statistics of Ljung and Box (1978) which indicate no significant residual autocorrelation. Although the statistical insignificance of some coefficients in the reported models suggests possible over-parameterisation,

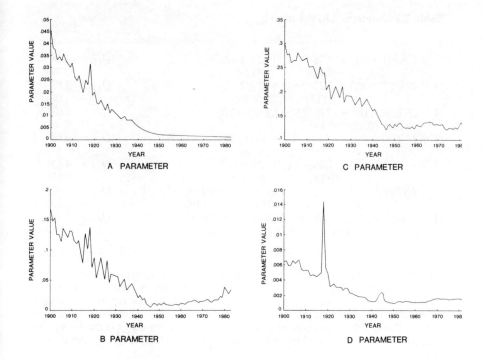

Figure 7.3 Heligman–Pollard parameters E–H: 1900–83, males

we have retained these insignificant coefficients since they improve forecasting performance. We attribute their lack of statistical significance to the large standard errors produced by the shortened sample. The use of second differences for four of the series may strike some as surprising, raising the issue of possible over-differencing. Again the choice of second differencing is based on the superior forecasting performance of the resulting stochastic trend models relative to that of the corresponding first-differenced, deterministic trend models.

To generate reliable forecasts of age-specific mortality probabilities (the q_x), our methodology requires that the time-series models be capable of providing satisfactory forecasts of the model schedule parameters. Forecasts of both the parameters and the mortality probabilities are evaluated using various criteria. Both updated (one year ahead) and non-updated (1–13 years ahead) forecasts over the 1971–83 period are compared with 'actuals', which were retained in the hold-out sample. The accuracy of these out-of-sample forecasts are evaluated using mean absolute percent error (MAPE), root mean squared error (RMSE), and Theil statistics. The Theil statistic reports the root mean squared error of the model forecast relative to that of the 'naive' no-change forecast, with values less than unity indicating greater accuracy for the model forecast.

Table 7.1 Estimated ARIMA models*

$(1 - L)^2 A(t) = e(t) - 1.08e(t-1) + .28e(t-2)$	$Q_{15} = $ 4.18
$\qquad\qquad\quad$ (0.18) $\qquad\quad$ (0.19)	(0.99)
$(1 - L)^2 B(t) = e(t) - 1.21e(t-1) + .39e(t-2)$	$Q_{15} = $ 3.83
$\qquad\qquad\quad$ (0.17) $\qquad\quad$ (0.18)	(1.00)
$(1 - .27L + .11L^2 + .22L^3)(1 - L)D(t) = e(t)$	$Q_{15} = $ 6.07
$\qquad$ (0.19) $\quad$ (0.19) $\quad$ (0.18)	(0.98)
$(1 - L)^2 E(t) = e(t) - .42e(t-1) - .23e(t-2)$	$Q_{15} = $ 12.65
$\qquad\qquad\quad$ (0.18) $\qquad\quad$ (0.18)	(0.63)
$(1 - L)^2 F(t) = e(t) - 1.26e(t-1) + .36e(t-2)$	$Q_{15} = $ 4.65
$\qquad\qquad\quad$ (0.18) $\qquad\quad$ (0.18)	(0.99)
$(1 - L)G(t) = -.015 + e(t) + .18e(t-1) + .39e(t-3)$	$Q_{13} = $ 7.41
$\qquad\qquad$ (0.014) $\qquad\quad$ (0.18) $\qquad\quad$ (0.19)	(0.88)
$(1 - L)H(t) = .0002 + e(t) + .27e(t-1) + .63e(t-3)$	$Q_{13} = $ 5.46
$\qquad\qquad$ (0.0002) $\qquad$ (0.15) $\qquad\quad$ (0.16)	(0.96)

*All models were identified and estimated using 30 observations from 1941 to 1970. Each parameter has been transformed into logarithmic form. No model is reported for C, which was identified as a random walk without drift. In each reported equation L represents the lag operator $LX(t) = X(t-1)$ and $e(t)$ is a white noise process. Numbers in parentheses below estimated coefficients are standard errors. Q is the Ljung–Box statistic with degrees of freedom shown as a subscript and level of significance given in parentheses.

The updated parameter forecasts are satisfactory according to these summary statistics (McNown and Rogers, 1988, Table 3). Only the one-step-ahead forecasts for H are substantially inferior to the no-change forecast, and this problem vanishes at the higher forecast intervals. The model forecasts are generally satisfactory according to the Theil statistic, and most show an improvement relative to the naive forecast as the horizon lengthens.

The non-updated forecasts naturally show larger errors, with considerable variation in quality, across the eight parameters (McNown and Rogers, 1988, Table 7.4). For example, overall errors as summarised by the mean absolute percent errors are quite small (less than 6.5) for parameters A, D, F, and H. Parameters B, E, and G have large percentage errors, averaging between 25% and 35% of actuals. The forecasts for E, for example, miss the actual decline in this parameter over the forecast period. The model for G does predict a decline, but the forecasted downturn is not as sharp as actually occurred. The importance of these forecasting errors for forecasting mortality probabilities is assessed in the following section.

MORTALITY PROBABILITY FORECASTS IMPLIED BY PROJECTED PARAMETERS

Non-updated forecasts of the model schedules are compared graphically with the observed schedules for the years 1971, 1975, 1980, and 1983 in Figure 7.4. The goodness of fit between the observed and forecasted schedules for each of

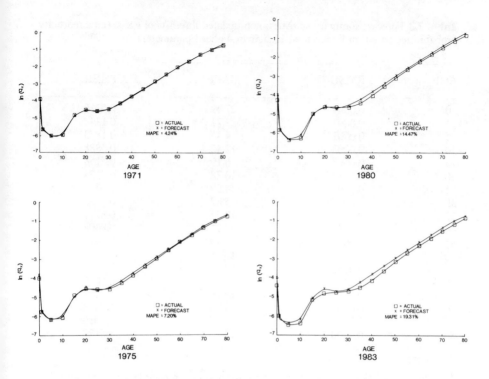

Figure 7.4 Actual and forecast mortality schedules: 1971, 1975, 1980, and 1983

these years is summarised by the mean absolute percent errors calculated at the 18 ages for which mortality rates exist. As expected, the association between the observed and forecasted schedules weakens at the longer horizons, with the mean absolute percent error rising from 4.24 for 1971 to 19.31 for 1983.

Summary statistics for the forecasts of the age-specific mortality probabilities over the 13 years 1971–83 are presented in Table 7.2. The disparities between actual and forecasted schedules can be traced to errors in the forecasts of individual parameters. The model for B is unable to capture the growth in B after 1975, reflecting smaller differences between infant and year-one mortality probabilities. Although mortality at age one is predicted with considerable accuracy (MAPE = 2.7 over the 13 years) due to the successful forecast of A, the MAPE in forecasts of infant mortality (27.4) is the largest of any age interval. This problem in tracking infant mortality is linked to the peculiarity of the Heligman–Pollard function at the lowest ages, which ties infant mortality rates to mortality at age one rather than representing infant mortality with an independent parameter. In addition, for data reported in five-year age intervals, exactly three mortality probabilities (at ages 0, 1 and 5) are represented by three parameters (A, B and C). Consequently there are no economies in the parameterization of the rate schedule at

Table 7.2 Forecast summary statistics: non-updated forecasts of age-specific mortality probabilities based on forecasts of Heligman–Pollard parameters, 1971–83*

AGE	RMSE	MAPE	THEIL
0	0.0044	27.43	0.5710
1	0.0001	2.71	0.1343
5	0.0001	4.35	0.1873
10	0.0003	12.42	0.5888
15	0.0005	6.19	0.5158
20	0.0012	10.78	0.8323
25	0.0005	4.99	0.7468
30	0.0006	5.67	0.4039
35	0.0025	18.25	0.8721
40	0.0041	20.25	0.8408
45	0.0050	14.49	0.7413
50	0.0059	10.71	0.6353
55	0.0083	10.15	0.5525
60	0.0112	8.63	0.6050
65	0.0188	10.19	0.7253
70	0.0269	9.96	1.0488
75	0.0356	9.05	1.2019
80	0.0500	10.70	1.6139

*Summary statistics are based on 13 non-updated out-of-sample forecasts for 1971–1983. RMSE is the root mean squared error, MAPE is the mean absolute percent error, and THEIL is the root mean squared error of the model forecast relative to that of the no-change forecast.

these ages, so that a direct forecast of mortality rates at these three ages may be efficient. The use of one-year age intervals would provide more data points for more precise estimation of the curvature of the model schedule associated with early-life mortality. Adequate representation of the curvature of the schedule also appears to be a problem at age 10 and, again, data with shorter age intervals could improve the forecast at this age.

The forecasted schedule is also too high at the accident peak, with age-20 mortality over-predicted in 1983 and a MAPE of 10.8 over the 13-year forecast period. Most of this error appears to have occurred after 1980, when there was a sharp drop in this peak (and correspondingly an unanticipated fall in D) after a decade of rather flat young adult mortality rates.

Senescent mortality is over-predicted, because of the upward bias in the forecast of the G parameter. This bias is in turn a result of a downturn in G in 1970, which was only partially captured by the univariate time series model. This drop in G reflects the unprecedented reduction in mortality at older ages stemming from the advances made against the degenerative diseases mentioned by Crimmins (1981). Improvement in forecasts of this component of mortality requires an ability to anticipate such advances and to incorporate them in a forecasting model.

Overall, the forecasts of the schedules and individual mortality probabilities are reasonably accurate. The Theil statistic is less than unity for all ages under 70 years, showing that the forecasts at these ages are more accurate than the assumption of constant probabilities. In fact, the gains in accuracy over the fixed probabilities assumption are quite dramatic at certain ages. The mean squared forecast errors from the model at ages 1 and 5 are less than 20% of those obtained using the assumption of constant mortality probabilities. Even for infant mortality, which showed the highest MAPE, the model forecast shows a 43% improvement in mean squared error over the no change assumption. The mean absolute errors are quite small in percentage terms for youth mortality (ages 1 and 5) and for young adults. At ages 35 and 40 we see some difficulty in capturing the curvature of the schedule (MAPEs of 18.3 and 20.3), but the forecasted mortality probabilities are still an improvement over the fixed parameter forecast.

To some extent, the strength of the methodology goes beyond the forecast accuracy statistics. Forecasts of the parameters produce a schedule that captures the fundamental characteristics of the age distribution of mortality. Smooth curves showing mortality probabilities at single-year age intervals can be inferred from the forecasted parameters as shown in Figure 7.4. The parameterised schedules and their forecasts provide a convenient summary of entire mortality distributions, and their representation by parameters provides a useful instrument for comparing mortality at different points in time. Without parameterisation, for example, it would be difficult to determine that the centre of the accident peak has shifted sharply towards younger ages during this century. Furthermore, forecasts of individual mortality probabilities can be traced to assumptions or projections of individual parameters, providing a convenient basis for the comparison of mortality forecasts obtained from different sources.

CONCLUSION

Previous modelling of mortality schedules has led to the question of how many parameters are necessary adequately to capture and reliably forecast age-specific mortality. Our initial work with the Heligman–Pollard function demonstrates that this eight-parameter model fits age-specific mortality probabilities for males at five-year age intervals with considerable precision. Changes in the age distribution of mortality over the 84 years beginning with 1900 are satisfactorily accommodated by the Heligman–Pollard model. More parsimonious representations would have difficulty in capturing the rise in young adult mortality that has occurred in the face of overall declining mortality rates at other ages. We have also found that the eight parameters of this model fitted over the 84 years can be modelled as a time series, although there is a severe change in structure around 1941.

Models fitted to each parameter, over the 30-year period from 1941 to 1970, provide adequate representations of the shorter time series, although the patterns for many of the parameters are not amenable to simple extrapolations. As Keyfitz (1982) points out, a schedule that yields a time series of parameters following a simple trend will be easily forecasted. The parameters of the Heligman–Pollard model, even over the shorter post-1941 period, do not satisfy this criterion. However, it is possible that shifts in the age distribution of mortality are such that no model that adequately captures this distribution will have smoothly trended parameters. Despite these difficulties, the Heligman–Pollard model has produced medium-range forecasts of age-specific mortality that are acceptable in terms of mean absolute errors and in comparison to those of a fixed-parameters model. Even the simple univariate forecasts of the parameters yield schedules that capture the fundamental characteristics of the age distribution of mortality.

The results presented in this chapter are sufficiently encouraging to warrant additional investigations. Improvement in forecast accuracy would probably be realised by a representation with more smoothly trended parameters. A step in this direction would be to model directly the mortality probabilities at the three youngest ages, since such rates tend to show smoother patterns than does the associated B parameter. Parameters A, B, and C can be solved algebraically from the mortality rates at ages 0, 1 and 5, so that the complete Heligman–Pollard schedule can be reconstructed. We also hope to obtain a time series of mortality by single years of age and to repeat the forecasting exercise with the re-estimated Heligman–Pollard model. The greater detail in age-specific mortality should allow a more accurate representation of the curvature of the schedules, particularly the early-life and middle-life components. The success achieved with the relatively short post–1941 series offers encouragement that similar analysis can be performed on cause-specific mortality schedules. We also intend to experiment with mutlivariate time-series models that allow interactions among the parameters of each of the three components of the Heligman–Pollard function and permit the introduction of socio-economic variables as predictors. Finally, we plan to test other models of mortality to see if alternative functional forms give rise to more accurate forecasts.

REFERENCES

Box, G.E.P. and Jenkins, G.M. (1976) *Time Series Analysis: Forecasting and Control*. San Francisco: Holden-Day.

Brass, W. (1971) 'On the scale of mortality' in W. Brass (ed.), *Biological Aspects of Demography*. London, Taylor and Francis, pp. 86–110.

Carter, L. R. and Lee, R.D. (1986) 'Joint forecasts of U.S. marital fertility, nuptiality, births and marriages using time series models', *Journal of the American Statistical Association*, vol. 81, no. 396, pp. 902–11.

Coale, A.J. and Demeny, P. (1966) *Regional Model Life Tables and Stable Populations*. Princeton NJ: University Press.

Coale, A.J. and McNeil, D.R. (1972) 'The distribution by age of the frequency of first marriage in a female cohort', *Journal of the American Statistical Association*, vol. 67, no. 340, pp. 743–9.

Coale, A.J. and Trussell, T.J. (1974) 'Model fertility schedules: variations in the age structure of childbearing in human populations', *Population Index*, vol. 40, no. 2, pp. 185–258.

Crimmins, E.M. (1981) 'The changing pattern of American mortality decline, 1940–77, and its implications for the future', *Population and Development Review*, vol. 7, no. 2, pp. 229–54.

Faber, J.F. and Wade, A.H. (1983), *Life tables for the United States: 1900–2050*. Actuarial Study no. 89. Washington DC: US Department of Health and Human Services, Social Security Administration.

Gompertz, B. (1825) 'On the nature of the function expressive of the law of human mortality', *Philosophical Transactions of the Royal Society of London*, vol. 115, no. 2, pp. 513–85.

Heligman, L. and Pollard, J.H. (1980), 'The age pattern of mortality', *Journal of the Institute of Actuaries*, vol. 107, pp. 49–80.

Keyfitz, N. (1968) *Introduction to the Mathematics of Population*, Reading, MA: Addison-Wesley.

Keyfitz, N. (1982), 'Choice of function for mortality analysis: effective forecasting depends on a minimum parameter representation', *Theoretical Population Biology*, vol. 21, no. 3, pp. 329–52.

Klebba, A.J., Maurer, J.D., and Glass, E.J. (1973) *Mortality Trends: Age, Color, and Sex, United States, 1950–69*, Series 20, no. 15. Rockville, MD: US Public Health Service, National Center for Health Statistics.

Land, K. (1986) 'Methods for national population forecasts: a review', *Journal of the American Statistical Association*, vol. 81, no. 396, pp. 888–901.

Lee, R.D. (1974), 'Forecasting births in post-transition populations: stochastic renewal with serially correlated fertility', *Journal of the American Statistical Association*, vol. 69, no. 347, pp. 607–17.

Ljung, G.M. and Box, G.E.P. (1978) 'On a measure of lack of fit in time series models', *Biometrika*, vol. 65, no. 2, pp. 297–303.

McDonald, J. (1979) 'A time series approach to forecasting Australian total live births', *Demography*, vol. 16, no. 4, pp. 575–601.

McDonald, J. (1981) 'Modeling demographic relationships: an analysis of forecast functions for Australian births', *Journal of the American Statistical Association*, vol. 76, no. 376, pp. 782–92.

McNown, R.F. and Rogers, A. (1988) *Time Series Analysis and Forecasting of Parameterized Model Schedules: Mortality*. Working Paper 88–2. Boulder, CO: Institute of Behavioral Science.

Miller, R.B. (1984) 'Evaluation of transformations in forecasting age specific birth rates', *Insurance: Mathematics and Economics*, vol. 3, pp. 263–70.

Mode, C.J. and Busby, R.C. (1982) 'An eight-parameter model of human mortality: the single decrement case', *Bulletin of Mathematical Biology*, vol. 44, no. 5, pp. 647–59.

National Center for Health Statistics (1986) *Annual Summary of Births, Marriages, Divorces, and Deaths: United States, 1985*, NCHS Monthly Vital Statistics Report, vol. 34, no. 13. Hyattsville, MD: US Public Health Service.

Rogers, A. and Castro, L. (1981) *Model Migration Schedules*. Research Report 81–30. Laxenburg, Austria: International Institute for Applied Systems Analysis.

Rogers, A. and Planck, F. (1983) *Model: A General Program for Estimating Parameterized Model Schedules of Fertility, Mortality, Migration, and Marital and Labor Force Status Transitions*. Working Paper 83–102, Laxenburg, Austria: International Institute for Applied Systems Analysis.

Saboia, J.L.M. (1977) 'Autoregressive integrated moving average (ARIMA) models for birth forecasting', *Journal of the American Statistical Association*, vol. 72, no. 358, pp. 264–70.

Siler, W. (1983), 'Parameters of mortality in human populations with widely varying life spans', *Statistics in Medicine*, vol. 2, pp. 373–80.

Thiele, T.N. (1872) 'On a mathematical formula to express the rate of mortality throughout the whole of life', *Journal of the Institute of Actuaries*, vol. 16, pp. 313–29.

Thompson, P.A., Bell, W., Long, J. and Miller, R.B. (1987) '*Multivariate Time Series Projections of Parameterized Age-specific Fertility Rates*, Working Paper Series 87–3. Columbus: College of Business, The Ohio State University.

Chapter 8

A MODEL WITH WHICH TO FORECAST EMPLOYMENT AND POPULATION CHANGE AT THE REGIONAL AND SUB-REGIONAL LEVEL[1]

P. Tyler and J. Rhodes

INTRODUCTION

This chapter presents work which is currently underway in Cambridge to produce a regional and sub-regional population and employment forecasting model. The programme of work is being undertaken jointly by the Department of Land Economy and PA Cambridge Economic Consultants (PACEC) and the construction of the model has involved a large number of people and has drawn on a body of expertise in the area of urban and regional economics built up over many years in the Department of Land Economy and the Department of Applied Economics in the University of Cambridge. This chapter describes the basic structure of the model and highlights aspects which are felt to be central to the Cambridge approach. The chapter concludes with an example of recent work which reflects the authors' basic approach to regional and sub-regional modelling.

THE REGIONAL MODEL

The model which has been developed is very similar in its overall structure to that outlined in the *Cambridge Economic Policy Review* (December 1982). For each region there are a set of 20 equations, 15 of which are estimated (described in Table 8.1 in broad functional form). The remaining five equations are identities. Most of the behavioural relationships link a regional variable to the same UK variable. The major exceptions to this are the treatment of employment in each region (which is modelled outside the main model and fed into the model using a form of shift-share analysis) and net working age migration which depends upon the differential between a region's job 'shortfall' and the national job 'shortfall'.

In this chapter the main emphasis is on explaining the methodology used to produce estimates of regional and sub-regional employment growth. A considerable amount of emphasis is given in the model to the modelling of the growth of labour demand at the regional and sub-regional level because in any area the growth of labour supply is endogenous to the growth of labour demand through the effects of the latter on migration, commuting and activity rates. There are obviously links the other way through the effects of changes in the number of people in an area on the demand for goods and services. The

Table 8.1 Basic relationships in the Cambridge model

Block of Equations for Region i:

---

1. Natural increase in population (PPNLi)
   PPNL$i = f$(PPNIUK, PPTUK, PPTi)
2. Total population (PPTi)
   PPTi = PPNLi + PPNMi + PPTi (-1)
3. Total net migration (PPNMi)
   PPNMi = NMWi(PPWTi/PPTi)
4. Working age migration (NMWi)
   NMW$i = f$(GAPi, GAPUK)
5. Working age population (PPWTLi)
   PPWT$i = f$(PPWTUK, PPTi, PPTUK)
6. Workforce (WFi)
   WF$i = f$(WFUK, PPWTi, PPWTUK)
7. Total employment (ETTi)
8. The regional component of the shift/share
9. Unemployment (EUi)
   EUi = WFi − ETTi
10. The job 'shortfall; (GAPi)
    GAPi = ((PPWTi − NMWi)(WFi/PPWTi)) − ETTi

The exogenous variables are:
1. Population (PPTUK)
2. Natural increase in population (PPNIUK)
3. Population of working age (PPWTUK)
4. Workforce (WFUK)
5. Job 'shortfall' (GAPUK)
6. National and sectoral employment forecasts

---

model developed attempts to incorporate these interrelationships between labour demand and labour supply explicitly.

Historically there is a strong relationship between the growth of population and the growth of employment in any area. The strength of this relationship depends on a number of factors, including the time period over which the relationship is examined and the size of the area considered. While it is intuitively obvious to expect that population change and employment change in an area should be related, it is perhaps surprising that much regional modelling work does not attempt to examine the links explicitly and thus the factors which condition these relationships.

As jobs are created in an area, there are a number of potential responses that can occur on the side of the labour supply. The first is that the resident population in the area will take the jobs and this may occur directly in that people already economically active, but currently unemployed in the area, take the jobs. It is also possible that people who are currently choosing not to make themselves available for work decide to enter the labour market. Thus, the participation rate among the population of working age rises. A common example of this labour-supply adjustment mechanism is the housewife who enters the labour market when it is clear that work is available. In an earlier period when jobs were not available the housewife did not indicate that she was looking for work. Another example where the population of workers is actually increased is the re-entry into the labour market of people who have retired. It is quite likely that the intensity with which the existing economically active population works will also increase, leading to double jobbing, with some of this perhaps occurring in the informal economy.

A second possibility is that the new jobs created in the local labour market affect migration flows and attract new workers into the area. In fact, the new jobs will actually affect *net* migration since in some areas people may well be considering leaving the area in search of a job but decide to remain once jobs are created locally. The degree to which a migrationary response will occur is a direct function of the characteristics of the jobs on offer, with some occupations being associated with national labour markets and thus migrationary responses over quite large distances.

A third possibility, more applicable to the sub-regional level, is that jobs created affect commuting flows into an area. The extent to which this is possible will be a function of existing settlement patterns, the openness of the area, and quality and quantity of both public and private infrastructure and real incomes.

In practice all of the above adjustments are likely to occur to some extent. In the case of a sub-regional area such as Cambridgeshire, for instance, there is at present a relatively strong labour market, in the sense that the degree of imbalance between the number of jobs available and the number of people looking for them is far less than in most other areas in the United Kingdom. At the present time unemployment rates in Cambridgeshire are amongst the lowest in the country. The extent to which any new jobs created in Cambridgeshire will reduce the existing levels of unemployment in the area further is probably relatively small. This is partly because many of the new jobs which are likely to be created will require different skills to those currently available from the existing pool of the unemployed. The available evidence does suggest that in the Cambridgeshire labour market there is some scope for increases in the participation rates from among the existing population of working age. Despite the possibility of some response from the unemployed and currently inactive, on balance the major labour-supply adjustments in the case of Cambridgeshire will continue to come from migration and commuting responses. (This is particularly true in an area like Cambridgeshire given the composition of the *new* jobs being created and the skills of the *traditional* Cambridge labour force.)

The relationships between components of labour supply and labour demand are usefully examined using labour-market balance sheets. By way of an example, Table 8.2 presents a set of labour-market balance sheets developed by the authors for the four traditional Development Area regions (Scotland, Northern Ireland, Wales and the North of England), All Other Regions and the United Kingdom in total.

The main components in the labour-market balance sheets are population, P; working-age population, W; total employment, E; the total number out of work, U; and total net migration in a given period, M. From these the following can be calculated:

Table 8.2 The relative job shortfall, migration and unemployment, 1951-81 (*thousands*)

	Four Development Area regions*			All other regions			United Kingdom		
	1951-61	1961-71	1971-81	1951-61	1961-71	1971-81	1951-61	1961-71	1971-81
Natural increase in labour force	131 (2.5)**	162 (3.0)	159 (3.0)	177 (1.0)	124 (0.6)	350 (1.7)	308 (1.4)	286 (1.2)	509 (2.0)
Plus Increase in participation	120 (2.3)	259 (4.8)	73 (1.3)	1848 (11.0)	634 (3.3)	144 (0.7)	1968 (8.9)	893 (3.6)	217 (0.8)
Less Increase in employment	-12 (-0.2)	42 (0.8)	-131 (-2.4)	2173 (12.9)	373 (1.9)	-336 (-1.7)	2161 (9.7)	416 (1.7)	-467 (-1.8)
Employment shortfall	263 (5.0)	378 (7.0)	363 (6.5)	-148 (-0.9)	385 (2.0)	830 (4.1)	115 (0.5)	763 (3.1)	1193 (4.7)
Net migration of labour force	201 (3.8)	229 (4.3)	102 (1.8)	-312 (-1.8)	-80 (-0.4)	82 (0.4)	-111 (-0.5)	149 (0.6)	184 (0.7)
Increase in numbers seeking work (unemployed)	62 (1.2)	149 (2.8)	261 (4.7)	164 (1.0)	465 (2.4)	748 (3.7)	226 (1.0)	614 (2.5)	1009 (3.9)
Relative job shortfall	224 (4.2)	250 (4.7)	140 (2.5)	-387 (2.3)	-179 (-0.9)	31 (0.2)†			

Source: Census of Population, 1951, 1961, 1971, 1981.

*Scotland, Wales, Northern Ireland and the Northern region of England.
**All figures in brackets are expressed as a percentage of the actual labour force in the base year of each period.
† The small relative job shortfall arises in non-Development Areas because of net outward migration abroad from these areas.

$$L = E + U$$
$$Y = L/W$$
$$X = W/P$$

where L is the size of the labour force; Y is the participation rate; and X is the proportion of the population of working age. Letting dZ denote the change in the variable Z, and the subscript -1 refer to the value of the relevant variable in the base year,

$$dL = L - L_{-1} + YXM \tag{8.1}$$

where dL is the *ex ante* change in the labour force. It is assumed that migrants have the same proportion of working-age population as the population as a whole and that these would have a similar activity rate to those that remain. (These assumptions are likely to lead to a slight under-estimation of the actual net migration of labour and the employment shortfall.)

The natural increase in the labour force, dN, is given by

$$dN = (W - W_{-1}) Y_{-1} + XMY_{-1} \tag{8.2}$$

The natural increase is found by applying the base year activity rates to the *ex ante* natural increase in working age population.

The increase dA due to changes in activity rate, A, is given by

$$dA = W(Y - Y_{-1}) + XM (Y - Y_{-1}). \tag{8.3}$$

We apply the change in activity rates to the *ex ante* working-age population. It is easy to check that $dL = dA + dN$.

The net change dS in employment shortfall, S, is expressed as:

$$dS = dL - (E - E_{-1}). \tag{8.4}$$

This is the increase in the *ex ante* labour force minus the increase in employment.

Rewriting equation (8.4) we find

$$dS = (L - L_{-1}) + YXM - (E - E_{-1}) \tag{8.5}$$
$$= (U - U_{-1}) + YXM.$$

The change in employment shortfall can be divided into two parts, the change in the out of work, plus the net migration of labour.

Row 4 of Table 8.2 shows the employment shortfall, derived by adding row 1 (the natural increase in the labour force in the area) to row 2 (the increase in participation among the labour force in the area) and subtracting row 3 (the increase in employment). These figures show the *change* in the difference between the supply and demand for labour over the decade rather than the absolute levels. An alternative name for this is the 'absolute job shortfall'. In the UK as a whole the absolute job shortfall gradually increased, rising from

115 000 jobs (0.5% of the labour force) in the 1950s to 1 193 000 jobs (4.7% of the labour force) in the 1970s.

In the 1960s the Development Area regions had an employment shortfall proportionately 3½ times greater than other regions. In the 1970s, however, the employment shortfall in the Development Area regions was much reduced relative to other regions.

Rows 5 and 6 show how the employment shortfall was divided between net migration and unemployment. In the 1950s and 1960s the largest response to job shortage in the Development Areas was net outward migration. This reached a peak in the 1960s and subsequently fell by about 50% in the 1970s. This was partly because the employment shortfall was lower in the 1970s but mainly because job shortage was reflected more in rising unemployment rather than in higher net outward migration.

Migration from the Development Areas goes partly to other regions and partly abroad. The 'Other Regions' group therefore receive population from the Development Areas but may gain or lose population from abroad. There was some *net* immigration to the UK as a whole in the 1950s but there was a net outflow in the 1960s and 1970s as the immigration of New Commonwealth citizens slowed down. The 'Other Regions' group experienced a net inflow of economically active population (312 000) in the 1950s, a much smaller net inflow in the 1960s and a small net outflow in the 1970s, when the net inflow of economically active population from Development Area regions was more than offset by a net outflow of population to Europe and the rest of the world.

THE CAMBRIDGE APPROACH TO FORECASTING THE GROWTH OF EMPLOYMENT IN THE REGIONS AND SUB-REGIONS OF THE UNITED KINGDOM

The approach to forecasting the growth of employment at the regional and sub-regional level is to break the factors affecting employment growth down into three major influences:

1. *National influences.* The major factors which will affect the growth of employment at the regional and sub-regional level in the UK will be national changes in the level of aggregate demand and, perhaps more slowly, changes in aggregate supply through the effect of innovation and technical change on production. Changes in aggregate demand will reflect the changing international competitiveness of the British economy and the accommodating policy stance undertaken by government.
2. *Structural influences.* The effects of changes in aggregate demand and aggregate supply do not affect all industries evenly through time. The process of change is different across industries and thus the local manifestation of national changes is differentiated by the type of industries which are to be found historically in a regional or sub-regional economy. In fact, the structure of industry found in a regional or sub-regional economy and its deviation from some national average is frequently based on industrial sectors. Although often forced on the regional modeller by data necessity, sectoral disaggregations are in fact a poor approximation to the factors which influence the impact of changes in national factors at the local level. A classification based on products, processes and industrial supply structures (reflecting such factors as the quality and quantity of the workforce, supply

chains and industrial organisation) is more appropriate. (For recent developments in this readers are referred to PACEC, 1987b.)

3. *Local influences.* Local influences embrace a number of factors and a convenient distinction to make is to divide the local economy into its traded and non-traded sectors. The traded sector will be influenced by factors which affect local competitiveness and local incomes and a range of factors are important here, notably wage and productivity levels of the labour force, the physical attributes of the area (and thus the transport costs), and many others. (For a detailed analysis of the range of factors which can affect local competitiveness and an empirical evaluation of the extent of geographical variations in England, the reader is referred to Tyler *et al.*, 1988.) The major influences on the non-traded sector will be essentially demographic and, at the sub-regional level, factors affecting commuting. The growth of population and changes in the pattern of commuting flows will affect the growth of employment in essentially non-traded sectors like health care, local service provision, and so on.

Historically, the growth of employment at both the regional and sub-regional level in the UK has differed, often quite dramatically, from the national level, even after allowing for the influences of industrial structure. Table 8.3 presents evidence from the recent past for the British regions and also a range of sub-regional areas classified according to settlement size. This difference, frequently termed the 'differential component', reflects the essentially local influences referred to earlier. Movements in this differential component between areas reflect the impact of a range of factors like the basic competitiveness of the traded base in the region, the growth of the area's non-traded employment base through sustained inward or outward migration, and the impact of a range of government policy measures, including regionally differentiated public expenditure on urban and regional policies and even factors like the Rate Support Grant.

The approach is to model the differential component in terms of the factors which it is felt affect it. A key factor affecting movements in differential employment growth at the local level is the competitiveness of the local industrial base. This competitiveness is a function of movements in the costs per unit of factor input which companies pay in an area and the output per unit of input (or productivity) which they obtain from their factor inputs. Thus local competitiveness depends upon:

$$\text{Competitiveness } f\left(\frac{w}{\lambda_1}, \frac{r}{\lambda_2}, \frac{\sigma}{\lambda_3}\right)$$

(8.6)

where w is wage per employee; λ_1 is labour productivity; r is rent per square foot of floorspace; λ_2 is floorspace productivity; σ is profit per unit of capital employment; and λ_3 is capital productivity. The most competitive geographical areas would thus enjoy below average input costs and above average levels of productivity. Areas with above average input costs, such as London, can only remain competitive if their productivity is also above average to the same extent.

The ratio of costs per unit is the efficiency wage of an area and is a basic measure of competitiveness. In recent years considerable efforts have been made in Cambridge to identify geographical variations in competitiveness in

Table 8.3 Changes in total employment by type of area, 1971–1984

	Actual change	% p.a.	National change	% p.a.	Structural change	% p.a.	Differential change	p.a.
1971–81								
London	−395.2	(−1.0)	−105.2	(−0.3)	241.7	(+0.6)	−531.8	(−1.3)
Conurbations	−541.0	(−1.2)	110.5	(−0.3)	−105.9	(−0.2)	−324.6	(−0.7)
Large towns	+94.2	(0.3)	−70.0	(−0.3)	−15.1	(−0.1)	+179.3	(0.7)
Free-standing areas	−115.4	(−0.4)	−76.0	(−0.3)	−59.9	(−0.2)	+21.4	(0.1)
Rural areas	+381.1	(+0.5)	−213.7	(−0.3)	−60.8	(−0.1)	+655.7	(+0.9)
Great Britain total	−576.4	(−0.3)	−576.4	(−0.3)	0.0		0.0	
1981–84								
London	−40.5	(−0.4)	−44.0	(−0.4)	+94.8	(0.8)	−91.3	(−0.8)
Conurbations	−166.7	(−1.4)	−45.0	(−0.4)	−21.2	(−0.2)	−100.7	(−0.9)
Large towns	−1.4	(0.0)	−33.5	(−0.4)	−7.1	(0.0)	+39.1	(0.4)
Free-standing areas	−81.2	(−0.9)	−34.2	(−0.4)	−16.5	(−0.2)	+30.6	(−0.3)
Rural areas	+74.1	(0.3)	−59.0	(0.4)	−50.0	(−0.2)	+183.5	(+0.2)
Great Britain total	−215.7	(−0.4)	−215.7	(−0.4)	0.0		0.0	

Source: Department of Employment

the UK (see Tyler *et al.*, 1988). The evidence points to large urban areas generally being at a disadvantage relative to more rural areas, particularly for modern industries. It is felt that the large-scale urban-to-rural shift which has occurred in the UK in recent years has its origins in this relative loss of competitiveness of urban areas relative to rural areas.

A further set of factors used in the modelling procedure is urban and regional policies. A considerable research effort has been devoted to identifying the employment impact of these policies on local areas (Moore *et al.*, 1986). Most recently the work undertaken to assess the effects of British regional policies has been broadened to include urban policies, including the Enterprise Zone programme (PACEC, 1987c).

One of the major influences on geographical variations in employment growth is the effect of geographically differentiated infrastructure expenditure (either initiated to achieve some specific policy goal or triggered automatically as the result of demographic change). It is thus appropriate at this stage to mention a further body of work which has been developed to assess what the local employment impact of major infrastructure projects is in the UK. Much of this work has been financed by the Department of the Environment with the principal objective of producing a manual for the policy-maker which allows an assessment of the local small-area impact of relatively large infrastructure projects (PACEC, 1987a).

The impact of infrastructure expenditures on the growth of employment at the sub-regional level was assessed using a conceptual framework which highlighted the different kinds of economic effect on local areas and regions which infrastructure projects could be expected to have. Empirical work was then undertaken to calibrate important parameters. This empirical work focused on 12 case studies. The specific case studies examined were the Severn Bridge; the Tyne Metro; the Dinorwig Pumping Station; Manchester Airport; government factory building in Consett; the Cambridge Science Park; the London Docklands Development; the M62; the Bournemouth Conference Centre; the Advanced Business Centre in Nottingham; the Yorvik Viking Centre at York; and the impact of digital telephone developments.

This work enabled a classification system to be established which identified likely economic effects on local areas for eight major types of infrastructure project. These were: roads and motorways (including bridges); rail improvements; ports; airports; utilities (coal, gas, electricity, water); tourist projects; communication improvements, and property provision. Conceptually, it was to be expected that the economic impact of each different type of infrastructure project would vary according to the economic characteristics of the study area. One characteristic related to the general level of economic activity in the area, with a principal distinction between 'advantaged' and 'disadvantaged'. The 'advantaged' regions were taken to be the South-East; the South-West; East Anglia; and the East Midlands. 'Disadvantaged' regions were the West Midlands; the North West; Yorkshire and Humberside; the Northern Region; Scotland; and Wales. Besides a regional classification, a further sub-regional distinction was made on the basis of the degree of urbanisation of the areas, with separate consideration given to rural areas, smaller towns, free-standing towns and larger conurbations. In the space available in this chapter it is not possible to describe the conceptual and empirical issues involved in the infrastructure work (the interested reader is referred to PACEC, 1987a. Some of the basic estimates of the impact of major infrastructure projects are given in Table 8.4.

The above classification of the factors affecting employment growth into national, structural and local is a valuable first step in modelling employment change at the regional or sub-regional level, although like most classification devices it has its difficulties. The most obvious is that there are clearly interactions between national, structural and local influences. In the absence of a fully specified model of how regional or sub-regional systems work, the modeller is forced to accept that these difficulties exist.

The broad structure of the Cambridge model is shown diagrammatically in Figure 8.1. The basic approach is to use the PACEC/Land Economy National Forecasting model to identify what change in employment is thought likely to occur at the national level over the forecast period and to disaggregate this into forecasts of employment change on an industry-by-industry basis. The industry forecasts are made using a disaggregated analysis of how individual industries have grown during the last 30 years in the UK and their relationship to national growth. The historic position is used to condition the relationship between individual sector and the nation, but the share which individual sectors are likely to take of national change in the forecast period requires some element of judgement derived from industry studies as to the factors which are likely to affect the growth of employment in each

Table 8.4 Employment generated by operating expenditures associated directly with the running of the infrastructure project, assuming no displacement (number of jobs per £10 million of capital expenditure)

	Depressed area		Advantaged area	
	Urban	Rural	Urban	Rural
Local jobs				
Roads	2	2	2	2
Rail	26–56	24–50	26–56	24–50
Ports	26–51	25–50	26–51	25–50
Airports	36–52	38–55	33–46	35–51
Utilities	20–26	20–26	20–26	20–26
Tourism	143–957	140–998	143–957	135–936
Communications	52–66	50–64	52–66	50–64
Property provision	5–161	3–126	5–172	3–126
Regional jobs (including local jobs)				
Roads	5	5	5	5
Rail	37–74	37–74	37–74	37–74
Ports	50–70	50–70	50–70	50–70
Airports	50–70	53–74	47–66	50–70
Utilities	32–49	32–39	32–49	32–49
Tourism	196–1203	203–1293	191–1143	198–1233
Communications	69	69	69	69
Property provision	5–185	5–193	5–185	5–193

industry (these factors relate to both demand and supply conditions in the respective industries).

The changes by industry at the national level are applied to base-year employment levels in the region or sub-region on an industry-by-industry basis. In this way forecasts of employment growth are obtained for the region which embody how employment would be expected to change if the industries represented in the region changed in line with the forecast of national change in each industry. Clearly it is desirable to adopt a fine level of industrial disaggregation in undertaking this procedure. A compromise has to be made which reflects the availability of data and computational ease. The model adopted uses 35 industrial sectors.

The total forecast of employment change for the area is obtained by adding the forecast of the differential component to the forecast of the national and structural component. The next section gives an example of the basic approach.

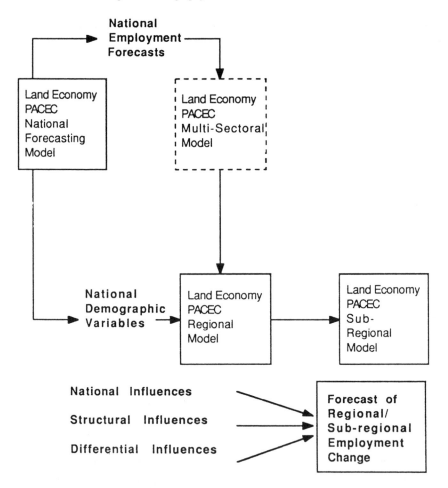

Figure 8.1 The basic regional modelling structure

AN EXAMPLE OF THE BROAD APPROACH

Forecasting the growth of employment, population and housing demand in the South-East.

The basic regional modelling work has been developed considerably in recent years and particular effort is currently being devoted to the sub-regional work. Some indication of the broad approach can be obtained from a recent forecasting exercise of the growth of employment in the South-East and its constituent parts (Tyler and Rhodes, 1987). This exercise represented something of a half-way position in the evolution of the Cambridge model, but the basic approach is useful for illustration purposes. The basis for the forecast of employment growth in the South-East region was to adopt a forecast of how national employment was expected to grow and then assess what share of this national change was likely to occur in the South-East region in the light of the structural and local factors described on pp. 129–30 above.

Figure 8.2 represents the share of the South-East in national employment over the period 1965–83. During the late 1960s and early 1970s, the South-East increased its share, reaching a peak of 33.5% by 1972. Thereafter, the share fell back somewhat to reach a low of 32.3% by 1979. By the end of the period, however, there had been a dramatic turnaround, with the South-East improving its overall share significantly as the severe recession beginning in 1979 affected the South-East less severely than the rest of the country.

Identifying what share of total national employment the South-East is likely to take in the future was of central importance in achieving the forecasting objective. The basic methodological approach of disaggregating past employment change into national, structural and differential change, described on pp. 129–30, was adopted. With respect to structural factors, the South-East has been characterised by a relatively favourable industrial structure because at different times in Britain's past it has been fortunate enough to have a large share of some of the fast-growing industrial and commercial sectors. Another 'structural' factor which has contributed favourably to employment growth in the South-East has been the large concentration of the headquarter operations of many of the largest firms in the UK. In recent years it has also become apparent that large urban areas have been the subject of large employment decline as industry and commerce have found such environments less desirable relative to more rural areas. Thus, the urban–rural mix of a region has thus been a further structural factor influencing the growth of individual regions, and the South-East with the largest urban area of all (London) has suffered in this respect.

A further set of factors which have been instrumental in influencing the growth of employment in the South-East relative to elsewhere has been central government policies such as regional policy and urban policy. These are incorporated as factors influencing differential employment growth, as described above. Historically, regional policies in the UK have sought to divert economic activity quite large distances from the relatively prosperous South-East to other less fortunate regions. The diversionary policies have consisted of financial inducements to companies to locate new capacity in assisted areas rather than in the South-East, but also the highly controversial physical control policy of Industrial Development Certificates. Urban policies, in contrast, worked until the late 1970s to displace economic activity relatively short distances from large conurbations to their more rural hinterlands, the most obvious examples being New Town and overspill dispersal policies. Both urban and regional policy objectives have been complemented, and in some cases initiated, by spatially differentiated infrastructure projects. (For a recent analysis of the impact of urban and regional policy on the movement of economic activity from the South-East the reader is referred to Fingleton and Tyler, 1988.)

Table 8.5 presents the historical position and the forecast for manufacturing employment for the national, structural and differential components. Movements in the differential growth effect are shown in column 3 of Table 8.5 and also on an annual basis in Figure 8.3. This growth component indicates how manufacturing employment has changed in the South-East region after allowing for national change and the industrial structure of the region.

This differential growth component was strongly negative between 1965 and 1975. This was a period of steady growth in national manufacturing output accompanied by active regional policies, active New Town and overspill

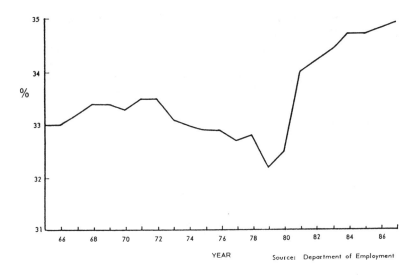

Figure 8.2 Total employment in the South-East as a proportion of total employment in Great Britain

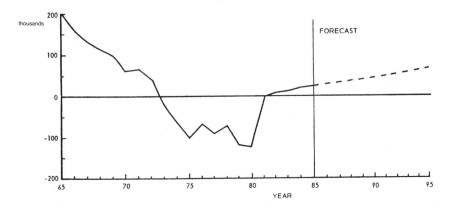

Figure 8.3 The growth of manufacturing employment in the South-East relative to that of the nation after allowing for differences in industrial structure

policy and restrictive local planning policies in many South-East counties, all of which took some manufacturing jobs out of the South-East region. After 1975 these policies were relaxed, abolished or reversed. The IDC policy which controlled new industrial building in the South-East was progressively relaxed after 1975 and finally abolished in 1981. New town and overspill policies were run down from the mid-1970s and to some extent reversed, through the new policies of inner-city economic regeneration signalled by the

Table 8.5 Components of manufacturing employment change in the South-East region, 1965–85, with forecasts to 1995 (*thousands of jobs*)

	National effect	Structural growth effect	Differential growth effect	Actual employment change	(%)
1965–70	−64	+41	−137	−160	(−6.7)
1970–75	−237	+49	−162	−350	(−15.7)
1975–80	−191	+69	−24	−146	(−7.8)
1980–85	−373	+73	+73	−227	(−12.8)*
Forecast					
1985–90	−80	+40	+20	−20	
1990–95	−53	+30	+27	+4	

*Provisional estimate based on quarterly estimates published in DE *Gazette*

1977 White Paper. Rising unemployment rates in the outer South-East persuaded some local authorities to relax their hitherto restrictive industrial planning policies.

As a consequence of these changes in policy stance, there was a substantial improvement in the South-East's differential growth effect in manufacturing between 1975 and 1985. The forecast for this component holds much of this gain over the next ten years to 1996 as the new policy stance is assumed to continue. However, further sizeable gains were not predicted relative to the UK. This was partly because Green Belt and restrictive planning policies were thought likely to be continued in some parts of the South-East within the foreseeable future, partly because competitive regions such as the East Midlands, the South-West and East Anglia will continue to divert some manufacturing activity from the South-East, partly because the older industrial regions will have some industrial recovery after the deep recession of the early 1980s and partly because high house prices, skill shortage, and other development pressures will provide some constraint on the attraction and growth of manufacturing firms in the South-East region itself.

Nevertheless, it was expected that the differential growth effect will remain positive for the South-East manufacturing sector and that this would generate an additional 47 000 manufacturing jobs between 1985 and 1995 (compared with a loss of almost 300 000 jobs between 1965 and 1975), which represent a substantial improvement on earlier decades.

The three components of change in Table 8.5 when added together indicate the manufacturing employment change for each period, including the forecast period. An absolute decline in manufacturing employment is still expected between 1985 and 1995, but this decline is very much smaller than the decline which occurred in any five-year period of the previous 20 years. In short, there is a strong relative improvement in the next ten years compared with the two previous decades.

Exactly the same analysis was carried out for non-manufacturing sectors in the South-East region, which consists mainly of public services, private services, construction, transport and utilities. The main results are shown in Table 8.6. When services grow at the national level, the South-East enjoys a large national effect because the service sector is relatively large in the South-East region. The period 1970–80 saw a rapid growth in services nationally and a large net gain in jobs for the South-East deriving from the national effect. This was off-set to some extent by a broadly neutral structural effect and an adverse differential growth effect, leaving an actual gain in the 1970s decade of 440 000 jobs. In contrast, in the period 1965–70 and 1980–5, the national effect was negative. These losses were more than offset by positive structural and differential growth effects.

The forecast of non-manufacturing employment nationally indicated continued growth. The national forecast of employment growth in this sector over the period is forecast to be strongly positive. Structural effects are expected to remain positive, but to be smaller in size than in the past because public sector service employment is no longer growing rapidly. Differential growth effects are expected to be negative but relatively small because the service industries in the South-East are already so large that it may not be possible to keep up with the national growth rate as easily as regions with currently smaller service sectors. The overall outcome is for the non-manufacturing sector in the South-East region to create an additional 433 000 jobs in the forecast period, 1985–95. This is above or near to the rate of employment growth achieved in this sector in previous decades. The combination of manufacturing and service employment change is shown in Table 8.7.

FORECASTING EMPLOYMENT CHANGE IN LONDON

The exercise which has been presented above for the South-East region as a whole was repeated for Greater London, again beginning with manufacturing industry (Table 8.8). The differential growth effect for London's manufacturing industries was strongly negative up to 1975 (see Figure 8.4), due principally to IDC policy, regional policy, overspill and New Town policies, and local authority planning, priorities for housing and commercial developments. The differential growth effect improved markedly after 1975 as IDC policies were phased out and overspill and New Town policies were gradually reversed. There was further improvement after 1980 as the recession hit the industrial regions harder than London. For the future it was considered that the differential growth effect for London's manufacturing industry will revert to being slightly negative as other industrial regions make some kind of recovery from the recession and as the cost pressures on land and premises in London continue. The three components of nations, structure and differential were combined to give a forecast of actual manufacturing employment which is declining but at a much slower rate than in previous decades.

The same analysis for London's non-manufacturing sector is shown in Table 8.9. A similar pattern emerged for the structural and differential growth effects to that found for manufacturing industry. The structural effect is positive, although becoming smaller in the future as the public sector ceases to grow. The national effect is, however, positive. The three effects combined suggest an increase in non-manufacturing employment in London over the

Table 8.6 Components of non-manufacturing employment change in the South-East region, 1965–85, with forecasts to 1995 (*thousands of jobs*)

	National effect	Structural growth effect	Differential growth effect	Actual employment change
1965–70	−143	+114	+41	+12
1970–75	+289	+133	−97	+325
1975–80	+237	−105	−18	+115
1980–85	−158	+108	+219	+168
Forecast				
1985–90	+193	+50	−50	+193
1990–95	+240	+50	−50	+240

Table 8.7 Components of employment change in the South-East region, 1965–85, with forecasts to 1995 (*thousands of jobs*)

	National effect	Structural growth effect	Differential growth effect	Actual employment change	(%)
1965–70	−207	+155	−96	−148	(−2.0)
1970–75	+52	+182	−259	−25	(−0.3)
1975–80	+46	−36	−42	−31	(−0.4)
1980–85	−531	+180	+292	−59	(−0.8)
Forecast					
1985–90	+113	+90	+30	+173	(+2.4)
1990–95	+187	+80	−23	+244	(+3.3)

Table 8.8 Components of manufacturing employment change in Greater London, 1965–85, with forecasts to 1995 (*thousands of jobs*)

	National effect	Structural growth effect	Differential growth effect	Actual employment change
1965–70	−34	+24	−180	−190
1970–75	−126	+52	−175	−249
1975–80	−95	+44	−52	−103
1980–85	−215	+24	+35	−156
Forecast				
1985–90	−30	+15	−30	−45
1990–95	−20	+10	−20	−30

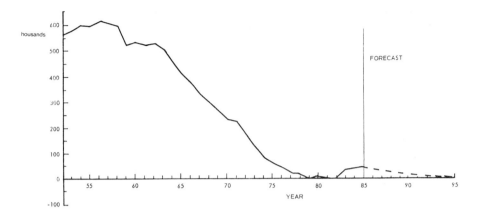

Figure 8.4 The growth of manufacturing employment in Greater London relative to that of the nation after allowing for differences in industrial structure

next decade which is larger than the fall expected in manufacturing employment. For the first time in over 20 years London's total employment is therefore expected to stop falling and even to increase a little. This is shown in Table 8.10, which adds together the results for the manufacturing and non-manufacturing sectors. The result is quite striking. It predicts that the rapid decline in employment in London which was persistent between 1965 and 1985 has come to an end and a small overall increase in total employment is now likely. In the three quinquennial periods up to 1980 it was a large negative differential growth effect which brought about London's decline (see Figure 8.5 for annual series). With the reversal in urban and regional policy in the late 1970s, this large negative differential growth effect came to an end in 1980. But the national recession of 1980–5, shown in Table 8.10 as a large negative national effect, ensured London's continued employment decline until 1985 (although most of this decline took place in 1980, 1981 and 1982). If the national forecasts adopted are correct, such a large-scale national recession will not be repeated in the forecast period; indeed, some growth in service industry employment is expected. The structural effect for London can confidently be predicted to remain positive in the forecast period because of its concentration on service industries. The differential growth effect may revert to being negative in the forecast period as the large service industries of London find it difficult to grow as rapidly as their counterparts in other regions due to pressures on the labour market and on premises, but the negative effect will be nothing like as large as in the 1960s and 1970s because of the reversal of urban policies and the weakening of regional policies. Overall, therefore, total employment is expected to increase in London between 1985 and 1995, although by a modest amount. But the turnaround, compared with previous periods of rapid employment decline in London, is swift and substantial.

Table 8.9 Components of non-manufacturing employment change in Greater London, 1965–85, with forecasts to 1995 (*thousands of jobs*)

	National effect	Structural growth effect	Differential growth effect	Actual employment
1965–70	−91	+110	−1	+18
1970–75	+170	+47	−183	+34
1975–80	+140	+14	−185	−31
1980–85	−114	+62	+20	−32
Forecast				
1985–90	+76	+35	−30	+81
1990–95	+103	+35	−40	+98

Table 8.10 Components of total employment change in London, 1965–85, with forecasts to 1995 (*thousands of jobs*)

	National effect	Structural growth effect	Differential growth effect	Actual employment	(%)
1965–70	−148	+134	−181	−172	(−4.1)
1970–75	+44	+99	−358	−215	(−5.4)
1975–80	+45	+58	−237	−134	(−3.5)
1980–85	−329	+86	+55	−188	(−5.1)
Forecast					
1985–90	+46	+50	−60	+36	(+1.0)
1990–95	+83	+45	−60	+68	(+1.9)

FORECASTING EMPLOYMENT GROWTH IN THE NON-LONDON SOUTH-EAST

A forecast of total employment change in the non-London part of the South-East region was made by subtracting the results for London as presented in Table 8.10, from the results for the whole South-East region as presented in Table 8.7. This is shown in Table 8.11. Although it is predicted that the South-East region as a whole will experience a substantial increase in total employment of 417 000 between 1985 and 1995, compared with small losses in earlier periods, the main reason for this improvement at the regional level is forecast to be the end of London's previously rapid decline. The outer South-East part of the region is therefore likely to experience continued employment growth at a rate similar to, or only a little faster than, that which occurred in the previous 20 years from 1965 to 1985. In other words, the pace of economic growth in the South-East region will substantially increase but the increase will occur because London will no longer be in decline. Growth

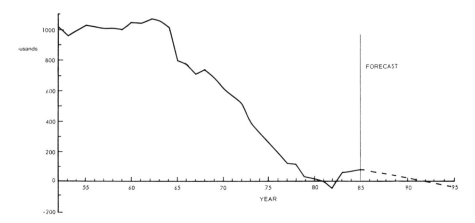

Figure 8.5 The growth of total employment in Greater London relative to that of the nation after allowing for differences in industrial structure

in the outer South-East will continue much in line with that experienced in previous periods.

FORECASTS FOR INDIVIDUAL COUNTIES WITHIN THE SOUTH-EAST

The forecast of total employment change for the outer South-East as a whole was allocated to individual counties on the basis of each county's growth performance between 1971 and 1981. (These forecasts are referred to as 'unadjusted' in Table 8.12.) Beyond this, however, some adjustments were made to allow for the fact that the allocation of growth between counties which prevailed in the 1970s may not be fully appropriate for the forecast period. There are good reasons based on historical evidence to suggest that the pattern of employment growth at county level would not change radically over a period as short as ten years. It is unlikely, for instance, that counties at the top of the growth league in the 1970s would be at the bottom of the league in the 1980s and 1990s, and vice versa. Moreover, this relative stability of position in the growth league table is reinforced by the fact that counties have not radically changed the direction and thrust of their structure plans relative to other counties, although some more minor changes have now been made. However, the forecasts incorporated the view that the pattern of employment growth by county in the 1980s and 1990s would differ from that of the 1970s in two main ways. First, there will be some reversal of the tendency for growth in the western counties (of the South-East) to be relatively high, and growth in the eastern counties to be relatively low. In other words, the differential growth between West and East will narrow, with the western counties growing a little more rapidly than previously and the eastern counties growing more slowly compared with earlier decades. However, only a partial correction of this imbalance—the fastest-growing counties, in absolute terms—will remain in the West.

Table 8.11 Total employment change in the South-East, Greater London and the outer South-East 1965-85, with forecasts to 1995 (*thousands of jobs*)

	South-East Region		Greater London		Outer South-East (Shire Counties)	(%)
1965-70	−148	(−2.0)[1]	−172	(−4.1)	+24	(+0.6)
1970-75	−25	(−0.3)	−215	(−5.4)	+190	(+4.6)
1975-80	−31	(−0.4)	−134	(−3.5)	+103	(+2.4)
1980-85	−59	(−0.8)	−188	(−5.1)	+129	(+2.9)
Forecast						
1985-90	+173	(+2.4)	+36	(+1.0)	+137	(+3.1)
1990-95	+244	(+3.3)	+68	(+1.9)	+176	(+3.8)

(1) Figures in brackets represent percent change in each five year period

A relative improvement in the growth performance in eastern counties was expected for the following reasons:

1. the designation of Stansted (on the Essex–Hertfordshire border) as London's third airport;
2. the completion of the M11 motorway in 1987 and its more recent connection to the M25;
3. the redevelopment and regeneration of London's docklands;
4. the continued growth in trading links with the rest of the EEC and Europe as a whole;
5. the distinct possibility of the Channel tunnel being built in the foreseeable future;
6. increasing development pressures in western counties;
7. the termination in the forecast period of the New Towns programme.

Second, some convergence (relative to the 1970s pattern) between counties with high growth rates and those with low growth rates was expected to occur. In other words, there will be some narrowing of the disparities in county growth rates in the 1980s and 1990s, compared with the 1970s. There are three reasons for expecting this. First, the counties which followed highly restrictive industrial planning policies in previous decades have tended to relax their tough planning stance a little, as a consequence of the 1981 recession. In particular, such counties now state some commitment to the rapid development of small businesses and to the safeguarding of employment in the larger indigenous enterprises.

Second, the fact that London is expected to stop losing jobs on anything like the scale experienced in the 1960s and 1970s (and may even increase employment between 1985 and 1995) means that the faster-growing areas will lose an important source of employment and population, since many of the jobs and people from London went to the Shires. The gradual elimination of the New Town programme will also serve to slow down the rate of growth of employment in the faster growing areas.

Third, all the national growth in employment expected to take place between 1985 and 1995 is in the private services sector, with manufacturing employment and public service employment expected to decline. Private sector

Table 8.12 Forecast of total employment change for South-East shire counties* 1985–95 (*percentage change*)

	Unadjusted forecast based on 1971–81 relative growth performance	Adjustment for phasing out of New Towns and reduced decline of London	Adjustment for slow decline of manufacturing	Adjustment for restrictive planning	Adjustment for shift of growth from East to West	Adjusted forecast	Actual 1971–81
Bedfordshire	8.4	-0.5			-1.1	8.4	7.5
Berkshire	11.1	-2.4			-1.5	9.5	10.1
Buckinghamshire	18.4				+0.7	14.5	18.2
Essex	7.6				+1.4	8.3	6.7
East Sussex	0.0			+1.0		2.4	-2.9
Hampshire	9.0	-0.5			-0.6	7.9	8.1
Hertfordshire	3.5	-1.0	+0.5	+1.0	+0.6	4.6	3.0
Kent	5.6				+0.3	5.9	4.8
Oxfordshire	5.6		+2.5	+1.0		8.1	4.9
Surrey	1.3				-0.1	2.2	1.1
West Sussex	13.1	-2.0			-1.5	9.5	12.2
Total Outer South-East	7.1					7.1	7.2
GLC						3.4	-16.1
South-East Standard Region						5.6	-4.3

employment, much of which will be in small businesses, can often expand without being affected by restrictive planning policies, particularly when many thousands of small businesses take on only one or two extra employees. This means that hitherto slow-growing areas will be able to expand employment faster than previously without being affected so much by restrictive planning policies.

In addition, the more industrial areas of Hertfordshire and Oxfordshire were expected to increase employment in the forecast period compared with more recent years, on the assumption that the large shake-out of manufacturing labour which took place in the 1970s and early 1980s will not be repeated in the forecast period—and indeed that some recovery in manufacturing employment might well take place.

In column 7 of Table 8.12 the adjusted preferred forecast of total employment change in the period 1985–95 by individual counties is compared with the actual changes in total employment recorded for each county between 1971 and 1981.

The estimation of the effects of the future course of urban and regional policy and major infrastructure changes on employment in the South-East has been achieved by drawing on previous work undertaken by PACEC into the effect of these factors on employment growth across urban and regional areas. The reader is referred to Moore *et al.* (1986), and PACEC (1987c 1988).

The county growth rates in the forecast period are not dissimilar to actual growth rates prevailing from 1971 to 1981, although the range of growth rates has narrowed and some growth has been 'diverted' from western to eastern counties. Employment in the outer South-East as a whole is predicted to increase by 7.1% between 1985 and 1995, which is almost identical to the actual change recorded between 1971 and 1981.

What is very different, however, is the position of London. The prediction for 1985–95 shows a small increase, perhaps of the order of 3.4%, although some of this increased employment will be taken up by non-London residents commuting into London. This small increase compares with a very large fall in employment in London between 1971 and 1981 of 16.1%.

This means overall that employment growth in the South-East region as a whole will be significantly more buoyant in the forecast period (+5.6%) than in the 1971–81 period (−4.3%) yet growth in the Shire counties as a whole will be very similar in the two periods.

Having derived forecasts of how employment was expected to change in the South-East and its constituent parts, the next step was to translate this into a consistent forecast of population. The basic underlying relationships between employment and population change described on pp. 124 *et seq* were used. In fact, the historic close relationship between movements of employment and population in the study area, which is such a central component of the Cambridge approach, is demonstrated by a cross-sectional regression of population change against employment change for the 96 districts of the South-East (excluding the London area) for the period 1971–81. The following equation was preferred:

$$\Delta P_i = 0.24 + 1.08 \; \Delta E_i \qquad\qquad R^2 = 0.78 \qquad\qquad (8.7)$$
$$\underset{(0.06)}{} \quad \underset{(18.5)}{}$$

(Figures in brackets are *t*-statistics.) It appears from this relationship that a 1% change in employment is reflected in a 1% change in population. The results of the modelling exercise are given in Table 8.13 where forecasts of population growth felt to be consistent with the forecasts of employment growth are presented.

There is an 'accuracy' problem associated with the modelling of aggregate variables of a regional labour market which is a general problem in economic modelling wherever the researcher is seeking to obtain results for a variable like the unemployment rate, which is the difference between two very large variables which have themselves been forecast; namely the growth of labour supply and demand. (The forecasts of the workforce also require estimates of how participation rates are likely to change). The only way by which consistent estimates of gap variables like unemployment can be obtained is by a careful reconciliation of employment and workforce forecasts to within realistic ranges on the basis of historic experience. Sensitivity analysis is employed to test for the variability of the forecast to change in the value of the key assumptions adopted. For a more comprehensive discussion of the problem the reader is referred to Ledent (1986).

Forecasts of population growth are crucially important in determining a wide range of socio-economic variables like the number of households and associated dwelling requirement. In the South-East forecasting work estimates of the future number of households and dwellings were produced and are presented in Table 8.13. To forecast how household formation and dwelling requirement were likely to change required a considerable amount of further data and estimation. This is because household formation is affected by a number of factors, demographic, economic and social. The size and structure of the population is obviously important as, for forecasting purposes, is how these variables are going to change. Also important is the way in which 'headship' rates are expected to change. (Headship rates are affected by a wide range of economic and social factors, like housing cost in relation to income levels, attitudes to cohabitation and marriage, and so on. There is an excellent literature on the factors influencing household formation; the work by Holmans, 1983, and Ermisch, 1983, is of particular note, but see also DoE, 1977.)

Recent work on the relationship between change in population and household formation is obviously assisted by the 1981 Census of Population. This data source has enabled the Department of Environment to examine the relationship between headship rates and household formation at different points in time—1961, 1966, 1971 and 1981—and the Department regularly publishes new forecasts of the likely number of households in the next five, ten and 15 years. These forecasts are made using the OPCS forecasts of population by sex and age (based on 1985 mid-year estimates), and DoE forecasts of likely changes in headship rates influenced by estimates of marriages status provided by the Government Actuarial Department. The forecasts indicate what level of population/headship rates/household formation is projected for 1991, 1996 and 2001 by region county and in some cases, metropolitan district of England and Wales. The projections have incorporated adjustments to the 1981 Census of Population to allow for the problem of 'concealed' households in relation to earlier years.

Table 8.13 The Cambridge forecasts of employment, population and household growth in the South-East, 1985–95 (*thousands*)

	Employment	Population	Households	Associated dwelling requirement
South East	413.0	832.1	341.3	+371.0
Greater London	104.0	136.5	58.1	63.4
Rest of South-East	309.0	695.6	+283.2	+307.6
Bedfordshire	+19.2	+42.3	+16.3	+17.4
Berkshire	+30.4	+64.5	+25.9	+27.8
Buckinghamshire	+37.5	+81.6	+31.3	+34.1
East Sussex	+6.0	+15.6	+7.5	+8.3
Essex	+53.0	+121.3	+49.5	+53.5
Hampshire	+50.8	+114.3	+46.1	+50.3
Hertfordshire	+20.7	+43.7	+18.0	+19.2
Kent	+36.1	+86.0	+35.0	+38.2
Oxfordshire	+18.9	+42.5	+16.9	+18.6
Surrey	+10.2	+21.8	+9.2	+10.0
West Sussex	+26.2	+62.0	+27.5	+30.2

The household population ratios forecast by the DoE for the selected years were used to translate the employment-based population forecasts into forecasts of the number of households. The next step was to translate the changes in the number of households into estimates of changes in the number of dwellings.

A considerable amount of research effort has been devoted to investigating the relationship between the number of households and the number of dwellings (see, for instance, DoE, 1977; Ermisch, 1983; Kleinman and Whitehead, 1988). The relationship is a complex one for both conceptual and statistical data reasons. The 1981 Census did not include a separate dwelling count. This is partly because previous Censuses have had difficulty in establishing *separate* dwellings and the 1981 Census classified a household space with a shared entrance from outside as self-contained (and thus a household), even though more than one household may have been inside. Some research effort has gone into deriving proportions to apply to the 1981 household space count in order to derive household spaces that are not self-contained in order to derive estimates of the number of dwellings. On the basis of this work, the Department of the Environment has been able to produce estimates of dwellings for 1981 (and more recent years) at the regional and sub-regional (county) level. These estimates, together with those of private households and the associated population, allowed an estimate to be made of how population and household formation have changed in relation to the stock of dwellings for the South-East region, Greater London, the outer metropolitan area and the outer South-East. These estimates were used to translate the future number of households into an associated stock of dwellings (as detailed in Table 8.13).

CONCLUSION

This chapter has presented the broad framework behind the regional forecasting model currently being developed in Cambridge. The model embodies certain key features which differentiate it from other regional models. Perhaps the most important of these is the emphasis given in the model to forecasting the growth of labour demand at the regional and sub-regional level. This emphasis reflects the view that labour demand affects labour supply through its influence on migration, commuting and activity rates. The model incorporates these interrelationships between labour demand and supply explicitly. The basic conceptual approach is demonstrated with reference to a set of labour-market balance sheets.

The chapter identifies those factors which need to be incorporated in the forecasting of labour demand at the small-area level within a country like the UK. The importance of national, structural and local influences was highlighted. Particular emphasis was placed on the modelling of urban and regional policies on local development, as well as the competitiveness of an area's traded base.

The basic approach was demonstrated with reference to a recent study which the authors had undertaken to forecast the growth of employment and population in the South-East and its constituent parts, including the Greater London area. The study also served to illustrate how the modelling approach could be adapted to incorporate forecasts of household formation and the demand for dwellings. Other adaptations were clearly possible.

NOTES

1. The main research team engaged on the current modelling work is Professor Gordon Cameron, Mike Anadyke-Danes, Bernard Fingleton, Morgan Holt, Barry Moore, Nick Mansley, Gavin Robertson, John Rhodes and Peter Tyler.

REFERENCES

Department of the Environment (1977) *Housing Policy, A Consultative Document*. Cmnd 6851. London: HMSO.
Ermisch, J. (1983) The Political Economy of Demographic Change, London: Heinemann
Fingleton, B. and Tyler, P. (1988) 'A cost based approach to the modelling of industrial movement in Great Britain'. Discussion Paper no. 20. Department of Land Economy, University of Cambridge.
Holmans, A. (1983) Demography and Housing in Britain, Recent Development and Aspects of Research, Social Science Research Council: London.
Kleinman, M.P. and Whitehead C.M.E. (1988) 'A Medium Term Forecast of Housing Demand, Department of Land Economy'. University of Cambridge, Occasional Paper.
Ledent, J. (1986) 'Consistent modelling of employment, population, labour force and unemployment in the statistical analyses of regional growth' in P.W.J. Batey and M. Madden (eds), *Integrated Analysis of Regional Systems*. London: Pion.
Moore, B.C., Rhodes, J. and Tyler, P. (1986) *The Effects of Government Regional Economic Policy*. London: HMSO.

PACEC (1987a) A Manual for Estimating the Local and Regional Impact of Different Types of Infrastructure Projects and Proposals, Final Report, Cambridge: PACEC.

PACEC (1987b) Towards a West Midlands Economic Regeneration Programme, Final Report, Cambridge: PACEC.

PACEC (1987c) *An Evaluation of the Enterprise Zone Experiment.* DoE Inner Cities Research Programme. London: HMSO.

Tyler, P. and Rhodes, J. (1987) 'South East Employment and Housing Study'. Discussion Paper No. 15, Department of Land Economy, University of Cambridge.

Tyler, P., Moore, B.C. and Rhodes, J. (1988) *Geographical Variations in Industrial Costs.* London: DTI HMSO.

Chapter 9

DEMOGRAPHIC-ECONOMIC IMPACT FORECASTING IN NON-METROPOLITAN REGIONS: AN AUSTRALIAN EXAMPLE

Peter Phibbs

INTRODUCTION

Over the last decade, input–output analysis has become a very popular tool of Australian regional scientists. The work of Jensen *et al.* (see, for example, Jensen *et al.*, 1979) has resulted in the development of an accepted semi-survey technique for the generation of consistent, cost-effective regional input–output tables in Australia. The major use of such tables is regional economic impact analysis.

While these tables have been widely used, earlier research by the author suggests that there are a number of problems with the impact forecasts that simple input–output tables generate. The major problem is their inability to forecast accurately changes in service employment. This chapter first examines these problems, and then describes how the use of a simple demographic-economic impact model can assist in overcoming them. The demo-economic model is then used to examine the impact of the expansion of a coal mine in the Central West of New South Wales.

PROBLEMS WITH THE SIMPLE INPUT–OUTPUT MODEL

Phibbs (1985) attempted to test the reliability of simple input–output forecasts by undertaking a historical study of the economy of a large mining town, Broken Hill, in western New South Wales. An input-output table for the town was constructed for 1971. Exogenous final demand changes between 1971 and 1976 were estimated and then fed into the input table in order to estimate 1976 employment levels. The major decrease registered in final demand could be accounted for by a large reduction in the lead-silver-zinc mining sector. These estimated 1976 employment levels were compared with 1976 Census estimates.

In general, the test revealed that the simple input–output table generated reasonably accurate estimates of the impacts of the exogenous final demand changes. However, the differences between the predicted and actual employment levels provided three main lessons for the users of simple input–output tables. First, the disaggregated sectoral multipliers generated using simple input–output tables are likely to contain large errors. For this reason, it might be wiser to view these multipliers as ranking measures rather than as definitive sectoral impact estimates. The second lesson is that changes in the activity levels of the housing sector can have major impacts on employment levels in the regional economy. Many Australian impact studies have erred in omitting the impact of changes in the residential construction sector. The third, and most important lesson, is that an alternative approach has to be found for modelling changes in service-sector employment in a region. The simple input–output model is incapable of reliably forecasting impacts in these sectors. This is a serious problem since for many non-metropolitan Australian regions, major impacts associated with new developments will be experienced in the service sector.

The next section focuses on an approach that provides an alternative methodology for modelling service-sector changes.

ALTERNATIVE APPROACHES TO MODELLING CHANGES IN SERVICE EMPLOYMENT

The main reason that traditional Australian input–output models have been poor estimators of service-sector employment is that a major component of the service sector, namely the public sector, is largely population-driven (as opposed to market-driven). Davis and Webster (1981, p. 60) argue that a detailed knowledge of in-migration is crucial in determining public sector employment since 'The number of public sector employees in a community is more a function of the total population than it is of the community's total income'. They are critical of previous impact studies for the lack of co-ordination between their demographic and economic components.

Phibbs (1985) explored the relationship between public service employment and population using a number of models. After testing various models using Australian Census data, he concluded that the model that generated the best results was as follows:

$$E_{t+1,t} = E_t R_{t+1,t}/R_t + [(1+R_{t+1,t}/R_t)r_t P_{t+1,t}] \qquad (9.1)$$

where $E_{t+1,t}$ = change in regional service[1] employment from time t to $t+1$;

E_t = regional service employment at time t;

$R_{t+1,t}$ = change in the service employment–population ratio from t and $t+1$ measured on a state-wide basis;

R_t = state service employment–population ratio at time t;

r_t = service employment population ratio in the statistical subdivision at time t;

$P_{t+1,t}$ = regional population change between time t and $t+1$.

This equation is made up of two components. The first term measures the change in service employment resulting from state-wide trends in the service employment-population ratio (SEPR). This term operates independently of population growth in the region. The second term measures the changes in service employment resulting from changes in population in the region. It does this by adjusting the base period SEPR for the region in line with state-wide trends, and then multiplying the resultant ratio by the population change in the region. Thus, the equation specifically allows for the observed ratio differences between regions.

The model was tested using Census data for non-metropolitan regions in three Australian states from 1971 to 1981. Equation (9.1) was used to generate an estimate of service employment in a Census year, using data from the previous Census. The correlation coefficient between the predicted change in employment and the actual change in employment was greater than 0.9 in all states.

The next section describes how the service employment–population model can be interfaced with a simple input–output model, in order to generate more realistic impact forecasts.

A SIMPLE DEMO-ECONOMIC MODEL

Integrating the service employment–population model within an input–output framework

The first stage in this process involves converting the SEPM model outlined above, into a service employment-population *impact* model (SEPIM). The SEPM models changes in total service employment as a result of population change in a region, while a SEPIM model is concerned with estimating the change in service employment resulting from population change attributable to a specific economic event.

The conversion process is a simple one, involving the removal of the first term in Equation (9.1) and redefining one of the variables in the second term. The resultant SEPIM model is shown in Equation (9.2) below:

$$E_f = [(1+R_{t+1}/R_t)r_t P_f] \qquad (9.2)$$

where E_f = forecast change in regional service employment;

R_{t+1} = change in the service employment population ratio between base period and forecast period measured on a state-wide basis;

R_t = state service employment-population ratio—base period;

r_t = service employment-population ratio in the study region—base period;

P_f = forecast population change in study region resulting from economic event under consideration.

Nesting this SEPM model within an input–output model seems, on first consideration, a straightforward exercise. The service sector can simply be removed from the input–output table, the two models run independently, and the results combined to generate the total economic impact of a particular development. However, when the service sector is completely removed from the input–output table, the feedback effects or linkages between the service sector and the remainder of a regional economy are not measured. This problem can be overcome if the following procedure is adopted: First, set all the service-sector row entries in the direct coefficients table to zero before calculating the traditional Type II impact multipliers. These multipliers could be termed Type IIs multipliers. Next, calculate the change in service employment using the SEPIM. Then estimate the linkages between the service sector and the remainder of the economy by applying the service-sector traditional Type II multiplier to the change in service employment generated by the SEPIM. The use of this procedure then enables the total impacts of a development to be estimated. The next sub-section demonstrates how this mechanism can be placed in an economic-demographic framework, in order to generate realistic regional impact forecasts.

A brief review of demographic–economic impact models

The integration of the SEPIM with the input–output model is an explicit acknowledgement of the importance of demographic factors in assessing regional impacts. Such an acknowledgment is consistent with recent trends in regional modelling, where attempts to model simultaneously demographic and economic variables have become widespread. One can only agree with Schinnar (1976, p. 455), who states: 'There is abundant evidence pointing to the fact that demographic variations have been induced by manipulations or movements in economic variables, and, conversely, that demographic changes have important "feedback" effects on economic matters.'

A large number of impact models which modelled these feedbacks were developed in the 1970s to analyse the impact of an expansion of the resources sector. However, many of these studies rely on the economic base model, which limits their utility in helping to solve the problem under consideration in this chapter. (See, for example, Monts and Bareiss, 1979; Cluett *et al.*, 1977; Anderson *et al.*, 1974). Moreover, the models that adopt an input–output framework in their economic modelling suffer from the problem of being unable accurately to measure service-sector impacts (see, for example, Beckhelm *et al.*, 1975).

Nevertheless, despite these limitations in the area of modelling economic impacts, the majority of these models adopt a consistent approach to modelling the demographic–economic interface, which seems suitable for incorporation into a demo-economic impact model. The approach adopted may be summarised as follows. The employment demands from the economic model are matched with estimates of labour availability from the demographic model. The supply factor is estimated by applying a labour-force participation rate (or a set of rates) to a projected base population. As a result of the matching process, projections of migrating labour are made, based on the imbalance between labour supply and demand. The demographic impacts of migrating workers are determined by applying a set of employment-related demographic characteristics (marital status, number of dependants, and so on).

A number of recent papers by Batey and Madden (Batey and Madden 1981; Madden and Batey 1983) also provide useful ideas about the structure of a demo-economic impact model. Batey and Madden build a demo-economic model around an activity-commodity framework, after identifying an inconsistency concerning unemployment in traditional input-output models. This inconsistency is explained in the following terms:

for forecasting purposes, the derivation of a household consumption vector . . . relies on an exogenous forecast of household numbers, and some assumption about the unemployment rate of the population making up those households. The consumption . . . must then be incorporated into a final demand vector, which . . . is premultiplied by the Leontief inverse. From these gross outputs labour demand figures may be obtained by means of coefficients relating employment to gross output. Labour supply is made up of the economically active members of the households whose consumption was incorporated into the final demand vector used to generate the forecast. Comparison of labour demand with labour supply yields an unemployment rate which is equal to the assumed rate only by chance (Batey and Madden, 1981, p. 1067).

One of the major thrusts of the Batey and Madden approach is to remove this inconsistency by specifically including household consumption coefficients for unemployed households. More specifically, Batey and Madden combine the traditional input–output matrix with disaggregated household consumption functions, a sub-model showing the interaction between demographic activities and commodities (for example, household formation) and a sub-model relating employment to industrial output.

Batey and Madden place the descriptive equations from each of these quadrants into a square matrix and solve the set of simultaneous equations by the usual method of inverting the matrix of coefficients. This process generates multipliers that can be interpreted in the traditional manner. Batey and Madden call these Type 4 multipliers and consider that they will be smaller than traditional Type 2 multipliers since:

consumption is treated as an increment—so that people moving into employment from unemployment increase consumption by a margin rather than by the amount they are newly receiving as income (ignoring savings), and vice versa—we can expect type 4 multipliers to be smaller than type 2 multipliers, but nevertheless larger than type 1 multipliers which ignore induced effects altogether (Batey and Madden, 1981, pp. 1072-3).

Batey and Madden's work clearly represents an important advance on traditional input–output modelling because of its ability to generate more realistic mutlipliers. The explicit modelling of the unemployed sector assumes added significance as unemployment in Australia and other Western economies continues to rise. Nevertheless, the model does have a number of problems in terms of modelling impacts under Australian conditions. First, the model is data-ravenous, necessitating a large amount of information in addition to the normal requirements of input–output models. Ledent (1982, p. 38) comments on this problem as follows: 'from a practical viewpoint, the model involves the use of many variables and parameters for which, owing to the paucity of disaggregate demographic and economic data commonly available at the regional level, pertinent data is not always available'.

Second, the model has not resolved the problem of forecasting changes in the service sector. The differences between type 4 and type 2 multipliers may be significantly different when non-market consumption in the service sector is considered.

Instead of this comprehensive modelling approach, a simpler approach would seem more appropriate for many Australian impact studies. The inter-sectoral linkages in many Australian regional economies are relatively weak. Thus, the use of a simpler demo-economic model with leaner data requirements, which attempts to incorporate some of the elements of the Batey–Madden approach, would seem to be a cost-efficient approach to impact analysis.

A SIMPLE DEMO-ECONOMIC IMPACT MODEL

This sub-section specifies in detail a demo-economic model that integrates the SEPIM within an input–output framework. The migration component of the model follows the example set by a number of US models and is estimated after matching labour supply and demand. The model does not include separate consumption functions for the unemployed because of Australian data limitations, although the stage of the model where they could be included is indicated in case the data situation changes. Nevertheless, it is considered that the unemployed have to be incorporated within the model in some manner. It is considered that the most promising option is to adjust the household row coefficients on the basis of the proportion of new jobs that are taken by the unemployed. For example, if the average wage in sector i is $200 per week (the average wage can be calculated by dividing the household income co-efficient by the employment coefficient and multiplying by an appropriate constant), and all the new jobs are taken by unemployed, with an average social security benefit of $100 per week, then the household row coefficient is reduced by 50%.

However, the ability of this technique to generate realistic results is limited by the need to specify in advance the number of previously unemployed people who will take up employment in each sector. As outlined above, in the discussion of the Batey–Madden model, the proportion of jobs that go to the unemployed in each sector could be affected by the size of the indirect and induced effects (flow-ons) associated with a particular development. This problem is related to the mechanistic process used to solve the input–output system of equations, namely the inversion of the $I-A$ matrix. A solution to this dilemma involves using an alternative approach to solve the system of equations, namely the use of the series $I + A^1 + A^2 + A^3 + \ldots + A^n$. This series was commonly used to estimate input–output multipliers before the widespread use of computers to estimate the Leontief inverse. The major advantage of the use of the series is that it enables the round-by-round indirect and induced effects to be estimated. Thus, it is possible to estimate the proportion of unemployed that will be able to enter the workforce at the end of each round by comparing the sex and skill structure of the unemployed with the sex and skill structure of the indirect and induced jobs. A round-by-round approach also has the advantage of allowing the analyst to assess whether capacity considerations will lead to bottlenecks in any sectors.

The model is best explained by decomposing its structure into a number of discrete modules or stages. These stages are shown in Figure 9.1 and discussed in detail below. In order to simplify the explanation of the model, the

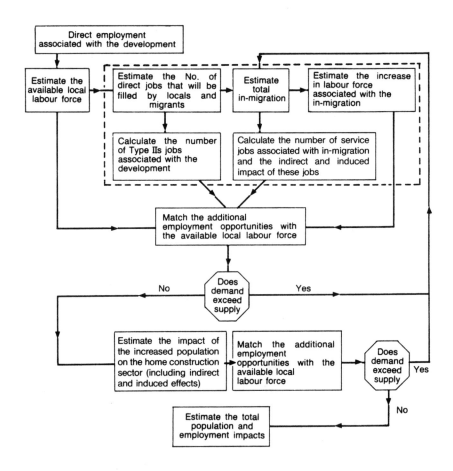

Figure 9.1 The demo-economic impact model

various stages describe the impact of an increase in direct employment. However, the model could also be used to estimate the impacts of a decrease in direct employment.

Stage 1.   Estimate the available local labour force
The locally available labour force, by sex, is estimated from regional unemployment statistics available from local Commonwealth Employment Service (CES) offices. In addition, female participation rates for the region are compared with the rates of other similar regions, in order to explore the extent of under-employment in the region. An appreciation of the skill characteristics can be gained by a discussion with the local CES officers.

Stage 2. Estimate the number of direct jobs associated with the development that will be filled by local residents, as opposed to migrants
The number of local residents who take up direct jobs at the development is estimated by comparing the sex and skill profile of the unemployed with the labour needs of the development. It is assumed that jobs that cannot be filled by local labour will be filled by labour migrating into the region.

Stage 3. Calculate the total in-migration associated with the direct employment effects
Total in-migration is calculated by establishing a demographic profile for the non-local direct employment component of the plant. This profile is derived, where possible, from empirical data for other similar developments in the region. Failing this, data from other regions or a state average are used.

Stage 4. Calculate the additional growth in the labour force due to this migration
Many simple impact models ignore the fact that some of the dependants of the migrants that take up the direct jobs at the development will also join the labour force. The model quantifies this increase in the labour force by applying an age-specific participation rate for dependant males in the 15–19 category, and a crude participation rate for female dependants. These rates are based on current regional values.

Stage 5. Calculate the number of Type IIs multiplier jobs
An input–output model is used to estimate the multiplier. (The technical coefficients of the development under consideration usually added as an extra row and column). The service sector row coefficients are set to zero and the Type IIs employment multiplier for the development are estimated using the $I + A^1 + A^2 + A^3 + \ldots + A^n$ series as discussed above. Round-by-round estimates of the number of unemployed people who will enter the workforce are inserted at the end of each round, and estimates of their foregone social security benefits are made on the basis of their sex and marital status. The household row coefficients are then adjusted downwards accordingly before the calculation of the next round of impacts. If disaggregated consumption coefficients are available for the unemployed, two rows of household coefficients and two columns of consumption coefficients could be included in the model before the direct and indirect effects were calculated, allowing for more accurate estimates of consumption-induced effects. Sex and skill characteristics of the labour force (available from the Australian Bureau of Statistics (ABS) Census matrix tapes) are used to disaggregate the multiplier impacts by sex and skill (see, for example, Phibbs, 1981).

Stage 6. Calculate the number of service jobs generated by the additional population and the indirect and induced impacts of these jobs
The total increase in population resulting from the in-migration identified in Stage 3 is fed into the SEPIM and the increase in service employment estimated. The sex and skill characteristics of these jobs are estimated from the ABS matrix tapes. The indirect and induced employment, disaggregated by sex and skill level, is calculated using the Type IIs multiplier for the service sector.

Stage 7. Match the additional employment opportunities with the available local labour force
Thus far, the supply of local labour is comprised of the local unemployed who

did not find employment at the development, plus the additional labour force generated by the in-migration. The demand for local labour includes the Type IIs multiplier jobs associated with the operation of the development under consideration, the service-sector jobs and their indirect and induced impacts identified in Stage 6.

Since both the demand and supply for labour are available by sex and skill level, it is possible to make reasonable estimates of the demand–supply balance. If demand exceeds supply then it is assumed that further in-migration will occur and hence the modelling process continues. If supply exceeds demand, then no further in-migration will occur and Stages 8, 9 and 10 are bypassed.

Stage 8.   Estimate the population impact of further in-migration
The total population increase associated with this further migration is calculated by applying a demographic profile to the migrants who move into the region to take up indirect and induced jobs. Since these jobs will be spread across many sectors, a state average is applied, rather than the more rigorous technique suggested in Stage 3. Since this round of migration is likely to be considerably smaller than the migration related to direct employment at the development, it is felt that this procedure is unlikely seriously to distort the accuracy of the model. The increase is the labour force associated with this further migration is also calculated in this stage (using a procedure identical to the one described in Stage 4).

Stage 9.   Estimate the increase in service employment and the associated indirect and induced jobs resulting from this additional in-migration
This increase in employment is calculated using the procedure outlined in Stage 6.

Stage 10.   Match the available supply of labour with the additional demand
The demand–supply labour balance is estimated using a similar procedure to Stage 7. If demand exceeds supply then the model reverts back to Stage 8. If this is not the case then the model proceeds to Stage 11.

Stage 11.   Estimate the impact of the total population increase on the home construction sector
A problem associated with previous Australian impact studies has been the exclusion of capital expenditure for the home construction sector. This stage of the demo-economic model attempts to overcome this problem by estimating the impact of population change on the home construction sector. This estimate is based on the following simple equation, suggested by Buchanan and Partners (1981):

$$D = PSV \qquad (9.3)$$

where D is dwelling demand; P is population increase; S is 1/(average household size of migrants); and V is 1/(percentage of occupied dwellings). The dwelling demand forecast by this model is converted to an annualised rate and compared with the trend in home completions (available from the Australian Bureau of Statistics). If it is considered that employment in the home construction industry will increase as a result of this increase in demand, the employment change can be estimated with the aid of the input–output table.

The Type IIs multiplier impacts for the construction sector are added to the direct change in construction employment. Using the method described in Stage 7, an estimate of the labour demand–supply balance is then made. If demand exceeds supply then further in-migration will occur and the model reverts back to Stage 8, otherwise the model proceeds to Stage 12.

Stage 12. Estimate the total population and employment impacts of the development
At this stage the results of the model are summarised by adding total in-migration and the total employment generation described by the model.

An empirical example
The demo-economic model described in the previous section was utilised to assess the economic impact of an expansion of the Ulan coal mines at Mudgee, in the Central West of New South Wales. In particular, the impact of the expansion of the operational workforce of the mine by 128 persons in 1983–4 was examined. The calculations for each stage are described below:

Stage 1.   As of 30 June 1983, 994 persons were unemployed in the Mudgee region, being comprised of 729 males and 265 females. It should also be noted that approximately 15% of the unemployed were skilled tradesmen.

Stage 2.   The high pool of skilled people that are currently unemployed in the region and the relatively low skill requirements of the development (only about 20% of the coal-mine jobs require skilled workers) suggest that a substantial proportion of the direct jobs will be taken by the unemployed. After consultation with the operators of the mine, a figure of 65% of the jobs going to those previously unemployed was considered reasonable. That is, 83 of the 128 jobs at the mine will go to local unemployed with the remaining 45 being taken by migrants. It is quite likely that there may be some job-switching where local people switch jobs in order to gain the good wages of miners. However, it is assumed that unemployed people will replace these people in their present jobs, and in the absence of marginal consumption coefficients, the estimation of consumption-induced effects will not be affected.

Stage 3.   Total in-migration was estimated by applying a demographic profile to the 45 in-migrants. This profile was based on data from the NSW Combined Colliery Proprietors Association, who conduct regular surveys on the demographic profiles of mine workers. Applying this typical demographic profile revealed that the total migration associated with the 45 jobs for migrants would total 130 persons, comprising 32 spouses, 45 male miners, and 53 children (27 female, 26 male, with five males in the 15–19 age category).

Stage 4.   The additional growth in the labour force was calculated by applying a crude participation rate of 0.315 (calculated using 1981 Census data) to the additional female population of 59, and an age-specific participation rate of 0.61 (calculated using 1981 Census data) to the estimated five dependant males in the 15–19 age category. The resultant increase in the labour force was estimated to be 18 females and three males.

Stage 5.   The Type IIs multiplier for the mining sector was calculated using an input–output table for the Mudgee–Merriwa shires. The coefficients for the service sector were set to zero and the total indirect and induced effects were calculated using the $I + A^1 + A^2 + \ldots + A^n$ series. At the end of each round the number of indirect and induced jobs by sector was estimated. The sex and skill characteristics of these jobs were then estimated using data from ABS matrix tape 21 of the 1976 Census (See Table 9.1) and these data were compared with the sex and skill profile of the unemployed in order to match supply and demand. In particular it was estimated whether the indirect and induced jobs were taken by: unmarried unemployed persons; married unemployed males; married unemployed females; or migrants. The breakdown between the different categories of unemployed worker was necessary in order to make reasonably accurate estimates of the amount of social security benefits forgone by the previously unemployed. For example, the unemployment benefit for married males is approximately double that of unmarried recipients, while unemployed married females receive no benefits. It was considered that the relatively small number of indirect and induced jobs, which were mostly relatively low-skill jobs in the trade and transport sectors, would be taken by people currently living in the region.

This round-by-round analysis was continued for five rounds, at which time the indirect and induced impacts were less than one job. The terms in the series were then added and the employment multiplier calculated in the normal manner. The resultant multiplier was 1.26, meaning that the 128 direct jobs at the mine would generate a further 33 non-service-sector jobs in the region.

Stage 6.   The SEPR for the region was calculated to be 0.0644 in June 1981. On a state-wide basis the SEPR has increased by 1.6% between June 1981 and May 1983 (ABS, 1984). It is considered that given the fiscal constraints of both the federal and NSW state governments this ratio is unlikely to increase between May 1983 and January 1984. Thus an adjusted SEPR (0.0654) was used to estimate that the additional 130 persons in the region will generate an additional 9 Service sector jobs. The traditional Type II employment multiplier for the service sector calculated using the round-by-round approach is 1.16, indicating that the 9 Service sector jobs will generate one additional indirect and induced job.

Stage 7.   Stages 5 and 6 identified 43 indirect jobs. It is considered that the sex and skill profile for these jobs suggests that the majority of these jobs will be taken by local unemployed people. However, it is estimated that because of the higher skill requirements of the service-sector jobs, four of these jobs will be taken by migrants.

Stage 8.   Using a demographic profile for multiplier jobs suggested by the demographic unit of the NSW Department of Environment and Planning, these four jobs will generate total in-migration of 12 persons, generating an increase in the female labour force of two persons.

Stage 9.   The in-migration of 12 persons will generate a further job in the service sector.

Stage 10.   The one job in the service sector will be filled by a local unemployed person.

Stage 11.   It is considered that the rate of home construction associated with the in-migration will not lead to an expansion of employment in the home construction sector.

Stage 12.   In total the initial expansion of 128 jobs directly created by the coal mine operation in 1983–84 will generate an additional 44 indirect and induced jobs and lead to an increase in regional population of 142 persons.

The 12 stages of the model are summarised in Table 9.2.

Table 9.1 Employment by sector by skill level, Mudgee region, 1976

Sector	PWC*	SWC	SEUWC	SBCME	SBCB	SBCO	SEUBC	RW	O	TOTAL
				Percent						
1. Rural	0.1	0.0	1.3	0.4	0.4	0.4	0.0	96.4	0.1	100
2. Mining	1.6	11.5	6.6	14.8	1.6	0.0	63.9	0.0	0.0	100
3. Food and beverages	0.0	4.8	8.2	3.2	0.2	28.4	46.7	7.6	0.8	100
4. Textiles, clothing and footwear	0.0	16.7	50.0	0.0	0.0	0.0	33.3	0.0	0.0	100
5. Basic metal	0.0	0.0	0.0	0.0	0.0	0.0	0.0	0.0	0.0	0
6. Fabricated metal products	0.0	0.0	12.5	25.0	0.0	0.0	62.5	0.0	0.0	100
7. Chemicals, petroleum and coal products	0.0	0.0	0.0	0.0	0.0	0.0	100.0	0.0	0.0	100
8. Glass, clay and other mineral products	0.0	11.8	0.0	0.0	0.0	0.0	88.2	0.0	0.0	100
9. Wood, wood products and furniture	0.0	0.0	25.0	0.0	0.0	0.0	75.0	0.0	0.0	100
10. Paper and paper products, printing	0.0	35.7	21.4	0.0	21.4	21.4	0.0	0.0	0.0	100
11. Other manufacturing	0.0	0.0	66.7	0.0	0.0	0.0	0.0	0.0	33.3	100
12. Electricity, gas and water	7.0	16.9	25.4	36.6	0.0	0.0	14.1	0.0	0.0	100
13. Building and construction	0.0	7.0	6.7	11.3	24.6	0.0	47.5	1.4	1.4	100
14. Wholesale and retail	1.0	15.6	55.3	11.0	0.5	4.4	11.5	0.5	0.2	100
15. Transport, storage and communications	2.4	6.6	12.3	12.0	0.0	0.0	64.8	0.6	1.2	100
16. Finance, business and professional services	12.2	9.9	68.0	0.0	0.0	0.0	9.9	0.0	0.0	100
17. Public authority and defence	9.1	10.6	20.7	2.0	4.0	0.0	40.4	8.1	5.1	100
18. Community and other services	14.7	27.0	22.1	0.6	0.8	3.6	29.3	1.6	0.2	100

*The skill level groupings are based on the classification of Craigie (1979). The skill categories include:

PWC	Professional white collar.	SBCO	Skilled blue collar (Other).
SWC	Skilled white collar.	SEUBC	Semi- and unskilled blue collar.
SEUWC	Semi- and unskilled white collar.	RW	Rural workers.
SBCME	Skilled blue collar (Metal and Electrical).	O	Other (including the armed services).
SBCB	Skilled blue collar (Building).		

Source: ABS matrix tape, no. 21.

Table 9.2 The demo-economic impact of the expansion of the Ulan coal mines, Mudgee, 1983–84.

Stage	Change in labour supply	Local labour demand M	Local labour demand F	Source and no. of jobs	No. of jobs to locals	No. of jobs to migrants	Total migration M	Total migration F
1.		122	6	128 coal				
2.	−77	45		Mine jobs	83			
3.						45	71	59
4.	21							
5.		20	13	33 IIs jobs				
6.		25	18	10 sepim jobs				
7.	−39	4			39			
8.	2					4	6	6
9.			1	1 sepim job	1			
10.	−1							
	Total*			172 jobs	123 jobs	49 jobs	142 persons	
12.	Impacts			128 direct				
				44 flow-on				

*Stage 11 produces no expansion in employment

Advantages and disadvantages of the demo-economic model

Advantages
The major advantage of the model is that it overcomes the errors associated with estimating service-sector impacts using simple input–output models. Moreover in avoiding these problems it reduces the amount of data relating to private consumption expenditure that needs to be collected. This reduction comes about since no private consumption data are required for the service sector.

A further advantage of the model is that it acknowledges the presence of unemployed persons within the economic system. Although data limitations restrict the comprehensive modelling of the unemployed, the demo-economic model outlined in this chapter is superior to the traditional input–output approach, and will generate reasonably accurate results, especially for rural regions.

Disadvantages
The major disadvantage of the model is that additional data are required, namely population forecasts and a forecast of likely changes in the SEPR. However, it should be noted that since most impact studies already include demographic forecasts, in most cases no additional work is required. Obviously, a reliance on population forecasts means that impact forecasts of the model are dependent on the accuracy of the demographic analysis. Nevertheless, while this procedure will build errors into impact forecasts, the errors associated with the alternative technique, traditional input–output models, are of much greater magnitude.

Impact forecasts based on the demo-economic model also require forecasts of the SEPR. The use of forecast SEPRs will obviously have the potential for generating larger errors than those identified in the historical analysis reported above. Nevertheless, it is felt that the availability of suitable data will allow reasonably accurate forecasts of the SEPR. Firstly, data are available from the Australian Bureau for Statistics, on current SEPR values. This means that the current year, rather than a Census year, can be used as a base year for the SEPR forecast. Secondly, governments at both the state and federal levels are being more explicit about forecast levels of public sector employment. Thus, it is considered that reasonably accurate forecasts of the SEPR seem plausible.

CONCLUSION

In this chapter, a model has been formulated for nesting the SEPIM within a demo-economic model based on an input–output framework. The advantage of this new approach is that it allows the obvious benefits of the input–output approach to be retained, while acknowledging the impact of the unemployed on regional economic systems. In addition, the approach remedies the major problem associated with traditional applications of the input–output models, by separately modelling service-sector impacts.

NOTE

1. The service sector here refers to those service sectors dominated by public sector employment and includes public administration and community services.

REFERENCES

ABS (1980) Matrix Tape 21, Magnetic Tape of Census data matrices. Canberra: Australian Bureau of Statistics.

ABS (1984) *The Labour Force*, Catalogue No: 8203.0. Canberra: Australian Bureau of Statistics.

Anderson, E., Chalmers, J., Hogan, T. and Beckhelm, T. (1974), *ATOM 2: Part I of Final Report*. Pheonix: Arizona Office of Economic Planning and Development.

Batey, P.W.J. and Madden, M. (1981) 'Demographic-economic forecasting within an activity-commodity framework: some theoretical considerations and empirical results', *Environment and Planning*, vol. 13A, pp. 1067–83.

Beckhelm, T.L., Chalmers, J.A. and Hannigan, W.M. (1975) *A Description of the ATOM 3 and of the Research Related to its Development*. Washington, DC: Four Corners Regional Commission.

Buchanan and Partners (1981), *The Population and Employment Impacts of the Proposed Stansted Airport*. Report to Essex County Council. London: Buchanan and Partners.

Cluett, C., Mertaugh, M.T. and Micklin, M. (1977) 'A demographic model for assessing the socioeconomic impacts of large-scale industrial development projects'. Paper presented at the 1977 Annual Meeting of the Southern Regional Demographic Group, Virginia Beach, VA.

Craigie, R. (1979) *Some Comments on the ABS Occupational Classification System, and the*

Impact of Occupational Grouping. Impact Preliminary Working Paper, no. 1P-08. Melbourne: Impact Project.

Davis, H.C. and Webster, D.R. (1981) 'A compositional approach to regional socio-economic impact assessment', *Socio-economic Planning Sciences*, vol. 15, no. 4, pp. 159-63.

Jensen, R.C., Mandeville, T.D. and Karunaratne, N.D. (1979), *Regional Economic Planning: Generation of Regional Input-Output Analysis*. London: Croom Helm.

Ledent, J. (1982) 'Long range regional population forecasting: specifications of a minimal demoeconomic model, with a test for Tucson, Arizona', *Papers of the Regional Science Association*, vol. 49, pp. 37-67.

Madden, M. and Batey, P.W.J. (1983) 'Linked population and economic models: some methodological issues in forecasting, analysis, and policy optimization', *Journal of Regional Science*, vol. 23, no. 2, pp. 141-64.

Monts, J.K. and Bareiss, E.R. (1979), *Community-Level Impacts Projection System (CLIPS)*. Austin: University of Texas Center for Energy Studies.

Phibbs, P.J. (1981) 'The cumulative and disaggregated impacts of new aluminium smelting capacity in the Hunter Valley' in B.A. Twohill and W.J. Sheehan (eds), *Input-Output Analysis and Regional Multipliers*. Proceedings of a Colloquium held at the University of Newcastle, May. Institute of Industrial Economics, University of Newcastle.

Phibbs, P.J. (1985) 'Estimating regional input-output multipliers in Australia: a methodological study'. PhD thesis, University of New South Wales, Sydney.

Schinnar, A.P. (1976) 'A multidimensional accounting model for demographic and economic planning interactions', *Environment and Planning*, vol. 8A, pp. 455-75.

Part III

MODELS FOR SETTLEMENT AND REDISTRIBUTION

Chapter 10

POPULATION REDISTRIBUTION IN WESTERN EUROPE: TRENDS SINCE 1950 AND THE DEBATE ABOUT COUNTER-URBANISATION

A.J. Fielding

INTRODUCTION: MIGRATION AND URBAN DEVELOPMENT IN WESTERN EUROPE

The period since the Second World War has seen first the growth and then the decline of three mass migrations. First, at the international level, millions of young adults, often followed by members of their families, migrated from the European 'periphery' to the 'core' countries of north-western Europe. Second, at the interregional level, even more young people and young adults migrated from rural areas and peripheral regions to the metropolitan and major industrial cities. Finally, at the intraregional level, still more people, most of them in nuclear family households, migrated from the pre-war built-up areas of the towns and cities to the new suburbs and peri-urban zones. During their growth phases, each of these migrations contributed to the population growths of the great cities of Western Europe. The first two provided the newcomers to these cities, and the age-structures of these migration streams ensured that these cities subsequently experienced high rates of natural increase. The third migration brought about the spatial expansion of the labour-market areas of the major cities, and hence the incorporation into those cities of what were previously independent small towns and rural areas.

After about 1970, however, each of these migrations underwent a transformation. The character and direction of the migration streams changed and the numbers of migrations decreased. The population growths of the major cities were checked, or even reversed, first, by the 'turnround' in interregional migration which occurred in many countries around 1970 and which brought about net migration losses in the great cities and net migration gains in small and medium-sized towns and in many rural areas; second, by the sharp decline in 'guestworker' migration after 1973, combined with significant levels of international return migration; and third, by the sudden decrease after 1973 in rates of suburbanisaton.

The two main sections of this chapter examine the migration turnround in Western Europe. However, the way in which this is explained has implications for an interpretation of the changes in the other two migrations. These implications are discussed in the final section of the chapter.

URBANISATION AND COUNTER-URBANISATION
IN WESTERN EUROPE

'Urbanisation' is a concept which is endowed with many meanings; too often, however, we do not specify which particular meanings we intend to convey. In this paper, 'urbanisation' will be used in its narrow sense to mean 'a process of population concentration that implies a movement from a state of less concentration in space to a state of more concentration' (Tisdale quoted in Berry, 1976). The opposite of urbanisation can then be called 'counter-urbanisation'; counter-urbanisation refers to the tendency for larger places to lose population, notably through migration, while smaller places gain. 'Larger' and 'smaller' are defined in terms of resident population, and 'places' are defined in terms of labour-market areas.

Operationally, in the empirical work on which this chapter is based, urbanisation and counter-urbanisation are measured in terms of the statistical relationship between net migration rate and settlement size (or population density). Where a significant positive relationship is found to exist, urbanisation is said to be dominant; where a significant negative relationship exists, then counter-urbanisation is dominant.

These relationships, together with the way in which a transition from urbanisation to counter-urbanisation might possibly occur, can be illustrated with the help of a schematic model (Figure 10.1). Does the evidence on population redistribution in Western Europe for the period 1950–85 provide support for this schematic model? To answer this question the statistical relationship between net migration and population density[1] was calculated for each of the 14 major countries of Western Europe (that is, those lying to the west of a line drawn from the Baltic to the Adriatic, at two (sometimes three) spatial scales, for each of the decades 1950–60, 1960–70 and 1970–80. In addition, for the eight countries of these 14 which had registration data, the relation-

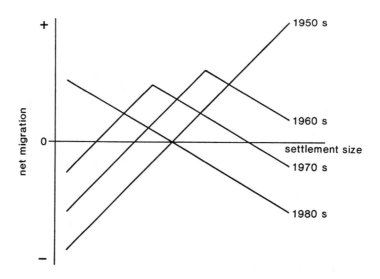

Figure 10.1 Migration and settlement size, 1950s to 1980s: a possible sequence

ship was also calculated for the early 1980s. The detailed results of this work are reported in Fielding (1982; Fielding 1986b).

Four main conclusions can be drawn from this analysis. First, the dominant characteristic of population redistribution patterns in the 1950s in each of the countries was urbanisation. Second, things began to change in the 1960s so that by the 1970s urbanisation remained dominant in only one country, Spain. In six of the remaining countries urbanisation had ceased but had not, as yet, been replaced by counter-urbanisation (Austria; Ireland; Italy; Norway; Portugal; and Switzerland). In the remaining seven countries counter-urbanisation was dominant (Belgium; Denmark; France; Netherlands; Sweden; UK; and West Germany). Third, in the early 1980s only two (Italy and West Germany) of the eight countries with registration data (Belgium; Denmark; Italy; Netherlands; Norway; Sweden; Switzerland; and West Germany), showed clear signs of counter-urbanisation; in all other cases the relationship between net migration and population density was very weak. This means that for several countries (Belgium; Denmark; Netherlands; and Sweden) the clear-cut counter-urbanisation of the 1970s had come to an end. Finally, using rather different data for France, it can be shown that the transition from urbanisation to counter-urbanisation proposed in the schematic model above, is, in general terms, supported by the facts of urban development, and that the peak period for the turnround was in the late 1960s and early 1970s[2] (see Figure 10.2).

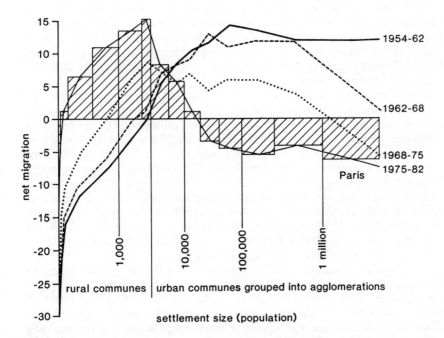

Figure 10.2 The relationship between migration and settlement size: France, 1954–82

INTERREGIONAL MIGRATION AND URBAN
DEVELOPMENT IN WESTERN EUROPE:
EXPLANATIONS OF COUNTERURBANISATION

Although affected by changing patterns of international migration, the turnround was very largely the result of a major shift in the pattern of inter-labour-market area (that is, interregional) migration.

Certain points about the explanation of this switch to counter-urbanisation are generally agreed. First, the turnround is now seen to be more than just suburbanisation 'writ large'. In the mid-1970s some writers asserted that counter-urbanisation was neither real nor new; rather it was an appearance produced by the failure of the administratively defined urban areas to encapsulate the continuously-expanding *de facto* functional urban regions. There is, however, a serious problem with this argument. The mix of processes which affect the changes taking place within labour-market areas is, in important respects, different from that affecting inter-labour-market area changes. The former are dominated by processes such as housing sub-market formation and social segregation; the latter are dominated by processes such as 'deindustrialisation' and the emergence of new spatial divisions of labour (see below). Of course the definition of labour-market areas is not unproblematic. The labour-market areas of certain kinds of worker 'nest' within those of other kinds, and the labour-market areas of those employed in the same type of work often overlap in a complex fashion. Nevertheless, the judgement that counter-urbanisation replaced urbanisation around 1970 is based upon information at several spatial scales, and, however broadly the metropolitan and industrial areas are defined, the results are consistent with the view that more than just suburbanisation was involved. Suburbanisation might just be able to explain some of the variation in the net migration rates of the Belgian provinces, but it is hardly equal to the task of explaining the variation in the rates for the French regions (seven times larger), or the turnround in Irish net migration (20 times larger).

The second point of agreement is that the turnround was assisted by the decline of rural depopulation. The argument is that since the net migration gains of the major cities was fuelled by rural depopulaton due to the decline of agricultural employment, it was the drying up of this source of migrants which was partly responsible for the turnround. Quite so, but two qualifications are in order. It is true that the proportion of the economically active population employed in agriculture had fallen to a very low level in many Western European countries by 1970, but this proportion continued to decline after 1970 even if the numbers of people thus released to sustain urbanisation were lower than in the 1950s and 1960s. More importantly, the turnround in net migration was as marked a feature of regions with high rural population densities as of regions with low rural densities.

Two other arguments receive broad support. The first is that developments in transport and communications technology have assisted the spatial decentralisation of economic activity. The second is that the effect of increased state activity has been a spatial standardisation of the 'general conditions of production', and the support of many groups of people in economically depressed areas through transfer payments (pensions, unemployment benefit, and so on).

But there the agreement ends. There are three main contending sources of explanation of counter-urbanisation represented in the literature, to which I shall add a fourth.

Explanation 1: Counter-urbanisation was caused by a marked shift in the place preferences of migrants away from large cities and towards small towns and rural areas.

This approach stresses the importance of values. It emphasises the way many people view life in the large city as stressful because of high crime rates, pollution, race hatred, run-down public services, traffic congestion, dirt and noise. Rural areas and small towns then take on all the opposite appearances; they are seen as havens of social harmony and of well-tried and trusted social values. The housing and job markets adjust to these preferences to produce a decentralisation of population and employment. It is true that the counter-urbanisation of the early 1970s coincided with a heightened sense of dissatisfaction with Western urban life. This was powerfully communicated in the neo-Malthusianism of the 'Limits to Growth' school of thought and in the disparate protest movements which came together under the banner of the 'green alliance'. It is also the case that circumstances can arise when individuals and families can exercise, in a relatively unconstrained manner, a choice of a place of residence between different towns and regions. This is most obviously so for the wealthy retired, but it can also happen when, in a highly segmented labour market, the supply of appropriate qualified persons for particular kinds of work is significantly less than the number of jobs on offer. In these cases the employee can accept an offer of a job at a preferred place and turn down one at a non-preferred place, and by this means help to create differential employment change between regions. This situation tends to arise most readily during times of general labour shortage such as existed in many Western European countries during the 1960s. However, even in times of high unemployment, the choice of place of residence can, for some, be relatively unconstrained.

Those who use this approach to explanation found support in the results of questionnaire surveys of migrants' reasons for moving which showed that environmental considerations figured prominently, and that the most preferred residential location was a small town within fairly easy travelling distance of a major city. They also point out that the opportunities for retirement migration had increased with the expansion of occupational pension schemes, and that the attractiveness of such a move had been increased through familiarity with other regions as a result of heightened geographical mobility during career development, increased leisure travel and a growth in the ownership of second homes.

However, this explanation, used as a principal approach to an understanding of counter-urbanisation, contains a fatal flaw. It ignores the fact that people who live in advanced industrial societies experience an inequality in their ability to choose where to live and work. Some can choose, most cannot. Most people are tied by their job location, and specifically by the location of jobs requiring their particular skills and experience. Most are also tied by family and other home-related commitments. This approach is therefore 'voluntarist';

it exaggerates the importance of human motivation in explaining behaviour. Migrants are subject to powerful social and economic forces; they exercise their decisions to move within the constraints of the law at the international level, and within the limits set by their wealth, income-earning capacity, qualifications and social status at the interregional level. These together determine how much 'freedom' they have in the national job and housing markets. In short, the explanation of migration trends must be located in the social relations and social processes of the wider society, and not in the motivations and aspirations of the individual migrant.

Explanation 2: On the basis of the economic theory of migration a reversal in the pattern of net migration must reflect a reversal in the pattern of employment opportunities.

Economic analysis sees migration as the means by which a spatially distributed population adjusts itself to the changing pattern of employment opportunities. These employment opportunities vary from one area to another in large part because of changes in demand for the area's products. Increases in demand for a particular region's goods and services will result in output growth and the recruitment of more labour; decreases in demand will result in falling output and redundancies. These differences in labour demand are expressed in regional variations in rates of unemployment and in average wage levels. Migration then takes place from the slack labour market, where people are pushed out by high unemployment and low wages, towards a tight labour market, where people are pulled in by low unemployment and high wages.

This approach to an explanation of counter-urbanisation has some distinct advantages over the emphasis on individual preferences. In particular, it correctly stresses the importance of employment opportunities in determining the distribution of population, and locates the key forces not at the level of the ordinary individual but at the level of institutions such as firms and government departments.

There is, however, one major problem with this explanation of counter-urbanisation. The economic changes required to bring about a reversal in net migration balances simply did not occur! The largest metropolitan areas continued to have employment structures biased towards high growth, they continued to have wage levels which were appreciably above average and their unemployment rates continued, generally speaking, to be below average. Indeed, what is so remarkable is how few of the predictions drawn from the economic theory of migration are borne out by the facts of contemporary migration in Western industrial countries (Zelinsky, 1983). For example, it would be expected on the basis of theory that there would be an inverse relationship between regional gross in-migration rates and gross out-migration rates; a high-growth region should have low out-rates and high in-rates, and a low growth region should have low in-rates and high out-rates. But the gross in- and out-migration rates are in fact positively correlated. This means that some regions, notably high-growth rural regions with small and medium-sized towns, have both high in- and high out-migration rates, while others, notably 'old industrial' regions, have low in- and low out-migration rates. These empirical problems facing the economic theory of migration do not constitute merely a 'naive falsification' of the approach; the world that the theory describes is one in which a redundant coal-miner from Scotland can take a post as a stockbroker in the City of London! This is not the real world of social classes, of wealth inequality, and of formal and informal rules of access to jobs and housing.

Another line of argument within this category is that the turnround occurred because of economic recession and the energy crisis. Energy scarcity can have multiple effects on the urban and regional system; it can encourage investment in resource-rich regions located well away from the existing centres of industrial activity such as northern Scotland and the west coast of Norway, and in this way assist the net migration turnround. On the other hand, it should have the overall effect of encouraging concentration since it puts a premium on the minimisation of transport costs and the achievement of spatial proximity. The economic recession argument rests partly on the experience of the 1930s when migration streams to the North-East and North-Central USA were temporarily checked by the very high unemployment rates to be found here. But the situation in the 1970s was importantly different. In most Western European countries the development of social welfare services in the period after the Second World War meant that the unemployed were cushioned against the desperate poverty experienced by their pre-war equivalents. Furthermore, the decline in agricultural employment and the concentration of agricultural land ownership in the hands of large capitalist farmers has resulted in a much reduced capacity of rural areas to absorb the urban unemployed. Thus, although much return migration to rural areas took place during the 1970s, very few of the migrants returned to agriculture. In any case, as many observers admit, the turnround came into being in many countries several years before the economic crisis of 1973–4; it occurred during the latter part of the long post-war period of growth and prosperity. It is pertinent to note that the recession argument is now coming to be used not as an explanation of the decentralization tendencies of the 1970s, but of their subsequent demise! (See below.)

Explanation 3: Counter-urbanisation was caused by state urban and regional development policies designed to check the growth of metropolitan cities and to promote the growth of peripheral and rural regions.

Migration is seen, as in the previous approach, as being primarily a response to changing employment opportunities. The geographical pattern of these opportunities has in this case, however, been determined by state redistribution policy. The strength of this approach lies in the fact that the state has become a formidable influence in the national economies of Western European countries, and that many Western European governments have spent considerable sums of money on area-development policies during the post-war period.

There remains, however, the difficult problem of judging the effects of state redistribution policy. First, two pitfalls must be avoided. It is all too easy for the observer to accept at face value government statements of intention which are not, in the event, matched by real resources. In Britain, for example, despite the political emphasis on regional policy in the 1960s and 1970s, government expenditure under this heading (which favoured northern and western regions) was massively outweighed by military spending (which favoured southern England). Also, it is tempting, since the turnround largely coincided with stated policy objectives, to assume that policy was the cause of the turnround. But what would have happened in the absence of state intervention? This is not an easy question to answer since Western European societies would be fundamentally different if their governments were not engaged in economic management, and in the ownership and control of important sections of their nations' economies. What can be said is that the assumption that urbanisation would have continued in the absence of state policy is poorly supported by the evidence. Commentators on counter-urbanisation in the US do not use this argument for good reason, since the turnround occurred there without a strong federal government redistribution policy. Also, if government policy was the determining influence, why in France did the net migration loss turn into net migration gain in rural regions (such as Brittany) but not in old industrial regions (such as Nord), regions which received roughly equal status in area-development effort?

Second, the effects of state intervention tend to be assessed by researchers only in terms of their positive impacts, notably the number of jobs created by state-aided manufacturing investment, plus the multiplier effects of this investment on the local economy. But the assisted firm may poach the best labour from other firms in the area thus endangering their profitability. It may also be producing, at lower cost because of the use of the latest technology, products which undermine the production of other firms located in this or in other problem regions. In these and other ways, state intervention may have been helping to create the very problems it was intended to solve.

To summarise, each of the three main paths towards an explanation of counter-urbanisation offered in the literature has serious weaknesses. Only the emphasis on the role of place preferences in the migration decisions of individuals and households has been upheld with any real enthusiasm, and then only for a minority of people in strictly limited situations. Clearly, other approaches need to be sought.

Explanation 4: Counter-urbanisation was produced by changes in the spatial division of labour; specifically, regional sectoral specialisation (RSS) was partially replaced by the so-called new spatial division of labour (NSDL).

This perspective on the causes of counter-urbanisation is, in my opinion, much more promising than those listed above. It emphasises the importance of job-creating and job-destroying investment decisions in determining population redistribution and trends in urbanisation, and it places these decisions within a historical and regional analysis of changing social class relations. The key concept is the 'spatial division of labour'. The migration turnround is seen as a by-product of the change from regional sectoral specialisation (RSS), a situation in which each place contained all the tasks involved in the production of one or a related set of goods or services (for example, Sheffield steel or Lancashire cotton textiles), to the new spatial division of labour (NSDL), in which places became differentiated on the basis of the role they played in the production process (for example, central planning and management in Paris, routine production in the Pays de la Loire).

Until the 1960s RSS had dominated, and because there was a common shift in Western European societies away from employment in agriculture and towards the expansion of employment in market-orientated mass-produced consumer goods, and public and private services, there was a major shift of population away from rural areas and old industrial regions (coal/textiles/shipbuilding), towards the largest industrial and commercial cities, especially when these were located in the core regions of the national territory. This redistribution of population produced an urbanisation relationship between net migration and settlement size (that is, positive).

By the 1970s it was clear that this relationship between sectoral employment structure and employment growth was breaking down. Thus rural regions, which, because of their agricultural employment, should have been declining were often experiencing employment growth in both manufacturing and services, and the major metropolitan areas, which, because of their bias towards modern industry and services, should have been growing, were in fact experiencing employment stagnation or slow decline overall, and rapid decline in their manufacturing employment. This puzzling situation is rather neatly explained by the notion that RSS had come to be replaced by the NSDL.

Under the NSDL, instead of the differences between places being due to the different parts they play in the social division of labour in society (a result of competition in the market), they arise from the planned separation of tasks within a particular production process (the technical division of labour). The emergence of the NSDL during the 1960s and 1970s implied nothing less than the creation of a new geography of production in the countries of Western Europe. Firms and government agencies evaluated places from the point of view of their needs for different kinds of labour and on the basis of the overall efficiency of their operations. In general, major metropolitan areas were judged to be necessary for the most specialised management functions and for those activities most closely linked to management such as financial services, banking and insurance, tax and other legal advice, and marketing services. High-amenity (prestige) environments near to or in easy contact with metropolitan cities tended to be chosen as sites for investment in research and development activities. Production which required industrial (craft) skills continued to be located in the long-established industrial areas. The remaining production tended to be dispersed to rural or peripheral regions or to places where there were people who had not previously been employed (such as women in certain old industrial areas). Although most clearly manifested in certain branches of non-public-sector manufacturing industry, similar separations tended to occur in state agencies and public corporations and in certain branches of private sector services.

The reasons for the change from RSS to NSDL are many and complex, but they include: the trend towards a concentration of ownership and control as multi-plant and multi-product companies became first national and then transnational in the scope of their operations; the equalisation of the general conditions of production between different places which accompanied the standardisation of publicly-provided goods and services such as the road, rail, air and telecommunications networks, electricity, gas and water provision and health and education services; and the effects of technological change which permitted a deskilling of many jobs as well as a reduction in the need for the production of goods and services to be serviced by very large workforces concentrated in single workplaces. All these factors facilitated the change from RSS to NSDL by allowing the separation of labour forces and the dispersal of routine production to small towns and rural areas. In addition, however, the rapid and fairly continuous growths of the Western European economies after 1945 led to a general shortage of labour during the 1960s, and thus to recruitment and industrial relations problems for employers with large workforces, working in large establishments in the major industrial and metropolitan cities. One solution was to seek out reserves of 'green' labour elsewhere. This was to be found among women in rural and old industrial areas (where female activity rates were often very low), and more generally among young men and women in smaller labour-market areas where the work practices and attitudes of the large factory or office were not endemic. These differences between towns and regions with respect to their social histories and political cultures were sometimes manifested in variations in levels of unionisation, but they were also revealed in the incidence of industrial conflict and in levels of labour turnover, both of which tended to be higher in larger industrial cities than in smaller towns and rural areas. The switching of investment towards these smaller places and more peripheral regions was accompanied by a major disinvestment, especially in manufacturing industry, in the largest cities.

From this perspective, counterurbanization is seen as a product of the rapid de-industrialisation of most of the largest cities and old industrial regions in Western Europe, accompanied by a stabilization of rural population levels following the long process of restructuring agriculture, and by a growth of manufacturing industry and services in small and medium-sized towns in rural and peripheral regions.

MIGRATION AND THE NEW SPATIAL DIVISION OF LABOUR

The change from RSS to the NSDL might be expected to produce certain migration outcomes in addition to that of bringing about the replacement of urbanisation by counter-urbanisation. First, it would be expected that overall levels of inter-labour-market mobility would decrease (i) because as sectoral diversification replaces sectoral specialisation, the push factor of job loss in an area's staple industry should be much reduced—for example, this diversification breaks the links between a decline in agricultural employment and rural depopulation; (ii) because, more generally, job creation in non-metropolitan labour markets would be expected to halt non-metropolitan to metropolitan migration; and (iii) because as female activity rates increase so also do the mobility problems of two-job households. Inter-labour-market migrations have indeed decreased during the period since about 1970.

Second, it would be expected that the social composition of migration streams would change (i) because manual worker mobility would be less, not only for the reasons listed above, but also because of the increasing importance of the social wage, and the increasing standardisation of its various elements (health, education, social security and so on) between places reduces the advantages to be obtained from moving away from unemployment, poor job security or low wages; and (ii) because, to obtain an efficient use of their higher-paid manpower, organisations would transfer technical and managerial personnel from one part of their operations to another. Again this is found to be the case. Transfers within organisations comprised over half of all interregional migrations in the UK in 1980-1, and the new middle class constitutes a large and increasing proportion of economically active migrants (Owen and Green, 1988).

Finally, the NSDL concept also suggests that, while deindustrialisation may well affect all large cities, those which house the highest-order functions of companies and public institutions may well sustain their employment levels through the further accretion of these kinds of activity and through the general growth of producer-services employment. There are some signs that this is the case, with capital cities such as London and Paris, and cities with major head office quarters maintaining their populations through migration in the 1980s, while other large industrial cities lose theirs. Paradoxically, however, this may well enhance the trends towards lower levels of mobility overall, and towards low levels of mobility for working-class households, since these major administrative and commercial cities will have costs of living (especially of housing) which reflect their increasing dominance by the new middle class (that is, their embourgeoisement). They thus become problematic as destinations for all those who are excluded from this class.

THE RELATIONSHIP BETWEEN INTERNATIONAL, INTERREGIONAL AND INTRAREGIONAL MIGRATIONS

Drawing upon the emphasis on the relationship between migration trends and the changing geography of production developed above, it is possible to speculate on the connections between the three great migrations mentioned at the beginning of this chapter.

In the period from 1945 until about 1970 suburbanisation was both an expression of the material gains made by ordinary working people through the expansion of the Western European economies, and also a major reason for that expansion, since it was the industries which fed suburban growth (cars, televisions and 'white goods' industries) which spearheaded economic growth. Rapid economic growth and higher wages led, however, to a crisis for the producers of these suburban products, because they found that their premises were obsolete and site-constricted, and that the labour they needed to expand production and remain profitable was too scarce, too expensive and too unmanageable in the major cities in which they were located at that time. Since the *in situ* restructuring of production was costly, usually resisted and often difficult to effect, further expansion required either the use of immigrant workers, who thus came to occupy many of the routine factory, building-site and other manual jobs in the major industrial cities from the early 1960s onwards; or the dispersal of the routine production of goods and services to regions with reserves of 'green' labour; this represented a new element in the geography of production and helped to produce the migration turnround. In this way, the international migration and counter-urbanisation trends of the late 1960s and early 1970s can be viewed as a product of the further development of Fordist forms of production and consumption and of the rapid suburbanisation with which these were associated.

After the mid-1970s, when this post-war expansion came to an end, there began a period of reorganisation of what, how and where goods and services were to be produced. Slower growth in household incomes, jobless growth and heightened competition from low-cost producers in the Far East and elsewhere led to a sharp decline in the mass production in Western European countries of standardised goods for mass markets and in its built-form equivalent, the suburb. International migrant workers had not been major beneficiaries of the suburbanisation process but it had been their labour on the building sites and in the car factories which had made that process possible. So the fortunes of these two migrations, the intra-regional and the international, were closely connected; both of them declined numerically and the composition and direction of their migration streams changed as well. Economic restructuring also brought about major changes in interregional migration. The counter-urbanisation of the late 1960s and early 1970s had been as dependent as foreign worker migration and suburbanisation on a continuation of the form and pace of post-war economic growth.

After 1973, forms of production, now popularly characterised as 'flexible specialisation', and associated with 'productive decentralisation', became more important. This change also contributed to counter-urbanisation since the urban contexts favourable to such activities were not the large industrial cities of Fordist production but the small and medium-sized towns found in prestige environments and in non-peripheral and/or near metropolitan rural regions. It is not surprising, therefore, that there has not been a simple return to an 'urbanisation' form of the relationship between net migration and settlement size.

We might, therefore, conceive of the existence of two phases of counter-urbanisation (or decentralised urbanisation) which overlap in time and space. In the first phase, which reached its peak in the late 1960s and early 1970s, the decentralisation of employment and population was spearheaded by branch-plant and back-office developments; it favoured smaller labour markets over larger ones and free-standing towns over large industrial cities. In the second phase, which developed during the late 1970s and 1980s, the decentralisation was led by small-firm growth and high-technology industry; it was far more selective spatially, and its distribution tended to reflect the location of the key agents of the emergent entrepreneurial culture—the private-sector segment of the 'service class' of professional, technical and managerial workers.

NOTES

1. For a justification of the use of population density in these calculations see Fielding (1982, p. 33).
2. For a discussion of the problem of statistical underbounding in this data see Fielding (1986a, p. 236).

REFERENCES

Berry, B.J.L. (ed.) (1976) *Urbanization and Counterurbanization*. Beverly Hills, CA: Sage.

Fielding, A.J. (1982), 'Counterurbanization in Western Europe', *Progress in Planning*, vol. 17, no. 1, pp. 1-52.

Fielding, A.J. (1984) 'Trends in urban development in Western Europe'. Crowthorne, Berks: Transport and Road Research Laboratory. WP/SRB 26, mimeo.

Fielding, A.J. (1986a) 'Counterurbanization' in M. Pacione (ed.), *Population Geography: Progress and Prospect*. London: Croom Helm, pp. 224-56.

Fielding, A.J. (1986b) 'Counterurbanization in Western Europe' in A. Findlay and P. White (eds), *West European Population Change*. London: Croom Helm, pp. 35-49.

Owen, D.W. and Green, A.E. (1988) 'Spatial aspects of labour mobility in the 1980s'. University of Warwick, Institute of Employment Research, mimeo.

Zelinsky, W. (1983) 'The impasse in migration theory: a sketch map for potential escapees' in P.A. Morrison (ed.), *Population Movements: the Forms and Functions in Urbanization and Development*. Liège, Ordina: pp. 19-46.

Chapter 11

TRENDS AND STRUCTURE IN LONDON'S MIGRATION AND THEIR RELATION TO EMPLOYMENT AND HOUSING MARKETS

Peter Congdon and Tony Champion

INTRODUCTION

This chapter considers the role of migration to, from and within London in the context of metropolitan labour and housing markets. It assesses the influence on migration of differentials in employment and housing availability between the constituent boroughs of Greater London, and conversely the extent to which migration gains or losses have impacts on the demand for labour and housing. The reciprocal relations involved are studied within a simultaneous equations framework, while the specifically labour-market role of migration is examined in more detail using a labour-market accounts procedure.

Many theories of metropolitan residential mobility, particularly of decentralisation to the suburbs or beyond, have placed primary emphasis on the stimulus to migration of changes in housing demand associated with life-cycle transitions. The labour-market role of intra-metropolitan migration has not often been studied, although there is evidence from a number of studies of an interaction between workplace and residential relocation within large urban areas (Brown, 1975; Verster, 1985). This is in turn a reflection of the decentralisation of employment and the development of dispersed polycentric employment markets in metropolitan regions, albeit with a high degree of commuting overlap (Smart, 1974; Gordon *et al.*, 1986). Such dispersal reduces the extent to which residential decentralisation takes place in relation to fixed monocentric workplaces in a unitary labour market covering the entire metropolis.

Specifically, the question can be asked whether migration to and from London and its boroughs has an equilibrating role between labour sub-markets in the London region, in the same way as classical push-pull theory argues for migration between economic regions. Alternatively, the parallelism hypothesis of higher migration turnover in areas of prosperity might provide a more appropriate framework for evaluating the labour-market role of migration in London (Gleave and Cordey-Hayes, 1977).

A test of the labour- and housing-market role of migration entails a recognition of the feedback between migration, jobs and housing. However, within the overlapping labour markets of London, there is also the question of substitution or complementarity between migration and other modes by which labour demand adjusts to supply, such as changes in economic activity and in commuting (Congdon, 1983; Evers, 1989; Chalmers and Greenwood, 1985). These interactions are recognised in the two formal quantitative analyses of the chapter.

Two major empirical issues are to be addressed in this chapter. One is the extent to which migration fluctuations in London and the major borough groups can be related to employment and housing opportunities. Recent estimates show a sharp fall in net migration loss from London (Table 11.1). The average annual rate of net out-migration from London fell from 9.2 to 3.5 per thousand between 1976–81 and 1981–6 with the fall in the inner London rate (from 16 to 6 per thousand) being most marked. In particular, gross migration from inner to outer London of 91 000 in the 1971 Census pre-censal year fell to 52 000 in 1980–1. Similar trends towards metropolitan population revival (primarily through migration shifts) have been observed in other countries, particularly the US where metropolitan growth has overtaken non-metropolitan growth (Richter, 1985). This chapter argues for a multi-factorial explanation for the migration turnround in London in terms of the strength of London's economy *vis-à-vis* the rest of South-East England and of Britain, a relaxation of policies of planned population and employment decentralisation, and improved housing supply within London due to public- as well as private-sector house-building.

The other main question to be addressed is the extent to which differentials in migration to and from individual London boroughs can be related to the employment situation of those boroughs as against factors such as the supply of housing or the migration proneness of borough populations. Thus some accounts of migration from inner to outer London stress the role of private housing construction in the suburbs as the major underlying factor, rather than high employment losses in some inner London boroughs (Buck *et al.*, 1986). Again, high migrant turnover in certain central London areas may be primarily attributable to the socio-demographic composition of borough populations, while low turnover in others reflects the tenure balance of borough housing stock. The simultaneous equation analysis is particularly intended to resolve the question of alternative sources of migration flow to and from boroughs, though it also considers the causes and consequences of changes in migration flow (that is, turnround) at borough level.

EXPLAINING MIGRATION TURNROUND IN LONDON

A number of possible explanations have been proposed for fluctuations in migration to, from and within London. One obvious explanation of the recent downturn in net out-migration from London is an increase in the net inflow to London from overseas, due primarily to a fall in foreign emigration, though the most recent years also show a sharp upturn in immigration (Bulusu, 1986).

However, Table 11.1 makes clear that until 1983–5 net migration to London with respect to the rest of the world was relatively low (under 10 000 gain or loss per annum) and that the main source of fluctuations in London's net migration is flows to and from the rest of Great Britain, and particularly the rest of the South-East region (ROSE) outside London. Migration data from

Table 11.1 Migration to and from London, 1970–86

Year	Start Population	Natural Increase	Net Migration MYE[1]	In Rest GB[2] NHSCR/CENSUS	Out Rest GB NHSCR/CENSUS	Net Rest GB NHSCR/CENSUS	In Rest World[3] IPS/CENSUS	Out Rest World[3] IPS/CENSUS	Net Rest World[3] IPS/CENSUS	In Rest SE NHSCR/CENSUS	Out Rest SE NHSCR/CENSUS	Net Rest SE NHSCR/CENSUS
(Census)				140[5]	247[5]	−107[5]	105[5]			73[5]	166[5]	−93[5]
1970–71	7530	31	−120									
1971–72[4]	7529	22	−108									
1972–73	7443	15	−95									
1973–74	7362	9	−107									
1974–75	7264	5	−90									
1975–76	7179	−3	−87	160	242	−82	68	60	8	80	148	−68
1976–77	7089	2	−79	152	225	−73	62	57	6	76	137	−62
1977–78	7012	2	−67	161	227	−67	56	50	7	79	141	−62
1978–79	6947	9	−68	149	214	−65	59	49	10	70	131	−62
1979–80	6888	14	−51	143	194	−51	61	49	12	66	117	−51
1980–81	6851	15	−60	159	197	−39	55	55	0	73	121	−47
(Census)				107[5]	147[5]	−39[5]	66[5]			53[5]	95[5]	−42[5]
1981–82	6806	13	−56	150	183	−33	56	59	−3	72	114	−42
1982–83	6767	15	−27	158	189	−32	55	51	4	75	117	−43
1983–84	6755	16	−16	151	193	−42	59	39	20	70	122	−52
1984–85	6756	20	−9	158	193	−35	62	41	20	71	116	−45
1985–86	6768	22	−14	161	214	−53	80	42	38	71	132	−61
1986–87	6775	24	−33	168	228	−60	71	52	20	73	138	−65
1987–88	6770											

[1] MYE = Mid-year Estimates, NHSCR = National Health Service Central Register, IPS = International Passenger Survey
[2] Rest of Great Britain includes South East outside London
[3] Census figures for the Rest of the World includes Northern Ireland and the Irish Republic; IPS figures relate only to places outside the British Isles
[4] Change of mid-year estimate population base
[5] Census figures

Sources: OPCS Monitors MN and VS Series; 1971 and 1981 Census Regional Migration Reports; Special NHSCR Tabulations

the National Health Service Central Register (NHSCR) show a fall in out-migration from London to ROSE and Great Britain outside the South-East in recent years, at least until 1984–5. There has also been some upturn in in-migration to London from Great Britain outside the South-East.

Migration and the housing market

Some studies have argued that a major influence on population decentralisation (and hence on fluctuations in outflow from London) is the level of private house-building in ROSE. Decentralisation within London is also attributed to higher rates of private house building in outer London. The slow-down in net out-migration from London is therefore attributed, in this view, to reduced rates of new housing construction in the recession. A statistical correlation of 0.33 between the rate of net out-migration from London and private house-building in ROSE (lagged by a year) over 1961–86 confirms a positive relationship, but implies that only about 11% of fluctuations in London migrations are explained in this way.

One reason for this lack of correspondence can be seen from data from the Nationwide Anglia Building Society for newly mortgaged houses in 1986 (SERPLAN, 1986; Congdon, 1988). These data show that the majority of moves are within the existing stock rather than to new houses. It is also apparent from this source that most moves to new houses in ROSE (67%) and to existing houses (73%) are from within a 10-mile radius, and under 20% (18% for new and 15% for existing houses) are from over 25 miles. This suggests that new building at local level is more important for meeting local housing needs (indigenous household formation) rather than responding to (or stimulating) in-migration.

For migrants into and within London, new house-building would also seem a relatively small influence on destination choice. The Nationwide data for 1986 show that 60% of those moving to new properties in London are from within a five-mile radius. The majority of private house construction in London (which has been running at about 5000–6000 in recent years) is in outer London. Assuming most new housing is taken by local households suggests that a low proportion of longer-distance migrant households move into new private houses. Thus annual migration to outer London (from the rest of Great Britain including inner London) has been running at over 100 000 persons according to the Census and over 150 000 according to the NHSCR.

A related argument is that house-price differentials encourage movement to outer London and ROSE, and that fluctuations in relative house prices underlie migration fluctuations. However, the ratio of London to ROSE house prices was at low levels in the mid-1970s when London out-migration was still at high levels, and has risen since then while net out-migration has fallen. In fact, there is a negative correlation between net out-migration from London and the London–ROSE house-price ratio over years for which data are available (1969–86).

A more promising explanation (particularly as an influence on migration from London) lies in the ratio of dwelling costs to household incomes in London. In the short term at least house price rises can outstrip rises in incomes—for example, as a response to changes in the flow of credit for house-buying—and fluctuations in the ratio of house prices to incomes over 1966–86 have been considerable, and have been proposed as a source of migration fluctuations (Ogilvy, 1979, p.39). There is a positive correlation of 0.31 in this period between the rate of net out-migration from London and the lagged ratio of new house prices in London to disposable incomes (as recorded by Family Expenditure Surveys).

A more general explanation relating housing availability to the migration turnaround in London, particularly reduced out-migration from inner to outer London and to ROSE is in terms of the improved balance of dwelling supply to household demand. Continued increases in London's dwelling stock have occurred in the last two decades while the number of households has remained virtually constant. At borough level this association is particularly apparent in inner boroughs such as Barnet, Hackney, Islington, and Southwark, boroughs where there were large increases in public housing for rent during the later 1970s.

Migration and employment growth

In contrast to explanations of migration fluctuations and turnaround which stress housing factors, an alternative explanation is in terms of fluctuations in London's employment growth *vis-à-vis* the rest of the South-East and Great Britain. For the post-1981 period evidence from the Annual Census of Employment shows service jobs in London (excluding transport and utilities) to have increased from 2.30 million to 2.45 million between 1981 and 1986, with financial service jobs growing from 0.57 to 0.69 million. These trends reflect London's role as a financial centre (including the effect of the 'Big Bang' financial services deregulation), and policy changes including the ending of office relocation and winding down of New Town schemes (both of which encouraged employment decentralisation). This is presumably a major factor in the upturn of immigration to London from the rest of Great Britain, which is primarily for employment reasons. Certainly the recent and increasing net inflow of young in-migrants to white-collar and personal/retail service jobs can be related to London's continuing role as a service employment centre. The net flow of migrants in the 16–24 age group changed from -4000 in 1970–1 to $+15\,000$ in 1980–1, and NHSCR estimates of age-specific migration since 1981 confirm the trend.

A role of employment availability as a factor in population decentralisation from and within London can also be supported. Table 11.2 shows that over 30% of migrants from central or the rest of inner London to outer London (in 1970–1) worked in an outer London workplace within (on average) six months of migrating, whereas only about 10% of non-migrant inner London residents in 1971 worked in outer London; this implies a workplace relocation rate of about 20% within six months of migrating. Among migrants from London who moved to the outer metropolitan area (OMA, just beyond London's boundaries), 44% had changed to workplaces in that zone by 1971 whereas very few non-migrants living in London in 1971 (about 3%) had workplaces there. Among migrants to ROSE workplace relocation is even higher at about 70% in the first six months.

Table 11.2 Workplaces of migrants and non-migrants within London, 1970–1 (10% sample figures)

Residence 1970	Migrants						Non-migrants			
Residence 1971	Central Boroughs Outer Boroughs		Rest Inner Boroughs Outer Boroughs		Outer Boroughs Outer Boroughs		Central Boroughs Central Boroughs		Rest Inner Boroughs Rest Inner Boroughs	
Workplace 1971	Number	(%)	Number	(%)	Number	(%)	Number	(%)	Number	(%)
Central Boroughs	694	54	1 162	32	35 273	19	19 654	80	28 515	29
Rest Inner Boroughs	173	13	1 283	35	24 834	13	2 740	11	58 129	59
Outer Boroughs	392	30	1 164	32	117 809	63	1 937	8	11 275	11
Greater London	1 259	98	3 609	98	177 916	96	24 431	99	97 919	99
Outside GL	30	2	75	2	7 913	4	214	1	1 278	1

This association between residential and workplace decentralisation may be interpreted as either: (a) reflecting employment-related moves (or moves where residential and employment considerations coincide) due to higher employment growth in ROSE or in outer London as against inner London; or (b) as an adjustment of workplaces to changes of residence to minimise the time taken for and costs of the journey to work (Brown, 1975; Gordon *et al.*, 1986). By implication, the downturn in decentralising migration from London to ROSE in the early 1980s may be partly attributable to the effect of recession in reducing job-related residential relocation or to the relative improvement in London's employment growth.

To assess this, a regression of the annual percentage rate of net out-migration (NETOM) over 1966-7 to 1986-7 on (a) the London house-price-income ratio (RATIO); (b) the percentage employment growth in London (ΔEMP); and (c) the number, in thousands, of new private houses in the rest of the South-East (ΔPRHOU), with all three predictors lagged by a year, was undertaken. This gives the following (*t*-ratios in brackets):

$$\text{NETOM} = -0.335 + 0.204\,\text{RATIO} - 0.148\,\Delta\text{EMP} + 0.016\,\Delta\text{PRHOU} \quad R^2 = 0.75$$
$$\phantom{\text{NETOM} = }(0.9) \quad (1.9) \qquad\qquad (4.1) \qquad\qquad (3.4) \qquad\qquad\qquad (11.1)$$

All signs are in the expected direction, but the influence of employment availability as an equilibrating influence on migration fluctuations over time is apparent.

The role of migration as an equilibrating mechanism between areas as well as over time is also apparent in the relatively strong positive correlation between population and (workplace) employment growth in the inter-censal period 1971-81 (Tyler and Rhodes, 1986). Specifically across the South-East counties the following regression was estimated

$$\Delta\text{POP} = 3.38 + 0.61\,\Delta\text{EMP} \qquad R^2 = 0.59$$
$$\phantom{\Delta\text{POP} = }(2.4) \quad (3.8) \qquad\qquad\qquad\qquad\qquad (11.2)$$

suggesting that a 1% change in employment is matched by a 0.6% increase in population. Within London, there is also a positive correlation at borough level over 1971-81 between population and employment growth, with the estimated relation

$$\Delta\text{POP} = -6.52 + 0.49\,\Delta\text{EMP} \qquad R^2 = 0.23$$
$$\phantom{\Delta\text{POP} = }(3.0) \quad (3.0) \qquad\qquad\qquad\qquad\qquad (11.3)$$

suggesting that a 1% change in jobs leads to a 0.5% increase in population.

Migration and policy shifts

The influence of policy changes in explaining fluctuations in London out-migration has often been played down, with the argument that planned moves to New and Expanded Towns (NETs) have accounted for a relatively small part of the outward shift. Nevertheless the NET programme has played a significant contributory role in explaining the level of and fluctuations in London out-migration, particularly in view of the occurrence of 'private' moves to owner-occupied housing in NETs as well as planned moves to public sector housing; the high rates of employment growth in NETs often as a result of moves of firms from London, which have attracted many migrants, particularly skilled workers; and the growth of the hinterlands of NETs as they became significant labour-market centres.

Figures from the 1971 Census show migration to larger NETs in South-East England or their hinterland districts to be at around 17% of total out-migration from London to the ROSE in 1970–71—this excludes moves to some smaller Expanded Towns.[1] By 1980–1 the outflow had fallen to every NET except Milton Keynes and had fallen proportionately more (by about half) than the total outflow from London to the ROSE. Thus while planned and private moves to NETs are a minority of the total outflow from London they have a significant role in explaining migration fluctuations, namely the peak out-migration in the late 1960s and early 1970s and the recent downturn in out-migration.

MIGRATION AND LABOUR MARKET ADJUSTMENT IN LONDON AND THE SOUTH-EAST

The above analysis points to an explanation for migration turnround in London in terms of both employment and housing markets, as well as policy changes. Analysis at individual borough level using labour-market accounts is now used to highlight one aspect of migration causation mentioned above: the positive correlation between population and employment change. These accounts will confirm that migration by the economically active has an equilibrating role between boroughs with different levels of employment growth, and how this role is modified by other modes of labour-force adjustment.

The difference between growth in workplace employment and changes in the resident labour supply through natural increase or change in participation rates provides a measure of employment shortfall or possibly surplus (Champion *et al.*, 1982). This may be met either by net in- or out-migration by the economically active, or, in the overlapping labour sub-markets of London, by changes in the flow of net out- or in-commuting between boroughs.

In so far as they are equilibrating forces in the labour market, net out-commuting and -migration are expected to increase in areas of job shortfall and to decrease in areas of job surplus, and thereby to lessen differentials in unemployment change due to mismatches of job supply and resident workforce. A lack of correspondence between net out-migration and employment shortfall may reflect other influences on migration (housing supply or population characteristics); failures in the equilibrating role of migration, because the largest migration is between areas of economic strength rather than from areas of low to high demand; or the more significant role of other adjustment mechanisms (changes in participation and commuting) in equilibrating between areas with different rates of employment growth and availability.

Table 11.3 focuses on the components which are together responsible for the overall change in the size of the resident labour force of the counties of the South-East and the London boroughs in the inter-censal period 1971–81 (for which sufficient data are available for this type of analysis). The main features of the migration component in the South-East are the reduction in labour supply caused by net out-migration from London, and the major contributions to labour supply made by net in-migration to the fast-growing counties of Buckinghamshire and West Sussex. In the London boroughs the dominance of net out-migration tends to produce different relationships between the components of labour-force change. In boroughs with increasing or stable economically active populations (which are all suburban boroughs), the pattern is generally that net out-migration offsets large increases in female economic activity.

This preliminary analysis simply of changes in the resident labour force suggests that increased activity may compensate for net out-migration, but that increased activity and net in-migration are complementary aspects of labour-force growth. Analysis of changes in the labour force in relation to changes in local job supply (workplace employment) is shown in Table 11.4. The top half of the table shows the strong relationship between net in-migration and employment growth in many of the counties of the South-East.

Increases in out-commuting have tended to be greatest in counties to the north and east of London where job shortfalls in relation to in-migration have been highest (for example, Bedfordshire). However, growth counties to the west and south of London, either in the M4/Heathrow corridor, or containing fast-growing New Towns (such as Crawley in West Sussex) have reduced out-commuting. The general pattern is therefore of high employment growth stimulating high in-migration (primarily from London) and increases in self-containment. This pattern does not conform to the picture sometimes drawn of discrepancies between employment availability and in-migration, leading to rises in out-commuting to fixed London workplaces by immigrants.

Within London also commuting has served primarily as an equilibrating mechanism—with the highest increases being from employment shortfall boroughs, and with a correlation of 0.77 between the two indicators (Vickerman, 1984). There is little evidence that marked increases in out-commuting are associated with net in-migration to suburban boroughs, as would be the case if in-migration were independent of employment availability.

It is also apparent that out-migration has generally acted in an equilibrating fashion, if to a lesser extent than commuting (there being a correlation of 0.49 between out-migration and employment shortfall). Rates of net out-migration of over 15% characterise not only high-status central boroughs (such as Westminster and Kensington and Chelsea), but working-class boroughs such as Hackney and Tower Hamlets. It is often argued that the out-migration response from such boroughs is constrained by the characteristics of the population (low income and skill), and by reliance on rented municipal housing, the allocation rules for which (on the basis of length of residence) may inhibit mobility between boroughs. However, it is obvious that considerable out-migration from these boroughs has occurred, though constraints on mobility may explain why employment shortfall leads to higher increases in unemployment than in higher-status boroughs.

A SIMULTANEOUS EQUATION MODEL OF LONDON MIGRATION

Labour-market accounts have illustrated the role of both migration and commuting as labour-market adjustment mechanisms in the growth counties of the South-East and employment shortfall boroughs of inner London. It remains to assess the relation between employment, migration and other forms of labour-supply change in a general model recognising both the alternative sources of migration (housing as against employment availability, for example) and the consequences as well as the causes of migration. A simultaneous equations model recognises these feedbacks. It may also be used to control for the endogeneity between migration and other modes of labour-force adjustment such as changes in commuting or in labour-force participation. The data used relate to the inter-censal period 1971–81, and thus pre-date the pronounced migration turnround of the early 1980s, though borough-level turnround during the 1970s is included in the analysis.

Unexpected effects in single-equation migration models may reflect not only simultaneity bias but different processes of labour-force adjustment than postulated in classical equilibrating theory. Instead of the highest rates of out-migration occurring from areas with employment deficit an alternative view is that both in and out-migration will be highest from areas of economic strength, where occupational turnover associated with employment growth generates vacancies for in-migrants and high levels of outflow (Cordey-Hayes and Gleave, 1977).

Alternative models of migration in the labour market have implications for migration selectivity. While push-pull theory argues for high out-migration by low-income workers from areas of labour surplus, the parallelism model argues that buoyant local economies attract disproportionate numbers of young non-manual migrants and that high out-migration is related to concentrations of the migration-prone in such areas (Kennett, 1982, p.43).

The simultaneous equations framework below recognises the reciprocal feedback between employment, housing and migration and the possibility of differential causation according to the distance of migration, as well as allowing for interactions between migration and other modes by which labour demand adjusts to supply. Appendix 11.1 presents definitions of the variables used; note that all endogenous variables are on an annualised basis to be consistent with one-year migration rates. The gross out and in-migration equations (11.4)–(11.6) and (11.7)–(11.9) express the dependence of migration on measures of growth in employment, housing and income (ΔEMP, ΔHOU, ΔY); on residential and occupational turnover; and on characteristics of the population and household stock.

In view of evidence for an interaction between metropolitan population and job relocation, employment growth is included as a migration predictor at all spatial scales: moves between London boroughs, between London and ROSE, and between London and Great Britain outside the South-East. Endogeneity between migration and changes in economic participation is expected to be reflected in a negative relation between immigration and increases in female activity—since the latter is an alternative source of increases in the labour force. Status upgrading through selective in-migration is represented by the indicator GENTRIF (Hamnett and Williams, 1980).

In-migration is expected to be positively related to measures of employment and housing availability. However, the relation of out-migration to employment and income growth will depend on the applicability of the push-pull as against the parallelism hypotheses of migration. An equation (11.10) for net in-migration turnround between 1971–76 and 1976–81 is also included—in terms of employment and housing stock growth, and status upgrading.

Table 11.3 Changes in labour-force size, South-East counties and London boroughs, 1971–81 (*as percentage of 1971 total*)

	MALES			FEMALES			
	Change in activity rate	Natural change	Net in-migration	Change in activity rate	Natural change	Net in-migration	TOTAL
County							
Bedfordshire	-3.1	4.9	1.7	3.3	3.2	1.4	11.5
Berkshire	-2.1	5.3	2.8	3.2	2.6	1.7	13.5
Buckinghamshire	-3.0	4.7	8.6	3.1	2.9	4.9	21.1
East Sussex	-2.9	-1.3	3.4	2.1	-3.1	2.5	0.7
Essex	-2.5	3.8	3.0	2.7	1.6	1.9	10.5
Greater London	-2.8	0.0	-5.6	1.0	-1.2	-3.1	-11.8
Hampshire	-2.4	4.8	1.5	4.2	2.2	1.1	11.3
Hertfordshire	-2.1	4.1	0.1	2.7	2.3	-0.3	6.8
Isle of Wight	-2.5	-0.6	4.7	2.9	-1.6	3.4	6.3
Kent	-2.5	3.3	2.2	3.5	1.0	1.4	8.9
Oxfordshire	-0.1	5.9	-4.6	4.8	2.7	-0.8	7.9
Surrey	-2.4	2.0	0.2	3.7	0.4	-0.1	3.8
West Sussex	-2.5	1.9	8.4	3.1	-0.5	6.3	16.6
Borough							
Barking and Dagenham	-3.2	0.4	-6.5	0.8	-0.8	-2.5	-11.7
Barnet	-2.3	-0.3	-2.6	1.8	-2.1	-0.5	-6.1
Bexley	-2.1	1.0	-1.5	3.6	0.2	-0.7	0.5
Brent	-3.2	0.1	-5.8	0.4	-0.7	-2.9	-12.0
Bromley	-2.4	0.9	-1.5	4.3	-0.6	-1.0	-0.2
Camden	-2.1	-1.5	-8.3	-1.5	-2.8	-5.6	-21.9
Croydon	-2.1	2.0	-3.1	3.1	0.2	-2.1	-2.0
Ealing	-2.9	-0.3	-3.6	0.7	-1.1	-0.9	-8.1
Enfield	-2.6	-1.4	-0.1	1.4	-2.0	0.3	-4.3

Greenwich	-2.7	1.3	-2.3	1.5	-0.4	-0.0	-2.6
Hackney	-4.4	0.9	-11.3	-0.9	-0.0	-6.9	-22.7
Hammersmith and Fulham	-3.2	-1.4	-9.9	-0.6	-2.5	-5.8	-23.3
Haringey	-3.5	0.9	-7.1	-0.1	-0.5	-4.0	-14.4
Harrow	-2.6	-1.1	-1.4	3.5	-1.7	-0.4	-3.8
Havering	-1.8	3.3	-4.8	2.6	1.3	-2.7	-2.0
Hillingdon	-2.6	1.0	-3.1	3.1	-0.1	-1.7	-3.5
Hounslow	-2.9	-0.0	-1.6	0.6	-0.7	-0.2	-4.7
Islington	-2.8	0.0	-11.3	-0.4	-0.7	-6.5	-21.7
Kensington and Chelsea	-1.8	0.6	-14.4	-2.1	-3.1	-10.8	-31.6
Kingston upon Thames	-2.8	-1.8	-2.4	1.7	-2.8	-1.2	-9.3
Lambeth	-3.6	1.3	-10.8	-0.2	-0.1	-7.1	-20.6
Lewisham	-2.8	0.9	-7.7	1.9	-0.2	-4.7	-12.6
Merton	-3.2	-1.4	-3.7	1.1	-2.6	-1.8	-11.6
Newham	-3.8	1.0	-7.1	-0.5	-0.2	-2.7	-13.3
Redbridge	-1.9	-1.0	-2.8	2.1	-2.2	-0.9	-6.8
Richmond upon Thames	-2.5	-1.9	-2.7	2.3	-3.3	-1.2	-9.4
Southwark	-3.7	0.4	-10.4	-0.7	-0.5	-6.6	-21.5
Sutton	-2.3	-0.3	2.1	3.4	-1.4	1.5	3.0
Tower Hamlets	-4.2	0.7	-9.1	-2.6	0.2	-4.9	-20.0
Waltham Forest	-3.4	-2.0	-4.8	1.0	-2.5	-2.0	-13.6
Wandsworth	-2.8	-0.3	-8.6	1.0	-1.4	-4.9	-16.9
Westminster, City of	-2.3	-3.2	-9.9	-2.0	-4.1	-6.0	-27.7
Central London	-2.1	-1.6	-10.6	-1.9	-3.4	-7.2	-26.7
Rest of Inner London	-3.4	0.5	-9.3	-0.2	-0.6	-5.5	-18.5
Outer London	-2.6	0.0	-2.8	2.0	-1.1	-1.1	-5.6

Note 3(a) Figures may not sum precisely because of rounding.
(b) Central London includes City of London.

Table 11.4 Employment shortfall by borough and county, 1971–81 (*as percentage of 1971 economically active*)

	Economically active population 1971	Natural increase	Plus rise in participation	Less rise in employment	Equals employment shortfall	Of which net out-migration	Rise in net out-commuting	Rise in unemployment
County								
Bedfordshire	221 150	8.1	0.2	3.4	4.9	-3.2	3.0	5.1
Berkshire	298 180	7.9	1.1	11.2	-2.2	-4.5	-0.4	2.7
Buckinghamshire	225 980	7.6	0.1	15.1	-7.4	-13.5	1.7	4.3
East Sussex	269 830	-4.4	-0.9	-2.4	-2.9	-5.9	0.2	2.9
Essex	622 630	5.4	0.2	3.5	2.1	-4.9	3.2	3.8
Greater London	3 824 120	-1.1	-1.9	-12.5	9.5	8.7	-2.3	3.0
Hampshire	620 790	7.0	1.8	7.0	1.8	-2.5	0.7	3.6
Hertfordshire	446 780	6.4	0.6	0.4	6.5	0.2	3.0	3.4
Isle of Wight	43 810	-2.2	0.4	1.1	-2.9	-8.1	-0.1	5.3
Kent	609 050	4.3	1.0	4.2	1.2	-3.6	1.1	3.7
Oxfordshire	229 760	8.6	4.6	3.8	9.5	5.4	0.6	3.5
Surrey	467 710	2.4	1.3	3.4	0.3	0.0	-1.3	1.6
West Sussex	253 530	1.4	0.5	15.0	-13.1	-14.6	-1.7	3.3
Borough								
Barking and Dagenham	80 000	-0.3	-2.3	-11.5	8.9	9.0	-3.8	3.6
Barnet	152 490	-2.4	-0.5	-1.2	-1.7	3.2	-7.0	2.1
Bexley	105 570	1.2	1.4	-3.4	6.0	2.1	1.7	2.2
Brent	146 350	-0.6	-2.8	-9.4	6.0	8.6	-6.2	3.6
Bromley	147 890	0.3	1.9	3.0	-0.8	2.5	-5.2	1.9
Camden	115 490	-4.3	-3.7	-25.5	17.6	14.0	1.1	2.5
Croydon	165 420	2.2	1.0	-5.2	8.4	5.2	0.6	2.7
Ealing	158 910	-1.4	-2.2	-15.3	11.7	4.5	3.2	3.9
Enfield	134 680	-3.3	-1.2	-8.7	4.1	-0.2	1.2	3.1

Area								
Greenwich	107 240	0.9	−1.2	−7.0	6.7	2.3	−0.4	4.8
Hackney	111 720	0.9	−5.4	−27.8	23.3	18.2	−0.6	5.7
Hammersmith and Fulham	103 000	−3.9	−3.8	−12.7	5.1	15.7	−12.7	2.1
Haringey	123 910	0.3	−3.6	−10.9	7.6	11.1	−7.9	4.4
Harrow	100 150	−2.8	0.9	−0.5	−1.5	1.8	−4.9	1.6
Havering	122 620	4.6	0.8	−3.3	8.7	7.4	−1.8	3.0
Hillingdon	119 940	0.9	0.4	−13.1	14.5	4.8	7.1	2.5
Hounslow	109 670	−0.7	−2.3	1.8	−4.7	1.7	−9.7	3.2
Islington	107 330	−0.7	−3.2	−17.9	14.0	17.8	−7.5	3.7
Kensington and Chelsea	106 130	−2.5	−3.9	−10.3	3.8	25.1	−21.4	0.0
Kingston upon Thames	72 300	−4.6	−1.1	−11.7	6.1	3.6	0.3	2.1
Lambeth	161 520	1.1	−3.8	−8.7	6.0	17.9	−16.0	4.1
Lewisham	133 300	0.8	−0.9	−6.8	6.7	12.4	−9.7	4.0
Merton	92 390	−4.0	−2.1	−14.1	8.0	5.5	0.6	1.8
Newham	116 660	0.8	−4.3	−22.4	18.9	9.8	3.8	5.3
Redbridge	120 060	−3.2	0.1	−5.4	2.3	3.7	−3.8	2.4
Richmond upon Thames	90 310	−5.3	−0.2	−5.3	−0.2	3.9	−5.6	1.5
Southwark	138 900	−0.1	−4.3	−11.5	7.0	17.0	−13.3	3.3
Sutton	82 260	−1.7	1.0	7.4	−8.1	−3.6	−6.6	2.2
Tower Hamlets	87 550	0.8	−6.8	−36.4	30.4	14.0	11.2	5.2
Waltham Forest	119 550	−4.5	−2.4	−9.1	2.2	6.8	−8.3	3.7
Wandsworth	157 020	−1.7	−1.8	−7.6	4.1	13.4	−12.2	2.9
Westminster	130 240	−7.4	−4.4	−61.1	49.4	15.9	32.1	1.3
Central London	355 410	−5.0	−3.9	−45.5	36.5	17.8	17.4	1.3
Rest of Inner London	1 240 910	−0.1	−3.6	−15.0	11.2	14.8	−7.6	4.0
Outer London	2 227 800	−1.1	−0.5	−5.9	4.3	4.0	−2.5	2.8

Note: Central London includes City of London

$$\text{IMRGB} = f(\Delta\text{EMP, }\Delta\text{HOU, }\Delta\text{Y, OM, OCCMOB, }\Delta\text{EAF, GENTRIF, RLA}) \quad (11.4)$$
$$\text{IMRSE} = f(\Delta\text{EMP, }\Delta\text{HOU, }\Delta\text{Y, OM, OCCMOB, }\Delta\text{EAF, GENTRIF, RLA, PERIM}) \quad (11.5)$$
$$\text{IMRGL} = f(\Delta\text{EMP, }\Delta\text{HOU, }\Delta\text{Y, OCCMOB, }\Delta\text{EAF, GENTRIF, RLA}) \quad (11.6)$$
$$\text{OMRGB} = f(\Delta\text{EMP, }\Delta\text{Y, OCCMOB, YAD, PRM, RLA}) \quad (11.7)$$
$$\text{OMRSE} = f(\Delta\text{EMP, }\Delta\text{Y, OCCMOB, YAD, PRM, RLA, PERIM}) \quad (11.8)$$
$$\text{OMRGL} = f(\Delta\text{EMP, }\Delta\text{Y, OCCMOB, YAD, PRM, RLA}) \quad (11.9)$$
$$\Delta\text{NETIM} = f(\Delta\text{HOU, }\Delta\text{EMP, GENTRIF, NETIM7176}) \quad (11.10)$$
$$\Delta\text{OUTCOM} = f(\Delta\text{EMP, IM, UNSK, YAD, CARCOM}) \quad (11.11)$$
$$\Delta\text{INCOM} = f(\Delta\text{EMP, }\Delta\text{EAPOP, EMPDEN}) \quad (11.12)$$
$$\text{OCCMOB} = f(\Delta\text{EMP, IM, }\Delta\text{OUTCOM, YAD}) \quad (11.13)$$
$$\Delta\text{EAF} = f(\text{IM, }\Delta\text{Y, MANU, UNEMP}) \quad (11.14)$$
$$\Delta\text{EAPOP} = f(\Delta\text{EMP, NETIM, }\Delta\text{INCOM, }\Delta\text{EAF, }\Delta\text{YAD}) \quad (11.15)$$
$$\Delta\text{Y} = f(\Delta\text{EMP, NETIM}) \quad (11.16)$$
$$\Delta\text{EMP} = f(\text{NETIM, }\Delta\text{NETCOM, }\Delta\text{EAF, }\Delta\text{Y, EMPDEN, FINAN, DIST}) \quad (11.17)$$
$$\Delta\text{UNEMP} = f(\Delta\text{EMP, NETIM, }\Delta\text{NETCOM, }\Delta\text{YAD, UNSK, GENTRIF}) \quad (11.18)$$
$$\Delta\text{HOU} = f(\text{IM, }\Delta\text{Y, }\Delta\text{YAD}) \quad (11.19)$$
$$\Delta\text{PRHOU} = f(\text{IM, }\Delta\text{Y, }\Delta\text{YAD}) \quad (11.20)$$

Other types of labour-force adjustment (such as commuting and occupational mobility in equations (11.11)–(11.13), and changes in economic participation (equations (11.14) and (11.15) depend on employment creation and characteristics of the labour force but are also influenced by interactions with each other and with migration.

Whether net in-migration to areas has a positive or negative sign in the income-growth equation (11.16) depends in part on the differential characteristics of in- and out-migrants and on the extent to which the demand shift associated with in-migration exceeds or is less than the supply shift. However, greater rates of suburban relative to inner-city income growth may be attributable in part to differential rates of employment growth or loss—a positive effect of ΔEMP on ΔY being consistent with this hypothesis.

Equations (11.17) and (11.18), representing the change in employment and unemployment, are intended to represent the effect of employment growth on unemployment, and the role of migration and commuting in reducing unemployment differentials. Net immigration is expected to raise both labour supply and demand, and thus stimulate employment growth. In-commuting is particularly expected to raise labour supply but may also raise demand for services in the receiving area (Berry and Kasarda, 1977). The relation of employment growth to existing concentrations of employment (a measure of external economies) is represented by employment density per hectare (EMPDEN), while the dependence of employment growth on distance from London's centre (DIST) reflects factors such as high land costs and lack of space for physical expansion in inner-city areas (particularly for manufacturing). The role of producer services (financial and business services, FINAN) in stimulating the recent employment turnround in London is also included.

The extent to which employment growth or loss reduces or enhances unemployment differentials (equation (11.18)) may be attenuated if such growth or loss is diffused over sub-labour markets by changes in commuting and perhaps migration (NETCOM and NETIM). Unemployment differentials may also reflect the skill characteristics of the labour force, and also perhaps natural increases in the labour force in excess of job increases (or typically job losses in inner London).

Changes in total and private dwelling stock are related to demand for housing through natural increase in potential households (ΔYAD). It is expected that demand will increase with incomes, this being particularly so of moves to new owner-occupied housing. In-migration is also expected to increase household formation and stimulate housing supply.

RESULTS

Migration equations

Regression coefficients for equations (11.4)–(11.20) are given in Table 11.5. The estimated coefficients for the long-distance immigration equations (11.4) and (11.5) show a strong influence of labour-market factors, though they point to turnover in areas of high occupational mobility as well as to a positive (equilibrating) influence of employment growth. Increases in the labour force through changes in (female) economic participation reduce the level of employment immigration (Chalmers and Greenwood, 1985).

The influence of the labour market is modified by housing supply and composition. Thus, boroughs with a large municipal sector have low rates of long-distance immigration. Nevertheless, increases in total housing stock (both public and private) enhance the rate of long-distance immigration, perhaps by creating vacancies in the private rented sector, which attracts disproportionate numbers of immigrants.

For immigration within London (equation (11.6)), only occupational mobility is used as a measure of turnover since the decentralising tendency of intra-metropolitan migration is not expected to be reflected in a positive relation between inflow and outflow. Occupational turnover in relatively buoyant local labour markets boosts such immigration, while employment growth is not significant. Immigration is also lower to boroughs with large stocks of public rented housing, though growth in total (public and private) housing stock has a positive effect on intra-London moves.

It is sometimes argued that the development of private housing in suburban London is a major influence on metropolitan decentralisation. However, when the rate of new private building is substituted for all types of housing development (equation (11.6′)) then an equilibrating role of intra-London migration in the labour market becomes apparent, and private housing growth has an unexpected negative sign. This suggests that the positive correlation between private housing growth and employment gain may suppress the role of employment availability as an influence on intra-London flows. One interpretation is that private housing growth has been concentrated in high-income suburban boroughs and is associated with relatively low inflow to high-cost developments (cf. Greenwood, 1980, p.492). Control for new private building also enhances the role of gentrification as a source of higher immigration from elsewhere in London.

Longer-distance out-migration (equations (11.7) and (11.8) shows some conformity to a parallelism model. In particular, out-migration to Great Britain outside the South-East is positively related to concentrations of the migration-prone—young adult non-manual workers—and to residential and occupational turnover. However, a secondary equilibrating role is apparent with higher out-migration from boroughs with higher employment losses.

Table 11.5 Two-stage least squares estimates of simultaneous migration model (regression coefficients with t-ratios in parentheses)

Equation		Variation explained (R^2)
11.4	IMRGB $= -1.37 + 0.18\ \Delta$EMP $+ 0.33\ \Delta$HOU $+ 0.02\ \Delta$Y $+ 0.15$ OM $+ 0.09$ OCCMOB (1.6) (2.6) (1.9) (1.0) (4.7) (2.9) $-1.31\ \Delta$EAF $- 0.01$ RLA $- 0.11$ GENTRIF (2.8) (2.4) (1.4)	0.93
11.5	IMRSE $= 0.13 + 0.27\ \Delta$EMP $+ 0.13\ \Delta$HOU $+ 0.00\ \Delta$Y $+ 0.07$ OM $+ 0.05$ OCCMOB (0.1) (2.0) (0.5) (0.0) (1.4) (1.1) $-1.06\ \Delta$EAF $- 0.01$ RLA $+ 0.07$ GENTRIF $+ 0.28$ PERIM (1.5) (1.0) (0.7) (1.5)	0.78
11.6	IMRGL $= 4.86 + 0.00\ \Delta$EMP $+ 0.66\ \Delta$HOU $- 0.12\ \Delta$Y $+ 0.19$ OCCMOB (1.4) (0.0) (1.0) (1.4) (1.6) $-2.23\ \Delta$EAF $- 0.04$ RLA $+ 0.33$ GENTRIF (1.5) (2.6) (1.0)	0.59
11.6'	IMRGL $= 13.57 + 1.30\ \Delta$EMP $- 5.43\ \Delta$PRHOU $- 0.25\ \Delta$Y $- 0.02$ OCCMOB (4.3) (2.6) (2.8) (3.2) (0.3) $-1.36\ \Delta$EAF $- 0.04$ RLA $+ 1.02$ GENTRIF (1.0) (3.5) (3.0)	0.68
11.7	OMRGB $= -1.93 - 0.09\ \Delta$EMP $+ 0.02\ \Delta$Y $+ 0.03$ OCCMOB $+ 0.10$ YAD (2.9) (1.5) (0.9) (1.7) (3.8) $+ 0.02$ PRM (4.4)	0.79
11.8	OMRSE $= 1.20 - 0.06\ \Delta$EMP $+ 0.01\ \Delta$Y $+ 0.05$ OCCMOB $- 0.05$ YAD (1.1) (0.5) (0.4) (1.5) (1.1) $+ 0.01$ PRM $+ 0.45$ PERIM (1.4) (2.4)	0.74
11.9	OMRGL $= -7.78 - 1.08\ \Delta$EMP $- 0.22\ \Delta$Y $+ 0.02$ OCCMOB $+ 0.79$ YAD (2.0) (2.8) (2.1) (0.2) (5.2) $+ 0.13$ PRM (3.8)	0.86
11.10	ΔNETIM $= -0.65 + 0.89\ \Delta$HOU $+ 0.34\ \Delta$EMP $- 0.20$ GENTRIF $- 0.45$ NETIM7176 (1.8) (2.8) (2.0) (1.0) (3.3)	0.58
11.11	ΔOUTCOM $= 0.18 - 0.18\ \Delta$EMP $+ 0.06$ IM $+ 0.03$ UNSK $+ 0.02$ CARCOM (0.2) (2.1) (1.0) (1.5) (1.8) -0.11 YAD	0.56

$$11.11' \quad \Delta\text{OUTCOM} = -1.39 - 0.17\,\Delta\text{EMP} + 1.22\,\text{IM(RGL)} + 0.30\,\text{UNSK} + 0.21\,\text{CARCOM}$$
$$(0.1)\ (1.7) \qquad (0.8) \qquad\qquad (1.2) \qquad (1.4)$$
$$- 0.99\,\text{YAD}$$
$$(2.2)$$
$$R^2 = 0.56$$

$$11.12 \quad \Delta\text{INCOM} = 0.64 + 0.19\,\Delta\text{EMP} - 0.06\,\text{OM} - 0.41\,\Delta\text{EAPOP} - 0.00\,\text{EMPDEN}$$
$$(2.3)\ (1.7) \qquad (1.1) \qquad (2.4) \qquad\qquad (1.9)$$
$$R^2 = 0.31$$

$$11.13 \quad \text{OCCMOB} = -3.32 + 1.66\,\Delta\text{EMP} + 1.09\,\text{IM} + 7.48\,\Delta\text{OUTCOM} + 0.55\,\text{YAD}$$
$$(0.3)\ (1.3) \qquad (2.1) \qquad (1.5) \qquad\qquad (0.8)$$
$$R^2 = 0.23$$

$$11.14 \quad \Delta\text{EAF} = 0.41 + 0.01\,\Delta\text{Y} - 0.05\,\text{IM} - 0.01\,\text{MANU} - 0.04\,\text{UNEMP}$$
$$(0.8)\ (0.9) \qquad (2.4) \qquad (2.5) \qquad\qquad (2.2)$$
$$R^2 = 0.70$$

$$11.15 \quad \Delta\text{EAPOP} = 0.40 + 0.20\,\Delta\text{EMP} + 0.85\,\text{NETIM} - 1.29\,\Delta\text{INCOM} - 0.74\,\Delta\text{EAF}$$
$$(1.4)\ (1.2) \qquad (6.2) \qquad\qquad (3.1) \qquad\qquad (0.9)$$
$$+ 1.07\,\Delta\text{YAD}$$
$$(2.4)$$
$$R^2 = 0.90$$

$$11.16 \quad \Delta\text{Y} = 27.56 + 0.70\,\Delta\text{EMP} + 2.04\,\text{NETIM}$$
$$(36.0)\ (0.8) \qquad\qquad (2.9)$$
$$R^2 = 0.50$$

$$11.17 \quad \Delta\text{EMP} = -0.76 + 0.74\,\text{NETIM} + 1.14\,\Delta\text{NETCOM} - 0.08\,\Delta\text{EAF} - 0.08\,\Delta\text{Y}$$
$$(0.3)\ (1.8) \qquad\qquad (1.9) \qquad\qquad (0.1) \qquad (0.9)$$
$$+ 0.05\,\text{FINAN} + 0.001\,\text{EMPDEN} + 0.08\,\text{DIST}$$
$$(1.6) \qquad\qquad (1.3) \qquad\qquad (1.9)$$
$$R^2 = 0.64$$

$$11.18 \quad \Delta\text{UNEMP} = 0.04 - 0.10\,\Delta\text{EMP} - 0.03\,\text{NETIM} + 0.16\,\Delta\text{NETCOM} + 0.30\,\Delta\text{YAD}$$
$$(0.5)\ (3.4) \qquad (1.0) \qquad\qquad (2.9) \qquad\qquad (3.1)$$
$$+ 0.01\,\text{UNSK} - 0.05\,\text{GENTRIF}$$
$$(2.0) \qquad (1.9)$$
$$R^2 = 0.93$$

$$11.19 \quad \Delta\text{HOU} = 1.81 - 0.04\,\text{IM} - 0.04\,\Delta\text{Y} + 0.90\,\Delta\text{YAD}$$
$$(1.2)\ (0.2) \qquad (0.7) \qquad (1.7)$$
$$R^2 = 0.34$$

$$11.19' \quad \Delta\text{HOU} = 1.14 + 0.30\,\Delta\text{NETIM} - 0.02\,\Delta\text{Y} + 0.96\,\Delta\text{YAD}$$
$$(1.9)\ (3.6) \qquad\qquad (0.7) \qquad (2.7)$$
$$R^2 = 0.54$$

$$11.20 \quad \Delta\text{PRHOU} = -0.73 + 0.01\,\text{IM} + 0.04\,\Delta\text{Y} - 0.10\,\Delta\text{YAD}$$
$$(1.5)\ (0.2) \qquad (2.6) \qquad (0.3)$$
$$R^2 = 0.29$$

$$11.20' \quad \Delta\text{PRHOU} = -1.02 + 0.09\,\text{IM(RSE/RGB)} + 0.04\,\Delta\text{Y} + 0.21\,\Delta\text{YAD}$$
$$(2.3)\ (1.3) \qquad\qquad (3.1) \qquad (0.6)$$
$$R^2 = 0.33$$

By contrast, short-distance out-migration from London boroughs to elsewhere in the metropolis (equation (11.9)) appears to be primarily a movement away from areas of high employment losses and low-income growth.[2] Hence the impression derived from labour-market accounts—that substantial out-migration has occurred from areas with large employment deficits—is confirmed by formal regression methods allowing for simultaneity between migration and employment. These results support the applicability of the push-pull model at least to shorter-distance decentralising moves, which account for the majority of out-migration from most London boroughs, and are particularly important in net out-migration from deprived low-income boroughs.

The estimated equations for gross migration rates suggest that employment losses have stimulated emigration, and job gains have stimulated immigration. The equation for turnround in net migration between the early and late 1970s confirms the role of employment growth as a source of reduced net out-migration. However, increases in housing stock are also a significant influence—for example, in inner boroughs such as Southwark and Islington with large increases in municipal housing in the late 1970s, and with pronounced reductions in net out-migration. The effect of initial net migration levels (NETIM7176) on migration shift expresses the greater reductions in net out-migration in previously high migration-loss inner-London boroughs. However, gentrification in inner London is not a source of migration gain, perhaps because the early stages of gentrification, with displacement of households from multiply-occupied privately rented dwellings, are associated with population loss (Hamnett and Randolph, 1982).

Commuting and occupational mobility

Increases in out-commuting are highest from boroughs with large employment losses, a 1% loss of employment leading to a 0.18 percent point increase in the rate of out-commuting—so that, like migration, commuting acts to equilibrate the supply and demand for labour. This is also apparent in the negative effect of indigenous labour force growth (ΔEAPOP) on in-commuting—such commuting offsets declines in labour supply throughout-migration which are in excess of the loss of employment.

However, unlike migration which is positively related to concentrations of prone social groups (young adult non-manual workers), out-commuting has increased most from boroughs with relatively low numbers of young adults, and is positively related to low skill. Hence the residentially immobile appear to commute as a substitute response to job losses. There is a secondary mode effect in that out-commuting has also increased in areas with high car commuting—for example, as a result of increased orbital worktrips in suburban London, where employment has been relatively buoyant.

It has been argued by some workers that population decentralisation within London and beyond has not been related to suburban job availability and is therefore associated with increased out-commuting to unchanged inner London workplaces (Buck *et al.*, 1986). The immigration coefficient in the out-commuting equation has the direction consistent with this, but is not statistically significant even when immigration is restricted to elsewhere in London (equation 11.11'). Similarly there is no evidence that in-commuting has increased most to those boroughs with the highest out-migration.

Occupational mobility tends to be higher in boroughs with employment growth (or lower job losses) where job vacancies are higher, and so is a positive function of excess demand (Cheshire, 1979). Such turnover interacts with migration, a 1% rise in the rate of in-migration being matched by a corresponding increase in occupational turnover. This effect and the positive relation of occupational turnover to concentrations of mobility-prone young adults tend to conform with the parallelism model of high labour mobility in prosperous boroughs (Gleave and Cordey-Hayes, 1977). However, occupational mobility has a secondary equilibrating role—as it complements increased out-commuting from areas of employment loss.

Changes in participation

Increases in economic participation, like commuting and occupational mobility, represent an alternative to migration in the face of employment growth or loss (Chalmers and Greenwood, 1985). Changes in participation show evidence of both a discouraged-worker effect—lower rises in participation in areas of high unemployment—and a positive relation to increases in average earnings. However, increases in labour supply through in-migration reduce increase in female participation, so that migration and changes in activity appear as substitute equilibrating mechanisms within London. Opportunities for women are also affected by employment structure, being less in boroughs with concentrations of manufacturing.

Changes in participation do not appear to be a major influence on changes in the economically active population, though this is partly because of a high correlation between the instruments for net in-migration and rises in female participation. Apart from the major contribution of migration to changes in the resident labour force (confirming the labour-market accounts) it is apparent that increases in in-commuting reduce the increase in the indigenous labour supply. Changes in the labour force through natural increase are also significant.

Employment and unemployment

The positive coefficient for net in-migration in the employment-growth equation confirms the link between migration and increases in prosperity, and suggests that employment decentralisation is in part a response to that of population. Conversely, employment losses in inner London are partly caused by net out-migration of the labour force and the associated reduction in demand for services and products. To the extent that population decentralisation outstrips that of employment, increased net in-commuting acts to counterbalance the loss of labour force through net out-migration, confirming the labour-market accounts. The positive sign for net in-commuting suggests that the demand effects of commuting reinforce those on supply; for example, increased in-commuting will raise demand for daytime services.

The links between population and employment decentralisation do not completely express the advantages of suburban location for new employment—since the distance variable remains significant. However, new employment in the suburbs tends to cluster around existing centres of employment—hence the positive effect of employment density. When the decentralising nature of employment change is controlled for, the structural advantage of high concentrations of financial and business employment becomes apparent.

Since migration and commuting equilibrate differences in excess demand for labour, they might be expected to reduce unemployment differentials. As the labour-market accounts suggest, changes in commuting have a more important role here—with increases in in-commuting tending to reduce jobs available for the local labour force, and hence raising unemployment, while increases in out-commuting reduce unemployment (Vickerman, 1984). The effect of net in-migration is positive though insignificant, suggesting that migration's effect in increasing labour supply is offset by its effect in raising product demand. The complete elimination of differentials in excess or deficit demand by migration or commuting would only occur if London were a single labour market. Hence employment losses in inner London explain at least part of the higher unemployment experienced there (cf. Buck *et al.*, 1986, Chapter 5), even if this link is attenuated by commuting across labour-market boundaries.

That labour force composition still has an effect on differentials in unemployment growth suggests that not all such differentials are explicable in terms of demand (Cheshire, 1979). Net out-migration has been socially selective and acted to increase concentrations of low-skill manual workers in inner-city municipal housing; such workers face a problem of mismatch of skills in relation to the growth of higher-level service jobs in inner areas. Increases in the young adult labour force—among whom unemployment rates are particularly high, especially for ethnic minorities—also tend to raise unemployment. Status upgrading in some parts of inner London may, however, displace low-skill workers prone to unemployment by high-skill workers and reduce the growth of unemployment (Evans and Russell, 1980).

Housing

The equations for housing growth (total and private) show relatively little dependence on total in-migration. However, when inflows are confined to those from outside London, in-migration becomes a significant positive influence on private housing supply (equation (11.20′)). This may be because longer-distance migrants include more high-income workers or because they lack information about the existing stock, while intra-metropolitan moves appear to be more likely to occur within that stock (Wyatt and Winger, 1971).

These results cast further doubt on the relation of metropolitan decentralisation and the location of private housing growth in suburban London. For total housing growth turnround in net migration rather than the rate of immigration appears most significant, illustrating the interdependence between turnround and the improved household–dwelling balance in the 1970s (equation (11.19′)). Household formation and effective demand for new private housing also depend on income, with the largest increases in private housing in suburban boroughs where incomes have also increased fastest (such as Sutton and Bromley). Changes in the demand for housing through natural increase of young adults is a more significant influence on total than private housing growth.

CONCLUSIONS

This chapter has considered the labour- and housing-market role of metropolitan migration both at the level of London and its main borough groups, and at the individual borough level. It has argued that migration turnround in the late 1970s and early 1980s can be explained in terms of changes in London's economy and policy shifts as well as in terms of housing supply. Investigation of migration differentials at borough level using labour-market accounts and a simultaneous equations model has found evidence for the influence of migration at all spatial scales in the labour market, and with much evidence pointing towards an equilibrating role. These results cast doubt on theories of residential mobility in metropolitan areas which do not take account of labour-market structure and job availability.

The equilibrating role for migration emerges despite constraints on migration from inner-city London boroughs with high unemployment, and despite some tendency for parallel migration between areas with the greatest turnover in employment. Particular counties in ROSE with the highest levels of employment growth depended on net in-migration (primarily from London) for such growth, as indigenous changes in labour supply were insufficient. Further support for the interdependence of employment and population relocation is provided by changes in commuting: out-commuting has not increased most from counties and boroughs where net in-migration has been highest, as would be the case if residential decentralisation occurred without employment relocation.

The primacy of housing supply in theories stressing housing rather than workplace adjustment is also thrown into doubt by the low level of new building in relation to that of in-migration, and evidence that most new private stock is occupied by local rather than immigrant households. The findings of this chapter, while specific to one city and to the last decade or so, thus point to the necessity for a re-evaluation of the role of metropolitan labour-market structure in stimulating differentials in gross and net migration between component metropolitan areas.

NOTES

1. The New and Expanded Town districts are Ashford; Aylesbury; Basildon; Basingstoke; Bracknell; Braintree; Crawley; Harlow; Hastings; Luton; Milton Keynes; Stevenage; and Welwyn/Hatfield. Together with Hemel Hempstead New Town, these accounted for 28 100 migrants from London to ROSE in 1970–1 out of a total of 166 000 but in 1980–81 for only 14 700 out of a total of 95 000.
2. Housing growth was found to have an unexpectedly positive influence on out-migration, and is not included in the final estimation.

REFERENCES

Berry, J. and Kasarda, J. (1977) *Contemporary Urban Ecology*. New York: Macmillan.

Brown, H. (1975) 'Changes in workplace and residential location', *Journal of the American Institute of Planners*, vol. 41, pp. 32–9.

Buck, N., Gordon, I. and Young, K. (1986) *The London Employment Problem*. Oxford: Clarendon Press.

Bulusu, L. (1986) 'Recent patterns of migration to and from the United Kingdom', *Population Trends*, vol. 46.

Chalmers, J. and Greenwood, M. (1985) 'The regional labor market adjustment process: determinants of changes in rates of labor force participation, unemployment and migration', *Annals of Regional Science*, vol. 19, pp. 1–17.

Champion, A., Gillespie, A. and Owen, D. (1982) 'Population and the labour market, with special reference to growth areas in the U.K.' in *Population Change and Regional Labour Markets*. OPCS Occasional Paper 28. London: HMSO.

Cheshire, P. (1979) 'Inner areas as spatial labour markets: a critique of inner area studies', *Urban studies*, vol. 16, pp. 29–43.

Congdon, P. (1983) 'A model for the interaction of migration and commuting', *Urban Studies*, vol. 20, pp. 185–95.

Congdon, P. (1988) Migration trends in and around London. Reviews and Studies 37. London: London Research Centre.

Evans, A. and Russell, L. (1980) 'A portrait of the London labour market' in A. Evans and D. Eversley (eds), *The Inner City: Employment and Industry*. London: Heinemann.

Evers, G. (1989) 'Migration, Population and Regional Labour Supply', Chapter 13 in *Advances in Regional Demography: Information, Forecasts, Models*. London, Belhaven Press.

Gleave, D. and Cordey-Hayes, M. (1977) 'Migration dynamics and labour market turnover', *Progress in Planning*, vol. 8, no. 1.

Gordon, P., Richardson, H. and Wong, H. (1986) 'The distribution of population and employment in a polycentric city: the case of Los Angeles', *Environment and Planning*, vol. 18A, pp. 161–73.

Greenwood (1980) 'Metropolitan growth and the intrametropolitan location of employment, housing and labour force', *Review of Economics and Statistics*, vol. 62, pp. 491–501.

Hamnett, C. and Williams P. (1980) 'Social change in London: a study of gentrification'. *The London Journal*, vol. 6, pp. 51–66.

Hamnett, C. and Randolph, B. (1982) 'How far will London's population fall? A commentary on the 1981 Census', *London Journal*, vol. 8, pp. 95–106.

Kennett, S. (1982) 'Migration between British local labour markets and some speculation on policy options for influencing population distributions' in *Population Change and Regional Labour Markets*. OPCS Occasional Paper 28. London: HMSO.

Ogilvy, A. (1979) 'Migration—the influence of economic change', *Futures*, vol. 11, pp. 383–94.

Richter, K. (1985) 'Non-metropolitan growth in the late 1970s: the end of the turn-around', *Demography*, vol. 22, pp. 245–63.

SERPLAN (1986) *Regional trends in the South East. The South East Regional Monitor, 1985–86*. RPC 535. London: SERPLAN.

Smart, M. (1974) 'Labour market areas: uses and definitions', *Progress in Planning*, vol. 2, no. 4

Tyler, P. and Rhodes, J. (1986) 'South East employment and housing study'. Discussion Paper no. 15. University of Cambridge, Department of Land Economy.

Verster, A. (1985) 'Commuting costs and the residential mobility of job changers', *Transportation Planning and Technology*, vol. 10, pp. 193–207.

Vickerman (1984) 'Urban and regional change, migration and commuting—the dynamics of workplace, residence and transport choice', *Urban Studies*, vol. 21, pp. 15–29.

Wyatt, G. and Winger, A. (1971) 'Residential construction, mover origin and urban form', *Regional Studies*, vol. 5, pp. 95–9.

APPENDIX 11.1 VARIABLE DEFINITIONS

Endogenous variables

OM(RGB/RSE/RGL): Out-migration to Great Britain outside the South East, the South East outside London and the rest of London (excluding intra-borough moves) as a percentage of Census population, average of 1970–1 and 1980–1 rates.

IM(RGB/RSE/RGL): In-migration rates defined as for out-migration.

OM = OM(RGB) + OM(RSE) + OM(RGL): Total out-migration rate.

IM = IM(RGB) + IM(RSE) + IM(RGL): Total in-migration rate.

NETIM = IM − OM: Estimated rate of annual net in-migration.

ΔNETIM: Change in rate of annual net in-migration, 1976–81 rate minus 1971–6 rate.

ΔOUTCOM: Percentage point difference (over 10) in rate of out-commuting between 1971 and 1981.

ΔINCOM: Percentage point difference (over 10) in rate of in-commuting between 1971 and 1981.

ΔNETCOM = ΔINCOM − ΔOUTCOM: Estimated annual change in net in-commuting.

OCCMOB: Percent of employed residents in each borough in 1980 who changed occupation or employer during 1980–1 (from 1981 EEC Labour Force Survey).

ΔEAPOP: Percentage change (over 10) in the economically active population in 1971–81.

ΔEAF: Percentage point difference (over 10) between 1971 and 1981 in percentage of women over minimum working age who are economically active.

ΔY: Percentage change (over 10) in household gross incomes (Source: 1971 and 1981 Greater London Transportation Surveys).

ΔEMP: Percentage change (over 10) in workplace employment in each borough during inter-censal period.

ΔUNEMP: Percentage point difference (over 10) in unemployment rate (percentage of economically active population out of work).

ΔHOU: Completions in 1971–81 (over 10) as a percentage of 1971 dwellings. (Source: Department of Environment Housing Statistics and 1971 Census)

ΔPRHOU: Private housing completions in 1971–81 (over 10) as a percentage of 1971 dwellings.

Exogenous variables

CARCOM: Percentage of commuters in a borough using a car for the trip to work (average of 1971 and 1981 rates).

DIST: Distance (in kilometres) of the population centroid of each borough from the City of London.

EMPDEN: Employment density, employment (in thousands) divided by area in hectares (average of 1971 and 1981 figures).

FINAN: Percentage of working population in each borough in 1981 employed in financial or business services (SICs 81–83, 85, 93–95).

GENTRIF: Equals one if rate of immigration by professional and managerial workers during 1980–1 (as percentage of 1981 economically active population) exceeds the London average, zero otherwise.

MANU: Percentage of the working population in a borough in manufacturing employment (average of 1971 and 1981 rates).

NETIM7176: Annual net in-migration during 1971–6 as recorded by Registrar General's mid-year estimates, divided by the average of the 1971 and 1976 estimates.

PERIM: Equals one for boroughs lying on outer boundary of London, zero otherwise.

PRM: Percentage of economically active males in professional and managerial occupations, socio-economic groups 1, 2, 3, 4, and 13 (average of 1971 and 1981 rates).

RLA: Percentage of households rented from a local authority (average of 1971 and 1981 rates).

UNEMP: Rate of unemployment, as percentage of economically active population (average of 1971 and 1981 rates).

UNSK: Percentage of economically active males in semi- and unskilled manual occupations, SEGs 7, 10, 11 and 15 (average of 1971 and 1981 rates).

YAD: Percentage of persons in each borough aged 15–24 (average of 1971 and 1981 rates).

ΔYAD: Percentage point difference (over 10) of persons in each borough aged 15–24 between 1971 and 1981.

Chapter 12

MIGRATION TRENDS AND POPULATION PROJECTIONS FOR THE ELDERLY

Philip Rees, John Stillwell and Peter Boden

CONTEXT AND REVIEW

There is increasing recognition that the process in which populations move from a regime of high mortality and fertility to one of low mortality and fertility via an intermediate stage of spectacular growth, has a long after-effect in which the age structure changes systematically. This is manifest in a dramatic ageing of the population, first because survival chances to and in the elderly ages improve, and second because the elderly from earlier high-fertility cohorts make up an increasing share of a population whose newest cohorts are either the same size or smaller than those that have gone before.

The British population, by and large, passed through this after-phase of the demographic transition between 1911 and 1981, when the percentage of the population aged 65+ rose from 5.1 to 15.1 (OPCS and CSO, 1984; Rees and Warnes, 1986). As the smaller cohorts born in the 1920s and 1930s move into the elderly population over the rest of this century, a cessation of the overall ageing process is anticipated with only 14.4% aged 65 or over in 2001 (projections reported in Rees, 1986). Other projections (OPCS, 1985; World Bank, 1984) see continued improvement in the survival chances of the elderly and a small increase (8%) is anticipated by the end of the century.

This picture of relative stationarity in Britain's elderly population is misleading if we look beyond the end of the twentieth century at ageing within the elderly population itself, or at the degree of spatial variation across the country in age composition at small or large scales. The spatial variation in the elderly population has been described in detail by Law and Warnes (1976), Warnes and Law (1984), OPCS and CSO (1984), Rees and Warnes (1986) and Champion et al. (1987), and we draw on these descriptions to build a picture of the geography of the elderly in the UK. The areas with the greatest concentrations of elderly are found in peripheral, rural and coastal locations away from the major metropolitan areas. Areas in which more than 20% of the population in 1981 was in the pensionable ages (65+ for men, 60+ for women) include coastal districts of Kent, East and West Sussex in the South-East region; most of Dorset, Devon and Cornwall plus the Cotswolds area in the South-West region; coastal and inland Dyfed, southern Powys, the Dwyfor, Merionnydd and Aberconwy districts of Gwynedd and coastal Clwyd in Wales; the Southport, Blackpool, Morecambe and Kendal areas of the North-West and Cumbria; the Harrogate and Scarborough areas of North Yorkshire; Norfolk and East Suffolk in East Anglia; the Hexham area of Northumbria; the Borders, Tayside and Western Isles regions of Scotland.

Pensioners are particularly under-represented in the Midlands outside the metropolitan cores, in the Outer Metropolitan ring around London, and in the counties just to the north and west of London. This geography is reported to have broadly persisted over at least the last four decades and is due very largely to the residential preferences of the elderly expressed through migration at or just after retirement.

Commentators also refer to the process of ageing in place as explaining some of the most dramatic increases in elderly population between 1971 and 1981 (Champion *et al.* 1987, pp. 36–7; Rees and Warnes, 1986, pp. 4–8). These have been observed in New or Expanded Towns with maturing populations such as Stevenage, Thetford, Bracknell, Harlow and Crawley. In these locations the in-migrants of the late 1940s, 1950s and 1960s have aged to become the elderly of the 1980s. However, very little analysis of the distribution of the elderly has focused on the exact contribution of these processes of migrational selectivity and ageing in place, or on the way in which the components of elderly population change might themselves be changing. Furthermore, it is important to compare the patterns of change in these components of the elderly with those of the non-elderly, in order to discover whether there are significant differences. In particular, to what extent does elderly migration contribute to the processes of population redistribution that have been identified by a careful comparison of the population numbers in labour-market areas and constituent zones between the 1971 and 1981 Censuses (Champion *et al.*, 1987)? Do elderly migrants constitute pioneers in these processes of change, given their relatively greater locational freedom after retirement from the world of work?

These are the questions which are addressed in this chapter using information on migration published in the 1971 and 1981 Censuses for a set of 20 regions (Figure 12.1). This set consists of the six former metropolitan counties, together with the former Greater London county area and the amalgam of local districts known as Central Clydeside. These eight regions constitute the main conurbation cores of the country. Added to these are the remainders of the standard regions in which the metropolitan cores are located together with the other standard regions. The South-East Remainder is divided into the outer metropolitan area (OMA) and the outer South-East, and Northern Ireland is included where data permit. It is useful to group these 20 regions into metropolitan (9) and non-metropolitan (11) zones, and into Northern (14) and Southern (6) zones, where the North–South divide is drawn roughly between the Severn and Humber estuaries.

In the next section, sources of data on elderly migration are introduced and trends across ages and between time periods are reviewed using a variety of derived measures of migration. The third section addresses the contribution of migration to elderly population redistribution drawing on an analysis of shift components over the period 1976–81. Finally, a set of population projections for the 20-region system is used to elucidate the ageing-in-place contribution to the projected redistribution over the period 1981–2031.

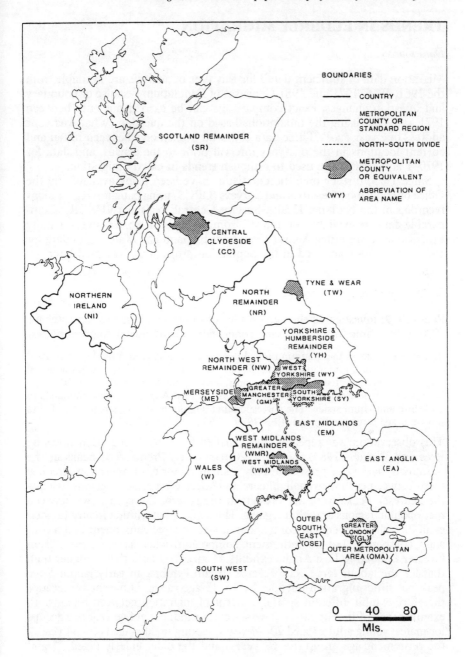

Figure 12.1 Metropolitan and non-metropolitan zones in the United Kingdom

TRENDS IN ELDERLY MIGRATION

Data sources

Migration data of sufficient detail for this type of analysis are available from the 1961, 1966, 1971 and 1981 Censuses of Population. Because of boundary and question changes, exact comparisons can be carried out only between 1971 and 1981 using the tabulations based on the question 'What was your address one year ago?'. These data count all 'transitions' between initial and current locations in the one-year interval prior to the census, and data for 1970-1 and 1980-1 are used to establish trends in elderly migration.

Since 1975, further migration statistics have been made available by the Office of Population Censuses and Surveys (OPCS) using patient reregistrations recorded in the National Health Service Central Register (NHSCR). Comparable data are available for 'moves' from 1975-6 to 1985-6 between Family Practitioner Committee Areas (95 units in England and Wales), and data for 1976-7 to 1980-1 are used in the population projections presented later.

The pattern of migration over age

Rees (1979) investigated the age profiles of interregional migration rates for 1970-1 and came to the following conclusions about elderly migration:

> Retirement peaks in the migration schedules are evident only at muted scale in total out-migration or in-migration flows (7 out of 10 regions). They are pronounced features of only selected migration streams, such as South East to South West . . . West Midlands to South West . . . South East to East Anglia . . . East Midlands to Yorkshire and Humberside. The corresponding migration counter-streams . . . fail to show marked retirement peaks (Rees 1979, p. 64).

This observation was repeated and clarified for 1980-1 migration flows by Rees and Warnes (1986) using the 20-region set. Pronounced peaks at the retirement ages were present in only a small minority of migration streams: those between each metropolitan core and selected retirement regions (usually the nearest). Peaks were not present in the reverse flows, in flows between metropolitan regions or within regions. Thus, migration within Greater London exhibits a child-dependant component, a labour-force component and a constant component but no retirement component, whereas the stream from Greater London to East Anglia exhibits a retirement peak that is higher than that for the labour force. The reverse stream exhibits an early labour-force peak but little migration outside the 15-35 age range. Different age groups therefore exhibit different spatial patterns of migration between regions. To examine these different patterns we select four individual five year age groups for males: young adults (aged 20-24 years), young middle-aged (40-44 years), the retirement age group (65-69 years) and the older elderly (aged 75 and over).

Levels of migration in 1970-1 and 1980-1

The levels of in-migration in the four selected age groups can be compared across 19 of the 20 regions (migration to Northern Ireland for 1970-1 was not available). The number of in-migrants to a region in 1980-1 is divided by the corresponding figure for 1970-1 and multiplied by 100 to yield a time-series index. Figure 12.2 indicates that levels of migration fell in virtually all instances (i.e. values are less than 100). The rates of migration fell further than the numbers indicated because each of the age groups chosen grew in population over the decade, particularly the pensionable ages. The overall increase in Great Britain's population was only 0.6% between 1971 and 1981, but the pensionable age population grew by 10% and 75+ age group by 24%. Hence the higher index values for the 75+ age group, which probably disguise a fall in rates equivalent to those in the other age groups.

What do the figures tell us about the shifts in migration destinations between 1970-1 and 1980-1? For the 20-24 age group the main contrast is between the greater than average decreases in level for regions in the North (except for Scotland Remainder where new oil jobs played a role), on the one hand, and Greater London on the other, which exhibits the least decrease. For migrants aged 40-44 years and 75+ years, the pattern of decreases above and below the national mean is not systematic with reference to our four-way classification of regions. For retirement-age migrants however, the principal contrast is between the three traditional regions of settlement at retirement, North West Remainder, outer South-East and the South-West, where decreases are greater than average, and the metropolitan regions, where decreases are less than average, or where increases are recorded.

Shares of internal migration

Another way of looking at changing migration patterns is to examine what shares of the national migration pool each region was able to capture in 1970-1 compared with 1980-1. Table 12.1, which summarises the percentages for a four-way grouping of regions, indicates that the Southern regions capture the lion's share of in-migration. Whereas the share of national population in the South was 47/49% (1971/1981), the share of in-migration was 60-70% depending on age group. There is, however, a sharp contrast between metropolitan and non-metropolitan regions in the South across the age groups. Greater London absorbed 15.6% (1970-1) and 18.8% (1980-1) of the UK's internal migrants in the young adult ages (20-24), but only 3.1% (1970-1) and 4.1% (1980-1) of retirement-age migrants (Figure 12.3). By contrast, the non-metropolitan regions in the South attracted 30.0% (1970-1) and 30.6% (1980-1) of 20-24 year old male migrants compared with 55.5% (1970-1) and 51.1% (1980-1) of 65-69-year-old male migrants. The shares for those aged 40-44 years and 75+ years in these two sets of regions are intermediate between these two extremes, but with the outer South East absorbing higher percentages of the older elderly migrants (75+) than the other regions relative to retirement-age migration (65-69).

The OMA is unique in that its share of in-migration in 1980-1 is highest for the 75+ age group. Rees and Warnes (1986) suggest this may be due to the concentration of residential homes and care institutions for the elderly in this settlement ring around London. In the North the metropolitan regions also fail to attract retirement-age migrants, but the non-metropolitan regions prove most attractive to middle-aged migrants rather than the elderly. This

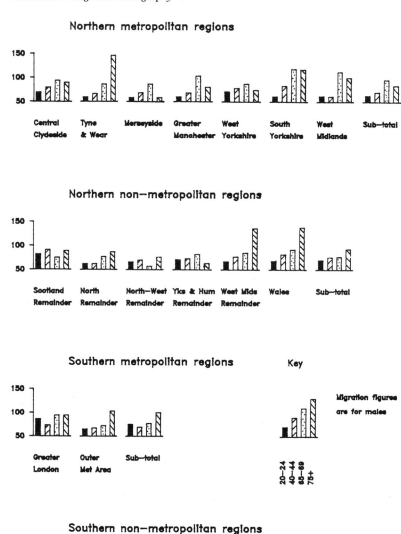

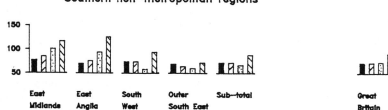

Figure 12.2 A Comparison of In-Migration Levels in 1970-1 and 1980-1

Table 12.1 The distribution of internal in-migrants in 1970–71 and 1980–81 for selected age groups (males) (percentage of GB total)

Broad region and metropolitan status	Age group at end of year 20–24	40–44	65–69	75+
	1970–71			
North				
Metro	17.2	14.8	6.8	13.7
Non-metro	22.1	25.0	23.8	22.4
Sub-total	39.3	39.8	30.6	36.1
South				
Metro	30.6	25.9	14.0	22.8
Non-metro	30.0	34.5	55.5	41.1
Sub-total	60.6	60.4	69.5	63.9
Great Britain				
Metro	47.8	40.7	20.8	36.5
Non-metro	52.1	59.5	79.3	63.5
Total	100.0	100.0	100.0	100.0
	1980–81			
North				
Metro	15.3	14.3	9.0	12.6
Non-metro	21.6	26.2	25.2	23.0
Sub-total	36.9	40.5	34.2	35.6
South				
Metro	32.5	24.9	14.9	25.0
Non-metro	30.6	34.5	51.1	39.5
Sub-total	63.1	59.4	66.0	64.5
Great Britain				
Metro	47.8	39.2	23.9	37.6
Non-metro	52.2	60.7	76.3	62.5
Total	100.0	100.0	100.0	100.0

suggests that a proportion of the Northern metropolitan region out-migrants choose Southern non-metropolitan destinations.

For elderly migrants the picture is one in which the majority chose non-metropolitan destinations rather than metropolitan, and this preference is much more marked than for younger ages. Elderly migrants could in this sense be said to be 'leading' this aspect of the population deconcentration occurring in Britain over the past two decades. However, when we compare the 1970–1 pattern with that in 1980–1, we see that the non-metropolitan preference has increased a little for the 20–24- and 40–44-year-old age groups, but has decreased for the two elderly age groups (79.3% to 76.3% for 65–69-year-olds, and 63.5% to 62.5% for those aged 75 and over), as has the prefer-

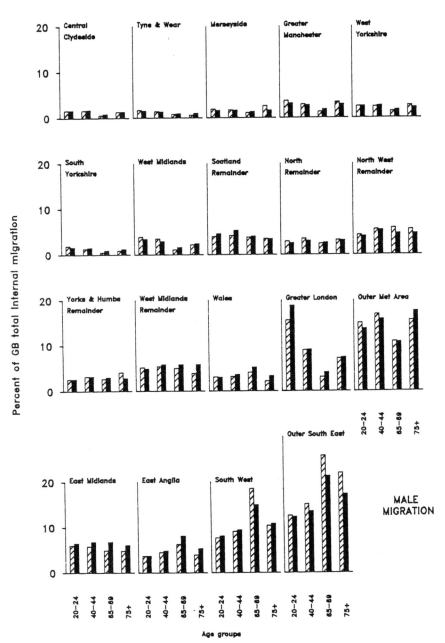

Figure 12.3 Shares of Internal In-Migration, 1970–1 and 1980–1

ence for the South over the North (69.5% to 66.0%) for 65–69-year-olds but not for the 75+ age group. Elderly migrants in 1980–1 were not quite as enthusiastic about moving to non-metropolitan retirement areas as they were in 1970–1. Among the younger migrants, the non-metropolitan share remains constant for 20–24-year-olds and increases for 40–44-year-olds.

Net migration patterns

A more traditional way of looking at the contribution of migration to population trends is to compute the net balance of in- and out-migration streams. Generally speaking, net migration levels are lower in 1980–1 than in 1970–1; the redistribution from metropolitan cores to non-metropolitan regions exceeds that from Northern to Southern; the contribution to the latter trend is predominantly in the retirement age group (65–69) rather than at older or younger ages. However, patterns in the young adult ages (20–24) do depart from those at the other ages. Metropolitan areas in the South gained in net terms in 1970–1 and 1980–1. In 1970–1, Greater London experienced net loss in 20–24-year-old migrants but this was compensated for by gains in the OMA. In 1980–81, OMA gains were much lower but Greater London switched to being a net gainer. This was a remarkable turnaround in Greater London's position given that 1980–81 saw massive job losses and rapidly rising unemployment in the national economy. Just as both metropolitan and non-metropolitan regions in the South gained migrants at ages 20–24, so both Northern region groups suffered net migration losses in 1980–1. Thus, the pattern of net migration in the 20–24-year-old age group was one of Northern loss and Southern gain, rather than metropolitan loss and non-metropolitan gain.

Summary

Patterns of elderly migration have been compared with those in other age groups and over the past two Censuses. Although, in general, the elderly are not very migratory compared with younger people, there is a minority who undertake long-distance (interregional) migration around retirement. They show revealed residential preferences that are more pronounced than those of both younger and older migrants, who are constrained by the location of employment and of careers, respectively. The exodus of retirement-age migrants from the nation's metropolitan cores to peripheral regions is the dominant pattern. The young elderly have been pioneers in the process of population deconcentration. However, the young elderly were more actively engaged in these processes at the beginning of the 1970s than they were at the start of the 1980s, when migration levels as a whole were depressed.

ELDERLY MIGRATION IN A COMPONENTS FRAMEWORK

Introduction

Regional projections of the elderly consist of population stocks broken down into appropriate ages at successive points in time. Each regional elderly cohort ages over a time interval and loses members through death, through out-migration to other parts of the same nation, and through out-migration to other parts of the world. Each regional cohort gains members from other regions and other countries. These gains and losses to each regional cohort can be viewed as composed of two parts: the national change; and the regional shift (or departure of the region from the national norm). The techniques of shift-share analysis are partially adapted to describe the extent to which regional populations depart from national expectations.

Of course, the elderly population as a whole does not disappear. New recruits are provided in successive time intervals by persons attaining an elderly age, defined operationally to be age 60. The fluctuation over time in new recruits to the elderly population attaining their sixtieth birthdays will reflect both the fertility history of the regional population 60 years earlier and the processes of migration and differential mortality between birth and age 60. These fluctuations can be examined in relation to national trends, although a full decomposition into birth and subsequent components of change is not attempted here. It would require full knowledge of regional population accounts back to 1916! The methods used for analysis of individual period-cohorts of the elderly population are first outlined and then used to examine the components of elderly population change across seven elderly period-cohorts for 20 UK regions in a recent five-year period (1976–81).

The components defined for the period cohort perspective

Adopting a projection viewpoint, we work with the period-cohort framework for the observation of demographic events. The following variables are defined:

$P(i, {}^*, a)$ = population of region i at the start of the time interval in period-cohort a;
$D(i,a)$ = deaths in region i to the period-cohort a in the time interval;
$M(i,j,a)$ = (internal) migrations from region i to region j by persons in period-cohort a;
$M(i,{}^*,a)$ = total (internal) migrations from region i to all other regions (*) by persons in period-cohort a;
$M({}^*,i,a)$ = total (internal) migrations to region i from all other regions by persons in period-cohort a;
$E(i,a)$ = emigrations from region i to other countries by persons in period-cohort a;
$I(i,a)$ = immigrations to region i from other countries by persons in period-cohort a;
$P({}^*,i,a)$ = population of region i at the end of the time interval in period-cohort a.

Initial and final populations in period-cohort a are linked by the following accounting identity:

$$P({}^*,i,a) = P(i, {}^*, a) - D(i,a) - M(i,{}^*,a) - E(i,a) \\ + M({}^*,i,a) + I(i,a) \qquad (12.1)$$

These components of change can be simplified into deaths plus net internal migration plus net external migration or just into deaths plus net total migration.

Parallel to these regional relations we can define the equivalent national variables, substituting N for i in the definitions above. The average population is adopted as the population at risk:

$$P(N,a) = (P(N, {}^* ,a) + P({}^* ,N,a))/2. \tag{12.2}$$

The national rates for each component are defined as:

$$d(N,a) = D(N,a)/P(N,a) \tag{12.3}$$
$$m(N,a) = M(N,{}^*,a)/P(N,a) = M({}^*,N,a)/P(N,a) \tag{12.4}$$
$$e(N,a) = E(N,a)/P(N,a) \tag{12.5}$$
$$i(N,a) = I(N,a)/P(N,a) \tag{12.6}$$

Each regional component can be decomposed into a national portion and a regional shift. The national part consists of the regional population at risk multiplied by the national rate for the event concerned. It represents the size of the component expected if the region reproduced national rates for that component. Regional shifts represent the change peculiar to the region itself and are computed as residuals (R before the variable concerned):

$$RD(i,a) \quad = D(i,a) \quad - d(N,a)\,P(i,a) \tag{12.7}$$
$$RM(i, {}^* ,a) = M(i,{}^*,a) - m(N,a)\,P(i,a) \tag{12.8}$$
$$RE(i,a) \quad = E(i,a) \quad - e(N,a)\,P(i,a) \tag{12.9}$$
$$RI(i,a) \quad = I(i,a) \quad - i(N,a)\,P(i,a) \tag{12.10}$$
$$RM({}^* ,i,a) = M({}^*,i,a) - m(N,a)\,P(i,a) \tag{12.11}$$

Another way of expressing these shifts is as differences between the national and regional rates. The ratio of regional to national rates when multiplied by 100 gives us sets of standardised rates, where the national mean is 100.

The shifts for the gross components can be reduced to net shifts by subtracting the outward migration shift from the inward. The net shift for the internal migration component reduces to the observed net internal migration. Each of the three net shifts can be expressed as a percentage of the total absolute value of the net shift to yield an assessment of the contribution of mortality differentials, internal migration flows or external migration differentials to the observed departure of regional population change from the national norm.

The arithmetic of the components analysis described above can be exemplified for Greater Manchester. The components derive from sets of multi-regional movement accounts described in Rees (1986). The population of 60–64-year-olds in Greater Manchester in 1981 (138 403) is the result of a reduction of the 55–59-year-old, usually resident, population there in 1976 (153 500) by 12 326 deaths, 469 foreign emigrations and 6395 out-migrations to other parts of the UK, partially compensated for by the addition of 253 immigrations from abroad and 3840 internal in-migrations from other British regions. The population reduction of 15 097 in this period-cohort is made up of 12 326 deaths, a net external migration loss of 216, a net internal migration loss of 2555 and therefore a net overall loss due to migration of 2771. Gross and net components of change can be expressed as annual equivalent rates per thousand average population in the time interval (1976–81). Greater Manchester's death rate is 16.89 per thousand in the 55–59 to 60–64 period-cohort and the internal out-migration rate is just over half this level at 8.76 per thousand. The internal in-migration rate is lower at 5.26 per thousand and the external and net migration rates much smaller (−0.3 and −3.5% respectively). The standardised rates place Greater Manchester in relation to the nation. The rate of population decline is 36.7% greater than that of the UK; the death rate is 13.9% higher; all the migration rates are lower than the national norms but, because the in-migration rates are lower than the out-migration rates, migration loss contributes 22.8% to the standardised population change rate.

When the pattern of population change expected if each region exactly mirrored the nation is calculated, all internal migration flows must balance. In Greater Manchester's case there are many fewer deaths (10 826) under these utopian conditions than we actually observe (15 097). Subtraction of the expected from the observed components yields the regional shifts (or departures from the national norm). Greater Manchester has 1500 more deaths, 320 less emigrations, 319 less immigrations, 1611 less internal out-migrations and 4166 less internal in-migrations than it would have if it repro-duced national demographic behaviour. The net shift of internal migration is a loss of 2555, but a tiny positive shift in external migration is recorded (the region loses through external migration but slightly less strongly than the nation). The percentage contributions of the net shifts to an absolute value sum of those shifts indicate that 63% of the depression of Greater Manchester's population below that of the nation is due to internal migration and 37% to higher mortality.

Shifts in components across the elderly ages

In Rees and Warnes (1986) a simple classification of the pattern of elderly population change was developed based on the direction of shift (positive or negative) for the deaths, net internal and net external migration components. Eight types of change were distinguished in relation to the national norm (Table 12.2). The classification represents, in part, a gradation from most

Table 12.2   Types of regional population shift

Type	Deaths	Internal migrations	External migrations
A	fewer	gain	more
B	fewer	gain	fewer
C	fewer	loss	more
D	fewer	loss	fewer
E	more	gain	more
F	more	gain	fewer
G	more	loss	more
H	more	loss	fewer

Table 12.3 Population-shift type for 20 UK regions and for seven elderly age groups, 1976–81

Region	Age group in 1976 to age group in 1981						
	55–59 to 60–64	60–64 to 65–69	65–69 to 70–74	70–74 to 75–79	75–79 to 80–84	80–84 to 85–89	85+ to 90+
Non-metropolitan regions							
South							
Outer South-East	A	A	A	A	A	A	A
South-West	A	A	A	A	A	A	A
East Anglia	A	A	A	B	B	B	B
East Midlands	A	A	A	E	E	E	A
North							
W. Midlands Remainder	A	E	E	E	E	E	E
Yorkshire and Humberside Remainder	A	A	A	E	A	A	A
Wales	E	E	E	F	H	H	H
Scotland Remainder	E	E	E	E	E	E	A
North West Remainder	E	E	G	G	G	E	E
North Remainder	F	E	H	H	H	H	F
Northern Ireland	H	G	G	G	H	H	G
Metropolitan regions							
South							
Outer metropolitan area	B	B	B	B	B	F	B
Greater London	D	D	D	D	D	D	D
North							
W. Midlands MC	G	G	G	G	G	G	G
S. Yorkshire	G	G	G	G	G	G	G
W. Yorkshire	G	G	G	G	G	G	G
Greater Manchester	G	H	G	G	G	G	G
Merseyside	H	H	H	H	H	H	H
Tyne and Wear	H	H	H	H	H	H	H
Central Clydeside	H	G	G	H	H	H	H

Note: see Table 12.2 for definitions of the population shift types A–H.

favoured region (in demographic terms) to least. For example, type A regions experience fewer deaths than the nation, gain through internal migration and show positive shifts in external migration (and often gains). Table 12.3 sets the population-shift types into which each region's population falls for seven elderly period-cohorts. There is a fair measure of agreement across the age groups in the pattern of population shift. Eight of the 20 regions retain the same classification across all age groups, and five more show only one deviation from a common pattern.

The East Anglian population moves from positive to negative shifts for net external migration from age 70–74 (in 1976), although the numbers involved are very small. The East Midlands population experiences a worse than national average risk of mortality for age groups 70–74 to 80–84 (in 1976), although the standardised mortality rates are only 1% or so above the national average. The Welsh population exhibits a transition from net internal migration gains and positive external shift to net internal losses and negative external shift as more aged populations are considered. Around retirement the region is attractive to migrants but not beyond age 70. The North-West Remainder's population shows variation in the internal migration component: gains from ages 55–59 to 60–64 (in 1976), losses from 65–69 to 75–79, and then gains again in the 80–84 and 85+ age groups. A somewhat similar pattern occurs for the North Remainder's population but along with a pattern of negative external migration shift. For Northern Ireland the deaths and internal migration shifts remain constantly negative but the relatively small external component varies between positive and negative. Finally, Central Clydeside shows positive external migration shifts in the 60–64 and 65–69 age groups (in 1976). The balance of external migration remains negative, however, in both these age groups. Overall, the changes that take place are confined to one component, and a majority involve the rather small and least reliably estimated external migration flows.

To generalise, the pattern of mortality shift during 1976–81 is one of a regional gradient from South and East regions (favoured) to North and West regions (unfavoured). The pattern of internal migration is one of a metropolitan (unfavoured) to non-metropolitan (favoured) gradient. The pattern of external migration is one of positive shifts for non-metropolitan regions and for the mid-Northern metropolitan counties which have been important destinations for overseas immigration in the past.

The classificatory analysis disguises somewhat the systematic change in the absolute size of changes as the population ages, and the change in the relative contribution of the different components of change. The older cohorts are much smaller than the younger, and much more subject to the influence of mortality. Figure 12.4 illustrates these age effects for Greater London and the South-West. The internal migration gains and losses are dominant in the first three age groups and are relatively less important after age 75. Mortality shifts rise to the 70–74 to 75–79 period-cohort as mortality rates rise faster than the populations at risk diminish but thereafter the shift diminishes as the population reduces rapidly. External migration shifts contribute only marginally and only in the first three period-cohorts.

The relative contribution of the deaths shift to the absolute value of the deaths and net migration shifts added together is listed in Table 12.4. The sign indicates whether regional deaths are less than the national norm (negative) or more than it (positive). After age 70–74, the contribution of the deaths shift dominates but in the first three age groups the situation is very variable. In the 'deepest North', in Central Clydeside, Scotland Remainder, Northern Ireland, Tyne and Wear and North remainder, the greatest contribution (more than 50%) to greater than average population attrition comes from the regions' poor mortality performance. For most other non-metropolitan regions, migration gains play the biggest role in reducing population losses below the national average. In Greater London and Birmingham the migration-loss component is dominant, and in the OMA the deaths shift predominates. The picture varies in the other regions over the first three age groups.

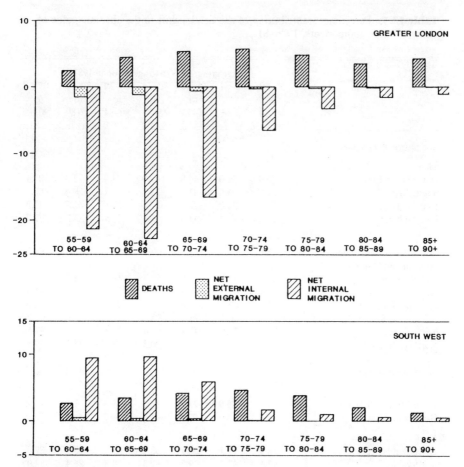

Figure 12.4 Shifts in the components of growth by age (1000's), 1976–81, selected regions

AGEING IN PLACE

A components framework for the period–age perspective

The analysis described in the previous section involves semi-closed populations that do not replace themselves, but merely exchange populations among themselves. Elderly cohorts disappear quite quickly over time. An alternative perspective is to use an open system in which the elderly population is replaced by new recruits, that is, persons attaining the starting age assigned to the elderly population. These are the elderly equivalent of new infants in the population as a whole. In this way we can estimate more precisely the contribution of 'ageing in place' to elderly population change. Here, the starting age is defined as a person's sixtieth birthday and attention is focused on the

Table 12.4   Percentage contribution of the deaths shift to the absolute value of shifts in three components, 1976–81

Region	Age group in 1976 to age group in 1981						
	55–59 to 60–64	60–64 to 65–69	65–69 to 70–74	70–74 to 75–79	75–79 to 80–84	80–84 to 85–89	85+ to 90+
Non-metropolitan regions							
South							
Outer South East	−26.9	−31.0	−44.9	−63.9	−71.4	−73.8	−87.4
South West	−21.0	−24.6	−41.1	−71.6	−79.1	−79.4	−80.5
East Anglia	−20.7	−21.0	−28.1	−53.1	−59.6	−62.7	−82.3
East Midlands	−19.1	−17.4	−11.3	7.7	53.5	57.7	−77.7
North							
W. Midlands Remainder	−8.0	8.5	19.5	40.4	51.2	66.8	83.7
Yorkshire and Humberside Remainder	−13.6	−13.2	−5.3	52.7	−60.5	−78.8	−83.5
Wales	26.9	41.5	61.0	84.4	92.5	88.9	93.0
Scotland Remainder	47.3	60.2	68.4	81.7	89.3	89.7	−81.6
North West Remainder	27.4	46.9	96.6	93.3	97.1	98.4	99.2
North Remainder	75.9	75.8	95.8	94.4	95.8	97.0	99.5
Northern Ireland	58.5	72.7	83.2	90.2	83.8	95.2	98.5
Metropolitan regions							
South							
Outer Metropolitan area	−77.1	−75.9	−71.1	−65.3	−69.1	3.9	−69.8
Greater London	−9.3	−14.8	−22.9	−45.5	−59.7	−64.1	−78.2
North							
W. Midlands MC	18.9	19.4	26.9	53.9	65.7	63.4	87.3
S. Yorkshire	43.4	47.4	79.5	82.3	88.8	86.4	87.9
W. Yorkshire	33.2	43.9	59.2	79.0	78.0	60.9	81.9
Greater Manchester	37.0	42.1	61.2	82.8	87.5	86.7	96.3
Merseyside	37.5	46.8	64.6	72.4	70.6	66.3	88.2
Tyne & Wear	56.1	62.8	71.2	83.4	81.8	78.1	90.5
Central Clydeside	68.3	74.0	78.3	80.0	79.2	86.3	84.5

elderly population as a whole across future years. The components of change for ages 60 and over are estimated by addition of the six oldest period-cohorts and half of the 55–59 to 60–64 period-cohort. Aggregate components for Greater Manchester are presented in Table 12.5. The number of new entrants exceeds the losses due to deaths but not those due to deaths and migration combined. Table 12.5 also contains the net components of change for the population aged 60 and over, where the 'natural increase' is computed as the difference between the numbers attaining their sixtieth birthdays and the numbers of deaths to persons aged 60+. Over the 1976–81 period the surplus of new entrants over deaths was some 220 000 for the UK as a whole. In only two regions was this surplus negative, and in only four regions were the natural

Table 12.5 Components of change for the population aged 60+: illustration for Greater Manchester, 1976–81

GROSS COMPONENTS OF CHANGE							
Initial pop.	Deaths	Internal out-migration	Emig-ration	60th birthdays	Internal in-migration	Immig-ration	Final pop.
521,100	139,642	18,735	916	145,952	12,255	516	520,530

NET COMPONENTS OF CHANGE						
Initial population	Population change	Natural increase	Net migration internal	Net migration external	total	Final population
521,100	−570	6,310	−6,480	−400	−6,880	520,530

ANNUAL RATES OF CHANGE (PER 1000 POPULATION)					
Death rate	Internal out-migration rate	Emigration rate	Birth rate	Internal in-migration rate	Immigration rate
53.6	7.2	0.4	56.0	4.7	0.2

Population change rate	Natural increase rate	Met migration rate internal	Met migration rate external	total
−0.2	2.4	−2.5	−0.2	−2.6

surpluses exceeded by migration losses. Table 12.5 contains annual equivalent rates per thousand for both gross and net components for Greater Manchester.

It is necessary not to take the term 'natural increase' too literally. The number of persons attaining their sixtieth birthdays in a region depends both on the number born there and the subsequent history of all regional cohorts. The task of linking the elderly back to their birth regions is not attempted here. What it is possible to do, however, is to peer into the future through a projection exercise. This makes possible the assessment of the influence of past population history, as represented by the regional distribution of 60-year-olds in five-year periods from 1976–81 to 2026–31, on fluctuations in the regional elderly populations. These fluctuations, due in the main to temporal variation in the size of birth cohorts in the past, have a profound impact on the national elderly population (Rees and Warnes, 1986, Section 7.1). In the next subsection, the regional impacts are described, focusing on the balance of sixtieth birthdays and deaths. Since the projections assume constant mortality and migration rates over the period of the projections, the patterns of such change replicate those described for the base period, 1976–81.

The balance of sixtieth birthdays and elderly deaths to 2031

The 'natural increase' rates (NIRs) for the 20 UK regions and the nation are graphed from 1976 to 2031 in Figure 12.5. The national pattern follows quite closely that of the projected population of 60–64-year-olds (Rees and Warnes, 1986) while the deaths part of the 'natural increase' calculation follows a much smoother trend as it involves the whole elderly population. The fall from 1976–81 to 1991–6 matches the fertility drop from 1916–21 to 1931–6; low NIR levels in 1996–2001 match continuing low birth numbers in 1936–41; rising NIRs in 2001–6 and 2006–11 correspond with the increasing births of the later Second World War years and the post-war baby boom (particularly 1947); the fall in 2011–16 reflects the trough for births in the early 1950s; the rise to 2021–26 and high level in 2026–31 represents the sustained fertility rise of the late 1950s and high fertility of the 1960s (only in 1971 did the total fertility rate drop back to replacement). The graphs for the regions have been arranged in groups corresponding roughly to the component shift groups identified previously, since the possibility exists of links between migration flow patterns and 'natural increase' patterns. Here several links are suggested in interpreting regional departures from the national trends, although ideally all need further careful verification. There are also clearly links to past regional fertility history. The following discussion focuses on the most extreme patterns of NIR fluctuation.

In 1976–81, the Northern Ireland elderly NIR is close to the UK figure, but it successively departs from it as time goes on, reflecting the arrival at their sixtieth birthdays of larger and larger cohorts. In the last 15 years of the projection period Northern Ireland elderly NIRs are double those for the UK as a whole. The OMA exhibits NIRs well above the national norm but they tend to converge over time towards those of the UK. Here the explanation is not that regional fertility was higher than that of the nation but that the history of migration to the region has been important. Persons attaining their sixtieth birthdays in the region in 1976–2001 were in their 20s and 30s in the period 1926–71 which saw massive expansion of suburbs, new towns, commuter settlements and industrial satellites in this peri-metropolitan belt which drew in large numbers of in-migrants. This bulge of in-migrants become the elderly of the region in the rest of the century and sustain the 'natural increase' of elderly in belt. The convergence of OMA and national NIRs in the 2001–31 period reflects the lesser growth rate in the region in the 1970s and the migration pattern of the 1976–91 base period. Until 2001, the outer South-East experiences negative NIRs. The number of deaths occurring in the region to persons aged 60 and over exceeds the numbers attaining age 60 in the region. This situation is fairly general in 1986–2001 but not in 1976–86. The excess of deaths probably reflects the considerable migration, after age 60, into the region making the 60+ population much larger than an 'ageing *in situ*' of the population attaining age 60 would sustain.

Up to the end of the century, Central Clydeside's NIRs do not depart from the national trend by much, but after 2001 they are substantially below the UK average. Persons attaining age 60 in 2001–31 will have been in their 20s and 30s in the 1961–2001 period, during which sustained out-migration from Greater Glasgow has occurred and is likely to occur. In part, this reflects suburbanisation beyond the boundary of Central Clydeside, but also the pro-

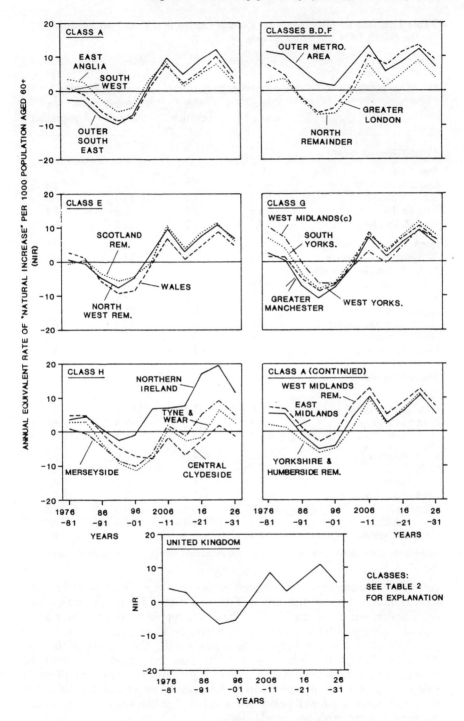

Figure 12.5 'Natural Increase' rates, UK regions, 1976–2031

Table 12.6 Annual rates of natural increase (ageing *in situ*) and net migration for the elderly (60+), selected periods

Region	Period			
	1996–2001		2026–2031	
	Natural increase	Net migration	Natural increase	Net migration
Non-metropolitan regions				
South				
Outer South East	−7.0	5.2	12.1	2.8
South West	−7.3	4.4	10.0	3.6
East Anglia	−4.6	5.6	7.6	4.3
East Midlands	−4.1	1.2	10.3	1.0
North				
W. Midlands Remainder	−0.1	1.6	12.6	0.1
Yorkshire and Humberside Remainder	−4.6	1.5	10.6	1.2
Wales	−8.3	1.4	8.9	1.7
Scotland Remainder	−4.6	1.1	11.1	0.7
North West Remainder	−4.6	0.5	10.9	−0.1
North Remainder	−5.8	−0.2	8.7	−0.0
Northern Ireland	−1.1	−1.2	19.4	−1.4
Metropolitan regions				
South				
Outer Metropolitan Area	1.7	−3.1	12.1	−3.2
Greater London	−4.9	−7.2	13.4	−6.6
North				
W. Midlands MC	−6.5	−4.0	9.9	−3.1
W. Yorkshire	−7.0	−1.4	10.1	−1.2
S. Yorkshire	−6.5	−1.1	11.4	−0.9
Greater Manchester	−7.9	−2.0	9.2	−1.6
Merseyside	−10.0	−2.6	9.0	−1.5
Tyne and Wear	−11.5	−1.7	6.4	−0.7
Central Clydeside	−7.2	−1.7	−1.9	−0.4

cess of abandonment of a devastated urban economy. These remarks apply also, although in lesser measure, to Tyne and Wear, Merseyside and Greater Manchester, but not to the West Midlands metropolitan county where a history of higher past fertility and an attractiveness to migrants persisting into the 1950s plays a role in keeping the region's NIRs above those of the UK. The national capital exhibits higher NIRs than the nation throughout the projection period. Here the factor at work is probably the massive retirement migration stream out of the metropolis after age 60 which reduces the size of the elderly population well below that which an 'ageing *in situ*' of those attaining their sixtieth birthdays would sustain.

Finally, what are the relative contributions of ageing in place (as measured by elderly natural increase) and migration (as measured by overall net migration) to changes in the numbers of elderly (aged 60 and over) over the next 50 years? Table 12.6 illustrates natural increase and net migration rates for two five-year periods: 1996–2001, in which Figure 12.4 indicates substantial decreases in the elderly due to smaller cohorts entering the elderly ages, and 2026–2031, when larger cohorts attain their sixtieth birthdays. The temporal and interregion fluctuation in the ageing-in-place indicator (natural increase rate) are clearly much more pronounced than those due to migration. Past history to age 60 has a much greater impact on population change than elderly migration *per se*, although elderly migration supplies a layer of icing on the non-metropolitan slices of the population cake and takes out small bites from the metropolitan slices.

CONCLUSIONS

The pattern of elderly migration has been shown to be one that favours non-metropolitan regions, particularly coastal areas and attractive inland country-side. In the decade around retirement, a substantial minority of the elderly 'vote with their feet' against continued metropolitan living. Beyond age 70, however, this preference is much less marked and is comparable to that exhibited in the late working ages. The contribution of these patterns of elderly migration to population change is most important before age 75; beyond that age, the influence of mortality differences between regions is more important. Even at the retirement ages, the influence of mortality differences is more important in accounting for population change in Central Clydeside and Tyne and Wear. Elderly migration has its greatest influence in shifting population from the nation's capital to the other regions of the South.

A simple extrapolation of this pattern into the future is disturbed by the influence of ageing in place. The smaller cohorts that will become elderly in the next two decades ensure that, unless mortality decreases substantially, all regions (of our 20) will see a decrease in the number of 70–74-year-olds in 2006 compared with 1981, and most regions will see decreases at ages 65–69 (Rees and Warnes, 1986, Figure 14). On the other hand, every region will see substantial increases in their populations aged 75 or more, which, if mortality continues to decrease, will mean gains of between 50% and 100% in these populations, with profound implications for the provision of care by the community for the infirm elderly.

Beyond 2006, the number of persons reaching their sixtieth birthdays increases substantially, leading to gains at all elderly ages compared with 1981 in all non-metropolitan regions together with South Yorkshire and the OMA (Rees, 1986, Figure 4). However, if the current migration patterns persist, absolute decreases in elderly population should continue in most metropolitan regions.

Are the current migration patterns likely to be maintained? Our comparison of 1970–1 flows with those of 1980–1 suggested that the 'high tide' of counter-urbanisation had passed, and that we should expect further diminution of this process. On the other hand, migration activity was particularly depressed in 1980–1, and detailed analysis of more recent migration information is needed. There is evidence to suggest that levels of internal migration have risen since 1981 and that some metropolitan regions, London particularly, are now gaining through external migration.

REFERENCES

Champion, A.G., Green, A.E., Owen, D.W., Ellin, D.J. and Coombes, M.G. (1987) *Changing Places: Britain's Demographic, Economic and Social Complexion.* London: Edward Arnold.

Law, C.M. and Warnes, A.M. (1976) 'The changing geography of the elderly in England and Wales', *Transactions, Institute of British Geographers*, new series, vol. 1, pp. 453-71.

OPCS (1985) *Population Projections, 1983-2053.* Series PP2, no. 13. London: HMSO.

OPCS and CSO (1984) *Britain's Elderly Population.* Census Guide 1. London: Information Office, OPCS.

Rees, P.H. (1979) *Migration and Settlement: 1. United Kingdom.* Research Report RR-79-9. Laxenburg, Austria: International Institute of Applied Systems Analysis.

Rees, P.H. (1986) 'How many old people will there be in the United Kingdom and where will they live?'. Working Paper 465, School of Geography, University of Leeds.

Rees, P.H. and Warnes, A.M. (1986) 'Migration of the elderly in the United Kingdom'. Working Paper 473, School of Geography, University of Leeds.

Warnes, A.M. and Law, C.M. (1984) 'The elderly population of Great Britain: locational trends and policy implications', *Transactions, Institute of British Geographers*, new series, vol. 9, pp. 37-59.

World Bank (1984) *World Development Report, 1984.* Oxford: Oxford University Press.

Part IV

MODELS FOR MIGRATION IN THE LABOUR MARKET

Chapter 13

MIGRATION, POPULATION AND REGIONAL LABOUR SUPPLY

G.H.M. Evers

INTRODUCTION

Recently, in several articles we have stressed the importance of understanding changes in regional labour supply as a main determinant of developments in unemployment (Evers and van der Veen, 1987, and Evers, 1987). It was demonstrated that changes in labour demand, related to a population-driven growth path, are less important than changes in labour supply in this respect. Hence, understanding the causes of (regional) unemployment can only be accomplished if changes in supply are taken into consideration.

In this chapter, it will be argued that changes in the stock of regional labour supply are no longer mainly due to natural increase of the population aged 15–64 years. On the contrary, changes in participation rates and the net effects of interregional migration and commuting have become increasingly important.

Spatial labour markets are generally characterised by a demand for specific skills that does not automatically match the supply of persons having such capabilities. Demand and supply are brought closer together by spatial mobility of workers. It can be argued that the evolution of industrialised societies into societies of specialised education and labour demand, requires a mobility policy designed to avoid a growth in discrepancies in spatial labour markets. Since both people and jobs become increasingly heterogeneous according to skills, qualifications and locational preferences this mobility is very important as a lubricant for the labour market. This is certainly true in a period where natural population growth is declining. Given the relatively short distances in the Netherlands, it is therefore of interest to study the relationship between two kinds of spatial mobility, namely labour migration and commuting.

The chapter opens with a brief recapitulation of the results of the descriptive analysis of components of change in regional labour supply and the developments in migration and commuting flows. The chapter then moves on to discuss the theory on the interdependencies between labour migration and commuting and to present two ways of dealing with these interdependencies: a macro-economic model and a micro-economic approach. Then estimation procedures and results are discussed. Finally, some general conclusions will be drawn. In this respect, the chapter can be considered as a brief overview of the various research efforts by the author and others in the Netherlands since 1980.

EMPIRICAL DEVELOPMENTS IN LABOUR SUPPLY, MIGRATION AND COMMUTING

It is important to point out that there is a difference between regional labour supply and the regional labour force. To derive the first, the latter has to be corrected for net interregional commuting (Burridge and Gordon, 1981; Gordon and Lamont, 1982, and Evers and van der Veen, 1986). Hence, changes in regional labour supply can be split up into changes in regional labour force and changes in net commuting.

Next, changes in regional labour force can be decomposed into several elements. The volume of the regional labour force can change because of natural growth of the 'native' labour force, or because of the net effect of interregional and international labour migration. Finally, the natural increase in the native labour force will be split into a demographic component and an economic component. The first is calculated by assuming a constant labour-force participation rate and applying this rate to the natural increase in population aged 15–64. The economic component reveals the effect of changes in participation rates under the assumption of a fixed population.

Details of the decomposition analysis can be found in Evers *et al.* (1983) and Evers and van der Veen (1986). Although the decomposition analysis is a rather simple descriptive device, it is quite useful in indicating the empirical magnitude of some of the components of changes in regional labour supply. Moreover, since the analysis is carried out for two periods separately, important trends and shifts can be revealed.

The periods under consideration are 1971–8 and 1978–86. Some key figures for these periods are given in Table 13.1. It is clear that the rise in labour supply is primarily due to females entering the labour market, especially in the period 1978–86. Also net interregional commuting has become increasingly important. The influence of these changes on the development of labour supply can be indicated as 10.4% and 12.4% of the total change in the two periods, respectively.

The components of change in labour force for the average Dutch region (province) are presented in the bottom half of Table 13.1, for males and females taken together. The results show that the economic component in the natural increase is by far the most important component and its influence has increased over time. So about 60% of the total change in regional labour force is due to a rise in participation rates. Detailed results for males and females separately show that in the case of males the influence of the above mentioned component is about 25% and decreasing over time, whereas for females this figure is about 80% and increasing steadily.

Furthermore, it is interesting to note that the influence of the demographic component is increasing. The net influence of spatial labour mobility (commuting, migration) on the development of labour supply in the average Dutch region can be indicated as 33.7% in the period 1971–8 and 21.2% in the period 1978–86. So, the net impact of spatial mobility has clearly deteriorated in favour of natural increases in the labour force.

Table 13.1 Components of regional labour supply, 1971–86

1971–78	1978–86	The Netherlands (in thousands)
82	209	Change in labour supply, males
271	688	Change in labour supply, females
353	897	Change in labour supply, total
41	127	Change in absolute net commuting
10.4	12.4	Influence of commuting (%)
		Average region: components (%)
15	26	Natural increase: demographic
59	64	: economic
18	7	Interregional migration
8	3	International migration

Sources: Statistics on foreign and internal migration, labour-force accounts

Finally, it is important to take into account interrelationships between components of change in regional labour supply. The interdependency between migration and commuting will be discussed in the next section. Also, there are indications, both from the literature as well from our own empirical research, that changes in participation status and spatial mobility are interrelated. Evers and van der Veen (1986) point out that people, especially females, who leave or enter the labour force, have twice the average propensity to migrate. Also, migration rates are particularly low for households with two adults workers and children. One-person household migrate more than average and commute shorter distances whereas the opposite is true for families. Hence, there is a clear indication that the economic component, on the one hand, and spatial mobility components, on the other, are correlated, due to the household context in which decisions are taken.

As already pointed out, the importance of net migration as a determinant of changes in regional labour supply decreased in the period 1971–86, whereas the opposite held for changes in net commuting. Because the spatial distribution of interregional migration and commuting flows in the Netherlands is remarkably stable over time (Evers and Bartels, 1981; Evers *et al.*, 1983), changes in net flows are due to changes in generation (that is, the total rate of outflow).

Table 13.2 provides information on the volume of migration and commuting. It is clear that both the volume of migration and the rate of migration have dropped considerably, from 2.5% of total labour force in 1971 to 1.3% in 1985. At the same time, interregional commuting has increased and rates more than doubled in the period 1971–86. From this one may conclude that migration and commuting should be analysed in an intertemporal context.

This leads to two questions: first, whether a substitution between migration and commuting has occurred; second, given the existence of these interdependencies, how to achieve an integrated framework for forecasting

Table 13.2 Volume of interregional labour migration and commuter flows (in thousands and as a percentage of total labour force)

Year	Migration		Commuting	
1971	119	2.5	125	2.6
1975	103	2.1	211	4.3
1977	94	1.9	248	4.9
1979	83	1.6	289	5.6
1981	77	1.4	309	5.6
1983	63	1.1	335	5.8
1985	77	1.3	354	5.9

Sources: Statistics on internal migration, labour-force accounts

changes in regional labour supply. These questions will be dealt with in the next sections.

ON THE INTERDEPENDENCY OF MIGRATION AND COMMUTING

The theory of interregional labour *migration* is extensive. From traditional neo-classical theory, in which differences in wage rates are the key stimulus (Clark, 1982), and Keynesian approaches where unemployment plays a crucial role (Hart, 1975) and vacancies are introduced (Harris and Todaro, 1970), there have been numerous modifications.

Detailed overviews of the developments in migration theory are given by Greenwood (1975), Shaw (1975), Clark (1982), Mueller (1982) and Evers and van der Veen (1986). The most important notion here is that migration cannot be analysed in a partial context, but calls for an integral approach, in which the many motives for migration and its interdependence with other labour-market responses are reflected. Motives in this respect are improvements in working conditions, in housing conditions, in physical-environmental conditions, in social-cultural environment and in amenities. Different categories of migrant will put different weights on each of the motives. Selectivity has been postulated and observed according to age, the distance of migration, income, profession, family context and so on (see Shaw, 1975, for an overview).

Other important topics are the time horizon and uncertainty. As Hart (1973) shows, migration decisions are based on expected regional differences rather than observed differences. This introduces an element of uncertainty, which is also present for the effects of migration on other members of the family (Sandell, 1977; Krumm, 1983). Since migration involves several costs, which have to be compensated by (discounted) expected earnings in the future, it can be considered as an investment decision. This has lead to the human capital theory of migration (Sjaastad, 1962). Empirical applications of this general migration theory, however, have not confirmed it (Navratil and Doyle, 1977; Grant and VanderKamp, 1980).

More recent theories on migration are based on discrete-choice analysis (Mueller, 1982; Amemiya, 1981). Location choice from a discrete set of alternatives is based on the (expected) utility of each alternative (Lancaster, 1966) and includes certain sub-decisions such as generation and distribution (Morrison, 1973; Moss, 1979; Clark *et al.*, 1979; and Bartels and Liaw, 1983), as well as the communication and information factor (Herzog and Schlottmann, 1981). The discrete choice approach has proved to be a powerful concept as it is capable of capturing individual differences in taste, risk behaviour, family type and so on.

Finally, the theory should incorporate dynamic and macro-elements as well. The influence of business-cycle effects on migration probabilities is pointed out by Grant and VanderKamp (1976), Bartels and Liaw (1983), Evers *et al.* (1983), and Molho (1984). As to the macro-elements, in some studies it is argued that theories which concentrate on individual behaviour ignore macro-economic influences and institutional constraints (Moore and Clark, 1980; Sheppard, 1980; Gardner, 1981; Anas, 1981).

The theory of *commuting* is largely restricted to urban economics, where the allocation of workplace and housing is studied within a city (Alonso, 1964). There also exists a fair amount of literature on commuting in transport economics, where modal split aspects are most relevant (Pickup and Town, 1983). Within the field of regional economics, only few studies pay attention to the determinants and effects of interregional commuting. This is quite extraordinary, given the sizeable influences of changes in net commuting on developments in regional labour supply (see Tables 13.1 and 13.2).

Theoretical contributions to interregional commuting in general are in accordance with the developments in migration theory as discussed in the previous section. The spatial dichotomy between workplace and residential location is explained by labour-market variables (wage, unemployment, vacancies), housing variables, amenities, socio-cultural environment and so on. Moreover, similarly to migration, commuting is selective by age, family type and income. Finally, since the trip has to be made twice a day, spatial variables (distance, time costs, physical infrastructure, car ownership) have been studied extensively.

From the brief description above it is clear that there is a considerable resemblance between migration theory and the theory of interregional commuting. Within the analysis of the *interdependencies* of migration and commuting, three approaches can be distinguished (Termote, 1980; Vickerman, 1984). First, if the work location is fixed, the relation reduces to the choice of residence, as in Alonso-type urban studies (Siegel, 1975; Simpson, 1980). Second, if residence is fixed (so no migration occurs), job-location choice remains (Beesley and Dalvi, 1974). Third, if both locations are not fixed beforehand, again two approaches are possible: partial studies on migration which take into account the accessibility of work locations (Graves and Linneman, 1979; Bonnar, 1979, Bartel, 1979; Krumm, 1983 and Linneman and Graves, 1983), and integral approaches in which the choice of a particular combination of work location and residential location forms the central issue. In this chapter we will restrict ourselves to the latter approach.

The interdependency of migration and commuting can be described with the concepts of substitution and complementarity. Suppose a person lives and works in the same region. If he decides to work outside this region, he may either migrate or commute to this new region (substitution). If he decides to live in a new region outside his work region, he migrates and then commutes daily to his former residential region (complementarity). Of course, many other cases are possible.

The modelling efforts in this respect contain two different approaches to catch this interdependency, namely a macro-economic model and a micro-economic model. Both approaches will be discussed in subsequent sections.

SIMULTANEOUS MACRO-MODELS FOR MIGRATION AND COMMUTING

Macro-level approaches towards migration and commuting have a long history. In an excellent review, Mueller (1982) discusses several approaches. Many of them are based on studies by Lowry who synthesizes neo-classical and Keynesian theories of migration, on the one hand, and the gravity model of human interaction, on the other. The gravity model not only contains population potentials but also so-called push- and pull-factors. The latter are necessary to allow for spatial asymmetry in migration flows.

The push-pull hypothesis, however, maintains that there is a strong negative correlation between in- and out-migration. In practice, in-migration and out-migration are highly and positively correlated (for the Netherlands this correlation is 0.98; see Evers and van der Veen, 1986), resulting in comparatively low net migration volumes. This has lead to the parallelism hypothesis, which states that migrants move from and to areas with high migration turnover and that low-turnover areas have both few in- and out-migrants.

The rate of out-migration (emission rate) is a good indicator. It appears that the emission rate is high for the region of Utrecht (in the centre of the Netherlands) as well as for the provinces of Groningen and Drenthe (in the North), whereas it is relatively low for Noord-Holland and Zuid-Holland (in the West) and for Noord-Brabant and Limburg (in the South). These differences remain fairly constant during the whole period and are not explained by differences in the composition of the labour force (Evers and Bartels, 1981).

Combined with the notion that the spatial distribution of migration is remarkably stable over time (see above), these results indicate that a two-stage modelling approach is necessary (see Bartels and Liaw, 1983; Moss, 1979). In the first stage the generation (total rate of out-migration) is explained, whereas in the second stage the distribution between destinations is studied. According to this, the macro-approach towards migration and commuting is based on a simultaneous equation model (van der Veen and Evers, 1983) and on an aggregate logit model (Evers and van der Veen, 1985).

Van der Veen and Evers (1983) developed a simultaneous model in which the overall level of migration activity is explained by national unemployment (to represent the business-cycle effect in a temporal context), the relative position of the region in the spatial configuration (core/periphery), and the size of the region. Specific push- and pull-factors such as regional unemployment and living conditions are only taken into account in the distribution model. Furthermore, with respect to commuting, both substitution and complementarity are introduced. The incommuting rate of a certain region, for instance, depends negatively on the rate of in-migration from adjacent regions (substitution effect) and positively on the rate of out-migration to adjacent regions (complementarity effect). The results show that the complementarity effect is difficult to handle at a macro level, due to spurious correlations. In fact, only complementarity relations proved to be significant. The overall results are reasonable, when elasticities of migration and commuting with respect to unemployment are considered (Evers and van der Veen, 1987). Increases in national unemployment reduce migration rates (with an elasticity of -0.26) and increase commuting ($+0.15$). Increases in regional unemployment reduce in-migration and in-commuting for that region and stimulate outward flows. In the latter case, out-migration reacts less ($+0.14$) than out-commuting ($+0.57$). As commuting involves a change in work location only and migration in this case probably involves both a change in work location as well as residential location, the trade-off between out-migration and out-commuting, which is in favour of the latter one, indicates a high degree of risk aversion in times of high unemployment.

Evers and van der Veen (1985) developed and estimated an aggregated logit model for labour migration and commuting. This model is based on a decision tree with respect to choices of work location and residential location. Since no individual or household characteristics are used in this model, it concentrates on the influence of macro-variables such as unemployment, living conditions, and distances. It appears that the choice between migration and commuting can very well be explained by using these macro-variables. However, again this aggregate level of modelling prohibits explicit statements on the interdependency of migration and commuting which are present at the level of the individual or household. This is why more sophisticated micro-models have been developed, which will be discussed in the next section.

SIMULTANEOUS MICRO-MODELS FOR MIGRATION AND COMMUTING

The simultaneous modelling of (changes in) residence and (changes in) work location—resulting in migration and commuting flows—has been advocated by Yapa *et al.* (1971). Termote (1978; 1980) has also studied this relationship. In the Netherlands, important work has been done by the Nederlands Economisch Instituut (1977; 1978; 1983).

Basically the analysis starts with the individual or household which is making decisions about where to live and where to work. All possible work and residential locations can be characterised by a so-called 'place utility' (see Wolpert, 1965). For each combination of workplace and residence we then can construct a 'joint utility' which is based on these two place utilities and of course on the disutility of the journey to work involved. Also, since the individual already has a residence and a workplace, a second disutility is associated with the monetary and other costs of a change in location. These joint utilities can be gathered in a preference matrix and the individual will choose the optimal combination. In this approach, a change in residence (migration) and in the journey to work (commuting) are logical outcomes of this decision-making process. Both are related to labour-market characteristics and housing or environmental characteristics of the different alternative locations (regions) in the individual's choice set, and to the characteristics of the individual or household.

The spatial choice model which we have used is based on the neo-classical theory of consumer behaviour. Under certain restrictions, the individual chooses a certain combination of goods which optimises his utility function. A spatial application of this theory asks for certain refinements, the most important being the notion that 'goods' as workplace or residential location are not perfectly and continuously divisible but instead discrete: they are all-or-nothing choices. The theory of the discrete choice models is capable of handling such phenomena. This theory is fairly well described in Domencich and McFadden (1975), Hensher and Johnson (1981), Amemiya (1981), Anas (1982) and Maddala (1983).

Discrete-choice models assume that individuals have a certain perception of the utilities associated with workplaces and residences. This perception is determined by the amount and quality of the information about the alternatives, the uncertainty of this information and the risk behaviour of the individual. This brings us to an important point, namely the uncertainty which is inherent to the way in which the utility of an alternative is measured. The theory assumes that this utility can be expressed in two components. The first, the so-called strict utility, is assumed to be a linear combination of observable characteristics of both the alternative and the individual.

The second component is random and represents stochastic influences. These stochastic influences have at least three sources. First, there will be measurement errors for the characteristics in the utility function. Second, the researcher is only capable of observing some of these characteristics and so it is possible that some of the determinants are not measured at all. Third and finally, as outlined above, there will be differences in individual taste, risk behaviour and so on. Any model which is based on observable characteristics thus can only try to explain the revealed choices with a certain degree of uncertainty. The model is essentially stochastic in nature. Empirical applications of the model have to assume a certain distribution function for this error term. In many cases a double negative exponential distribution is used which leads to the well-known logit model (see McFadden, 1973).

When the number of alternative workplaces and residences increases, so does the number of possible combinations. It is not reasonable to assume that any individual is capable of comparing too many alternative combinations simultaneously. Instead one could argue that the choice process can be broken down into a number of sequential or consecutive steps or levels. This implies a decision tree in which the choice process at a certain level is conditional on the outcome of the choice process at higher levels in the tree. This concept of a decision tree is a way out of the problem of dealing with many alternatives. One solution is to assume that choices are strictly sequential, leading to the pure sequential logit model. Another solution assumes the process to be simultaneous, but treats computation in a sequential way. Estimating a simultaneous model in this way hardly affects the parameters (see McFadden, 1978). However, one should include a feedback effect from lower decision levels to higher levels in order to restore the simultaneous nature of the model. The feedback is assumed to be complete and the breakdown is merely done for technical and computational reasons.

A further generalization is to assume that the magnitude (the parameter) of this feedback (often referred to as 'inclusive value' or 'logsum') is not fixed to be either one or zero (as in the pure sequential model) but is allowed to be determined by the data. This version of the model is known as the nested logit model. It permits an answer to the question whether the decision process can be characterised as purely sequential, as fully simultaneous, or as something inbetween.

Crucial in this modelling effort is the design of the shape of the decision tree, the subsequent levels and the number of alternatives available at each level. Each individual has a certain residence at the beginning of the decision-making process. The most important question then is whether the individual first determines the work region and next the residential region or vice versa. In general the literature supports the first alternative: the choice of the workplace is dominant and the choice of a residence is conditional upon the outcome of this workplace decision (see Okabe, 1977; Beesley and Dalvi, 1974; Vickerman, 1984; Nederlands Economisch Instituut, 1983). This seems reasonable at a spatial level of regions. We will use this sequence as a working hypothesis in this chapter. The magnitude of the feedbacks will reveal whether the real decision process is sequential or simultaneous.

In his search for a work region, the individual will normally have strong preferences for a workplace close to his residence, which means in the same region as where he lives. This minimises the journey to work. Moreover, the individual normally has the best information on jobs available in this region. So, as the first step or level we model the decision whether or not to choose a job outside the (old) residential region. Once he decides to work elsewhere, the next choice to be made is between partial and total displacement (Roseman, 1971). Partial displacement means that the workplace is still rather close (for instance, adjacent) to his old region of residence, so many family and social contacts and ties can be maintained. A total displacement means that the work location is at a greater distance and the individual or household has to build a new social environment or accept a long journey to work.

After a decision as to the degree of displacement, the individual chooses a particular work region and next determines what his residence will be. This latter choice also includes a zero option, which is to stay in the old residential region.

The choices at the four different levels of the tree are shown in Figure 13.1. Decision-making starts at the top and then proceeds towards lower levels. Possible feedbacks are marked with a dotted line in the reversed direction. Hence, the model is based on six different choices (sub-models) and there are four feedbacks to deal with. This means that the decision tree has two binary choices (levels 1 and 2) and four multinomial choices (levels 3 and 4). In the latter choices there are three to six alternatives, so the breakdown of the decision process results in an attractive number of alternatives from a computational point of view. Estimation is based on maximum likelihood since the model is non-linear in variables. Incorporation of feedbacks makes it necessary to start the estimation procedure at the lowest level and consecutively work up towards higher levels (see McFadden, 1978).

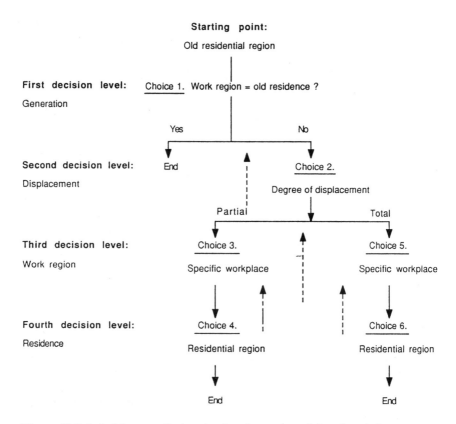

Figure 13.1 A decision tree for housing-location and work-location choice

RESULTS AND ESTIMATION

The model was calibrated on data from a housing market survey (Woningbehoeftenonderzoek, 1981) which contains 66 000 household records and about 200 variables. We restricted ourselves to 3000 households based in the northern part of the Netherlands in 1978, and analysed their behaviour in the period 1978–81. As can be seen from Figure 13.1, the model has six submodels, each with a different population at risk. The model uses different characteristics (explanatory variables) for each choice. After calibration, several validation tests are carried out. We exemplify two choices and present the validation results for the total model.

The two choices to be elaborated in this chapter are choices 3 and 1 from Figure 13.1, namely the choice of a particular work region in case of a partial displacement and the choice whether or not to work outside the old residential region. In the third choice, the individual chooses a work region from three to six alternatives. All these regions are adjacent to his old residential region (partial displacement). Several factors explain observed choices. First, the inclusive value or feedback from the residential choice submodel (choice

4) is relevant. It is possible that when choosing a particular work region, the individual already takes into account the utility of the residential choice at the next level. The degree to which this feedback exists is measured by the magnitude of the parameter for this variable. This parameter will vary between 0 and 1, denoting a whole range between pure sequential and pure simultaneous relationships between these choices respectively. Second, we take the distance between the old residence and the alternative work regions as an indicator of both the amount of information available and the possible journey to work involved. Third, we use a number of aggregated macro-variables to represent the labour-market conditions for each region. Note that these variables do not vary over individuals. Unfortunately we have no information on education, work experience or detailed profession of each individual, so it is difficult to measure one individual's place utility with respect to a work region (for the use of such variables, see Anas, 1981). In the analysis we use employment, both in absolute value to indicate the labour turnover and the number of vacancies) and in relative terms (divided by population, to measure labour-market tensions). Unemployment rates, the degree of urbanisation and the average wage rate are also used to denote the relative favourability of each region. Finally, as an individual characteristic, we take the work region of other members of the household as a dummy variable. This reflects the necessity of fine-tuning of workplace choice for households with more than one worker.

The estimation results are shown in Table 13.3. After the first round we deleted all variables with the wrong sign. This did not affect the likelihood noticeably. We were left with four variables in the second round. The inclusive value was not significantly from zero, which means that in the case of a partial displacement, first a work location is chosen, and, purely conditional on this outcome, a residential region is then chosen. Further, distance and employment variables are significant, as are the work locations of other household members. So the family context is relevant.

In the first choice, the individual has to decide whether or not to work outside his old residential region. Analogous to the two-stage type of migration modelling, this choice explains the generation of spatial mobility. For the

Table 13.3 Work-location choice in the case of a partial displacement. Estimation results for choice 3

Variable	Expected sign	First round Parameter	First round t-ratio	Second round Parameter	Second round t-ratio
Inclusive value	+	−0.12	−0.8	*	*
Distance	−	−2.55	−7.6	−2.81	−9.1
Employment (abs.)	+	1.25	1.4	1.12	2.3
Employment (rel.)	+	1.07	0.8	0.87	1.5
Unemployment	−	0.62	0.2	*	*
Urbanisation	+	−3.45	−0.6	*	*
Average wage	+	−1.01	−0.1	*	*
Work region other members	+	2.76	5.8	1.89	4.4

Table 13.4   The generation of mobility. Estimation results for choice 1

Variable	Expected sign	First round		Second round	
		Parameter	t-ratio	Parameter	t-ratio
Inclusive value	+	0.16	4.7	0.16	4.8
Family size	−	−0.10	−0.6	−0.10	−0.6
Age	−	−0.35	−3.4	−0.36	−3.3
Participation members	−	0.03	0.1	*	*
House ownership	−	−0.89	−0.4	−0.87	−0.4
Income	+/−	0.12	1.4	0.12	1.5
Profession	−	−0.87	−2.2	−0.87	−2.2
Distance	−	−0.57	−7.5	−0.57	−7.7
Employment	−	−8.83	−1.7	−8.80	−2.0
Unemployment	+	−0.36	−0.1	*	*
Average wage	−	−0.23	−0.2	−0.23	−0.2

explanation of the revealed choices we use eleven variables. First, an inclusive value determines the magnitude of the feedback from the second level (degree of displacement) to this generation choice. Second, we use a number of individual- or household-specific characteristics, such as the size of the household, age, and the labour force participation of other household members. An increase in any of these variables is likely to increase the resistance towards mobility and hence affect the generation in a negative way. Other variables of this type are the ownership of one's house (a negative influence expected), income (both negative and positive influences) and a dummy variable for certain professions (people who work at their home address, such as shop owners; negative). Finally a number of macro-variables will affect mobility as well. The distance to other regions (negative) and the relative labour-market situation in the old residential region (employment, unemployment and wages) are such variables. Estimation results are presented in Table 13.4.

The results show that almost all variables are relevant. The relative unemployment situation does not affect mobility, which is a surprising result. The parameter for the inclusive value is clearly significantly different from zero and also from one. So the feedback is neither absent nor complete. The relationship between the choices 2 and 1 is therefore neither purely sequential nor purely simultaneous, but rather something inbetween. This is called a 'sequential-recursive decision structure'.

After calibration of the submodels we carried out some tests to evaluate the *goodness of fit*. These validation criteria are twofold, namely a likelihood-ratio index and a prediction-success index. The likelihood-ratio index compares the value of the likelihood function at the optimum with the value which can be obtained by using the prior information on the aggregate shares of the alternatives (see Tardiff, 1976; Hensher and Johnson, 1981). This latter value then provides a point of reference to determine whether the full model, using individual information, is capable of substantially improving the goodness of fit. The two likelihood values are divided and normalized in the 0–1 interval. The

Table 13.5 Overview of the quality and feedback structure of the sub-models

Choice number	Short description	Likelihood-ratio index	Prediction-success index	Feedback parameter
1.	Generation of mobility	0.19	0.26	0.16
2.	Partial or total displacement	0.11	0.11	0.33
3.	Workplace choice (partial displacement)	0.26	0.27	0
4.	Residential choice (partial displacement)	0.63	0.48	none
5.	Workplace choice (total displacement)	0.12	0.10	0.77
6.	Residential choice (total displacement)	0.33	0.39	none

resulting index is to a certain extent comparable with the well-known R^2 statistic. However, values between 0.2 and 0.4 are considered extremely good fits (Hensher and Johnson, 1981, p. 51).

The second validation test is the prediction success index. This index measures the quality of the model by comparing observed and predicted choices for each individual separately. Again, a correction is made for the prior information on the aggregate shares of the alternatives. This index is developed by McFadden (1978) and is normalized in the 0–1 interval.

In Table 13.5 we summarize the results of the validation tests and the feedbacks in the model. As Table 13.5 reveals, in general the results are quite satisfying. The two exceptions are sub-models 2 and 5, in which cases model quality is less good. As for the feedback parameters, it appears that in the case of partial displacement, there is no feedback from housing choice to workplace choice. This indicates a purely sequential relationship. In the case of total displacement, the parameter (0.77) is significantly different from zero but not from one. Hence in this case we cannot reject the hypothesis that workplace and residence are simultaneously determined. The possible outcomes for the workplace choice do not affect the choice of the degree of displacement itself. The parameter (0.33) is not significantly different from zero, so again we accept a purely sequential decision structure. Finally, as mentioned in the section above, the choice of the degree of displacement affects the generation of mobility. The parameter (0.16) is different from both zero and one, so there is a sequential-recursive relationship.

We summarize the most important features of the estimation for the six submodels. First, the results show that, with respect to the interdependency of commuting and migration, substitution is far more important than complementarity. Also, when mobility takes places over short distances (up to 80 km), commuting is more attractive than migration. This is in line with the empirical observations made in Table 13.2.

Second, family-context variables such as household size and work status and work region of other members are important in the case of a partial displacement. When one decides to relocate work and residence over larger distance, these family variables are no longer important. As for age, it appears that when a partial displacement is chosen, elderly people prefer to commute, whereas in the case of total displacement these people are more likely to migrate because of the journey to work they would otherwise face.

Third, the model shows that not only individual characteristics should be used. Area characteristics such as employment, unemployment and wages also seem relevant. These macro-variables are not necessarily only used because of lack of adequate individual data but play an important role themselves in setting the social, economic and psychological environment in which the individual operates (for an extensive discussion see Navratil and Doyle, 1977; Gardner, 1981).

A final conclusion is that it is sensible to break down the total model into six sub-models and to allow for different feedback structures. It appears that the model cannot be estimated in its entirety at one go, since the number of alternatives then is far too large. However, the relationships between the submodels are purely sequential only in part, so it is necessary to include a possibility for feedbacks. Nested logit models seem to be a very powerful tool for entangling complex choice structures into a series of sub-choices and still maintaining a reasonable degree of behavioural validity.

CONCLUSIONS

The analysis of components of regional labour supply shows that economic rather than demographic components are dominant. The influence of changes in net commuting is surprisingly high, whereas the volume of net migration has decreased. Overall, the contribution of net effects of spatial mobility has decreased.

An examination of the changes in the volume of commuting and migration reveals that migration is at historically low levels by the end of the period. From the literature it is not fully clear whether this indicates a structural change in the kind of spatial mobility chosen (increased commuting as a substitute for migration) or business-cycle effects. Empirical results cannot resolve this question because of the short time series of commuting and labour-migration data. By the end of 1986 the volume of migration had recovered.

Finally, it should be clear that any national or regional labour-market model should incorporate endogenous relationships for labour supply. Only too often this component is exogenised and reduced to a simple demographic factor. Since it has been demonstrated that changes in labour supply do contribute heavily to developments in unemployment, explicit attention should be paid to the supply side. Moreover, in regional economic modelling, relatively little attention has been paid to commuting as such, and to inter-relationships between participation, commuting and migration.

The discussion has made clear that these interdependencies exist and should be incorporated because of their importance. However, this can only be done properly within a micro-economic model for workplace and residential location choice. The micro–macro debate is one of the most important topics in economic theory. Several authors state that the explicit attention to individual behaviour neglects broader, societal constraints which restrict freedom of choice. Also, individuals could be satisficers rather than maximisers (Sheppard, 1980). Models estimated from aggregated data could be far more adaptable to practical prediction and policy analysis (Anas, 1981). On the other hand, as Navratil and Doyle (1977) show, the process of aggregation seriously distorts some of the factors important to the individual's decisions. Taken together, these notions result in a plea for a kind of synthesis of macro- and micro-approaches, where the basic level of analysis is micro and is represented by the introduction of personal or household characteristics, whereas all kinds of geographical, institutional and other environmental constraints are taken into account by using macro-variables as well. This prerequisite certainly introduces many complications in a research environment in which many labour-market models are still exclusively macro-economic in nature and where a proper transmission mechanism to synthesise macro- and micro-approaches has yet to be fully developed.

REFERENCES

Alonso, W (1964), *Location and Land Use*. Cambridge, MA: Harvard University Press.
Amemiya, T. (1981) 'Qualitative response models: a survey', *Journal of Economic Literature*, vol. 29, pp. 483–536.
Anas, A. (1981) 'The estimation of multinomial logit models of joint location and travel mode choice from aggregated data', *Journal of Regional Science*, vol. 21, pp. 223–42.
Anas, A. (1982) *Residential Location Markets and Urban Transportation: Economic Theory, Econometrics and Policy Analysis with Discrete Choice Models*. New York: Academic Press.
Bartel, A.P. (1979) 'The migration decision: what role does job mobility play', *American Economic Review*, vol. 69, pp. 775–86.
Bartels, C.P.A. and Liaw, K.-L. (1983) 'The dynamics of spatial labor mobility in the Netherlands', *Environment and Planning*, vol. 15A, pp. 329–42.
Beesley, M.E. and Dalvi, M. (1974) 'Spatial equilibrium and the journey to work', *Journal of Transport Economics and Policy*, vol. 8, pp. 197–222.
Bonnar, D.M. (1979) 'Migration in the South East of England: an analysis of the interrelationships of housing, socio-economic status and labour demand', *Regional Studies*, vol. 13, pp. 345–59.
Burridge, P. and Gordon, I. (1981) 'Unemployment in the British Metropolitan Labour Areas', *Oxford Economic Papers*, vol. 33, pp. 274–97.
Clark, W.A.V. (1982) 'Recent research on migration and mobility: a review and interpretation', *Progress in Planning*, vol. 18, no. 1.
Clark, W.A.V., Huff, J.O. and Burt, J.E. (1979) 'Calibrating a model of the decision to move', *Environment and Planning*, vol. 11A, pp. 689–704.
Domencich, T.A. and McFadden, D.L. (1975) *Urban Travel Demand: A Behavioral Analysis*. Amsterdam: North-Holland.
Evers, G.H.M. (1987) 'The dynamics of regional labour supply and unemployment, The Netherlands, 1971-1986', *Tijdschrift voor Economische en Sociale Geografie*.
Evers, G.H.M. and Bartels, C.P.A. (1981) *Policy-relevant characteristics of spatial labor mobility in the Netherlands*, WP-81-157. Laxenburg, Austria: International Institute for Applied Systems Analysis.
Evers, G.H.M., van der Veen, A. and Heerink, N.B.M. (1983) *Pendel, migratie en deelname aan het beroepsleven: partiele en simultane benaderingen*. Groningen: Institute for Economic Research.
Evers, G.H.M. and van der Veen, A. (1985) 'A simultaneous non-linear model for

labor migration and commuting', *Regional Studies*, vol. 19, pp. 217–29.

Evers, G.H.M. and van der Veen, A. (1986) *Pendel, migratie en deelname aan het beroepsleven: macro- en micro-economische benaderingen*. Proefschrift, Febo, Enschede. (Commuting, migration and labour force participation, Ph.D. dissertation, Tilburg University).

Evers, G.H.M. and van der Veen, A. (1987) 'Regional unemployment and inter-regional labour supply mobility' in R. Funck and J. Oosterhaven (eds), *Problems of Regional Underemployment*. Karlsruhe.

Gardner, R.W. (1981) 'Macrolevel influences on the migration decision process' in G.F. de Jong and R.W. Gardner (eds), *Migration Decision Making*. New York: Pergamon Press.

Gordon, I. and Lamont, D. (1982) 'A model of labour market interdependencies in the London region', *Environment and Planning*, vol. 14A, pp. 237–64.

Grant, E.K. and Vanderkamp, J. (1976) *The Economic Causes and Effects of Migration, Canada, 1965–71*. Ottawa: Economic Council of Canada.

Grant, E.K. and Vanderkamp, J. (1980) 'The effects of migration on income: a micro study with Canadian data 1965–71', *Canadian Journal of Economics*, vol. 13, pp. 375–406.

Graves, P.E. and Linneman, P. (1979) 'Household migration: theoretical and empirical results', *Journal of Urban Economics*, vol. 6, pp. 383–404.

Greenwood, M.J. (1975) 'Research on internal migration in the United States: a survey', *Journal of Economic Literature*, vol. 13, pp. 397–433.

Harris, J.R. and Todaro, M.P. (1970) 'Migration, unemployment and development, a two sector analysis', *American Economic Review*, vol. 60, pp. 139–49.

Hart, R.A. (1973) 'Economic expectations and the decision to migrate: an analysis by socio-economic group', *Regional Studies*, vol. 7, pp. 271–85.

Hart, R.A. (1975) 'Interregional economic migration: some theoretical considerations (part I)', *Journal of Regional Science*, vol. 15, no. 2.

Hensher, D.A. and Johnson, L.W. (1981) *Applied Discrete Choice Modelling*. London: Croom Helm.

Herzog, H.W. and Schlottmann, A.M. (1981), 'Labor force migration and allocative efficiency in the United States: the roles of information and psychic costs', *Economic Inquiry*, vol. 19, pp. 459–75.

Krumm, R.J. (1983) 'Regional labor markets and the household migration decision', *Journal of Regional Science*, vol. 23, pp. 361–76.

Lancaster, K. (1966) 'A new approach to consumer theory', Journal of Political Economy, vol. 74, pp. 132–157.

Linneman, P. and Graves, P.E. (1983) 'Migration and job change: a multinomial logit approach', *Journal of Urban Economics*, vol. 14, pp. 263–79.

Maddala, G.S. (1983) *Limited-Dependent and Qualitative Variables in Econometrics*. Cambridge: Cambridge University Press.

McFadden, D.L. (1973) 'Conditional logit analysis of qualitative choice behavior' in P. Zarembka (ed.), *Frontiers in Econometrics*. New York: Academic Press.

McFadden, D.L. (1978) 'Modelling the choice of residential location' in A. Karlqvist, L. Lundqvist, F. Snickars and J. Weibull (eds), *Spatial interaction theory and planning models*. Studies in regional science and urban economics, Vol. 3. Amsterdam: North-Holland.

Molho, I. (1984)'A dynamic model of interregional migration flows in Great Britain', *Journal of Regional Science*, vol. 24, pp. 317–36.

Moore, E.G. and Clark, W.A.V. (1980) 'The policy context for mobility research' in W.A.V. Clark and E.G. Moore (eds), *Residential Mobility and Public Policy*. Beverly Hills, CA: Sage.

Morrison, P.A. (1973) 'Theoretical issues in the design of population mobility models', *Environment and Planning*, vol. 5A, pp. 125–34.

Moss, W.G. (1979), 'A note on individual choice models of migration', *Regional Science and Urban Economics*, vol. 9, pp. 1–11.

Mueller, C.F. (1982) *The Economics of Labor Migration, A Behavioral Analysis*. New York: Academic Press.

Navratil, F.J. and Doyle, J.J. (1977) 'The socioeconomic determinants of migration and the level of aggregation', *Southern Economic Journal*, vol. 43, pp. 1547–59.

Nederlands Economisch Intituut (NEI) (1977) *De samenhang tussen woonmigratie, werkplaatsverandering en woon-werk bereikbaarheid, een methode van onderzoek*. Rotterdam: NEI.

NEI (1978) *Residential mobility, work mobility and home-to-work accessibility*. Rotterdam: NEI.

NEI (1983) *Woon- en werkplaatsverandering in de Noordvleugel van de Randstad, deelrapport 3: Theorie, data-organisatie en deel-analyses*, Rotterdam: NEI.

Okabe, A. (1977) 'Formulation of the intervening opportunities model for housing location choice behavior', *Journal of Regional Science*, vol. 17, pp. 31–40.

Pickup, L. and Town, S.W. (1983) *Commuting Patterns in Europe: An Overview of the Literature*. Report 796. Crowthorne, Berkshire: Transport and Road Research Laboratory.

Roseman, C.C. (1971) 'Migration as a spatial and temporal process', *Annals of the Association of American Geographers*, vol. 61, pp. 589–98.

Sandell, S.H. (1977) 'Women and the economics of family migration', *Review of Economics and Statistics*, vol. 59, pp. 406–14.

Shaw, R.P. (1975) *Migration, Theory and Fact*. Bibliography Series no. 5. Philadelphia: Regional Science Research Institute.

Sheppard, E.S. (1980) 'The ideology of spatial choice', *Papers of the Regional Science Association*, vol. 45, pp. 197–213.

Siegel, J. (1975) 'Intrametropolitan migration: a simultaneous model of employment and residential location of white and black households', *Journal of Urban Economics*, vol. 2, pp. 29–47.

Simpson, W. (1980) 'A simultaneous model of workplace and residential location incorporating job search;, *Journal of Urban Economics*, vol. 8, pp. 330–49.

Sjaastad, L.A. (1962) 'The costs and returns of human migration', *Journal of Political Economy*, vol. 70.

Tardiff, T.J. (1976) 'A note on the goodness-of-fit statistics for probit and logit models', *Transportation*, vol. 5, pp. 377–88.

Termote, M. (1978) 'Migration and commuting in Losch Central Place system' in R. Funck and J.B. Parr (eds), *The Analysis of Regional Structure: Essays in Honour of August Losch*. London: Pion.

Termote, M. (1980) *Migration and Commuting: A Theoretical Framework*. WP-80-69. Laxenburg, Austria: International Institute for Applied Systems Analysis.

Van der Veen, A. and Evers, G.H.M. (1983) 'A simultaneous model for regional labor supply, incorporating labor force participation, commuting and migration', *Socio-economic planning sciences*, vol. 17, pp. 239–50.

Vickerman, R.W. (1984) 'Urban and regional change, migration and commuting—the dynamics of workplace, residence and transport choice', *Urban Studies*, vol. 21, pp. 15–29.

Wolpert, J. (1965) 'Behavioral aspects of the decision to migrate', *Papers and Proceedings of the Regional Science Association*, vol. 15, pp. 159–69.

Yapa, L., Polese, M. and Wolpert, J. (1971) 'Interdependencies of commuting, migration and job site relocations', *Economic Geography*, vol. 47, pp. 59–72.

Chapter 14

COMPOUND AND GENERALISED POISSON MODELS FOR INTER-URBAN MIGRATION*

R. Flowerdew and A. Lovett

INTRODUCTION

Inter-urban migration (like other forms of spatial interaction) has been modelled in many different ways with varying degrees of success. Since the entropy-maximising derivation of Wilson's (1970) family of spatial interaction models became well known, these models, with or without origin and destination constraints, have dominated the study of inter-urban migration. Flowerdew and Aitkin (1982) developed an alternative approach to spatial interaction modelling using a form of regression analysis based on the Poisson distribution. This method makes it easier to introduce new explanatory variables and to evaluate the model's goodness fit. These two approaches have been shown to give equivalent results (Baxter, 1982).

In common with others using Poisson regression to analyse migration flows (for example, Constantine and Gower, 1982), Flowerdew and Aitkin found that the model did not fit. The Poisson method, as operationalised in the computer program package GLIM, produces a goodness-of-fit statistic, the deviance, which should have an approximately chi-squared distribution if the data could have been generated by the model. With a data set of 15 750 observations and a model with four parameters (a constant, plus coefficients for the logarithms of origin population, destination population and distance), the calculated deviance was 77 188 with 15 746 degrees of freedom. This is nearly five times higher than it should be if the model provides an acceptable fit to the data (the critical value of χ^2 at the 5% significance level is 16 095). The implication is that the data are over-dispersed in relation to the Poisson assumption, or equivalently (Breslow, 1984) that there is 'extra-Poisson variation' in the data. Although the poor fit may result in part from the absence of important explanatory variables from the model, its main cause is likely to be the inappropriateness of the Poisson assumption.

*We are indebted to Murray Aitkin for help in developing the algorithm, and to several members of the Centre for Applied Statistics and the Computer Centre at the University of Lancaster, especially Charles Daly, for help in computation. An earlier version of this work was presented at the British Regional Science Association Conference, University of Stirling, 2–4 September 1987.

The Poisson distribution refers to counts of events which are independent of each other; in this case, a Poisson model assumes that each migrant from i to j moves independently of the others. In practice, of course, this is not true. People live together as households and normally, if one household member migrates, the others will do so, too (there are, of course, exceptions, such as a young adult leaving home or a marital partner leaving if the marriage breaks up). It is more reasonable to suppose that households, not individuals, move independently of one another, and hence that household moves should be modelled by a Poisson distribution. If this assumption is made, the number of people moving should have a generalised Poisson distribution, the Poisson process describing household moves being generalised by the size distribution of households.

In this chapter, we describe the Poisson regression model and its extension to take account of household size. We also review other attempts to construct models with extra-Poisson variation in this context. The household-size model is then applied to the data set mentioned above, and the results are evaluated according to the model's performance and the empirical conclusions that can be drawn from it.

POISSON REGRESSION METHODS

Poisson regression analysis can be regarded as part of a family of statistical models, which includes log-linear and logit models as well as ordinary least squares regression. Nelder and Wedderburn (1972) first proposed the concept of generalised linear modelling in which the response variable is regarded as linked to a linear function of a set of explanatory variables. The specific model depends on the probability distribution assumed for the response variable and the nature of the link between its mean and the linear combination of explanatory variables. In ordinary least squares regression, the probability distribution is the normal and the link function one of identity; in Poisson regression, the probability distribution is Poisson and the link logarithmic. A log-linear model is equivalent to a Poisson regression model in which all the explanatory variables are categorical. Poisson regression can, however, include not only such categorical variables but also other explanatory variables at any scale of measurement. The technique is available as an option in the GLIM, GENSTAT and LIMDEP statistical packages. A brief treatment is given in Maddala (1983, pp. 51–4) and an introductory guide has been written by Lovett (1984).

The fit of a generalised linear model is evaluated by a statistic which Nelder and Wedderburn (1972) term the 'deviance'. The lack of fit of a particular model to observed data is measured by minus twice the log-likelihood, and the deviance of a particular model is the difference in this quantity for the model concerned and for the saturated model of the original observations (in which there are as many parameters as observations). In Poisson regression, the deviance is equivalent to the log likelihood-ratio statistic (sometimes denoted G^2). The formula is:

$$D = 2 \sum_{\substack{i \ j \\ i \neq j}} \sum n_{ij} \ln (n_{ij} / \hat{\lambda}_{ij}) \tag{14.1}$$

where n_{ij} is the observed flow from i to j and $\hat{\lambda}_{ij}$ is the estimate produced by the model. The deviance measures the variation in the data that the model fails to explain; a high value consequently indicates a poorer fit than a low value. If the model is correct, the deviance has an approximately chi-squared distribution with $n - p$ degrees of freedom (where there are n observations and p parameters have been fitted). If the deviance exceeds the critical value of χ^2 at an appropriate significance level, the model does not fit.

The impact of changing the set of explanatory variables in a model can also be evaluated using a chi-squared test. If a new parameter is added to the model, its contribution can be regarded as significant if the reduction in deviance is greater than the critical chi-squared value (at an appropriate significance level) for the degrees of freedom lost.

The interpretation of Poisson regression parameters is similar to that for ordinary least squares regression conducted in logarithmic form. A gravity-model equation produced using ordinary least squares might be written:

$$\ln \hat{y}_{ij} = \hat{\beta}_0 + \hat{\beta}_1 \ln P_i + \hat{\beta}_2 \ln P_j + \hat{\beta}_3 \ln d_{ij} \tag{14.2}$$

where the left-hand side of the equation is the estimated mean for the logarithm of the movement from i to j, P_i is origin population, P_j is destination population, d_{ij} is the distance from i to j, and the $\hat{\beta}$ terms are the parameters estimated by the model. A Poisson regression involving the same variables might be written:

$$\hat{\lambda}_{ij} = \exp\left(\hat{\beta}_0 + \hat{\beta}_1 \ln P_i + \hat{\beta}_2 \ln P_j + \hat{\beta}_3 \ln d_{ij}\right) \tag{14.3}$$

where the exponential term reflects the logarithmic link function. In equation (14.2), the term $\ln y_{ij}$ is the mean of a normal distribution and in equation (14.3) λ_{ij} is the mean of a Poisson distribution. The difference in format between equations (14.2) and (14.3) is intended to emphasise that it is the flows themselves, not their logarithms, that are being estimated. The interpretation of the $\hat{\beta}$ terms is identical; for example, $\hat{\beta}_3$ (which we would expect to be negative) can be interpreted as the rate at which interaction is predicted to change as the logarithm of distance increases.

Residuals can be computed for each observation in several ways, according to the purpose of the analysis. For example, the estimated flow can simply be subtracted from the observed flow; or the difference can be standardised by dividing by the square root of the estimate. A further way of assessing the relationship of individual flows to the overall model is to calculate their contribution to the total deviance, a statistic easily calculated though not automatically provided in GLIM. The size of these contributions to deviance, and the identity of the observations concerned, can be very useful in evaluating the model and in suggesting other explanatory variables that may be important.

A POISSON REGRESSION ANALYSIS OF INTER-URBAN MIGRATION IN GREAT BRITAIN

In this section, we will report briefly on an application of Poisson regression, with the intention of illustrating the points made above and setting the scene for the subsequent discussion of compound and generalised Poisson models. This application has been reported in more detail by Flowerdew and Aitkin (1982).

The data used consist of observations from the 1971 British Census of people recorded as living in one Standard Metropolitan Labour Area (SMLA) at the time of the census and in another SMLA one year previously. SMLAs were defined by Drewett *et al.* (1974) for Great Britain on the basis of commuting criteria; they are intended to represent functional labour markets. There are 126 SMLAs, containing about 80% of the population of Great Britain, and hence 15 750 (126 × 125) flows connecting pairs of places, omitting flows from each place to itself. The total number of migrants recorded is 89 101, the largest flow being 681 migrants from London to Brighton, and with many flows being very small or, in 8150 cases, zero. The data are based on responses to questions given to a 10% sample of households; the numbers are therefore only some 10% of those actually migrating during 1970–1.

The largest flows, as might be expected, are those between the largest SMLAs, together with a number of shorter moves from large centres to smaller SMLAs nearby, often corresponding to overspill schemes (for example, London to Basildon, Liverpool to Wigan). Size and distance do seem to be important factors, as the gravity model predicts. There are also large flows involving the naval bases, Plymouth, Portsmouth and Rosyth (in Dunfermline SMLA) and between some pairs of contiguous SMLAs. A detailed account of the data set and its empirical implications can be found in Flowerdew and Salt (1979).

As reported in Flowerdew and Aitkin (1982), fitting a Poisson model to this data set produced results more satisfactory than those derived from ordinary least squares regression. The parameters were different and more in accord with expectations, the overall goodness of fit (as measured by a chi-squared statistic comparing observed and estimated values) was much better, the total migration estimated was identical to that observed (instead of being a small fraction of it), and the regression seemed less influenced by very small flows.

The model fitted had the following form:

$$\hat{\lambda}_{ij} = \exp\left(-14.94 + 0.954 \ln P_i + 0.804 \ln P_j - 1.134 \ln d_{ij}\right) \qquad (14.4)$$

However, the deviance value obtained, 77 188 for 15 746 degrees of freedom, showed that the model clearly did not fit. The critical value of χ^2 at the 5% significance level is 16 095; hence the deviance is nearly five times what it should be for the model to be considered adequate.

Such situations occur frequently in Poisson regression modelling. There are two likely explanations for a poor fit. There may be other variables which affect the dependent variable in the regression; or the Poisson assumption may be inappropriate. We attempted to improve the model fit by introducing additional explanatory variables (contiguity, unemployment, and naval base dummy variables) and by incorporating origin and destination constraints (Flowerdew and Lovett, 1988). These were successful in that they reduced the deviance significantly, but unsuccessful in that it remained well in excess of the critical value of χ^2.

There may, of course, be other important variables which have not been included; such variables may in practice be unobtainable, or even unmeasurable. If this is so, or if there are reasons to suppose that the phenomena being counted (for example, the migrants) are not independent of one another, some form of compound or generalised Poisson distribution may be worth investigating.

COMPOUND AND GENERALISED POISSON MODELS

There are two main ways in which Poisson models can be modified when the Poisson assumption is inadequate. First, a compound Poisson model may be used where the Poisson parameter is subject to variation. This variation can be represented as a nuisance parameter ε_{ij} which is added to the linear predictor. The term ε_{ij} can be regarded as representing the effects of omitted variables (Davies and Crouchley, 1985). As Davies and Guy (1987) show, the nature of the compound Poisson model will depend on the probability distribution of exp (ε_{ij}). If this distribution is gamma, for example, the resulting model is negative binomial.

Second, relaxing the assumption that all events are independent (in this context, that all migrants move independently) leads to a generalised Poisson distribution. This can be thought of as representing a series of independent events (for example, household moves) modelled by the Poisson distribution, each event having a magnitude (for example, number of household members) modelled by the generalising distribution. If the generalising distribution is logarithmic, the resulting model is again negative binomial.

Both compound and generalised Poisson models have variances greater than their means and hence may be useful in accounting for extra-Poisson variation. Davies and Guy (1987), however, have shown that they give the same estimates for parameters and for fitted values as the ordinary Poisson model (assuming the same set of explanatory variables is used). The standard errors of the parameters are nevertheless likely to be larger, and this may affect whether a particular variable can be regarded as making a significant contribution to the model. Furthermore, the deviance of a compound or generalised Poisson model will be less than that of the Poisson model with the same parameters. In our migration example, such a model (which can be argued to be more theoretically appropriate) may have a much better fit to the data than a standard Poisson model.

One of the simplest ways of adjusting a Poisson model to account for extra-Poisson variation is the quasi-likelihood approach (Wedderburn, 1974; Baxter, 1985) where the variance is set equal to the mean multiplied by a constant. If the main goal is to get the model to fit, this constant can be derived by dividing the deviance by the degrees of freedom. This variance value can be incorporated into a GLIM model using the $SCALE directive. The model will then fit perfectly. However, its interpretation may be difficult. It may be noted, for example, that such a model can be made to fit regardless of the explanatory variables used.

Aufhauser and Fischer (1985) adopt a related approach, but provide more theoretical justification. They were concerned with modelling migration within the city of Vienna, and recognised that the units migrating were households rather than individuals. This means that the independence assumption of the Poisson model is violated; they therefore suggest that the migration of households may be Poisson, but the number of migrating individuals should be treated as generalised Poisson. They use a quasi-likelihood approach, in which the variance is taken to be the mean multiplied by the constant 2.2 (which appears to be the mean household size in the city of Vienna). They do not discuss why this is an appropriate way to incorporate household size into the model; it is effectively a generalised Poisson model in which all households have exactly 2.2 members! At least some theoretical justification is provided for the quasi-likelihood approach.

Hinde (1982) developed a compound Poisson model for the case where poor model fit is the result of omitting an important variable. If this variable is assumed to be normally distributed, it can be incorporated by fitting a Poisson model with a normally distributed error term, and Hinde has written macros in GLIM for fitting such models. This type of model also has the effect of mopping up all the extra-Poisson variation, but has the problem of relying on an unknown normally distributed variable which may be hard to interpret.

As discussed earlier, it is also possible to produce compound or generalised Poisson models by combining the Poisson with another known distribution (as was frequently done in the point-pattern analysis studies of the 1960s). The most frequently encountered model of this type is the negative binomial. Macros exist to fit negative binomial models in GLIM, but a problem arises because the negative binomial has two parameters, and in the absence of any theoretical guidance an iterative procedure is necessary to estimate the best value of the second 'nuisance' parameter. In the present context, a negative binomial model would be appropriate if households were assumed to move according to a Poisson process, with their sizes distributed logarithmically.

In practice, this is not necessary. We do not have to fit a logarithmic or other distribution to model household size because the distribution of household sizes in Great Britain is known from the Census. The most appropriate model for the analysis of inter-urban migration flows, therefore, is a Poisson model for household migration generalised by the observed household-size distribution.

THE HOUSEHOLD SIZE MODEL

This model, unfortunately, is not easy to fit in GLIM as it requires a complex and time-consuming recursive algorithm. The parameter estimates and fitted values are identical to the estimates from the standard Poisson model, as with any compound or generalised Poisson model, but calculating the deviance presents more difficulties and necessitated writing a FORTRAN program. For each migration flow, the log-likelihood $L(n_{ij})$ of the observed value must be calculated, where n_{ij} is the number of migrants from i to j. This must be done using an iterative procedure, because the log-likelihood of observing any given number of migrants, p, is calculated from the log-likelihood of observing smaller numbers of migrants.

The rationale behind the iterative procedure can be outlined by considering how a migrant stream of size n_{ij} may be constituted. If there is 1 migrant, his (or her) household must have size 1 (we are concerned with moving households, not households as they may exist before or after migration). A stream of 2 migrants may be made up of one household of size 2 or two households of size 1. A stream of 3 migrants may consist of one household of size 3, or one of size 2 added to a single-person household, or one of size 1 added to 2 migrants composed in either of the ways in the previous sentence.

The probabilities of a household consisting of 1, 2, . . ., 9 members are known, as is the probability of a household consisting of 10 or more members. The latter is sufficiently small that little error is introduced by treating all such households as if they had exactly 10 members. The log-likelihood of p migrants from i to j, therefore, is made up of ten components: a household of size 10 added to $p-10$ other migrants, a household of size 9 added to $p-9$ other migrants, a household of size 8 added to $p-8$ other migrants, and so on down to a household of size 1 added to $p-1$ other migrants. Of course, if p is less than 10, some of these situations cannot arise.

The starting point is the calculation of $L(0)$, the log-likelihood of a zero flow. The value of $L(1)$ is then a function of $L(0)$, representing the case of a one-person household being added to no other migrants. $L(2)$ is a function of $L(0)$ plus a two-person household and $L(1)$ plus a one-person household; $L(3)$ is a function of $L(0)$, $L(1)$ and $L(2)$; and so on up to $L(10)$ which is a function of $L(0)$, $L(1)$, . . ., $L(9)$. However, because we are assuming that no households have more than ten members, the recursive relationship never includes more than ten terms. Thus $L(11)$ is a function of $L(1)$, $L(2)$, . . ., $L(10)$ and $L(p)$ is a function of $L(p-10)$, $L(p-9)$, . . ., $L(p-1)$. Each $L(p)$ is then the sum of up to ten terms representing the probability of a migrant stream being made up by households of any possible combination of sizes.

The initial term $L(0)$ is equal to $-\hat{\theta}_{ij}$, where $\hat{\theta}_{ij}$ is the Poisson parameter for the number of households migrating from i to j. This can be calculated simply by dividing $\hat{\lambda}_{ij}$, the Poisson parameter for the number of migrants from i to j as calculated in an ordinary Poisson regression, by the mean household size. For Great Britain in 1970–71, this had the value 2.885. For subsequent values, $L(p)$ can be obtained from $L(p-1)$, $L(p-2)$, . . ., $L(p-10)$ by the following relationships:

$$L(p) = \ln \hat{\theta}_{ij} + \ln \sum_{k=1}^{p^*} \exp \left(\ln (k/p) + g(k) + L(p-k) \right) \qquad (14.5)$$

where p^* is the minimum of p and 10 and $g(k)$ is the logged probability of a given household containing k members, $k = 1, 2, . . ., 10$. The algorithm works by computing $L(p)$ for each successive value of p until n_{ij} is reached, a lengthy process when n_{ij} is large.

This method gives values for $L(n_{ij})$ applicable to the Poisson regression model whose fit is being evaluated. This must be compared with the value for $L(n_{ij})$ for the full model. A similar process is necessary to calculate this quantity, except that here the parameter $\hat{\theta}_{ij}$ is computed by dividing n_{ij} by the mean household size. The contribution of this flow to the overall deviance is then minus twice the difference between $L(n_{ij})$ for the fitted model and $L(n_{ij})$ for the full model. The deviance is equal to the sum of this quantity for all observations.

RESULTS

The household size model was fitted to the inter-urban migration data set described earlier. The deviance value was 21 476. This value is still in excess of the critical chi-squared value, but it is very much closer than values obtained using the Poisson model, and it suggests that the generalised Poisson approach is indeed a better way of modelling inter-urban migration, at least in a context where many of the migrants form complete households. It should be remembered, however, that the model does not provide an acceptable fit to the data. This may not be altogether surprising, given that it is based only on population and distance variables, and there are many other things known or believed to influence migration patterns. Indeed, incorporating into the model the contiguity and unemployment variables mentioned earlier reduced the deviance below 18 000.

Another way of evaluating the regression is to inspect the residuals to see how useful they are in identifying those cases where the model performs worst. The estimates derived from a compound or generalised Poisson model are identical to those derived from the Poisson, so most standard types of residual are identical, too. However, the deviance is computed in a different way for such models. The contribution of each case to the total deviance is a natural way to identify those flows which have been least successfully estimated, and using this measure instead of the residual allows a comparison of the Poisson and household size models in terms of the prediction of individual flows.

Table 14.1 lists the flows making the largest contribution to overall deviance for the Poisson model and Table 14.2 gives the equivalent information for the household size model. In both cases, the flows between naval bases are prominent. There are also several flows from major cities to smaller satellite SMLAs which in some cases reflect planned decentralisation to New and Expanded Towns (for example, London to Basingstoke, Liverpool to Wigan), and some to resort cities (for example, London to Bournemouth, Manchester to Blackpool), which may be swelled by retirement migration. Some flows may be inflated by the contiguity of the spatial units concerned and resulting inclusion of some short-distance moves (for example, Norwich to Great Yarmouth, Slough to Reading), and one (Glasgow to Corby) probably reflects the recruiting policy of a major employer (British Steel) at the time. Some negative residuals (for example, Manchester to Sheffield, Liverpool to Manchester) are found, where there is less migration between major cities than their sizes and distance apart would suggest. Such flows seem more important as residuals in the household-size model. Overall, the lists are similar and, as might be expected, there is a tendency for the household size model to pick out those residuals involving large estimated and observed flows, rather than those with few observed migrants and a tiny estimated flow.

Additional analysis was carried out with the Aufhauser and Fischer model. Using the quasi-likelihood approach with their scale parameter of 2.2 gave a deviance value of 35 088, again much better than the standard Poisson model. However, 2.2 represents average household size for Vienna and is unlikely to be appropriate for Great Britain. Using the equivalent British value, 2.885, and the same method produced a deviance of 26 756—considerably better, but not as good as we obtained with the household size model, which also, we feel. has a better theoretical rationale.

Table 14.1 Major residuals from the Poisson regression model

Origin	Destination	Observed flow	Estimated flow	Standardised residual	Contribution to deviance
Plymouth	Portsmouth	211	4.8	94.1	1184.4
Liverpool	Wigan	514	114.9	37.2	741.8
Portsmouth	Plymouth	145	5.2	61.4	686.3
Glasgow	London	376	83.8	31.9	544.8
London	Basildon	651	262.9	23.9	404.3
London	Brighton	681	298.9	22.1	357.4
Edinburgh	London	195	35.3	26.9	347.3
London	Basingstoke	364	114.2	23.4	344.4
Slough	Reading	170	29.7	25.8	312.7
London	Bournemouth	373	131.2	21.1	295.9
Manchester	Blackpool	241	63.7	22.2	286.7
Glasgow	Corby	69	3.9	33.2	267.8
Manchester	Sheffield	42	248.5	−13.1	263.6
Norwich	Great Yarmouth	108	13.6	25.6	258.4
Chatham	Portsmouth	81	7.0	28.0	249.0
Newcastle	London	253	77.6	19.9	247.0
Portsmouth	Dunfermline	41	0.8	44.2	240.0
Plymouth	Dunfermline	35	0.5	50.0	231.6
Luton	Bedford	113	17.8	22.5	227.1
Dunfermline	Portsmouth	37	0.7	44.4	224.2

CONCLUSION

The use of compound or generalised Poisson models can clearly be very effective in reducing the deviance of a Poisson model that does not fit. Some forms of these models can also be justified on theoretical grounds. Recognising that migrants move in household groups of varying sizes seems more sensible than assuming that they move entirely independently of one another. It would have been preferable, however, to use data on the sizes of wholly moving households rather than of all households, had the former been available.

The household-size model seems the most appropriate for the inter-urban migration problem under study, and it should have applications in other migration studies. It seems less relevant for other spatial interaction problems, such as the journey to work, where the Poisson assumption may be more reasonable.

This analysis can be seen as one example of a set of Poisson and Poisson-related models which may be appropriate for the analysis of a large range of data sets in geography, regional science and other fields. Discrete distribution models offer several theoretical and practical advantages over ordinary least squares regression for count data, and it is becoming clear that compound or

Table 14.2 Major residuals from the household-size regression model

Origin	Destination	Observed flow	Estimated flow	Standardised residual	Contribution to deviance
Plymouth	Portsmouth	211	4.8	94.1	238.6
Liverpool	Wigan	514	114.9	37.2	177.9
Portsmouth	Plymouth	145	5.2	61.4	143.1
Glasgow	London	376	83.8	31.9	130.7
London	Basildon	651	262.9	23.9	101.6
London	Brighton	681	298.9	22.1	90.4
London	Basingstoke	364	114.2	23.4	84.9
Edinburgh	London	195	35.3	26.9	82.1
Manchester	Sheffield	41	248.5	−13.1	79.0
Slough	Reading	170	29.7	25.8	73.8
London	Bournemouth	373	131.2	21.1	73.6
Manchester	Blackpool	241	63.7	22.2	69.8
Newcastle	London	253	77.6	19.9	60.9
Norwich	Great Yarmouth	108	13.6	25.6	59.5
Glasgow	Corby	69	3.9	33.2	58.0
Liverpool	Manchester	129	358.5	−12.1	56.0
Chatham	Portsmouth	81	7.0	28.0	55.8
Plymouth	London	149	32.3	20.5	53.4
Luton	Bedford	113	17.8	22.5	53.2
Manchester	Liverpool	148	377.4	−11.8	51.8

generalised Poisson models offer a better approach to modelling count data when the Poisson assumption of independence is not met. Such models are, as yet, less straightforward to use than the Poisson, but current and future developments in statistics and computing are likely to see them becoming increasingly prominent.

REFERENCES

Aufhauser, E. and Fischer, M.M. (1985), 'Log-linear modelling and spatial analysis', *Environment and Planning*, vol. 17A, pp. 931–51.
Baxter, M.J. (1982) 'Similarities in methods of estimating spatial interaction models', *Geographical Analysis*, vol. 14, no. 3, pp. 267–72.
Baxter, M.J. (1985) 'Quasi-likelihood estimation and diagnostic statistics for spatial interaction models', *Environment and Planning*, vol. 17A, pp. 1627–35.
Breslow, N.E. (1984) 'Extra Poisson variation in log-linear models', *Applied Statistics*, vol. 33, no. 1, pp. 38–44.
Constantine, A.G. and Gower, J.C. (1982) 'Models for the analysis of interregional migration', *Environment and Planning*, vol. 14A, pp. 477–97.
Davies, R.B. and Crouchley, R. (1985) 'Control for omitted variables in the analysis of panel and other longitudinal data', *Geographical Analysis*, vol. 17, no. 1, pp. 1–15.
Davies, R.B. and Guy, C.M. (1987) 'The statistical modeling of flow data when the

Poisson assumption is violated', *Geographical Analysis*, vol. 19, no. 4, pp. 300–14.

Drewett, R., Goddard, J., Spence, N., Connock, C. and Pinkham, R. (1974) 'Urban change in Britain: 1961–71', Working Reports 1 and 2, Department of Geography, London School of Economics.

Flowerdew, R. and Aitkin, M. (1982) 'A method of fitting the gravity model based on the Poisson distribution', *Journal of Regional Science*, vol. 22, no. 2, pp. 191–202.

Flowerdew, R. and Lovett, A. (1988) 'Fitting constrained Poisson regression models to inter-urban migration flows', *Geographical Analysis*, vol. 20, no. 4, pp. 297–307.

Flowerdew, R. and Salt, J. (1979) 'Migration between labour market areas in Great Britain, 1970–1971', *Regional Studies*, vol. 13, no. 2, pp. 211–31.

Hinde, J. (1982) 'Compound Poisson regression models', in R. Gilchrist (ed.), *GLIM82*. New York: Springer-Verlag, pp. 109–21.

Lovett, A. (1984) 'Poisson regression using the GLIM package' in *Computer Package Guide 5*. University of Lancaster, Department of Geography.

Maddala, G.S. (1983) *Limited-Dependent and Qualitative Variables in Econometrics*. Cambridge: Cambridge University Press.

Nelder, J.A. and Wedderburn, R.W.M. (1972) 'Generalized linear models', *Journal of the Royal Statistical Society*, vol. 135A, no. 3, pp. 370–84.

Wedderburn, R.W.M. (1974) 'Quasi-likelihood functions, generalized linear models and the Gauss–Newton method', *Biometrika*, vol. 61, no. 3, pp. 439–47.

Wilson, A.G. (1970) *Entropy in Urban and Regional Modelling*. London: Pion.

Chapter 15

US MIGRATION PATTERN RESPONSES TO THE OIL GLUT AND RECESSION OF THE EARLY 1980s: AN APPLICATION OF SHIFT-SHARE AND CAUSATIVE-MATRIX TECHNIQUES*

David A. Plane

Peter A. Rogerson

INTRODUCTION

In this chapter we set out an application of two recently developed methods designed for examining temporal change in the geographic structure of migration systems. We use the methods to explore how streams of migration flow among nine broad regions of the US responded during the first half of the 1980s to a recession that affected, particularly, the oil-dependent economies of states in the West South Central portion of the nation (see Figure 15.1).

The first major section of the chapter is comprised of a discussion of the two methods. The first of these is a spatial adaptation of the shift-share technique that is commonly used in analyses of regional employment. As in Plane (1987), changes in the level of net migration to each region k of a migration system may be decomposed into a series of factors and components representing distinctive system-growth, system-mobility, proportional-shift (or geographic-mix) and differential-shift (or competitive) perspectives on spatio-temporal change. Taking the place of the economic sectors used in traditional applications of shift-share analysis are the source regions of in-migration to, and the destination regions of out-migration from, each region k.

The second method, that of causative matrices, was previously applied to migration systems in Rogerson and Plane (1984) and Plane and Rogerson (1986). Unlike the shift-share method, which results in an additive decomposition of net migration change for each of the regions of the system, the focus here is on changes in the Markov transition probabilities of individuals

*We wish to thank Peter Congdon for encouraging us to carry out the comparative applications reported upon in this chapter and for his helpful, substantive comments on an earlier draft.

migrating between specific pairs of regions. The causative matrix approach affords a perspective on non-stationarity in transition probabilities. A causative matrix is one which maps, either through pre- or post-multiplication, an earlier period transition matrix to one for a later time period.

The two methods provide substantially different, yet quite complementary, views on changes in the geographic patterns of migration. They differ in that one results in an additive set of descriptive measures focused on net migration change, whereas the other is based on changes in transition probabilities. They are very similar, however, in their emphasis on *interregional interdependencies* in migration-system structure. By this we mean that they both posit that the volume of flow in any migration stream from region i to region j depends on conditions not only in regions i and j, but also in all the other regions of the system.

The systemic interdependency perspectives of the two methods are exploited in the second major section of the chapter. Here we investigate how the geographic patterns of interregional migration in the US responded to a significant economic event: a recession that differentially affected the economies of the states—as grouped into the nine US Bureau of the Census divisions (see Figure 15.1). Using the nine Census Divisions we are able to paint a fuller picture of the nature of temporal change in broad-scale US migration than would have been possible with a core/periphery (see Vining *et al.*, 1981; Vining and Pallone, 1982) or 'rustbelt'/'sunbelt' dichotomous regionalisation. At the same time, however, the divisions may easily be placed within such overarching conceptual frameworks. Together, the New England, Middle Atlantic, and East North Central divisions fairly closely approximate the historical national core region as employed in the previous analyses of Vining and associates,[1] whereas the East North Central covers much of the traditional American manufacturing belt region now popularly referred to as the 'rustbelt'.

During the recessionary period of the early 1980s, the diversified, highly urbanised economies of Middle Atlantic states fared much better than previously and net out-migration slowed from the historic peak levels of the 1970s. Particularly important for the New York metropolitan area was its role as the primary national concentration of control and information functions. Also contributing to the better economic fortunes of the North-East was the growth in financial and business services. On the other hand, the heavily production-orientated economic structure of the Midwestern portion of the historical national core (as represented by the East North Central division) meant significantly worsened economic conditions during the recession, but reduced mobility stemmed consequent additional erosion of migration attractiveness. We show, however, that by far the largest changes occurring in the first half of the 1980s in the previously existing pattern of core-to-periphery population dispersal are those likely to be traceable to the effects of the 'oil glut', the impact of which was a significant slowdown in the energy-driven economies of the West South Central division, and, to a somewhat lesser extent, in parts of the Mountain and other divisions. Economic events herein affected all other divisions through the interdependent system of migrant interchange. By looking not simply at temporal change across the entire study period, 1980–5, but also at annual changes, we are able to detect, furthermore, how the impacts of this regionally focused economic event rippled throughout

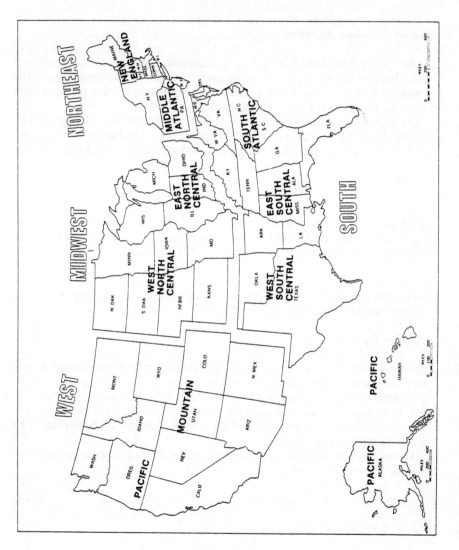

Figure 15.1 The nine geographic divisions of the USA used in the study, as defined by the US Bureau of the Census

the historically established network of region-to-region channels of population redistribution.

THE METHODS

Spatial shift-share decomposition

In the spatial shift-share framework, the economic sectors used in a traditional shift-share model are replaced by the source regions of in-migration and the destination regions of out-migration. It is *changes* in migration patterns from one time period to the next which are decomposed.

Let m_{ij} represent the gross movement of persons that takes place over time period t from origin region i to destination region j. Total gross in-migration, total gross out-migration, and net (in-)migration to region k may be denoted:

$$I_k = \sum_{i \neq k} m_{ik}; \quad O_k = \sum_{j \neq k} m_{kj}; \quad N_k = I_k - O_k. \tag{15.1}$$

Let $\Delta N_k = N_{k,t+1} - N_k$ represent the change in net migration to region k taking place from time period t to $t+1$. Note that in our notation, if a time subscript is omitted, reference is to a quantity for period t.

System-wide components.
Change in net migration to region k is decomposed first into system-growth, system-mobility, and total-shift components:

$$\Delta N_k = G_k + U_k + S_k \tag{15.2}$$

where G_k is the system-growth component, which reflects the changing total pool of persons in the nation who might potentially become migrants; U_k is the system-mobility component which controls for the changing national propensity to make moves; and S_k is the 'total' shift, that is, the amount of net migration change for each region of the system that cannot be explained by the two national-scale factors.

The two system-wide components are computed for each origin–destination-specific migration stream as:

$$g_{ij} = \gamma \, m_{ij} = (\Delta P/P) \, m_{ij}. \tag{15.3}$$

$$u_{ij} = \mu \, m_{ij} = [(\Delta M/M) - \gamma] \, m_{ij}. \tag{15.4}$$

Here γ may be termed the system-growth factor and μ the system-mobility factor. P is the total population of the system and M is the total number of migrants in it. Aggregating:

$$G_k + U_k = \sum_{i \neq k} (g_{ik} + u_{ik}) - \sum_{j \neq k} (g_{kj} + u_{kj}) = (\gamma + \mu) \, N_k. \tag{15.5}$$

The two system-wide components posit the effects of an equal, system-wide increase or decrease in the volume of flow in all migration streams, as if there were no changes in the pre-existing spatial pattern of movement.

Proportional-shift components.
The first of the two constituent components of the total shift is termed, following the convention of more standard shift-share applications, the proportional shift. The proportional shift may be subdivided into gross in- and gross out-migration sub-components. The in-migration shifts give expected flows into region k from each origin i on the assumption that changes in total out-migration from i are allocated to each destination h in base-period proportions, after controlling for systemwide effects:

$$y_{ik} = \Delta O_i \left(m_{ik} / \sum_{h \neq i} m_{ih} \right) - g_{ik} - u_{ik}$$ (15.6)

$$= [(\Delta O_i / O_i) - \gamma - \mu] \, m_{ik} = \rho_i \, m_{ik}.$$

Similarly, the proportional shift associated with each out-migration stream from k to specific destination j is:

$$z_{kj} = -\Delta I_j \left(m_{kj} / \sum_{h \neq j} m_{hj} \right) + g_{kj} + u_{kj}$$ (15.7)

$$= [(-\Delta I_j / I_j) + \gamma + \mu] \, m_{kj} = \sigma_j \, m_{kj}$$

The terms ρ_i and σ_j are called the origin and destination proportional-shift factors, respectively.

Summing over all potential origins and destinations yields the total proportional shift component, X_k, made up of origin and destination subcomponents, Y_k and Z_k. Because positive values of Y_k indicate that region k has a historical specialisation in receiving in-migrants from origin regions that are, on balance, experiencing *increasing* out-migration between time period t and $t+1$, and because positive Z_k values mean that k has traditionally sent out-migrants to destination regions that are now, on balance, experiencing *decreasing* in-migration, the proportional shift may also be termed a 'geographic mix' effect. Much as in traditional shift-share analysis, it tells us whether historical specialisation of the region has been 'favourable' or 'unfavourable' for accelerating growth during the current time period.

Differential-shift components.
After controlling for the system-wide and proportional effects, the remaining portion of the change in migration flow in each stream is referred to as the differential shift. For each in-migration stream to k:

$$d_{ik} = \Delta m_{ik} - y_{ik} - g_{ik} - u_{ik}$$
$$= [(\Delta m_{ik} / m_{ik}) - (\Delta O_i / O_i)] \, m_{ik}$$ (15.8)
$$= \delta_{\iota\kappa} \, \mu_{\iota\kappa}$$

and for each out-migration stream from k:

$$e_{kj} = \Delta m_{kj} - z_{kj} + g_{kj} + u_{kj}$$
$$= [(-\Delta m_{kj} / m_{kj}) + (\Delta I_j / I_j)] \, m_{kj} \qquad (15.9)$$
$$= \varepsilon_{kj} \, m_{kj}.$$

The inflow and outflow differential shift factors, δ_{ik} and ε_{kj}, respectively, are useful quantities expressing the relative ability of specific movement streams to change in- and out-migration to region k, beyond that portion attributable to changes in overall out- or in-migration for region j.

The total inflow and outflow differential shift subcomponents, D_k and E_k, respectively, are obtained through aggregation, with the sum of these, C_k, termed the total 'competitive' component for region k. C_k is a summary measure of how the net-migration fortunes of region k have changed due to factors not attributable to either total system-wide effects or to the changing levels of total gross in- or out-movement for each of the other regions. A positive value indicates that region k has become relatively more attractive, *vis-à-vis* alternative regions, as a migration destination (positive D_k), or that it has increased its relative capability to retain existing population (positive E_k), or both.

Causative matrices

A common practice in representing and forecasting migration flows is to assume that the interregional probabilities of movement remain constant, as in a Markov chain (see, for example, Rogers, 1968). A non-stationarity assumption about these probabilities is, however, clearly more appropriate. A causative matrix method assumes that there exists a matrix, **C**, that maps one transition probability matrix, **P**, into the next. That is,

$$\mathbf{P}_{t+1} = \mathbf{P}_t \, \mathbf{C}_R, \text{ or } \mathbf{P}_{t+1} = \mathbf{C}_L \, \mathbf{P}_t. \qquad (15.10)$$

where the subscripts on the **C** matrices reflect the possibility of defining two alternative models because matrix multiplication is not commutative. In our application, the 'right' and 'left' causative matrices prove to be extremely similar and we consequently focus our interpretations exclusively on $\mathbf{C}_R$.

Note that the stationary Markov model may be obtained as the special case where **C** is equal to the identity matrix. For short-term systemic change, causative matrices are, in fact, quite close in structure to identity matrices; elements only slightly deviating from one are ranged down the principal diagonal, and very small positive or negative quantities are found for the off-diagonal elements.

Early study of the causative matrix model focused on the existence and nature of equilibrium (Harary *et al.*, 1970; Pullman and Stynan, 1973; Ledent, 1978), with one notable application to the study of brand choice and new product introduction in marketing research (Lipstein, 1968). In Rogerson and Plane (1984) and Plane and Rogerson (1986) we focus considerable attention on interpreting elements of the **C** matrix in applications to the analysis of migration flows. We shall only briefly review such interpretation here, referring the interested reader to these earlier papers.

Interpretation of causative-matrix elements.
When a transition probability matrix is post-multiplied by a causative matrix, the elements of C_R reflect the changing competitive ability of regions to attract migrants. Similarly, when the transition matrix is pre-multiplied by a constant causative matrix C_L, the elements reflect the changing competitive ability of regions to supply other regions with migrants. The use of C_R, therefore, results in a competing-destinations perspective on system change, while the use of C_L results in a somewhat less intuitive, perhaps, but equally valid competing-origins perspective.[2]

A negative off-diagonal element of the C_R matrix, c_{kj}, reflects an increasing ability of region k to divert migrants from all origins away from region j toward k, including a direct effect represented by the change in the p_{kj} transition probability. A positive c_{kj} reflects a declining ability of region k to compete with j for migrants from all origins. Thus the sign of the elements pertains to the change in attractiveness of the column region, j, *vis-à-vis* the row region, k. The elements of c_{kj} are determined not only by direct changes in the transition elements, p_{kj}, but also by changes in the probabilities of migrating from other regions, p_{ij} ($i = 1, 2, \ldots r, i \neq k$). The latter changes are weighted by the strength of interaction between i and k. The changing influence of k on j is thus measured in relative terms, reflecting both the direct influence of changes in p_{kj}, and the offsetting or enhancing effects of changing interaction probabilities between other regions and j. For more explicit explanation of these embedded systemic properties, see Plane and Rogerson (1986).

Given the above interpretation of the individual elements of C_R, which focusses on the changing competitive position of region j, it can be seen that a column sum of C_R, which we denote as ξ_j, provides a summary measure of the changing attractiveness of the region. Column sums greater than one indicate increasing attractiveness, and sums less than one reflect declining attractiveness.

Estimation of causative matrices.
When two successive transition probability matrices, P_t and P_{t+1} are available, the C matrix may be determined through straightforward matrix algebra:

$$C = P_t^{-1} P_{t+1}. \tag{15.11}$$

Causative matrices may thus be used to provide measures complementary to those of shift-share in showing changes in relative regional attractiveness; in the present applications, we simply use equation (15.11) to determine the causative change in migration probabilities that has occurred between two periods of time. Causative matrices, however, are not confined to such use for single, discrete-time intervals. When a series of more than two P matrices is available, the best-fitting causative matrix across the entire time-span may be found via a non-linear least squares approach (details are given in Rogerson and Plane, 1984). The technique also presumably has a place in continuous-time applications. No truly analogous multi-period shift-share measures are derivable (but see the simple 'dynamic shift-share' concept set forth in Barff and Knight, 1988a, involving the summation of a series of single-year proportional- and differential-shift components).

TEMPORAL CHANGE IN US INTERDIVISIONAL MIGRATION, 1980-5

Monitoring migration with individual income-tax return data

A time series of state-to-state flow matrices for the 1980s
Spatial shift-share components and causative matrices were derived from a short time series of five migration tables representing consistent estimates of population movement occurring within the US during the first half of the 1980s. Available were state-to-state migration flows based on year-to-year matches of individuals' federal income-tax returns filed during 1980, 1981, 1982, 1983, 1984, and 1985.[3] Because the vast majority of Americans procrastinate until quite close to the 15 April deadline in filing their returns, movement is essentially estimated between the beginnings of the second quarters of each year. (For full descriptions of this data source, see Engels and Healy, 1981, and Isserman *et al.*, 1982).

The five migration matrices permit construction of four sets of shift-share and causative-matrix measures of year-to-year change in migration-system structure, as well as one set of measures of temporal change across the entire half-decade study period (1980-1 to 1984-5). The periods over which temporal change in the geographic patterns of population movement are thus measured very nicely span the previously mentioned national recession and its aftermath. This recession, which, as we shall show in the latter parts of this section, had significant repercussions in modifying migration-system structure, reached its point of greatest severity during 1982, when the overall US unemployment rate peaked at 9.6% of the national labour force.

Coverage adjustment.
Before computing the relevant shift-share components and causative matrices for these periods of temporal change in migration-system structure, we first adjusted the state-to-state flow matrices to represent estimates of 'full' population movements.[4] This was desirable because of geographic variability in the completeness of coverage. The state-to-state migration flows reported in the unadjusted matrices are obtained at the US Bureau of the Census by elaborate computer matching of limited information taken from individual income-tax returns. Tax filers are matched, by social security numbers, from one year to the next. Addresses listed on each pair of matched returns are then compared to determine whether a move has occurred. Spouses, children, and other financially dependent individuals are assumed to have moved with those filers whose addresses differ from one year to the next. Because certain households with below a minimum level of income are not required to file returns, and because others who are so required sometimes do not, our procedure to inflate the unadjusted population flows involved origin-state coverage ratios which ranged from 1.09 to 1.34. In general, these ratios were highest (and thus the coverage the least complete) for states with low median income, but the geographic pattern of coverage is not a simple one. At a national level, the mean population-coverage adjustment factor across the five years of our study period was 1.21.

Estimated interdivisional in-, out- and net migration for the study period
After the state-specific adjustment ratios were applied, we aggregated the 51
× 51 (50 states plus the District of Columbia) flow tables into 9 × 9 tables
according to the Census Bureau division boundaries shown in Figure 15.1.
These widely used regional demarcations correspond, to a fair extent, with
traditional cultural and economic regionalisations of the nation. A lower level
of geographic disaggregation than that represented by the states was desired
for this study in order that we might report full tables of shift-share components and full causative matrices, as well as to allow us to focus upon
specific origin–destination streams of movement in some detail.

Table 15.1 shows our estimates of total gross in-migration, total gross out-
migration, and net migration for each division as derived from the five 9 × 9
matrices of adjusted interdivisional flows. When the relatively sophisticated
systemic measures of temporal change in the patterns of interdivisional flow
are presented in the subsequent subsections of the chapter, the reader may
find it helpful to refer back to this table to aid understanding of our interpretations of dynamic change in the patterns of broad-scale population redistribution extant during the first half of the 1980s.

System-level views of temporal change in interdivisional migration

The first two components of the shift-share spatial decomposition (system
growth and mobility) are explicitly system-wide measures of temporal
change. In addition, the proportional- and differential-shift components may
be aggregated by taking absolute values and summing across all regions to
obtain an indication of their relative contributions to 'explaining' all temporal
change throughout a migration system.

A system-wide measure may also be derived from the causative-matrix
method. A summary measure of the systemic properties of a causative matrix
is afforded by examining its largest real eigenvalue. If all eigenvalues are less
than or equal to unity, the non-stationary Markov chain converges; all
regions in the system will eventually contain stable population proportions. If,
on the other hand, one or more eigenvalues are greater than one, a divergent
process is indicated, that is, one or more regions would eventually absorb all
the population. Thus Lipstein (1968) suggested (for a marketing application)
that the largest eigenvalue, λ^*, may be interpreted as an index of stability; the
further it differs from one, the greater are the convergent or divergent
properties possessed by the system. A previous application of this notion to
temporal change in migration-system structure may be found in Plane and
Rogerson (1986).

Table 15.2 summarises the various system-wide measures of migration-
system change across the entire study period and for the four year-to-year
periods.

Systemwide mobility
Shown first are the shift-share, system-mobility parameters, μ. Recall that
these measure the change in total number of migrants in the system, after
overall population growth has been controlled for. The parameter is thus a
close relative of a traditionally computed mobility rate. System-wide mobility,

Table 15.1   Annual estimated gross in-migration, gross out-migration, and net migration (in thousands) for US divisions, 1980–1 to 1984–5

Division		1980–1	1981–2	1982–3	1983–4	1984–5
New England	In	227	220	215	250	247
	Out	245	254	228	242	227
	Net	−18	−34	−13	+8	+20
Middle Atlantic	In	405	412	399	430	412
	Out	649	628	560	610	611
	Net	−244	−216	−160	−180	−199
East North Central	In	510	500	486	549	553
	Out	858	928	823	847	812
	Net	−348	−428	−337	−298	−259
West North Central	In	356	342	332	363	345
	Out	416	450	404	419	428
	Net	−60	−108	−72	−56	−83
South Atlantic	In	1057	1035	1012	1130	1141
	Out	804	829	740	770	757
	Net	+252	+206	+273	+360	+383
East South Central	In	365	375	349	363	354
	Out	397	410	371	392	381
	Net	−31	−35	−21	−28	−27
West South Central	In	748	916	740	671	607
	Out	507	502	558	619	614
	Net	+241	+414	+182	+52	−8
Mountain	In	599	609	526	544	531
	Out	440	453	441	469	464
	Net	+159	+156	+84	+75	+68
Pacific	In	711	708	662	712	718
	Out	661	663	598	645	614
	Net	+50	+45	+64	+68	+104
Total interdivisional migrants:		4978	5116	4722	5012	4908

Sources: Computed by the authors from unpublished data from the US Internal Revenue Service and US Bureau of the Census.

thus measured, generally declined across the study period, although it was actually on the rise, slightly, as the decade began, and also for the 1982–3 to 1983–4 time-span. The greatest drop in mobility occurred when the recession was at its worst in 1981–2 to 1982–3. The subsequent period's increase can be viewed, therefore, as a recovery to a more normal level.

A longer-term declining trend in US interregional mobility is consistent

Table 15.2 System-wide measures of temporal change in US interdivisional migration flow patterns, 1980-1 to 1984-5

	1980-1/ 1984-5	1980-1/ 1981-2	1981-2/ 1982-3	1982-3/ 1983-4	1983-4/ 1984-5
Shift-share measures:					
Mobility parameter, μ	−0.0555	+0.0169	−0.0874	+0.0515	−0.0304
Net migration change, $\sum_k \mid \Delta N_k \mid$	724	401	606	333	224
System-growth component, $\sum_k \mid G_k \mid$	58	15	17	12	11
System-mobility component, $\sum_k \mid U_k \mid$	78	24	143	62	34
Total shift component, $\sum_k \mid S_k \mid$	714	401	519	345	229
Geographic mix component, $\sum_k \mid X_k \mid$	141	81	112	82	40
Origin subcomponent, $\sum_k \mid Y_k \mid$	68	29	55	22	18
Destination subcomponent, $\sum_k \mid Z_k \mid$	94	69	57	65	32
Competitive component, $\sum_k \mid C_k \mid$	703	321	467	306	190
Inflow subcomponent, $\sum_k \mid D_k \mid$	401	280	259	261	135
Outflow subcomponent, $\sum_k \mid E_k \mid$	326	122	216	67	81
Causative-matrix index of stability					
Largest real eigenvalue	1.0028	1.0006	1.0030	.9990	1.0014

with the ageing of the US baby-boom cohorts; whereas 'baby boomers' were in their highest mobility and/or early labour force years during the 1970s, when the rate of core-to-periphery net outflow from the traditional national core region of the US tripled in volume (see Vining *et al.*, 1981; Vining and Pallone, 1982; Plane 1984; Plane, 1988), persons in these cohorts were entering their relatively less mobile mid-career years by the 1980s. For some further thoughts on the longer-term evolution of US mobility rates, see Rogerson (1987).

Decreased geographic mobility is also an oft-noted characteristic of recessionary periods. In contradiction to the popular misconception that movement should increase as a result of greater speculative migratory flows, overall volumes of US interregional flow sharply decline when regional labour markets tighten and employed workers retain existing jobs rather than seeking new opportunities further afield. During expansionary periods, more migrants move as greater labour turnover takes place; there are more opportunities to entice the bulk of prospective migrants—those who will move from positions of economic strength, rather than of economic weakness. (See Silvers, 1977, for further development of the motivations of 'contracted' versus 'speculative' migrants.)

Aggregate measures of temporal pattern shifts
In terms of total absolute net migration change, and its most aggregate decomposition into system-growth, system-mobility, and total-shift components, it can be seen that the period at the depth of the recession, 1981-2 to

1982–3, was that when the most significant short-term temporal shifts in net migration occurred. Not only did mobility decline dramatically, as indicated by the large aggregate absolute value of the system-mobility components (column 3 of Table 15.2), but there was also considerable geographic restructuring of the streams of net population interchange, as indicated by the extremely high magnitude of the aggregate of the absolute total shifts. The most recent time-span for which we currently have consistent data, 1983–4 to 1984–5 is, by contrast, characterised as one for which little further change in the patterns of interdivisional migration is detectable.

Disaggregation of the aggregate total shift measure into its constituent components and subcomponents is also revealing. Note, especially, the relative sizes of the aggregates of the origin and destination absolute proportional shifts, $\sum_k |Y_k|$ and $\sum_k |Z_k|$ respectively and of the inflow and outflow absolute differential shifts and $\sum_k |D_k|$ and $\sum_k |E_k|$, respectively. As has been found in a previous application of the spatial shift-share methodology (Plane, 1987, pp. 291–2), the sub-components driven by the cross-regional changes in in-migration tend to be greater than those associated with the variation across regions in out-migration. Recall that the origin proportional shift, Y_k, is derived by applying the proportional change in total out-migration for each origin region i from time period t to period $t+1$ to each of the migration streams into region k (after controlling for the system-wide components of change), whereas the destination proportional shift, Z_k, results from similarly applying the proportional changes in in-migration to each of the destinations for migrants from region k. Recall, too, that the in-migration differential shift sub-component, C_k, is composed of residual changes in the in-migration streams to region k, whereas the out-migration differential shift, D_k, is composed of residuals in that region's out-migration streams. As was demonstrated in Plane *et al.* (1984), there are structural reasons to expect, in general, greater cross-regional variation in in-migration than in out-migration within a migration system.

With respect, further, to the relative size of the sub-components driven by in-migration and out-migration change, note that the period 1981–2 to 1982–3 was somewhat anomolous to the general tendency observed above: for this period, the aggregate of the absolute out-migration differential-shift subcomponents exceeded the aggregate of those for in-migration, and the aggregate of absolute-origin proportional shifts was almost as large as the aggregate of the destination shifts. As we shall see in greater detail in the next subsection, the initial impact of the 'oil-glut' recession was to significantly speed up the rate of out-migration from the divisions of the nation most dependent on energy industries—the West South Central, in particular. It was not really until the subsequent period, 1982–3 to 1983–4, that the traditionally strong in-migration streams to these divisions were seriously weakening. The lag between an initial out-migration response and a subsequent in-migration one to worsened economic conditions in a growing area is one of the more intriguing findings of our study. It is suggestive of the importance for migration dynamics of such concepts as information diffusion, perceptual lags, and system inertia.

Indices of stability

Finally, the indices of stability, computed as the largest eigenvalues of the causative matrices, should be noted. The time-span as a whole, 1980–1 to 1984–5, was one of diverging trends in transition probabilities, with the 1981–2 to 1982–3 period accounting for the largest break in system structure. During the following period, 1982–3 to 1983–4, the system did exhibit a reversal toward convergence properties, but the force of this opposite tendency was not particularly great.

Measures of relative competitiveness of the divisions

We now turn from system-level measures of the nature of temporal change in US interdivisional migration during the first half of the 1980s, to the perspectives that shift-share and causative matrices offer on the relative competitiveness of the various divisions to attract in-migrants and to retain potential out-migrants. We examine first 'competitive' components derived from the shift-share procedure, then we present the column sums of the causative matrices, which are also summary measures of the competitiveness of the divisions in terms of increasing their probabilities of both attracting in-migrants and of retaining existing population. Finally, we break the shift-share competitive components into their in- and out-migration constituent parts to explore further the interesting rippling or lag effects of the 1982 recession hinted at by the previously presented system-wide measures.

Shift-share competitive components.
Table 15.3 discloses the signs and magnitudes of the competitive components of net migration change for the overall time-span of the study and the four shorter periods which it encompasses. These provide a more refined view of 'competitiveness' than would be gained simply by looking at total net migration change. By summing up all the stream-specific differential shifts we have controlled for general effects of changes in total system population, changes in total system mobility, and changes in the levels of in- and out-migration in each of the other regions of the system—apportioned according to a historical geographic pattern of flow. What we are looking at, therefore, are essentially summary measures of the abilities of each region k to effect change within the origin–destination-specific channels of population redistribution represented within the interdependent system of flows. The quantities reported are easily interpretable, being simply the population change (in thousands) attributable to region k's competitive component.

Most striking in the components for the entire time span, 1980–1 to 1984–5, are the competitive losses of the West South Central and Mountain divisions. The West South Central includes such preeminent oil-producing states as Texas, Oklahoma and Louisiana, whereas in the Mountain division, Colorado is a large state with a heavily oil-based economy; Arizona, one of the other more populous states of the Mountain division, was affected not so much by the drop in world oil prices, but by synchronous lows in world copper prices. The West North Central division was the other significant 'loser' over the period. The most recent manifestations of the American 'farm problem' engendered by massive productivity increases over the course of the current century hit particularly hard in this division of the Great Plains with its largely agricultural base.

Among the divisions showing overall competitive gains, most significant

Table 15.3 Shift-share competitive components, C_k, of net migration change (in thousands) for US divisions, 1980–1 to 1984–5

Divison	1980–1/ 1984–5	1980–1/ 1981–2	1981–2/ 1982–3	1982–3/ 1983–4	1983–4/ 1984–5
New England	+50	−15	+27	+24	+13
Middle Atlantic	+74	+18	+55	+8	−11
East North Central	+72	−64	+49	+50	+26
West North Central	−40	−37	+9	+10	−28
South Atlantic	+136	−39	+86	+61	+67
East South Central	+4	−0	+7	−6	+1
West South Central	−221	+142	−172	−121	−52
Mountain	−91	−3	−61	−20	−4
Pacific	+16	−2	−1	−6	+29

are those of the traditional national 'core' region, the Middle Atlantic, East North Central, and New England, as well as the South Atlantic. As we discussed in Rogerson and Plane (1985), the diversified economies of certain north-eastern metropolitan areas, such as New York's, seem to have fared well during the recent recession. It also should be noted that in the 1980s we have witnessed a reversal of the 1970s trend of higher aggregate growth rates in non-metropolitan than in metropolitan areas. Many of the broad regional trends described in this chapter seem consistent with the waning of counter-urbanisation. However, we are hesitant to infer too much in this regards because the data we here employ do not permit metropolitan–non-metropolitan disaggregations by division.

In fact, the Middle Atlantic's 'gain', as well as the positive competitive component for the East North Central division, which encompasses much of the traditional American manufacturing belt, may be a bit misleading. They actually indicate that population losses during the 1980s have somewhat lessened from the astonishingly high levels that came to be characteristic of the nation's core during the 1970s. Net migration for the Middle Atlantic states went from an estimates −244 000, during 1980–1, to −199 000 by 1984–5; net out-migration from the East North Central declined from 348 000 during 1980–1, but was still high during 1984–5, when the division lost an estimated 259 000 in population to other divisions. New England, on the other hand, did witness a changeover in the sign of net migration during the study's time-span: from −18 000 for 1980–1 to +20 000 for 1984–5. The economic 'turn-around' in New England during the 1980s has received considerable attention of late in both popular and scholarly (see, for example, Barff and Knight, 1988b) writings, with much focus on the roles of high-technology industry and military-related spending. We shall postpone consideration of the South Atlantic division's positive competitive gain until a later section, in which we examine the specific division-to-division streams of movement giving rise to these overall components.

Causative-matrix measures of changing attractiveness of the divisions
The column sums of causative matrices provide somewhat different, though complementary perspectives on the changing ability of regions within an

Table 15.4 Scaled* causative-matrix column sums, US interdivisonal migration, 1980-1 to 1984-5

Division	1980-1/ 1984-5	1980-1/ 1981-2	1981-2/ 1982-3	1982-3/ 1983-4	1983-4/ 1984-5
New England	+22	-9	+20	-0	+11
Middle Atlantic	+7	+7	+12	-2	-11
East North Central	+18	-24	+16	+18	+7
West North Central	-16	-26	+22	+0	-12
South Atlantic	+43	-13	+12	+40	+5
East South Central	+10	-4	+20	-10	+4
West South Central	-87	+72	-87	-49	-24
Mountain	-14	+1	-12	-10	+6
Pacific	+19	-3	-3	+12	+13

* Scaled column sums computed as 10 000 (ξ_j − 1.0000), where ξ_j is a column sum of the causative matrix, **C**.

interdependent system to become more attractive to potential in-migrants and to retain existing population. The focus, here, is on probabilities of movement and of making specific destination choices.

Table 15.4 gives the column sums, ξ_j, for the right causative matrices computed for the entire time-span of the study, as well as for the individual, consecutive periods of temporal change. Because the column sums of the left causative matrices are virtually identical, we do not report them in the interests of brevity. Column sums greater than one indicate increased attractiveness, be it to draw additional in-migrants or to hold in place potential out-migrants, whereas those less than one suggest a decreased ability to attract in-migrants or to retain existing population. To facilitate interpretation, in the table we use a simple, scaled transformation of the column-sum measures expressed in terms of their deviations from unity.

Although the signs of these Table 15.4 measures are almost identical to the shift-share competitive components given in Table 15.3, the magnitudes suggest a somewhat different view of the relative importance of the temporal trends for the various divisions. The units of the shift-share components are impacts on total net migration; thus the different population bases of the various divisions are, to an extent, picked up in the competitive-component measures. Importance is measured in the sense of overall impact on the redistribution of national population. The causative-matrix technique, however, provides more direct measures of the changes in the *relative* attractiveness of regions.

For the time-span as a whole, a ranking of the most significant changes in attractiveness emphasises the abrupt turnabout in the West South Central division's fortunes. The biggest deviations from unity were all found for this division: its loss of attractiveness during 1981-2 to 1982-3, which reversed a dramatic gain just experienced for 1980-1 to 1981-2; and its continued decline in attractiveness during 1982-3 to 1983-4.

The column-sum summary measures are limited in the sense that they provide only a single measure of changing regional attractiveness. We turn now to a bifurcation of the US divisions' overall shift-share competitive components into in- and out-migration sub-components; we also explore the timing of the in- and out-migration responses to the economic shock of the 1982 oil-glut recession.

Shift-share inflow and outflow sub-components

Table 15.5 reports the nine divisions' sub-components, D_k and E_k, respectively.

The rows disclosing the West South Central division's sub-components are of particular interest. Note that the division went from a situation of a significant positive in-migration gain for 1980–1 to 1982–3, to a large loss for 1982–3. There was, however, considerable inertia in its in-migration streams, which had been pumping unprecedented levels of new population into the division ever since the drive for energy 'independence' was launched after the 1973 Arab oil embargo. Despite a dramatic increase in gross out-migration from the region concomitant with the peak of the recession, as evidenced by the $-85\ 000$ out-migration competitive sub-component for 1981–2 to 1982–3, the division was still experiencing substantial net in-migration; net migration to West South Central states dropped from a very large $+414\ 000$ for 1981–2, but only down to $+182\ 000$ for 1982–3. In many ways the economic hardships faced by these states as the bottoms suddenly dropped out of their oil-driven booms were intensified by the lack of an immediate capping off of migration-induced population growth. Net migration did not turn negative until 1984–5. For 1983–4 the division gained an estimated additional 52 000 persons through its interdivisional migration exchanges. Even its net migration loss for 1984–5 of 8000 was still far too small to halt population growth, due to significantly greater natural increase.

The underlying cause for the West South Central's growth momentum may be found in the fact that it was not until well after the 1982 peak of the recession that the most dramatic slowdown in in-migration occurred, as witnessed by the $-109\ 000\ D_k$ sub-component for 1982–3 to 1983–4. Significant deceleration of gross in-movement continued, however, into 1983–4 to 1984–5, with D_k at $-50\ 000$. The differential shifts in West South Central out-migration streams, by contrast, responded much more quickly than the in-migration streams. Peak acceleration of outflow took place during the 1982–3 to 1983–4 time period, with only modest further increases found for the subsequent two periods.

Among the other divisions, the in- and out-migration subcomponents for New England, the Middle Atlantic, and the East North Central divisions as well as the South Atlantic, seem to be mirror images of those for the West South Central division whereas the Mountain division's trend seems to have generally foreshadowed that of the West South Central division. Because the three divisions of the nation's historical core were those largely fuelling the population boom of the West South Central division, the zero-sum-game nature of an internal migration system makes it logical that these divisions were those gaining the most in their ability to retain population when one of the premier growth regions of the nation experienced economic difficulties. We might speculate that the South Atlantic division benefited as a result of providing a sunbelt alternative for potential core-to-periphery migrants.

Table 15.5 Shift-share competitive subcomponents, D_k and E_k, of net migration change (in thousands) for US divisions, 1980–1 to 1984–5

Division	1980–1/ 1984–5	1980–1/ 1981–2	1981–2/ 1982–3	1982–3/ 1983–4	1983–4/ 1984–5
Inflow subcomponents, D_k					
New England	+28	−10	+15	+21	+1
Middle Atlantic	+18	−7	+22	+9	−6
East North Central	+47	−21	+22	+31	+12
West North Central	−13	−24	+9	+9	−9
South Atlantic	+107	−44	+61	+51	+36
East South Central	−10	−2	−1	−6	−3
West South Central	−116	+140	−87	−109	−50
Mountain	−60	−6	−38	−16	+1
Pacific	−1	−25	−3	+10	+17
Outflow subcomponents, E_k					
New England	+22	−6	+12	+3	+12
Middle Atlantic	+56	+25	+33	−1	−5
East North Central	+25	−43	+27	+19	+14
West North Central	−27	−13	−0	+0	−19
South Atlantic	+29	+5	+26	+10	−9
East South Central	+15	+2	+8	+0	+3
West South Central	−105	+2	−85	−12	−3
Mountain	−31	+3	−23	−4	−5
Pacific	+17	+23	+3	−16	+12

A hypothesis regarding the Mountain division trends derives from the fact that it contains a number of states whose energy sectors have been more focused on exploration and the opening of new reserves than on the maintenance of older production and the corporate-control functions more characteristic of Texas. We might expect that the more speculative operations were those initially affected by retrenchments brought about by the oil glut. We shall be able to be more explicit about these sorts of interpretation when we turn later to examine the most salient interdivisional differential shifts underlying these summary measures and specific division-to-division elements of the causative matrices. At this point, however, we can observe that the geographic evidence points to the centrality of the oil glut in accounting for much of the systemic change in the broad-scale interdivisional patterns of movement during the first half of the 1980s.

Underlying the primary trend, however, we can also detect the continuance of at least two other underlying patterns of economic/geographic restructuring. The ongoing farm problem is evidenced by the only very short-term turnaround of the West North Central's inflow and outflow sub-components, and the trends particularly for the Middle Atlantic division, but also, to a lesser extent, the East North Central and New England divisions, suggest that the massive core–periphery deconcentration of the 1970s has not totally run its course. The recession of the early 1980s slowed the process somewhat, aiding, especially, the East North Central division, which was experiencing the worst of the net outflows as the decade began. Going beyond the strictly energy-sector effects, national-scale dispersal of population is dependent on capital investment in the traditionally more peripheral sections of the nation. A cyclical national recession reduces availability of capital, and thus can be expected to slow the longer-term deconcentration. We may tentatively speculate that as the economy recovered in the later 1980s, the pre-existing channels of broad population redistribution began to reassert themselves.

Some longer-term optimism for the North-East and Midwest is, however, provided by the previously mentioned ageing effect, which should serve to stanch the flow of population from the traditional core divisions throughout the 1980s and beyond. The bulk of US 'baby boomers' grew up in the eastern/mid-western American manufacturing belt, where economic opportunity during the previous industrialisation era had fixed in place their parents' and prior generations. During the 1970s, however, the excessively large baby-boom cohorts came into their early labour-force years, a stage in the life-cycle when individuals are most poised to move. Unlike the cyclical effect of the recession of the early 1980s, which led us to predictions for revived broadscale dispersal by the late 1980s, the consideration of fairly predictable age–mobility relationships (see, for example, the work on model migration schedules by Rogers *et al.*, 1978) should suggest somewhat diminished levels of out-migration from the core divisions. In a certain sense, we could contend that much of the 'excess' labour force which came of age in the national core during the 1970s had already been 'bled off' as the 1980s were getting under way.

To expose fully the systemic nature of temporal change in a migration system, one would wish to examine the time-path of evolution in the interdependent volumes of flow coursing throughout the entire network of place-to-place streams of movement. We now conclude our analysis by summarising some of the more striking evidence exposed via the causative-matrix and spatial shift-share perspectives on the nature of the interdependencies in stream-specific channels of population redistribution extant within the USA during the first half of the 1980s.

Shifts in the structure of interdivisional flow

The causative-matrix perspective
Causative matrices are suggestive of the relative ability of the various divisions of the US to compete with each other for migrants during the study period. In Table 15.6 we show the right causative matrices for the middle two time periods: 1981–2 to 1982–3, when the shifts in migration structure occasioned by the oil-glut recession came to the fore, and 1982–3 to 1983–4, a period of intensification of these trends. To facilitate comprehension of the systemic interdependencies embedded in the individual elements, we have used the same deviation-from-unity transformation as employed in Table 15.4.

Perhaps most readily noticeable in both of the panels of the table is the tendency of the diagonal elements to predominate. In essence, the diagonal elements show the ability of a division to 'compete with itself' for potential

Table 15.6 Scaled* causative matrices of temporal change in US interdivisional migration, 1981–2 to 1982–3 and 1982–3 to 1983–4

1981–82/1982–3	NE	MA	ENC	WNC	SA	ESC	WSC	Mtn	Pac
1981–82/1982–3									
New England (NE)	+22	−3	−2	−1	−6	−1	−3	−3	−3
Middle Atlantic (MA)	−1	+19	−2	−0	−5	−1	−4	−2	−3
East North Central (ENC)	+0	−1	+25	−2	−1	−2	−14	−4	−3
West North Central (WNC)	+0	−1	−4	+28	+0	−2	−13	−6	−3
South Atlantic (SA)	−1	−3	−4	−1	+27	−5	−8	−2	−3
East South Central (ESC)	−0	−1	−4	−1	−6	+29	−13	−2	−2
West South Central (WSC)	+0	+2	+9	+4	+3	+2	−16	−3	+0
Mountain (Mtn)	+0	+0	−0	−3	+0	+1	−8	+21	−11
Pacific (Pac)	+0	−0	−2	−2	−1	−1	−8	−11	+24
1982–3/1983–4									
New England (NE)	−11	+5	+2	+0	+5	+0	−2	−0	+1
Middle Atlantic (MA)	+4	−13	+2	+0	+8	+0	−2	−0	+0
East North Central (ENC)	+1	+2	−6	+3	+6	+1	−8	−0	+1
West North Central (WNC)	+1	+1	+5	−8	+4	+0	−7	+1	+3
South Atlantic (SA)	+1	+1	+3	+0	−5	+1	−2	+0	+1
East South Central (ESC)	+0	+1	+4	+1	+10	−13	−5	+0	+1
West South Central (WSC)	+1	+1	+2	+2	+5	+1	−18	+2	+5
Mountain (Mtn)	+1	−0	+3	+0	+5	−5	−5	−15	+12
Pacific (Pac)	+1	+1	+3	+1	+3	+0	−0	+2	−11

* The quantities reported are the elements of the matrix: 10 000 ($\mathbf{C}-\mathbf{I}$), that is, diagonal elements are shown in terms of their deviations from 1.0000, multiplied by 10 000, and the off-diagonal elements in terms of their deviations from 0.000, similarly multiplied by 10 000.

migrants. As discussed at some length in Plane and Rogerson (1986), the diagonal terms are related to region-specific mobility rates. As may also be seen in Table 15.1 the 1981–2 to 1982–3 recessionary period was one of substantially reduced migratory movement from all divisions except the West South Central, which, as we have previously observed, experienced dramatically increased out-movement.

In order most readily to interpret the off-diagonal elements, it is necessary to read down the columns of the matrices. For example, consider the entry in the East North Central division's column, West South Central row for 1981–2 to 1982–3. The +9 value indicates that the temporal changes in flow patterns traceable to the West South Central division had significant, positive influences on the East North Central division's attractiveness as a migrant destination, *relative to* the influences traceable to all the divisions. Part of the West South Central division's influence is expressed directly through changes in the transition probability of migrating from this division to the East North Central (the absolute number of such interdivisional migrants, in fact, increased from 78 000 to 88 000), but the causative-matrix element also builds in the offsetting or enhancing effects of the changing competitive positions of other divisions *vis-à-vis* the West South Central in influencing the attractiveness of the East North Central. It is thus in a truly relative sense that the West South Central division contributed toward increasing the competitiveness of the East North Central division. On the other hand, the latter was seeing its attractiveness diminish relative to the other divisions, particularly the West North Central, South Atlantic, and East South Central.

The largest number of significant negative elements are found in the column for the West South Central division, which experienced relative losses of attractiveness with respect to all other divisions, particularly the two Mid-western ones, the East and West North Central, and the East South Central. The mid-West had been the primary source region for the West South Central's explosive population growth during the 1970s, and was the biggest beneficiary of the slowdown of that growth in terms of retaining potential out-migrants during this recessionary period. Note, too, in the top, 1981–2 to 1982–3, portion of the table that the East South Central and South Atlantic divisions were both contributing to the decreased attractiveness of the other, as were the Mountain and Pacific divisions.

For the later time period represented by the causative matrix elements in the bottom panel of the table, a general recovery in mobility levels is sug-gested by the negative signs of all nine diagonal elements. The principal bene-ficiary of the return to higher rates of movement appears to have been the South Atlantic division; all other divisions contributed positively to its increased attractiveness. The largest relative increase in attractiveness was that occasioned by the East North Central division; note that, unlike for the previous period, there is no symmetrical effect represented in the East South Central column/South Atlantic row. With the continuing economic problems of the West South Central division, movement out of the East South Central was apparently redirected eastward to the South Atlantic states. In general, the slackening of the recession meant a return to higher levels of population dispersal from the historic national core to the South Atlantic division, which was simultaneously reaping increased attractiveness with respect to other portions of the formerly thriving 'sunbelt'. But note, too, the relative attractiveness gains experienced within the North-East; significant positive elements indicate increased relative importance for the New England–Middle Atlantic and Middle Atlantic–New England flows.

Spatial shift-share differential-shift factors
Whereas overall mobility effects and the changing relative attractiveness of regions are treated simultaneously in the causative-matrix perspective on dynamic, flow-pattern change, the spatial shift-share perspective takes an alternative tack. It seeks to 'net out', progressively, broader-scale influences on the changing level of flow in specific migration streams until differential shifts are distilled, these reflecting simply the changing relative competition for dominance in origin–destination-specific net migration exchanges. The two sets of differential-shift *factors*, for in-migration streams, (δ_{ik}), and out-migration streams, (ε_{kj}), as previously defined in equations (15.8) and (15.9), may be used to assess changes in pattern within the flows into and out from region k. The first set focuses on the changing sources of overall in-migration to k, whereas the second pertains to changing destinations of overall outflow from k.

Table 15.7 reports the most highly salient differential shift factors derived

Table 15.7 Differential-shift factors of highly salient changes in US interdivisional* migration streams, 1980–1 to 1984–5

1980–1/ 1984–5	1980–1/ 1981–2	1981–2/ 1982–3	1982–3/ 1983–4	1983–4/ 1984–5

Inflow differential shift factors, δ_{ik}, greater than .150 or less than −0.150

.313 WSC–ENC	.390 ENC–WSC	.291 WSC–ENC		
.201 ENC–NE	.242 WNC–WSC			
.184 Pac–SA	.165 NE–WSC			
.179 WNC–SA	.165 ESC–WSC			
.156 ENC–SA	.160 MA–WSC			
−.239 MA–WSC		−.168 WSC–Mtn	−.236 ENC–WSC	
−.207 ENC–WSC		−160 ENC–WSC	−.192 MA–WSC	
−.203 MA–Mtn			−.188 NE–WSC	
−.187 NE–Mtn				
−.184 WSC–Mtn				
−.166 ESC–WSC				
−.164 SA–WSC				

Outflow differential shift factors, ε_{kj}, less than −0.150 (no outflow factors greater than 0.150)

−.439 WSC–ENC	−.247 ENC–WSC	−.432 WSC–ENC		
−.238 WSC–MA		−.219 WSC–MA		
−.230 WSC–NE		−.207 WSC–WNC		
−.213 WSC–WNC		−.170 WSC–ESC		
−.202 WSC–ESC				
−.186 WSC–SA				

* Division abbreviations are as defined in Table 15.6.

from the changing interdivisional patterns of flow in the US during our 1980–5 study period. We show all inflow and outflow factors greater than 0.15 in absolute value, meaning that more than a 15% change in the volume of inter-divisional movement took place *beyond the percentage that may be accounted for by the proportional shift and system-wide factors.* The focus here, unlike that in interpreting causative-matrix elements, is purely on geographic pattern changes, not the relative amount of overall changing attractiveness experienced by the divisions.

Table 15.7, perhaps more clearly than any other, highlights the dominant role of the West South Central division in effecting temporal change in broad-scale population redistribution patterns. Every single one of the highly salient factors for the four individual periods of temporal change involves this division as either the origin or destination region.

During the 1980–1 to 1981–2 period the West South Central division gained growth momentum through accelerated in-migration from, especially, the two mid-West divisions, but also from the two north-eastern ones, as well as the nearby states of the East South Central division. Looked at from the perspective of the contributor regions, however, it was only for the East North

Central division that the increased flow to the West South Central represented a salient change in pattern.

For the 1981–2 to 1982–3 period there were seven highly salient differential shifts involving the West South Central division. The East North Central significantly benefited from increased in-migration originating in the West South Central. Substantially decreased in-migration to the West South Central from the East North Central also took place, and the West South Central contributed significantly fewer in-migrants to the Mountain division than previously. The four highly salient, negative ε_{kj} factors represent the impact of increased out-migration in slowing growth in the West South Central division; in rank order, the streams having the greatest percentage changes were those to the East North Central, the Middle Atlantic, the West North Central, and the East South Central.

It is intriguing to compare the 1981–2 to 1982–3 ordering of highly salient, negative ε_{kj} factors to that of the positive δ_{ik} factors for the prior period. We might speculate about the effects of return migration, which would suggest that when the fortunes of a growing region change, the changes in out-migration flow should mirror the previous in-migration ones. The higher placement of the Middle Atlantic in the salient out-migration shifts than in the prior in-migration ones is, however, interesting in this context and worthy of further investigation.

For the 1982–3 to 1983–4 period, the three salient streams all are for slowdowns in in-migration to the West South Central. An even more significant response than for the previous period was found for the East North Central, and it is joined by the two north-eastern divisions in contributing significantly fewer in-migrants. The lagged response of in-migration streams as opposed to out-migration streams is apparent here—there were no highly salient ε_{kj} factors for this period, which came somewhat after the worst year, 1982, of the recession.

No further significant pattern changes took place during the final period of the study, 1983–4 to 1984–5, as witnessed by the lack of salient differential shift factors. By then, the effects of the oil-glut shock had largely rippled throughout the system, and this period could be characterised as one in which the force of the change was dissipating.

Finally, the first column of Table 15.7, which reports the most highly salient differential-shift factors for the entire time-span, contributes some further understanding of some changes in the system that do not involve, directly anyway, the West South Central division. For example, the general, increased attractiveness of the South Atlantic can be viewed as being occasioned, in part, by its greater relative ability to draw in-migrants from the Pacific, West North Central, and East North Central divisions. And the Mountain division's slowdown was effected by a stemming of in-migration from the North-East divisions—both the Middle Atlantic and New England.

CONCLUSIONS

In this chapter we have employed two different, yet complementary methods for examining temporal changes in the patterns of broad-scale population movement in the US. The methods prove useful in pointing towards interconnections between economic events in one region and the population growth and decline of all other regions of a nation. Both the spatial shift-share framework, which focuses on decomposing temporal change in each region's net migration, and the causative matrices, which highlight changes in interregional patterns of migration probability, emphasises the systemic nature of internal migration.

Analyses based on these methods have allowed us to understand the dominant role that was played by the West South Central division in restructuring long-distance channels of population redistribution as the oil-glut recession of the early 1980s unfolded. The East North Central division, in particular, was perhaps critically aided by the slowdown of growth in, and what may well be return migration from, the West South Central. These analyses have provided tantalising insights into the swells and swales of the landscape of US internal movement and are suggestive of the relevance of cyclical economic events to the processes of regional population growth and decline.

NOTES

1. The two most significant differences are that the Wilmington, Delaware, Baltimore, Maryland, and Washington, DC metropolitan areas, which perhaps truly belong in the national 'core', are included for historical reasons by the Census Bureau in the South Atlantic division; and that the major portion of the St Louis metropolitan area lying to the west of the Mississippi River is included in the (primarily agricultural) West North Central division.

2. The term 'competing destinations' is used by Fotheringham (1981; 1984) to refer to a modelling technique to represent the spatial structure of destinations in both cross-sectional spatial interaction models and longitudinal semi-Markov models. Our use of the term derives from a consideration of *changes* in destination preferences, where it is recognised that all regions play both direct and indirect roles in determining the change for individual regions.

3. A sixth table obtained from the Internal Revenue Service (IRS), based upon a match of returns filed in 1985 and 1986, proved to have been generated at the US Bureau of the Census in a manner inconsistent with the earlier five matrices for the decade. After discussion with Census Bureau personnel, and after learning that the consistent matrix for 1985–6 has still not been cleared through the IRS for release, we were forced to limit our analysis to the period up through the first quarter of 1985.

4. Our procedure for adjusting the coverage of the IRS migration matrices is based on deriving Markov transition probabilities from the unadjusted tables of flow and then applying these to estimates of the full, resident population of (origin) states. Transition probabilities were obtained by dividing each unadjusted matrix element, m_{ij}, by its row sum (including diagonal elements representing both non- and within-state movers). The 1 April estimates of state populations for 1981 to 1985 were derived through linear interpolation of official US Bureau of the Census intercensal population estimates. These give populations of states for 1 July of each year. For 1980, 1 April decennial Census figures were used.

REFERENCES

Barff, R.A. and Knight, P.K., III (1988a) 'Dynamic shift-share analysis', *Growth and Change*, vol. 19, no. 2, pp. 1–10.

Barff, R.A. and Knight, P.K., III (1988b) 'The role of federal military spending in the timing of the New England employment turnaround', *Papers of the Regional Science Association*, vol. 65.

Engels, R.A. and Healy, M.K. (1981) 'Measuring interstate migration flows: an origin-destination network through Internal Revenue Service records', *Environment and Planning*, vol. 13A, pp. 1345–60.

Fotheringham, A.S. (1984) 'Spatial structure and distance-decay parameters', *Annals of the Association of American Geographers*, vol. 71, no. 3, pp. 425–36.

Fotheringham, A.S. (1984) 'Spatial flows and spatial patterns', *Environment and Planning*, vol. 16A, pp. 529–43.

Harary, F., Lipstein, B. and Styan, G.P.H. (1970) 'A matrix approach to nonstationary chains', *Operations Research*, vol. 18, no. 6, pp. 1168–81.

Isserman, A.M., Plane, D.A. and McMillen, D.B. (1982) 'Internal migration in the United States: an evaluation of federal data', *Review of Public Data Use*, vol. 10, no. 4, pp. 285–311.

Ledent, J. (1978) *Stable Growth in the Nonlinear Components-of-change Model of Interregional Population Growth and Distribution*. Laxenburg, Austria: International Institute for Applied Systems Analysis, RM-78-28.

Lipstein, B. (1968) 'Test marketing: a perturbation in the market place', *Management Science*, series B, vol. 14, no. 8, pp. 437–48.

Plane, D.A. (1984) 'A systemic demographic efficiency analysis of U.S. interstate population exchange, 1935–80, *Economic Geography*, vol. 60, no. 4, pp. 294–312.

Plane, D.A. (1987) 'The geographic components of change in a migration system', *Geographical Analysis*, vol. 19, no. 4, pp. 283–99.

Plane, D.A. (1988) 'The interregional impacts of U.S. core–periphery net migration' in L.J. Gibson and R.J. Stimson (eds), *Regional Structural Change: Experience and Prospects in Two Mature Economies*, Peacedale, RI: Regional Science Research Institute.

Plane, D.A. and Rogerson, P.A. (1986) 'Dynamic flow modeling with interregional dependency effects: an application to structural change in the U.S. migration system', *Demography*, vol. 23, no. 1, pp. 91–104.

Plane, D.A., Rogerson, P.A. and Rosen, A. (1984) 'The cross-regional variation of in-migration and out-migration', *Geographical Analysis*, vol. 16, no. 2, pp. 162–75.

Pullman, N. and Styan, G. (1973) 'The convergence of Markov chains with nonstationary transition probabilities and constant causative matrix', *Stochastic Processes and Their Application*, vol. 1, no. 3, pp. 279–85.

Rogers, A. (1968) *Matrix Analysis of International Population Growth and Distribution*. Berkeley: University of California Press.

Rogers, A., Raquillet, R. and Castro, L.J. (1978) 'Model migration schedules and their applications', *Environment and Planning*, vol. 10A, pp. 475–502.

Rogerson, P.A. (1987) 'Changes in U.S. national mobility levels', *Professional Geographer*, vol. 39, no. 3, pp. 344–51.

Rogerson, P.A. and Plane, D.A. (1984) 'Modeling temporal change in flow matrices', *Papers of the Regional Science Association*, vol. 54, pp. 147–64.

Rogerson, P.A. and Plane, D.A. (1985) 'Monitoring migration trends', *American Demographics*, vol. 7, no. 2, pp. 26–9, 47.

Silvers, A.L. (1977) 'Probabilistic income maximizing behavior in regional migration', *International Regional Science Review*, vol. 2, no. 1, pp. 29–40.

Vining, D.R., Jr. and Pallone, R. (1982) 'Migration between core and peripheral regions: a description and tentative explanation of the patterns in 22 countries', *Geoforum*, vol. 13, no. 4, pp. 339–410.

Vining, D.R., Jr., Pallone, R. and Plane, D.A. (1981) 'Recent migration patterns in developed world: a clarification of some differences between our and IIASA's findings', *Environment and Planning*, vol. 13A, pp. 243–50.

INDEX